STILL MORE
Tell Me Why

How can birds fly?

How do snails walk?

Who was Socrates?

How was the
Grand Canyon formed?

What is the smallest
country in the world?

What happens
to bees in winter?

STILL MORE
Tell Me Why

By ARKADY LEOKUM

Illustrations by
CYNTHIA ILIFF KOEHLER
and ALVIN KOEHLER

**Answers to
hundreds
of questions
children ask**

DEAN

This edition first published 1991 by
Dean, an imprint of Reed Children's Books Limited,
Michelin House, 81 Fulham Road, London SW3 6RB,
and Auckland, Melbourne, Singapore and Toronto.

Reprinted 1994 , 1996

ISBN 0 603 55014 2

British Library Cataloguing-in-Publication Data.
A catalogue record for this book is available from
the British Library.

Printed by The Thomson Press

CONTENTS

Chapter I

The World We Live In

What is botany? Page 12
Where did plants come from? 12
How do plants get their food? 13
What makes the rings on a tree? 14
Why do trees have bark? 15
What is eucalyptus? 16
How do weeds spread? 18
How does asparagus grow? 19
What makes sap go up a tree? 20
Where do nuts come from? 21
How does a nettle sting? 22
How many kinds of apples are there? 23
What is a banyan tree? 23
How does a coconut grow? 25
Where do toadstools come from? 26
Why do figs have so many seeds? 27
What is tapioca? 27
How are herbs used? 28
What are lichens? 29
What is nutmeg? 30
What is mould? 31
What is a virus? 32
What are vertebrates? 32
What is centrifugal force? 34
Why does ice float? 34
What is pollination? 36
How did man find out about heredity? 37
Why are the colours in a rainbow
  arranged as they are? 37
How does light travel? 38
What is noise? 39
What is perpetual motion? 40

What is a vacuum? Page 40
What is matter? 42
How big is a molecule? 43
Does a molecule have weight? 43
What is air? 44
What are the elements? 45
What is metal? 45
What is quicksand? 47
What is fallout? 48
What is gypsum? 48
What is slate? 50
What is dust? 50
What is milk made of? 51
What is carbon? 52
What is nitrogen? 53
What is uranium? 53
What makes some diamonds more
  valuable? 55
How were diamonds formed? 56
What is granite? 57
What is platinum? 58
What is alcohol? 59
What is aluminium? 60
What is talc? 61
What is latitude and longitude? 61
Is there any kind of life in the
  antarctic? 62
How are fossils formed? 64
What is archaeology? 65
Who were the cave men? 66
What was the Stone Age? 67
What happened to animals in the
  Ice Age? 68
Who was Neanderthal man? 68
What is conservation? 70
Are deserts always hot? 71

What is soil?	Page 72	What is a cyclone?	Page 105
Are ocean tides useful?	72	Is thunder dangerous?	106
Why is it hot inside the earth?	73	What is condensation?	106
What's the difference between a spring and an artesian well?	74	What is snow?	107
		What causes hail?	108
How was the Grand Canyon formed?	75	Why is it warmer in summer?	109
How does an earthquake start?	76	Who was St. George?	110
How does a glacier move?	76	Why is America so called?	111
How does a volcano form?	77	What is a boycott?	112
How were the oceans formed?	79	Did people ever speak Latin?	112
How do rivers form?	79	Why do people collect stamps?	113
Why is the day 24 hours?	80	How old are English folklore and customs?	114
Does the universe ever end?	81		
What is the solar system?	82	Why is the census taken?	115
How did ancient astronomers picture the universe?	83	What is a Whig?	116
		Who was David Livingstone?	117
What are meteors made of?	84	What was the Alamo?	118
Can a comet explode?	85	What is the Cabinet?	119
What are the rings around Saturn?	86	What is a totem pole?	120
What is a Radio Telescope?	87	What was the lost continent of Atlantis?	121
What is a star made of?	88		
How many stars can we see at night?	88	What is the Dead Sea?	122
What are the nearest stars?	90	Is there any life in the Dead Sea?	122
What makes the stars shine?	90	What was Pompeii?	123
Why are some stars brighter than others?	91	What is Stonehenge?	124
		Who were the Anglo-Saxons?	125
Does the sun shine the same all the time?	92	Why do cannibals eat people?	126
		What is civilization?	126
What is the origin of the sun?	93	What are the fine arts?	128
How hot is the sun?	93	What is a bachelor's degree?	128
How long will the sun last?	94	When was Buckingham Palace built?	130
What causes an eclipse of the sun?	94	What is "the riddle of the Nile"?	131
What are sunspots?	96	'What is the smallest country in the world?	131
Why does the moon shine?	97		
Is there gravity on the moon?	97	Who designed St. Paul's Cathedral?	133
Why can we see only one side of the moon?	98	Why does Venice have canals?	134
		Why do gipsies keep their own customs?	134
How do clouds stay up in the sky?	99		
What makes the weather?	100	What are mermaids?	136
What makes a wind?	101	Who were the Amazons?	137
How do tornadoes start?	102	What are the Easter Island statues?	138
What's the difference between a hurricane and a tornado?	103	Who were the Druids?	139
		What is a gladiator?	140
What is a monsoon?	104	Who was Homer?	141

What is a leprechaun?	Page 142	Can dogs see colours?	Page 174
What was Custer's Last Stand?	143	What makes dogs go mad?	174
Who were the cliff-dwellers?	144	Do all cats purr?	174
Why do we have counties?	145	What do goats eat?	176
Who were the Incas?	146	Are a donkey and jackass the same?	177
Who were the Aztecs?	147	Do elephants ever forget?	178
Where did the American Indians come from?	148	Are there any white elephants?	179
		Are elephants afraid of mice?	179
Who was Hercules?	149	How tall is a giraffe?	180
Who was Pythagoras?	150	Does the giraffe have a voice?	181
Did King Arthur ever exist?	150	Why does the camel have a hump?	181
Who were the vikings?	151	What are guinea pigs?	183
Who was Lord Nelson?	152	How do we get ermine from a stoat?	184
Who was Copernicus?	153	What do beavers eat?	185
Who was Achilles?	154	Why does an opossum hang by its tail?	186
Who was Socrates?	155		
Who was Robin Hood?	156	Which insect has the longest life?	187
		Can plants eat insects?	188
		Why was the mosquito man's great enemy?	189
Chapter II		Can grasshoppers hear?	190
		What is a praying mantis?	190
Animal Life		How do spiders spin their webs?	191
		What is a scorpion?	192
Did dragons ever exist?	158	Do ants always live in colonies?	193
Why did the dinosaurs become extinct?	159	Where do termites live?	194
		What is a weevil?	195
How do we know what dinosaurs were like?	160	Do butterflies migrate?	196
		How many kinds of insects are there?	197
How do plants and animals live in the desert?	161	What is an aphid?	198
		What does a butterfly eat?	198
What were centaurs?	162	What does a fly eat?	199
What was a unicorn?	163	How are flies born?	200
Why do animals like salt?	164	How can a fly walk on the ceiling?	201
Can animals count?	164	What happens to bees in winter?	202
Why can't animals learn to talk?	165	To what family do worms belong?	203
Which animal resembles man the most?	166	Are rats of any use to man?	204
		What is an asp?	205
Can any animals use reason?	167	What is the deadliest snake?	206
Do animals' eyes shine in the dark?	168	Do snakes lay eggs?	207
What is moulting?	169	Do snakes have bones?	208
Is the chimpanzee a monkey?	170	Why don't snakes have legs?	208
How were different breeds of dogs started?	172	Why do snakes have scales?	210
Why do dogs bury bones?	173	Can a snake really be charmed?	210

Why do birds migrate? Page 211
Does the ostrich have a voice? 212
What are birds of paradise? 213
What bird lays the largest egg? 213
What birds can talk best? 214
How can birds fly? 215
How do pigeons find their way
  home? 216
What was the first land animal? 217
What are amphibians? 217
Does the turtle have a voice? 219
What do fish eat? 220
Can fish hear? 220
What is an electric eel? 221
Are jellyfish dangerous? 222
Where do sharks live? 223
What does an octopus eat? 224
How are oysters born? 225
How do oysters make pearls? 225
How do snails walk? 226
What is a mammal? 227
What are flatfish? 228
What is a manatee? 228
What is the world's fastest mammal? 230
Why are whales considered
  mammals? 230
What is the biggest whale? 232
What do we get from whales? 233
What is a dolphin? 234
Why do bats hang upside down? 235
Why were kangaroos found only
  in Australia? 236
What is an echidna? 237
Do bats have teeth? 238

Chapter III

Our Body and What Happens To It

Why does the body need water? 240
How long can man go without food? 240
What does the body do with food? 241
Why is the body warm? 242

How do we breathe? Page 243
What causes different skin colours? 244
What is an albino? 245
How does the body tan? 246
What are cells? 246
What does a cell do? 247
What does the liver do? 248
What is the pituitary gland? 249
What is the pineal gland? 250
How do our kidneys function? 250
What do our tonsils do? 252
How many sets of teeth do we grow? 253
How does a broken bone heal? 253
Why is one of our feet bigger than
  the other? 255
Why do we have a skeleton? 256
When do you stop growing? 258
How does hair grow? 258
Why do humans have hair? 259
What causes dandruff? 260
What are birthmarks? 261
Why do we get pimples? 262
What causes mumps? 262
What is meningitis? 263
What causes scarlet fever? 264
What causes stomach ulcers? 265
What is rheumatic fever? 266
What is rheumatism? 267
What is intoxication? 268
What is the appendix? 269
What is athlete's foot? 270
How is diphtheria controlled? 271
What is ringworm? 272
What does blood do for the body? 273
What is a stroke? 274
Why do muscles ache after
  exercise? 275
How much blood is in our body? 276
What is high blood pressure? 276
What is anaemia? 277
What is leukaemia? 278
How does the heart work? 279
What is a heart attack? 280
What are nerves? 281

How do we read? Page 282
Why do people walk in their sleep? 283
Why do onions make you cry? 284
How does the brain help us see? 285
What is an optical illusion? 286
How do we see in three dimensions? 287
How do we hear different sounds? 288
How do we sing? 288
What does the tongue do? 289
What is smell? 290
Why does the nose have mucus? 291
What is the speed of thought? 292
What is the theory behind ESP? 293
Why do we get tired? 294
Why do we sleep? 295
How much sleep do we need? 295
Is what we dream our own idea? 296
How do we lose our memory? 297
Why can we balance ourselves on
  two legs? 298
Can two people have identical
  fingerprints? 299
How do our teeth grow? 300

Chapter IV

How Things Began

How did nursery rhymes originate? 302
Who started the first zoo? 302
How old is the sport of wrestling? 304
How did some children's games
  begin? 305
Who invented skating? 305
How did skiing begin? 306
Where did the game of ice hockey
  originate? 307
How did duelling originate? 308
Where were card games first played? 309
Where did golf originate? 309
What was the first music? 311
Who first wrote music? 311
Who invented the accordion? 312

Who invented the drum? Page 313
How was the first recording made? 314
Who made the first photograph? 315
When was the first book written? 316
Who made the first printing press? 316
Who made the first paintings? 318
What was papyrus? 319
When were the first coins made? 319
When was money first used? 320
When did the first aeroplane fly? 322
When did smoking begin? 323
Who built the first car? 324
How did some fish get their names? 325
How did trees get their names? 326
What do our names mean? 327
Who started vaccination? 328
Who started short haircuts for men? 329
When was honey first used? 330
Where did melon originate? 331
How did the pineapple get its name? 332
Where did the cabbage come from? 333
When were flags first used? 334
Who built the first canals? 335
Who was the first astronaut? 336
Who were the first pirates? 336
What was the first gun like? 337
Why do we celebrate the New Year? 338
How were beards named? 339
How did pins originate? 340
When was brick first used? 341
Who gave the first wedding
  presents? 342
When did the wedding cake
  originate? 342
Why do brides wear a veil? 343
Why is a married man called a
  husband? 344
When did people begin to make
  homes? 344
When was gas first used? 345
When was furniture first used? 346
How long has man been making
  beds? 347
When was the first world's fair? 348

Who made the first needle?   Page 349
Who discovered Alaska?   350
When did the first Negro go to
  America?   351
When was the Tower of London
  built?   352
How was Hawaii formed?   353
How did cities begin?   354
Who invented plastic?   355
When was the first university started?   355
How did arithmetic start?   356
Why did people start to have schools?   357
How did the major religions start?   358
Who were the first nuns?   360
When did the Red Cross start?   361
Why is a black cat considered
  bad luck?   362
How did trial by jury begin?   362
Why do we have gravestones?   363
Why did people believe in witches?   364
Why are some people head-hunters?   365
How was oil formed?   366
When was gold discovered?   367
Where did the Eskimoes come from?   368
When were the first posters used?   369
When did people settle in Canada?   370

When did tattooing begin?   Page 370
When did advertising begin?   372
When were silkworms first used?   373
When was the umbrella invented?   374
How long have handkerchiefs been
  used?   375
How did the wearing of gloves
  begin?   375
Who invented stockings?   376
Who made the first engine?   376
When did chemistry begin?   377
When did man first use electricity?   378
How did science begin?   379
How did laundries start?   380
What was the Pony Express?   381
What is the Coronation Stone?   382
What is real estate?   383
How did the postal system start?   384
How did the handshake
  originate?   385
How did income tax start?   386
Who invented the broom?   387
How did the Civil Service originate?   388
When did acrobats first appear?   388
Who invented the helicopter?   390
Index   391

Chapter 1

The World We Live In

Because in early times the study of plant life dealt mainly with plants as food, it became known as botany, from a Greek word meaning "herb".

WHAT IS BOTANY? The first people to specialize in the study of botany were primitive medicine men and witch doctors. They had to know the plants that could kill or cure people. And botany was closely linked with medicine for hundreds of years.

In the sixteenth century, people began to observe plants and write books about their observations. These writers were the "fathers" of modern botany. In the nineteenth century, the work of an English scientist, Charles Darwin, helped botanists gain a better understanding of how plants, as well as animals, evolved from simpler ancestors. His work led botanists to set up special branches of botany.

One of these branches is "plant anatomy", which has to do with the structure of plants and how they might be related. Experiments on plant heredity were performed to find out how various species came to be and how they could be improved. This study is called "genetics".

"Ecology", another branch of botany, deals with studies of the distribution of plants throughout the world, to find out why certain species grow in certain places. "Paleobotany", another branch, works out plant evolution from the evidence of fossil remains.

Other branches of botany include "plant physiology", which studies the way plants breathe and make food, and "plant pathology", which is concerned with the study of plant diseases.

According to the theories of science, there was a time when there were no plants on earth. Then, hundreds of millions of years ago, tiny specks of protoplasm appeared on the earth. Protoplasm is the name for the living

WHERE DID PLANTS COME FROM? material that is found in both plants and animals. These original specks of protoplasm, according to this theory, were the beginnings of all our plants and animals.

The protoplasm specks that became plants developed thick walls and settled down to staying in one place. They also developed a kind of green colouring matter known as "chlorophyll". This enabled them to make food from substances in the air, water and soil.

These early green plants had only one cell, but they later formed groups of cells. Since they had no protection against drying out, they had to stay in the water. Today, some descendants of these original plants still survive, though they have changed quite a bit. We call them "algae".

One group of plants developed that obtained their food without the use of chlorophyll. These non-green plants are the "fungi".

Most of the plants on earth today evolved from the algae. Some of them came out of the sea and developed rootlets which could anchor them in the soil. They also developed little leaves with an outer skin covering, as protection against drying. These plants became mosses and ferns.

All the earliest plants reproduced either by simple cell division or by means of spores. Spores are little dustlike cells something like seeds, but containing no stored food in them as seeds do. As time went on, some of these plants developed flowers that produced true seeds.

Two different types of plants with seeds appeared; those with naked seeds and those with protected seeds. Each of these two types later developed along many different lines.

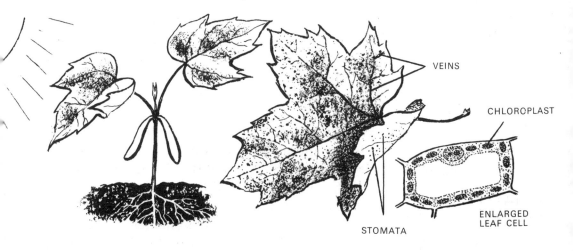

VEINS

CHLOROPLAST

ENLARGED
LEAF CELL

STOMATA

Plants have "factories" to manufacture their food, and these factories are the leaves.

HOW DO PLANTS GET THEIR FOOD?

Leaves of fruit trees manufacture the food which helps to make fruit. Both peaches and maple sugar, for example, are sweet. So peach and maple leaves must be able to make sugar. They do this by taking materials from the air and the ground.

One of these materials is carbon dioxide, a gas which is taken from the air. The other material is water, which comes from the soil. From the water and carbon dioxide the leaves manufacture sugar. This process of making food is called "photosynthesis".

Many kinds of plants seem to have no sugar in them because the sugar is soon changed to other kinds of food, such as starch and protein.

The food "factory" needs machines, and the machines of the leaf are many little green bodies called "chloroplasts". They are green because they have in them a green matter called "chlorophyll". The power that runs the machines is sunshine.

The roots of the plant take water from the soil. The water goes through the roots, through the stems and branches, and then into the veins of the leaves. The veins carry water to the cells. This is where the chloroplasts are.

Veins also carry the food which the leaves have made and not used to storage places such as roots, fruits and seeds.

Leaves must also get rid of waste materials. The air that goes into a leaf has carbon dioxide in it. When the sun is shining, the leaves use the carbon dioxide to make sugar. The rest of the air, with additional oxygen, is given off through the stomata, which are openings between cells on the underside of the leaf.

If you were to cut down any tree more than one year old and look at the cross-section, you would see alternating bands of light and dark wood. The two bands together are called "the annual ring", and they make up

WHAT MAKES THE RINGS ON A TREE?

the amount of wood formed by the tree during a single growing season or year.

Why are the bands lighter and darker? This is because the wood grows in a different way during the different seasons. In spring and early summer, the cells of the wood are bigger and have thinner walls. This makes them look lighter. In late summer, the cells are smaller, have thick walls, and are closely packed together. This makes a darker band.

The age of a tree can be told by counting the annual rings. When you look at the rings of a tree, you will notice that they vary in width and in many other details. These variations are caused by the weather conditions that prevailed during the given season. A difference in the light, the amount of rain, and the minerals in the soil, will produce a difference in

the rings of a tree. That is why scientists often use the rings to obtain a clue to the weather conditions that prevailed years ago in certain parts of the world.

When a tree grows, the wood of the tree is not the only thing that increases in size from year to year. Additions are also made to the bark of the tree. This is done by means of a thin band of living, dividing cells between the wood and the bark. This layer is called "the cambium". The new cells which are formed on the wood side of the cambium become wood. The cells formed towards the outside become bark.

The outer portion of a woody stem or root is called "bark". Sometimes it is hard to tell how much of the stem should be called bark. In the palm tree, for example, there is no clear separation between bark and wood.

WHY DO TREES HAVE BARK? What does bark do for the tree? One of its main functions is to protect the inner, more delicate structures. It not only keeps them from drying out, but also guards against outside injuries of various sorts.

The thick, fibrous barks of some redwood trees in America show scars as a result of fires near the ground, but the inner portions of the tree escaped injury.

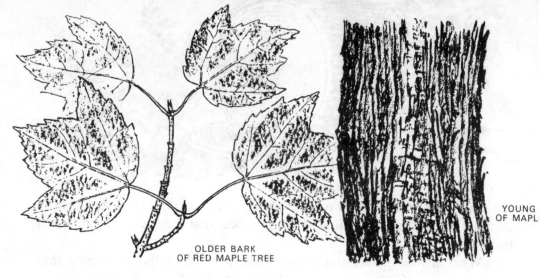

OLDER BARK
OF RED MAPLE TREE

YOUNG BARK
OF MAPLE

The process by which bark is formed may go on year after year. In the very young branch of a maple, for example, there is no rough bark as such. The surface of the shoot is nearly smooth. As the twig forms more wood and grows in size, the outer portions may split open. The injury caused in this way is healed from the inside.

Some of the outer portions become dry and die. The dead, broken portions give the bark a rough appearance. Some of the dry pieces are shed or broken off as the twig grows larger and older.

Man finds the bark of many trees very useful. Commercial cork is obtained almost entirely from the cork oak tree. The bark of the hemlock tree is used in the tanning of leather. The spice we know as cinnamon is the powdered bark of a tree which grows in India and Malaya. Quinine is obtained from the bark of the cinchona tree. Extracts from the bark of other trees are used for flavouring, and the bark of the roots and branches of many trees are used in medicines.

The eucalyptus is a native tree of Australia, where it is sometimes called the "gum tree" or "string-bark" tree. It has now been introduced into Europe, Algeria, Egypt, India, South America and the southern United States.

WHAT IS EUCALYPTUS?

The eucalyptus is one of the most striking trees in appearance. Its leaves are leathery and hang down vertically in most cases. The trunk is tall and straight, and grows at a remarkable pace. Saplings of the eucalyptus tree have been known to grow as much as 4 metres in a single year! In height, a eucalyptus can even

16

equal the giant sequoias of California. There are eucalyptus trees that are nearly 140 metres tall.

The eucalyptus is an extremely useful tree. It requires a great amount of moisture, so it is often planted in swampy regions. By drawing water out of mosquito-infested swamps, it can actually help fight malaria in certain regions of the world.

One of the most remarkable things about this tree is that it actually provides man with a medicine. The leaves are dotted with pores that hold a straw-coloured oil, which smells something like camphor oil. This is eucalyptus oil. This oil is sometimes given to patients to be inhaled to clear the nasal passage.

Eucalyptus oil is also used as medicine internally. It has an effect on the kidneys, and it also depresses the nervous system so that it slows up breathing. It has even been used by surgeons as an antiseptic!

The wood of this tree is adaptable and durable. Eucalyptus wood is valuable in building docks and ships, and it is in great demand for the interiors of houses because it can be given an attractive, highly polished finish.

There are actually no such things as weeds. When a farmer plants certain seeds which he hopes will produce a valuable crop, he calls any other plant which grows up in his field and interferes with his crop a weed!

HOW DO WEEDS SPREAD?

Basically, though, weeds are plants that do harm. Some are poisonous to cattle and horses. Others injure crops by robbing them of sunlight, soil, minerals and water. Others act as parasites, or serve as hosts to insects or plant diseases that cause harm.

Weeds are spread by various means. Some are carried from place to place in fodder, in dust, in rubbish and in manure. But most weeds that cause so much trouble do not spread because of man's carelessness. They have their own devices for spreading their seeds.

Some weeds, such as pimpernel, nightshade, dodder and grasses, produce their seeds in such great quantities that some of them are likely to survive practically no matter what the conditions.

Other weeds have hairlike or winglike projections on their seeds and fruits. These make it possible for the seeds to be carried by the wind for considerable distances. Such weeds include dock, sorrel, thistle and dandelion. Still other weeds have little hooks or spines on their seeds. These hooks catch in the fur of animals or in the clothing of man, and in this way the seeds are spread to new territory.

Some of the most successful weeds do not even spread by means of seeds. They have spreading underground stems which send up erect branches. If the underground stem is cut, these erect branches merely become separate plants.

Because of the harm they can do, weeds are fought and controlled by man. Today there is a whole variety of chemicals that have been developed to destroy weeds or prevent them from appearing.

Asparagus has been considered one of the finest table delicacies since the days of the ancient Greeks and Romans. Yet strangely enough, asparagus grows wild around the coasts of Europe and in other sandy

HOW DOES ASPARAGUS GROW?

places. In fact, it is so common on the steppes of Russia that the cattle pasture on it!

Of the 150 species of asparagus widely distributed in tropical and temperate countries, many species are only cultivated for ornamental purposes. Wild asparagus grows on the south coast of England.

The remarkable thing about the asparagus plant is that it produces both the tender shoots which we eat, and the fern-like foliage which we use for decorative purposes. Asparagus for the table is cut while the leaves are still in bud and the shoot is less than ten inches high.

Asparagus is a member of the lily family and has many varieties. If it is left to grow, it becomes a plant two or more feet high with spreading branches bearing small, white flowers and brilliant, red berries. When the crop is gathered, some of it is tinned, and some rushed fresh to city markets where it is sold in bunches. In Europe, asparagus is often dried so it can be used in the winter.

Even though asparagus is delicious, and can be used to make soup, or eaten hot or in cold salads, it provides very little nutritive value because of its large water content.

Asparagus may be grown from seeds, or roots may be planted in a shallow trench which is later filled in gradually. The soil must be deep, rich and sandy. If the plant is allowed to grow for three years before it is cut, it will continue to bear an annual supply for some nine years or more, but the soil must be fertilized every year to maintain a good yield.

Every single part of the human body receives a constant supply of blood which is pumped by the heart. In plants and trees, every single part receives water and nourishment, which we call sap. But a tree has no pump because it has no heart. So how does the sap go up a tree?

WHAT MAKES SAP GO UP A TREE?

Science still cannot explain this mystery exactly. Of course, there are several theories about it, but no single theory seems to offer the complete answer. Scientists believe that there are several forces at work to make this possible.

One explanation has to do with "osmotic pressure". In living things, liquids and dissolved materials pass through membranes. This is called "osmosis". When there are dissolved chemicals in contact with a membrane, they press against the membrane. This is called "osmotic pressure". If there are many particles in a solution, more particles press against the membrane and seep through than in solutions with fewer particles.

Minerals and water used by plants come from the roots. Since the soil contains more minerals than the plant, the osmotic pressure causes the minerals to enter the plant. The dissolved minerals remain in the plant cells. The water evaporates. In this way, water from the soil continuously moves upward through plants.

Another way of explaining how sap goes up a tree has to do with "transpiration" and the cohesion of water. The evaporation of water from leaves is called "transpiration". The attraction of one water particle to another is called "cohesion".

Transpiration provides the upward "pull". As water evaporates from the cells of the leaves, it creates a vacuum in the cells directly below the surface. So these cells draw on the cells below them for a new supply of sap. And this continues right down to the roots of the tree. Cohesion holds the water particles together as they move up.

The hard-shelled fruits we call nuts differ widely in size and flavour. Walnuts, with their wrinkly, hard shells enclosed in a round, smooth husk, are a favourite in this country. Long ago, Oriental princes sent them as presents to rulers of lands where the walnut tree did not grow.

WHERE DO NUTS COME FROM?

The chestnut, too, has long been valued. There are famous old chestnut trees reputed to be over 500 hundred years old, and, in Spain especially, this tree is highly prized.

A nut that is very hard to crack but most delicious to eat is the Brazil nut. These three-sided nuts grow in clusters of twenty or more, tightly packed in a hard, round shell. As soon as the nut is ripe, it falls to the ground, and, as the trees are often over thirty metres high, it is not surprising that the natives will avoid them in a strong wind!

The almond tree with white blossoms produces bitter almonds, which are used in the manufacture of flavouring extract and drugs used in medicine. Sweet almonds come from the tree with pink blossoms, which is grown extensively in Western Asia, in the Mediterranean region and in California.

The most valuable of all nuts, however, is the coconut. At first, it grew only along the East Indies coast and in the South Sea Islands, but it is now found in the tropics of all the continents. Its food value is high because it contains much oil and some protein.

One native English nut is the hazel, which is grown mainly in Kent. Hazelnuts lie in leafy cups in clusters of two, three, or four, and from their light brown shade we get the colour "hazel".

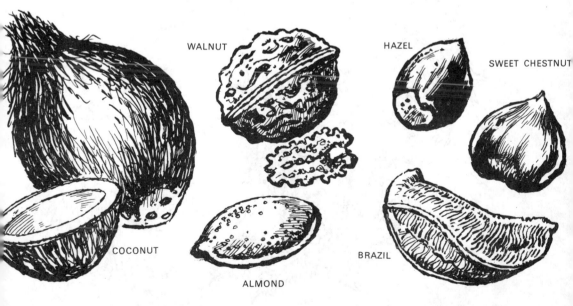

WALNUT

HAZEL

SWEET CHESTNUT

COCONUT

BRAZIL

ALMOND

There are several species of nettle, not all of which have stinging hairs. Most people, however, have suffered a nettle-sting at one time or another; and of those nettles that do sting, the common nettle and the Roman nettle are the best known. The latter has the most painful sting of all nettles.

HOW DOES A NETTLE STING?

The stinging action of a nettle is very similar to the stinging cells in the tentacles of the sea-anemone. It has a delicate, trigger-like coil in a cell, its sharp point being released on the slightest touch. The nettle-sting is developed from a single cell with the walls of the hair silicified, a small knob protects the fine point until touched, when it breaks and allows the trigger to penetrate the skin. It is an acrid juice which causes irritation and, sometimes, inflammation of the skin.

If one is careful, however, to grasp the nettle in such a way that the hairs are pressed to the stem, they cannot pierce the skin, and the nettle can be plucked painlessly.

In many countries, boiled nettles have a special food value for pigs and poultry. The roots boiled in alum produce a yellow dye, and the leaves and stalks give a green dye. The "ramie" (fibres) of different species of nettle are used to make lace, cloth, rope and yarn.

The nettles proper are annual or perennial herbs, sometimes with shrubby bases, and they make up the genus Urtica. Several trees of different genera, in particular the giant nettle of Australia, are given that name.

There are enough varieties of apples to satisfy everybody's taste. In the United Kingdom alone, more than 2,000 varieties of apples have been recorded. And when you consider the whole world, there are probably a few thousand more.

HOW MANY KINDS OF APPLES ARE THERE? We know that it is one of the earliest fruits raised by man. The apple probably originated in South Eastern Europe and South Western Asia, and was raised and eaten by the very earliest inhabitants there. More than 2,000 years ago, different varieties of apples were already being grown in Europe. In ancient Rome, the inhabitants enjoyed seven different varieties of apples.

How are all these varieties obtained? A great deal of experimenting is always being carried out by apple growers. When you graft a bud or twig of any variety on to any kind of young apple tree, the mature tree yields apples of the same variety as the graft. So nurserymen always experiment with grafting and by fertilizing the blossoms to cross-breed them.

Up to the 17th century there were two main kinds of apples grown in Britain, known as Costards and Codlins.

During the 14th century, however, grafts of good quality dessert apples were introduced from France. They had a red skin and became known as Pippins, but it was not until 1830 that a Mr Cox of Slough produced his famous Cox's Orange Pippin. Another famous apple, the Worcester Pearmain, was introduced by a Mr Hale of Worcester in 1873. Even today, in spite of the 2,000 varieties recorded in the United Kingdom, only about 20 are grown commercially.

The banyan tree is one of the giants among trees. Anything in nature that is a "giant" presents all kinds of problems, and trees are no exception. For example, a giant tree has the problem of drawing moisture from the

WHAT IS A BANYAN TREE? roots to the top. The trunk of the tree must be strong. A tree cannot grow too tall and remain slender, or it would break. So a giant tree must be wider at the base to support the load above it. And if the branches are large and heavy, they could pull down the trunk to one side or another.

The banyan tree is a giant tree that has solved these problems in an interesting way. It is a tree of the mulberry family, and it is found in Eastern India and Malaysia.

The most unusual thing about the banyan tree is the way its branches grow. They spread out in all directions all around the trunk. And even though the trunk is huge, it cannot support these branches. So thick roots grow from the underside of the branches directly to the ground.

When these roots take hold, they provide support and nourishment for the tree. They also develop into new trunks. The result is that the banyan tree grows more in circumference than in height. Eventually, "arcades" of these roots are formed, and a banyan tree may have a circumference that reaches 450 metres.

These arcades of roots are actually used as marketplaces by people who find it a perfect sheltered place to gather and do business. If these roots are cut, they are useful for making tent poles and the fibre is used for making rope.

The banyan tree produces tiny figs. When they become ripe they are bright red and are eaten by birds and bats.

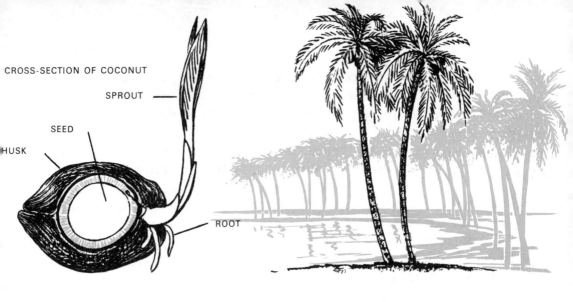

CROSS-SECTION OF COCONUT

SPROUT

SEED

HUSK

ROOT

The coconut is the fruit of the coconut palm tree. The husk of the coconut is there so that the inner seed, or nut, will be cushioned when it falls to the ground.

HOW DOES A COCONUT GROW?

This nut is about 8 to 20 centimetres long. Just inside the hard, dark shell is a layer of dense, white meat. The centre of the coconut is filled with a watery liquid which is called "coconut milk".

If you have ever seen a coconut, you have noticed it has three "eyes", which are really undeveloped buds. When a coconut is planted in the ground in its husk, a new sprout pushes through one of the eyes. And if a new palm begins to grow it takes about eight years before it bears any fruit.

A mature coconut palm flowers throughout the year and almost always has a few ripe nuts. It may take a nut a year or more to mature, depending on the place and the kind it is. A palm produces an average of 50 nuts a year.

The coconut palm grows from 6 to 27 metres high and has a tuft of long, feathery leaves at the top. A leaf may be 3 to 6 metres long. Coconuts can be grown at elevations as high as 900 metres above sea level, but they are usually planted at lower elevations.

An unusual thing about this tree is that it can live in salt water, but it does not require salt water. The palm grows near the sea because its shallow roots can find moisture there.

The husk of the coconut is not harmed by salt water either. Which means that if a coconut falls into the sea it can be carried a long way and take root on some far-away beach.

Sometimes toadstools seem to appear as if by magic on a lawn after a rainy day. But, of course, no magic is involved. Toadstools grow from spores. And toadstools and mushrooms are exactly the same thing. There

WHERE DO TOADSTOOLS COME FROM?
is no difference between them.

A typical mushroom consists of a cylindrical stem, or "stipe", supporting a circular cap, or "pileus". On the stipe is a collar known as a ring, or "annulus". Radiating from the stipe to the margin of the cap on its underside are gills, or "lamellae". This is where the spores are formed.

Spores have a similar purpose to that of seeds, but they should not be confused with seeds. Spores are produced in great quantities. In fact, so many are produced by a mushroom, that there is a good chance the wind will carry some of them to spots favourable for growth.

PILEUS

GILLS

STIPE

ANNULUS

MYCELIUM

If a spore falls in a place that is warm and moist and where food is available, the spore, which consists of a single cell, begins to absorb nourishment. It grows by division until long chains of cells resembling threads are formed. Such a chain is called a "hypha". A tangle of them is called a "mycelium". At various points along the mycelium, tiny balls no bigger than pinheads develop and become mushrooms.

So you see that when mushrooms or toadstools seem to appear suddenly, it is really the end of a long process that started with the spores leaving some mushroom that could have been quite a distance away!

The fig is one of the most remarkable fruits in the world. It has been valued as a food by man since prehistoric times. At one time it was a delicacy that emperors enjoyed, at another time it was the staple diet of slaves.

WHY DO FIGS HAVE SO MANY SEEDS?

From the juice of figs are made alcohol, wine, and a dye for cloth. The leaves are used to polish ivory, while cord is made from the bark of the fig tree.

There are many varieties of figs, but the most delicious one known to most of us is the Smyrna (Izmir) fig, which is named after the city in Turkey. This fig is now cultivated in California.

When we look at the large, fleshy fig what we see is really a baglike structure, nearly closed at its top. Inside are many true flowers which produce the pollen and what we call "seeds". But these are not seeds at all. They are the true fruit of the fig!

In the cultivation of Smyrna figs, a very interesting process takes place. The Smyrna fig can be pollinated only by pollen from the Capri fig. Although the Capri fig bears a great deal of pollen, this can be released from the Capri fig and reach the fruit of the Smyrna fig only with the help of a tiny wasp-like insect known as the fig wasp.

The fig wasp lives in the Capri figs until it is ready to lay its eggs. It then leaves the Capri fig and carries the pollen from the Capri fig on its body. It crawls into the Smyrna fig and rubs off the pollen on the flowers.

The tapioca pudding that you eat is not something "manufactured". It is a product of nature. Tapioca is made from the roots of a large shrub which grows in warm countries.

WHAT IS TAPIOCA?

The shrub is called "manioc". The roots of this plant consist of about one-third starch and two-thirds water. And it takes quite a bit of time to prepare manioc roots.

The first step is to wash them and peel them. Then they are put into water and left to soak for a few days. Or they may be grated or pounded into a paste without soaking. The paste can be cooked and eaten, or it can be dried and made into flour.

To make tapioca, the grated root is mixed well with clean water and left to stand. The pure starch grains slowly settle to the bottom, and any dirt can be poured off with the water.

The starch is then taken out and mixed with clean water again, and this may be done four or five times. When the starch is perfectly clean it is spread on a metal plate over a low fire and cooked. As the starch grains cook they stick together to form little balls.

After the pure starch is cooked it is called tapioca. Most of the tapioca used in Europe and the United States comes from Java, Brazil and Madagascar.

In Europe and the United States tapioca is used to make puddings or to thicken soups and sauces. But in South America and Africa, manioc is eaten in the form of a paste or as a dry flour.

A herb is a plant of which the leaves can be used for food, medicine, perfume, or for flavour in cooking. Herbs and spices can transform an ordinary, everyday meal into something special. As some herbs are very

HOW ARE HERBS USED?

strong and piquant in flavour, however, they should be used sparingly. Some of the most popular herbs in this country are listed below.

Basil, a sweet, mild herb with a rather peppery taste, goes well with all kinds of savoury and salad dishes.

Sage is good with rich meals. It is strong in flavour, with a rather bitter fragrance. Sage leaves are sometimes wrapped round cheeses to give them flavour.

Thyme. There are several varieties of thyme, which originated in the Mediterranean countries. The best-known varieties are garden thyme and scented lemon thyme. It is a strong, spicy herb, and it is used fresh or dried.

Cloves can be used in sweet or savoury dishes. They are the flowers of the clove-tree, which grows in the Molucca Islands. Cloves are sweet,

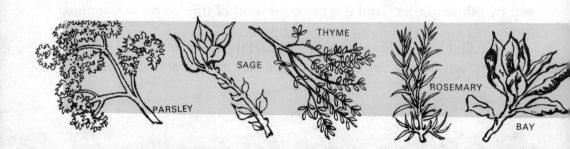

PARSLEY
SAGE
THYME
ROSEMARY
BAY

fragrant spices, and can be used either whole or ground.

Mint, popular for its flavour and fragrance, is named after Mintha, a nymph of Greek mythology! The goddess Persephone, according to the story, in a jealous rage turned her beautiful rival, Mintha, into this plant.

The mints belong to the family *Labiatae,* which also includes many other herbs such as thyme, sage, marjoram and rosemary. The commonest wild species of mint in this country is the water mint, but we generally use garden mint for flavouring mint sauce or chewing-gum. Catmint, or catnip, which is so attractive to cats, also belongs to this family.

Lichens are plants without roots, leaves, or flowers. Even though they have no leaves or flowers, they can be quite attractive and range from a pale grey or whitish colour to bright green when they are moist.

WHAT ARE LICHENS? There are about 16,000 species of lichens, and they are found in every conceivable kind of place. They grow in sun-baked deserts and on exposed antarctic rocks. They grow in waste places, on bare rocks, bare soil, dead wood, and tree bark, and can live through heat, cold, dampness, or dryness. About the only place where they do not thrive is near a city, where they are killed by smoke, dust, and coal gas!

Lichens are really two plants growing together—a "fungus" and an "alga". The greater part of a lichen plant is greyish, thread-like fungus material. Held among the fungus fibres are bright green cells of algae.

Algae, being green plants, can make their own food, but the non-green fungi cannot. Lichen fungi use food made by the algae. The algae use water absorbed by the fungus, which also shelters and supports the algae. Such a relationship where each member benefits from the other is called "symbiosis", from Greek words meaning "life together".

Lichens grow very slowly but live a long time. Some colonies are thought to have lived as long as 2,000 years! In some lichens, the fungus produces spores. But most lichens are reproduced by broken-off bits blown or carried to new places, or by special structures that break off easily and become new lichen plants.

Lichens are the first plants to grow on bare rocks. They loosen rock particles, and these particles plus decaying lichens form the first thin layer of soil on which other plants can grow.

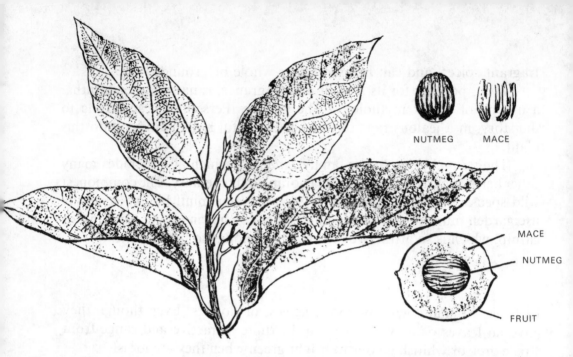

NUTMEG MACE

MACE
NUTMEG

FRUIT

Nutmeg is one of the best-known fragrant spices. It is the name given to the kernel of the fruit of a tropical tree.

Most nutmegs come from the Philippines, West Indies, Moluccas or Spice Islands and Brazil. There are about 80 species of nutmeg trees and shrubs. The most common, whose botanical name is *Myristica moschata,* is a handsome evergreen with a straight trunk about 7 metres high. It is covered with branches from base to tip. The flowers are small and yellow, with a perfume like lilies of the valley.

WHAT IS NUTMEG?

After about eight years of growth, the tree begins bearing fruit. The tree blooms and bears fruit in continuous succession all the year round, but the principal harvests occur about three times a year.

The fruit is about the size and shape of a pear. When ripe it is golden yellow in colour. The fruit opens in halves. Inside is a red, fleshy part called "the mace", and the nut-like seed. Inside this seed is the portion of the nutmeg used as a spice.

After the nuts are separated from the mace, they are dried in ovens until the kernels rattle in the shells. Then the shells are removed. Although nutmegs are usually exported while still whole in order to retain their flavour, they are used for flavouring food only after they have been grated.

Nuts that are considered inferior are ground and the oils are extracted. This is called "oil of mace" or "nutmeg butter".

How is it that if you leave a piece of damp bread around in the kitchen of your home, it will be covered with a furry, green coat in a few days? We say the bread has become "mouldy", which means mould is now

WHAT IS MOULD?

growing on it. But where did the mould come from?

The answer is that the spores of green and black mould exist in the air almost everywhere. The spores are the reproductive bodies of the mould. And if you provide them with a suitable place for obtaining food, they will settle and reproduce.

If you looked with a microscope at the web-like threads of the mould, you would see that it is made up of many long, colourless threads with two kinds of branches. One branch is topped by little black balls which contain the spores.

The other kind, which is shorter and which penetrates into the bread, serves as an absorber of food, like roots. All moulds and mildews have them and they are both types of fungi; simple, dependent plants.

The most common moulds that people know are the black and green moulds, named after the colour of their spores. And since these spores are floating about in the air all around us, when food, fruit, preserves, or even leather are left about in warm, moist places, the spores quickly "attack" and begin to grow.

The green mould that grows on bread is called *penicillium glaucum.* There is a mould very much like it which grows in soil, called *penicillium notatum,* from which we get penicillin!

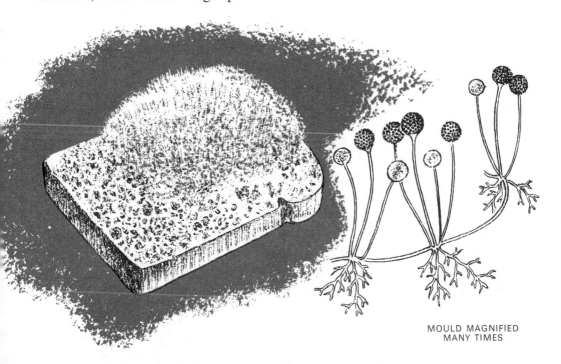

MOULD MAGNIFIED
MANY TIMES

Viruses are very small particles which may cause disease in man, animals, and plants. That word "particles" seems a strange way to describe them, so let's see why it is used.

WHAT IS A VIRUS? Viruses are so small they will pass through the finest filters. They cannot be grown in sugar solutions, but will grow and multiply in the presence of living tissue. They are parasites and depend completely upon their host. Viruses are too small to be seen by ordinary microscopes—they have to be photographed through electron microscopes.

Because they are so small and need so many things to make them grow, many scientists think viruses are not living matter at all, but something between living and non-living matter.

Viruses cause many diseases with which we are all familiar. In attacking organs of the body, each group of viruses causes a different group of diseases. Some of the diseases caused by viruses that attack the skin are chickenpox, smallpox, measles, German measles and fever blisters.

Other viruses cause diseases of nerve tissue, such as rabies, brain fever and infantile paralysis. A third group of viruses cause diseases in the internal organs. Yellow fever, influenza, the common cold and viral liver inflammation are examples of this group.

One of the things that birds, snakes, fish, frogs, cows and men all have in common is a backbone, or vertebral column.

It is made up of many small pieces of bone called "vertebrae".

WHAT ARE VERTEBRATES? These forms of life are therefore called "vertebrates". Creatures that do not have a backbone, such as crabs, snails, grasshoppers and sponges, are called "invertebrates".

True vertebrates also have a bony, boxlike structure at one end of their backbone which contains the brain. Their nerves run together into large bundles which are carried in a cavity in the backbone to the brain. The nerves make contact with every part of the body in a vertebrate.

Vertebrates also have fine, hair-like blood vessels which carry food to every cell in the body. And they combine to form large arteries and veins which run the length of the body to the heart.

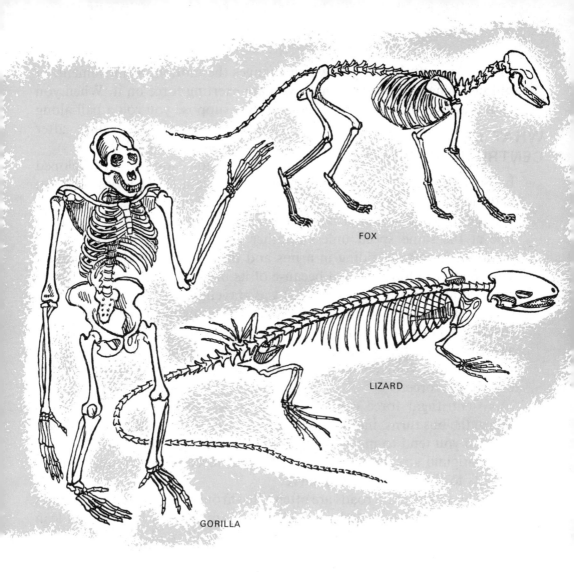

FOX

LIZARD

GORILLA

Another thing that distinguishes vertebrates from boneless animals is their muscular system. Their digestive system is well developed. To the vertebrae of their backbones are attached the ribs and also the bones which carry the limbs.

Vertebrates never have more than four limbs. In fish, the two pairs of paired fins correspond to the limbs. In some vertebrates, such as the snakes, these limbs are entirely lacking. In others, such as birds, one pair of limbs has developed into wings. In man, one pair is arms, the other, legs.

Typical vertebrates have tails. But just as other vertebrates have lost their limbs during development, so man has lost his tail.

"Force" is a push or a pull which changes the motion, or movement, of objects. When you push a chair, you are exerting force on it. When you stop pushing, the chair stops moving. But suppose you roll a ball along the ground. It keeps on rolling after you have stopped pushing it! Why?

WHAT IS CENTRIFUGAL FORCE?

The explanation for this (developed by Sir Isaac Newton, the first scientist to explain the theories of force) is the idea of "inertia". Inertia makes an object keep up whatever motion it has. Every bit of matter has inertia and will keep moving in a straight line at the same speed unless another force changes its motion. For example, if you are riding in a bus and the driver jams on the brakes, your body will hurl forward because of its inertia—it will keep on going forward at the same speed the bus was travelling.

Now let us get to centrifugal force. All of us have experienced this force. We notice it whenever an object travels in a curved path. Let us say you are on that same bus and it suddenly turns a corner. You will probably find yourself falling off the seat into the aisle! The reason is centrifugal force.

Centrifugal force can be explained by using the idea of inertia. When the bus turns, inertia tends to keep your body moving in a straight line. So you tend to move toward the outside of the curve so as to keep your original straight motion. Centrifugal force always seems to push objects to the outside of the curve.

This is why main roads are often tilted around a turn; why aeroplanes bank when they turn; and why, when you are riding a bicycle, you lean inward! This leaning inward, and the banking of roads and aeroplanes, helps to balance centrifugal force, which would otherwise tend to hurl objects outward. The leaning inward balances the tendency to move outward and you can make the turn properly.

Ice is a solid. When the temperature is cold enough, liquid water becomes solid ice. Water expands greatly when it freezes. Ten litres of water make about 11 litres of solid ice.

WHY DOES ICE FLOAT?

Objects in water float or sink according to a principle that was first discovered by Archimedes, a Greek mathematician who lived in the third century B.C. This law, known as "Archimedes' Principle", states

that any object placed in liquid is buoyed up or held up by a force equal to the weight of the liquid displaced.

Wood is one-half as heavy as water, therefore one-half its volume of water will hold it up. Cork is one-fifth as heavy as water. Ice is about nine-tenths as heavy. This is why about nine-tenths of an iceberg is under water and an iceberg may really be much larger than we think it is when we see it.

Ice near the freezing point may be melted by adding pressure, but it refreezes quickly when the pressure is released. When you squeeze a snowball, you melt some of the ice crystals but they freeze again to make a hard ball when you stop squeezing.

Because water expands greatly when it freezes, a great force is put forth when ice is formed. Rocks are often split by water freezing in tiny cracks or crevices. This is important in the slow breaking down of mountains. In fact, in the quarries of Finland, workmen split great blocks of rock by filling cracks in the rock with water and allowing it to freeze.

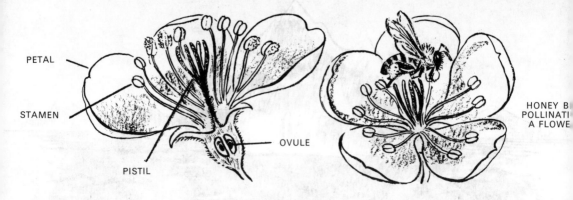

PETAL

STAMEN

PISTIL

OVULE

HONEY B
POLLINATI
A FLOWE

The flower is the means by which the plant can reproduce new plants like itself. A botanist defines a flower as a group of parts whose function is to produce pollen or seeds or both.

WHAT IS POLLINATION?

The most important parts of the flower, from this point of view, are "pistils" and "stamens". Many flowers contain both, the pistil or pistils in the centre, surrounded by the stamens.

In the enlarged, bottom part of the pistil there are tiny bodies called "ovules". Each ovule may develop into a seed. The most important part of an ovule is a tiny egg cell, so small it can only be seen under a microscope.

The stamens contain a pollen sac at the end of a stalk. When these pollen sacs open, they release the pollen they contain as a fine dust which is usually yellow.

In order to produce new seeds, the pollen grains from the stamens must be transferred to the pistils. This transfer of pollen is always called "pollination".

Pollination is brought about in many different ways. Sometimes the pollen simply falls on to the pistil, but usually the wind or insects are needed for pollination.

Among the plants that are pollinated by the wind are the grasses; not just the grasses of the meadows, but wheat, corn and other grains. The stamens wave in the breeze. The pollen is shaken off and flies through the air and lands on pistils.

Another form of pollination is carried out by insects. This usually happens with flowers that have bright colours or fragrance, and thus attract insects. Insects visit the flower for nectar which they make into honey, and for pollen which they use as food. As an insect collects pollen from a flower, some of it rubs off on the insect's body. Then, when the insect visits another flower, some of the pollen rubs on to the stamens.

Every living and growing thing in the world, whether animal or plant, produces young of its own kind or species, and no other. This takes place because of heredity.

HOW DID MAN FIND OUT ABOUT HEREDITY?

However, the offspring of any two parents need not all be the same in their traits, such as looks, colouring, and physical and mental condition. Their differences also result from heredity.

Hereditary traits are traits which form from something inside the baby at the very second that his life begins. The first facts from which the whole modern science of heredity was developed were discovered by an Austrian monk, Gregor Mendel, in the mid-nineteenth century.

Mendel was experimenting with sweet peas in his garden. He discovered that in the seeds from parent plants, there were a large number of different factors that always worked by certain rules to control what a plant growing out of the seeds would look like. We now call these factors "genes". But it was not until 1900, 16 years after Mendel's death, that other scientists saw how important his findings were. They called his discoveries "the Mendelian Laws".

We speak of ordinary light as being "white"; we call it white light, or sunlight. But this light is really a mixture of colours.

When sunlight strikes the bevelled edge of a mirror, or the edge of a

WHY ARE THE COLOURS IN A RAINBOW ARRANGED AS THEY ARE?

glass prism, or the surface of a soap bubble, we see the colours in light. What happens is that the white light is broken up into the different wave lengths that are seen by our eyes as red, orange, yellow, green, blue, indigo and violet.

These wave lengths form a band of parallel stripes, each colour grading into the one next to it. This band is called a "spectrum". In the spectrum, the red line is always at one end and the indigo and violet lines at the other end, and this is decided by their different wave lengths.

When we see a rainbow, it is just as if we were looking at such a spectrum. In fact, a rainbow is simply a great curved spectrum caused by the breaking up of sunlight.

When sunlight enters a droplet of water, it is broken up just as if it had entered a glass prism. So inside the drop of water, we already have the different colours going from one side of the drop to the other. Some of this coloured light is then reflected from the far side of the droplet, back and out of the droplet.

The light comes back out of the droplet in different directions, depending on the colour. And when you look at these colours in a rainbow, you see them arranged with red at the top and violet at the bottom of the rainbow.

A rainbow is only seen during showers when rain is falling and the sun shining at the same time, but on opposite sides of the observer. You have to be between the sun and the droplets of water with the sun at your back. The sun, your eye, and the centre of the arc of the rainbow must all be in a straight line.

One of the great mysteries of the world in which we live is light. We still do not know exactly what it is. It can only be described in terms of what it does.

HOW DOES LIGHT TRAVEL?

We know light is a form of energy. Like some other forms of energy—heat, radio waves and X-rays—the speed, frequency and length of its waves can be measured. Its behaviour in other ways makes it similar to these other forms of energy, too.

We know the speed of light. It travels at about 186,000 miles per second. This means that in a year, a beam of light travels 5,880,000,000,000 miles. That is the distance which astronomers call a "light year", and it is the unit used to measure distances in outer space.

In trying to understand what light is and how it travels, many theories have been developed. In the seventeenth century, Sir Isaac Newton said that light must be made up of "corpuscles", somewhat like tiny bullets shot from the light source. But this "corpuscular" theory of light could not explain many of the ways in which light behaves.

At about the same time, a man named Christian Huygens developed a "wave theory" of light. His idea was that a luminous or lighted particle started pulses, or waves, much as a pebble dropped into a pool makes waves.

Whether light is waves or corpuscles was argued for nearly 150 years. Gradually, as certain effects of light became known, the idea of light corpuscles died out.

Scientists now believe that light behaves both as particles and as waves. Experiments can show either idea to be true. So we simply cannot give a complete answer to "What is light?"

Sound is the result of vibrations. Vibration is simply the moving back and forth of some object. But in order for these vibrations to be heard, they must take place in some medium, something to carry the sound

WHAT IS NOISE? from its source to the hearer. That medium may be air, a liquid, or a solid.

When the vibration is very regular, that is, when the sounding body sends out waves at absolutely regular intervals, the result is a musical sound. If the vibration is not regular, the effect on your ears is not at all pleasing. The resulting sound is "noise".

The three differences between one sound and another are loudness, pitch, and tonal quality. Loudness of a sound depends partly on the distance from the object to the ear and partly on the amplitude of vibration of the sound-making object. Amplitude means the distance the vibrating body moves in its to-and-fro motion. The greater this movement is, the louder the sound will be.

The highness or lowness of a sound is called its "pitch". Pitch depends on the speed of vibration of the sounding object. The greater the number of vibrations that reach the ear every second, the higher will be the pitch.

Even when two sounds may be of the same pitch and loudness, they can sound different. The quality of a musical sound depends upon the number and strength of the "overtones" present in the sound. If a violin string is made to vibrate in one long vibration throughout its entire length, it gives the lowest tone that it can make. This note is called "the fundamental". If the string vibrates in more than one part, higher pitched notes are heard. They blend with the fundamental to create the particular "violin" quality. These higher notes are the overtones. They create the tonal quality of a sound.

The words "perpetual motion" by themselves just mean motion that goes on forever. But usually when we say perpetual motion we are referring to a very special thing.

WHAT IS PERPETUAL MOTION?

For hundreds of years, men have had the dream of creating a machine that, once it is set in motion, would go on doing useful work without drawing on any external source of energy. Every machine now known has to have a source of energy.

A perpetual motion machine, however, would create its own energy in the form of motion. Every time a complete cycle of its operation was finished, it would give forth more energy than it had absorbed.

Most of the people who tried to create perpetual motion machines had practical purposes in mind. They thought it would be wonderful to have machines that could raise water or grind corn without the need of supplying any energy to the machine.

Is it possible to create a perpetual motion machine? Any scientist will tell you that the answer is no. The reason is based on what is one of the most important laws of science, the principle of the conservation of energy. According to this principle, energy cannot be created and cannot be destroyed in nature. Energy can be transferred from one place to another, energy can be freed or unlocked, but energy cannot be created. This means that any machine that does work must have a source of energy.

In the course of history, thousands of attempts have been made to create perpetual motion machines. The first attempts were made at a time when the law of the conservation of energy was still unknown. A great many others were simply fakes that were later exposed.

Most people think a vacuum is a place where there is absolutely no matter, a place that contains absolutely nothing.

WHAT IS A VACUUM?

According to scientists, however, such a thing is impossible. They believe there can be no region where there is not a single bit of any substance, not a molecule of gas or the tiniest particle of dust. So a vacuum is actually a region where there is very little matter. A good vacuum means an almost total lack of air, dust, and other samples of matter. But the key word is "almost".

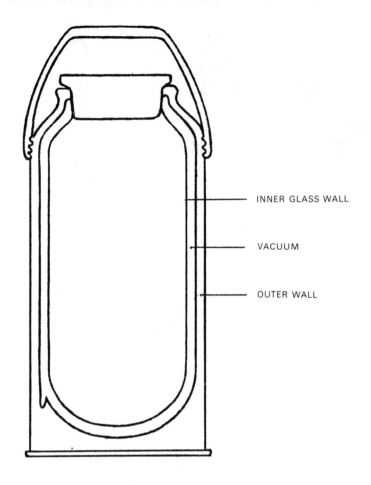

INNER GLASS WALL

VACUUM

OUTER WALL

One of the simplest ways to develop a vacuum is to pump the air out of the container in which the vacuum is to be formed. Very efficient vacuum pumps which are able to create good vacuums are used in many important ways in industry. For example, the electric bulb is worked on by a vacuum pump when it is being manufactured. If air were to remain in the bulb, the oxygen in the air would cause the filament to burn up in a fraction of a second.

In most modern bulbs, almost all the air is removed by a pump. The same is true of the vacuum valves in radio or television sets. Just before they are sealed, as much air as possible is removed.

Probably one of the most familiar uses of a vacuum is the vacuum flask in lunch boxes. There is a double wall inside and a vacuum is produced between the two walls. Since there are very few molecules in a vacuum and they are far apart, the conduction of heat is prevented. This keeps the cold milk in a vacuum flask cold. And if a hot liquid is put in the flask, conduction of heat does not take place and the liquid stays hot.

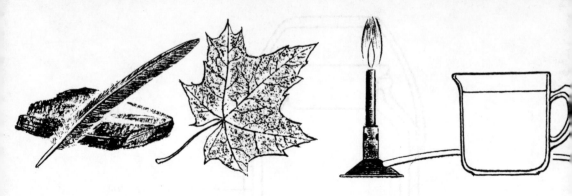

Anything that takes up room anywhere in the universe is called "matter". Matter may be a liquid, a solid, or a gas. These are known as the three "states of matter".

WHAT IS MATTER? Matter may also be "organic", or "inorganic". Human beings, trees, animals and flowers are examples of organic matter. Lumber, cotton and woollen cloth, and breakfast cereal are also organic matter, for they were once part of something alive. Things that are not living, or were never alive, such as iron, tin, glass and water, are inorganic matter.

All matter is put together in very much the same way. All matter, regardless of what form it is in, is built of "atoms". And atoms are made up of still smaller things called "electrons". Electrons are tiny, always-moving sparks of pure electricity.

Even though an atom is so small that you cannot even imagine it, there is a good deal of space between the particles that make it up. And so matter is really mostly space! A brick wall, or a living person, is really mostly space. In fact, if there were some way to take all the space out of you, leaving only solid matter, you would be the size of a small pill.

If all the atoms were exactly alike, there would be only one kind of matter in the world. But there are more than 100 kinds of atoms, and each of these is an "element", the simplest kind of matter. An element is matter built of only one kind of atom. Gold, iron, iodine, and oxygen are among the many elements.

Matter that is made up of more than one kind of atom joined together is called a "compound". The smallest bit of compound is a "molecule". The more closely atoms and molecules are packed together in matter, the "denser" we say it is. Matter that has great density is also heavy, like gold. Wood is less dense, and therefore lighter.

Matter can be changed from one state (liquid, solid, gas) to another, but it can never be completely destroyed. But it can be changed into energy.

A molecule is the smallest particle of a substance that can exist and still keep the properties of the whole. For example, if you broke down a molecule of sugar, the elements would not have the characteristics of

OW BIG IS A MOLECULE?

sugar—its taste or its colour, among other things.

Sometimes molecules are very simple, others have thousands of atoms arranged in a complicated pattern. In some gases, such as helium and neon, a molecule consists of only one atom. Some molecules contain two or more atoms of the same kind. A molecule of water, for example, is made up of two atoms of hydrogen and one of oxygen.

In contrast, the molecule of pure natural rubber is thought to contain about 75,000 carbon atoms and about 120,000 hydrogen atoms. So you can see that molecules differ greatly in size.

Simple molecules like that of water are only a few billionths of an inch in length. The rubber molecule is thousands of times larger. Some molecules are shaped like footballs, others are long and threadlike.

It is really impossible for us to imagine how small molecules are. For example, let us take 10 cubic centimetres of air. In this space there are over 300 million billion molecules (3 with 20 zeroes after it). And that bit of air is not packed tightly because it actually contains a great deal of empty space.

The weight of a molecule is measured by scientists on a relative scale. The weight of the molecule depends upon the weight of the atoms that form it. And the weight of the atom, in turn, depends upon the number

DOES A MOLECULE HAVE WEIGHT?

of protons and neutrons in the nucleus of the atom.

A molecule of water is made up of two atoms of hydrogen plus one of oxygen. Hydrogen is a simple atom with only one proton in the nucleus. Its atomic weight is 1. The weight of other elements is in multiples of the weight of hydrogen. Oxygen has eight protons and eight neutrons, making an atomic weight of 16. So, water has a molecular weight of 2×1 plus 16, which makes its molecular weight 18.

Molecules are held in their places in a solid or a liquid by the forces of attraction between molecules. This attraction is of an electrical nature, and this force is strong enough to account for the strength of most solid materials.

Air is everywhere about you. Every crack, hole and space that is not already filled with something else is filled with air. Every time you breathe, your lungs are filled with air.

WHAT IS AIR?

Even though you cannot see air, nor taste it, nor feel it (unless the wind is blowing), air is "something". It is a substance or material which scientists call "matter". Matter may be a solid, a liquid, or a gas. The matter called "air" is almost always a gas.

In fact, air is made up of certain gases. Two of these, nitrogen and oxygen, make up 99 per cent of the air. They are always found in the same proportion of about 78 per cent nitrogen and about 21 per cent oxygen. There is also a small amount of carbon dioxide in the air which is added to it by living things. The remaining part of 1 per cent is made up of what are called rare gases: argon, neon, helium, krypton, and xenon.

The great ocean of air extends for many miles above the surface of the earth. Because air is something, gravity attracts, or holds it, to the earth. Thus air has weight. The weight of the air exerts pressure. The air presses on your whole body from all directions, just as water would if you were at the bottom of the sea.

If you climb a high mountain or go up in an aeroplane, there is less air above you, so the pressure is less as you go up. About eight miles up, the pressure is only one-eighth of that at sea level. At 62 miles, there is almost no pressure.

All material things on earth are made up of one or more elements. Elements are substances that have atoms of only one kind.

WHAT ARE THE ELEMENTS?

Any one element may have some of the same properties that other elements have, but no two elements are exactly alike. For example, hydrogen and helium are both colourless, odourless, and tasteless gases. They are both light, but helium is heavier. Hydrogen burns, but helium will not.

All elements have a certain weight. They can be a solid, a liquid, or a gas. Some will dissolve in water. Others must be heated to a certain temperature before they will change from a solid to a liquid or to a gas. These characteristics are called "the physical properties" of elements.

After scientists studied the physical and chemical properties of elements, they grouped the elements that were alike together. These elements are called "chemical families".

All the families were combined into "the periodic table of elements". They were listed in order of their "atomic number". The atomic number of an element depends on how many protons, particles with a positive charge, the atom of each element contains. A hydrogen atom has one proton and its atomic number is one, so it is first on the periodic table.

Some elements are named after people or places or countries: Einsteinium, Europium, Germanium, Californium, and Scandium. Among the familiar elements are carbon, copper, gold, iron, lead, mercury, nickel, platinum, tin, radium and silver.

WHAT IS METAL?

It is not easy to define what a metal is. Physically, a metal is a substance that has a bright lustre and is a good conductor of heat and electricity. Metals have varying degrees of hardness, density, malleability, and ductility. (Malleability concerns being able to be rolled out and hammered. Ductility has to do with being drawn out, as into wire.)

Metal has a definite melting point and will fuse with other metals to form "alloys". With the exception of mercury, all metals are solids at ordinary temperatures.

Some metals are found in the pure state, but most of them are found in combination with other elements. These metals are in the form of

45

sulphides, oxides, carbonates, and silicates, usually mixed with rock and earthy materials. Some of the common metals found in combination in ores are lead, zinc, iron, copper, chromium, nickel, and mercury.

Some metals are so rare that tons of ore must be treated to get even a small amount of the pure metal. Radium is one of these. The science of recovering metals from their ores is called "metallurgy".

Many metals, when they are in the pure state, have properties that are undesirable. This is why most of the metals commonly used today are either alloys or compounds. Examples of alloys are table silver, gold coins, and aluminium pans. Pure iron is too soft to be of much value, so it is used most frequently as steel, which is a compound.

There are a few metals which, in tiny amounts, are necessary to animal life. Among these are iron, potassium, calcium, magnesium, and sodium. The body even uses minute quantities of copper, aluminium, and manganese.

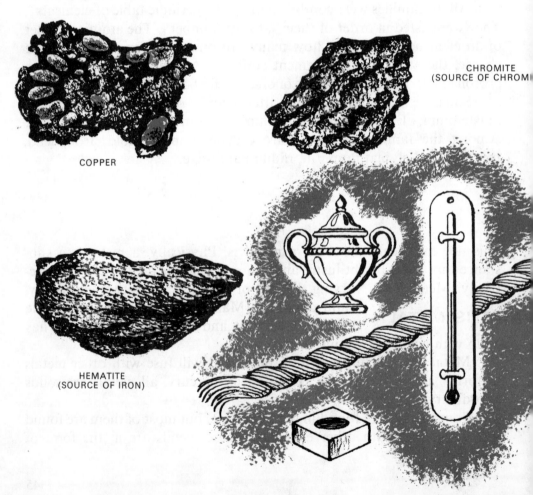

COPPER

CHROMITE
(SOURCE OF CHROM

HEMATITE
(SOURCE OF IRON)

People have been terrified of quicksand for centuries. It is supposed to have the mysterious power of sucking victims into it until they disappear.

The truth is, quicksand has no such power. And the fact is that if you

WHAT IS QUICKSAND? know what it is and how to deal with it, it cannot hurt you at all.

What is quicksand? It is a light, loose sand which is mixed with water. It does not look different from sands which might be right next to it. But there is a difference: quicksand will not support heavy objects.

Quicksand usually occurs near the mouths of large rivers and on flat shores where there is a layer of stiff clay under it. Water is collected in the sand because the underlying clay keeps the water from draining away. This water may come from many different places, such as river currents or pools.

The grains of quicksand are different from ordinary grains of sand because they are round instead of being angular or sharp. The water gets between the grains and separates and lifts them, so that they tend to flow over one another. This makes them unable to support solid objects.

Some quicksand is not even made of sand. It can be any kind of loose soil, a mixture of sand and mud, or a kind of pebbly mud.

People who step into quicksand do not sink out of sight. Since it contains so much liquid, it will enable them to float. And as quicksand is heavier than water, people can float higher in it than they do in water.

The important thing is to move slowly in quicksand. This is to give it time to flow around the body. Once it does this, it will act like water in which you are swimming.

The dust and other materials that are in the air as the result of a nuclear explosion—that is, from atom bombs—is fallout. It contaminates, or poisons, the air, soil, and water.

WHAT IS FALLOUT? Fallout contaminates the world around us because it is radioactive. This means that it contains certain kinds of atoms that are breaking down. As they break down, they give off tiny amounts of energy and matter, which are called "radiations".

A nuclear explosion produces a huge blast, a lot of heat, and many radioactive atoms. These radioactive atoms become mixed with particles of soil and dust from the earth. Tons of radioactive dust are blown or sucked into the atmosphere by a nuclear explosion. This returns to earth as radioactive fallout.

The heaviest particles of this debris drop to earth within minutes or a few hours of a nuclear explosion. The lighter particles are carried up and come down more slowly. They may circle the earth for months or even years. Eventually, they fall to the earth, mostly in snow, rain, and mist.

Fallout that falls on the outside of the human body can be washed away. But if fallout radiation gets inside the body, it may stay there for years. Fallout enters the body with the air, water, and food taken in. Mainly it comes from food. Fallout dusts the leaves of plants and their fruits. It falls on the soil and is taken into plants through their roots. Animals eat the plants, then human beings and other animals eat these animals.

Inside the body, radioactive atoms from the fallout send off radiations. When too much radiation passes through living cells, it may damage the cells or weaken the body's defences against disease.

The use of gypsum has increased so much that the production of gypsum has more than doubled in recent years.

WHAT IS GYPSUM? Gypsum is used to make wall-board and tiles because it resists fire and water so well, and because it insulates a building against both heat and cold. The boards or blocks of gypsum can be nailed and sawed like wood.

A mixture of gypsum with a little cement and certain other materials forms a light building material called "staff". This is generally used in constructing temporary buildings.

What is gypsum? It is a mineral of calcium sulphate in combination with water. There is a translucent kind of gypsum that is known as "selenite", and another which has a special lustre that is called "alabaster".

Most gypsum is mined from thick beds. Some deposits of it are near the surface, while others are far below. Gypsum beds over 100 metres thick are found in parts of Texas over areas of hundreds of square miles.

Gypsum has been used as a plaster and a building material since the time of the ancient Egyptians. If gypsum is used alone or mixed with sand or lime, it can be moulded into casts, stucco, tiling, or finishing plasters. Or it can be made into wall-board or blocks.

Many stage and film-sets are made of gypsum wall-board and plaster of Paris. Sculptors, surgeons, and dentists also use it for making casts.

Gypsum is found in Cheshire and other parts of England, but it occurs in the largest quantities in the United States.

Millions of years ago, fine-grained clay particles settled on the bottoms of lakes and inland seas and formed a soft mud. This later hardened into the mud-rock that is called "shale".

WHAT IS SLATE? During this period, the earth's crust moved and shifted. The layers of shale, covered by beds of other rocks, were folded up into wrinkles. These were flattened and squeezed so hard that the shale became slate.

The clay particles making up the slate were deposited by the lakes and seas in layers. Even after the pressure changed the shale to slate, the many separate layers of the deposits remained. And today we can split slate into wide, thin plates because it did stay in layers.

The most common colours of slate are dark grey and black, though it may also be red, green, or various shades of grey. The reason it is chiefly black is that the living matter in the original muds left carbon material.

Slate occurs only where mountain-making pressure and earth changes have been active upon the layers of old shale.

Slate is used for many purposes. One of its chief uses is as a roofing material for homes and buildings of all kinds. Among other things made from slate are blackboards, table tops, and draining boards.

Dust consists of tiny particles of solid matter that can be carried in suspension by air. Dust is usually lifted by the wind from the place it originated and is carried along by air currents until it finally settles because of gravity, or it comes down with rain.

WHAT IS DUST? Dust is produced by a wide range of conditions. It may come from soil that is being blown about, from the exhaust of heavy traffic, from the burning of fuel in homes and industry, and from volcanic activity, forest fires, and ocean spray.

You probably never thought of ocean spray as a producer of dust in the air. But did you know that ocean spray produces about 2,000,000,000 tonnes of salt dust in the air each year? After the water has evaporated in the spray, the chemical elements found in salt are left in the air.

We have all heard about "dust storms". These originate in areas where drought has removed natural vegetation. Such storms put thousands of tonnes of dust into the air, and this dust may end up somewhere as far as 2,000 miles away! For example, during the great dust storm that hit the South Western part of the United States in 1933, about 25 tonnes of dust per square mile were deposited in New England. Dust from the desert region of the Sahara has been noted to fall in London!

There is always an amazing amount of dust in the air. It is estimated that about 43,000,000 tonnes of dust settles over the United States every year. About 12,000,000 tonnes is due to human activities.

It was air pollution and unusual weather conditions that caused the dreadful London smogs—today, with a system of smoke-controlled areas, this serious health hazard seems to have been overcome.

Many people consider milk to be the most nearly perfect food we have. And when you consider all the good things for your body that you obtain when you drink milk, you can see why this is so.

WHAT IS MILK MADE OF? Proteins used to build and repair muscles are found in milk. Another important part of milk is fat, an energy-giving food. The fat in milk is called "butterfat". When globules (tiny, round pieces of fat) are present in milk, butter can be made.

Milk also has sugar, which is an energy-giving carbohydrate. Lactose, the sugar found in milk, is less sweet than cane sugar, and is more easily used by the body than is any other kind of sugar.

Milk also supplies the body with important minerals. The body uses minerals as bone-building and blood-building foods. Calcium and phosphorus make up a large part of the mineral content of milk. There is more calcium in milk than in any other food.

Other minerals in milk are iron, copper, manganese, magnesium, sodium, potassium, chlorine, iodine, cobalt, and zinc. And we're not finished yet! Milk also provides us with many vitamins. Milk is rich in vitamins B_2, A, B_1. It also contains vitamins C and D. And, of course, milk also contains water. But the amazing thing is that there is about 110 grams of food solids in each litre of milk!

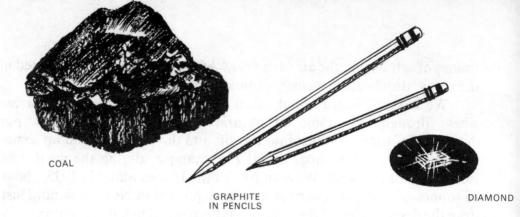

COAL

GRAPHITE
IN PENCILS

DIAMOND

Carbon is important to all forms of life. It makes up less than 1 per cent of all matter, but everything that lives or has lived contains this element. The bodies of all living things are made up of compounds containing

WHAT IS CARBON?   carbon, and where it is found in any quantity in the earth, life has probably existed.

Plants get carbon from the carbon dioxide gas of the air and use it in building up their roots, stems, and leaves. Animals get it for food from plants. At the same time, carbon dioxide is being returned to the air by animals when they breathe, and by plants when they decay.

Of all the forms of carbon, the best known, and perhaps the most valuable to man, is coal. Coal is about four-fifths carbon, the rest being hydrogen and other elements. The attraction between carbon and oxygen is almost like that between a magnet and iron.

This is one of the reasons why coal is so valuable. When coal is put into fire, its elements, particularly its carbon, burn, or combine with the oxygen in the air. This burning produces heat energy, which is used by man in many ways.

Carbon is found in forms that vary a great deal. Two of its most different forms are graphite and diamonds. Graphite is soft and slippery. It makes an excellent lubricant for machinery. When it is mixed with clay and hardened enough, it is used as the "lead" in lead pencils. Diamonds are the hardest substance known.

Carbon atoms can attach themselves to each other and to the atoms of other elements. They combine in many different ways to form many carbon compounds. One of the simplest ones is carbon dioxide, which is given off into the atmosphere when carbon burns in oxygen. Carbon monoxide, a poisonous gas, forms when carbon burns where there is not enough oxygen.

Carbon does not combine easily with other elements or compounds. However, it does react freely with them at high temperatures.

All living things are constantly searching for nitrogen in a form their bodies can use. Nitrogen makes up an important part of the bodies of humans, plants, and animals.

WHAT IS NITROGEN? Nitrogen is a necessary part of the protein substance which is man's body-building material. Without this substance, no one could grow or repair damaged or worn-out tissues.

Nitrogen makes up 78 per cent of the air we breathe, while oxygen is only 21 per cent. There are about 20,000,000 tonnes of nitrogen above every square mile of the earth's surface.

It is a colourless, odourless, tasteless gas that dissolves only slightly in water. When extreme cold or pressure is applied, it changes to a liquid. The temperature at which it becomes liquid is -218 degrees Centigrade.

It would seem easy for living things to get the nitrogen they need since it is all around them in the air. But in nature, only a few plants known as "legumes" are able to use pure nitrogen from the air. Human bodies cannot use pure nitrogen. We get the nitrogen we need by taking in proteins. These proteins are obtained by eating certain plants or plant-eating animals.

We breathe in nitrogen but do not use it in our lungs. We simply breathe it out again unchanged. What the nitrogen does is dilute the oxygen of the air so that we do not get too much at one time.

Nitrogen is useful only when combined with other chemicals to form compounds. It is chemically inactive and does not combine easily with other elements.

Uranium has existed in the earth for billions of years, but until man tried to make an atomic bomb and use atomic energy, most people did not know it existed.

WHAT IS URANIUM? Uranium is a metal, an ore, and one of the heaviest elements. Uranium is actually more common in the earth's surface than mercury or silver. And it has been found in rich deposits in many different places, including Zaire, Canada, the United States, and Russia.

When you look at clean, pure uranium metal, it is as shiny as silver. But after a few minutes of exposure to air, the uranium surface becomes dull and turns brown. The film that forms is uranium and oxygen—and it serves to protect the metal underneath.

The biggest difference between uranium and other metals is that uranium has natural radioactivity. This means the metal slowly changes by giving off certain rays that come out of the atom of the uranium. They are called alpha, beta, and gamma rays.

By giving off radiation, the uranium atom changes and becomes another radioactive element. This element in turn changes by giving off more radiation. And this process goes on as long as a radioactive element is left.

There are 14 steps in this series. One of the steps produces radium, and the last one produces lead. After that the series is ended, because lead is not radioactive. To change from uranium to lead in nature takes billions of years.

The uranium used in atomic bombs or in reactors for atomic energy is U-235. It is one of the natural forms of uranium, and is called an "isotope". Plutonium, which is also used in atomic energy, is a man-made product of uranium.

PROSPECTING FOR URANIU

Basically, a diamond is a beautiful gem. So we might say that its beauty makes it desirable and valuable. The diamond is also the hardest substance known to man, and this hardness is very useful. So this also makes the diamond valuable.

WHAT MAKES SOME DIAMONDS MORE VALUABLE?

Now why should one diamond be more valuable than another? Well, the diamonds that are offered for sale in jewellery may vary considerably in colour and quality. They occur in all colours of the rainbow. Some colours are rarer than others. The highest values are placed on those tinged with red or blue, and clear, colourless diamonds. Another factor which has an important bearing on value is purity. Diamonds may be as pure as a drop of water, or may show defects from a small pinpoint to a large flaw.

There are many diamonds that have been so valuable they have actually played a part in history. The most famous of these is the Koh-i-noor (Mount of Light), which has the longest history of any diamond in the world. Possession of this stone was so greatly desired by the rulers of Asia that practically all of the conquests of India from 1400 to 1828 were the result of it!

The Hope, an unusually blue diamond weighing about 44 carats, has also passed through many hands. The Hope is said to bring misfortune to all who possess it. Other famous diamonds are the Orloff, a former Russian crown jewel; the Regent, now in the Louvre in Paris; and the Cullinan, whose pieces are in the British crown and sceptre.

Inferior grade diamonds are used in industry. Many are manufactured into diamond-grinding wheels which are used to sharpen tools and to grind lenses. Industrial diamonds are also used in drills by mining companies to drill through rock.

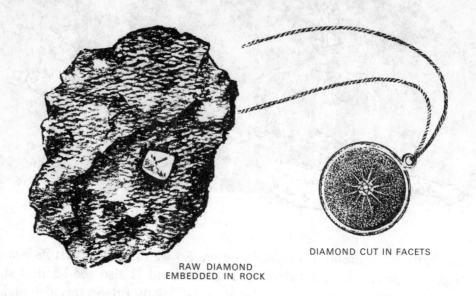

RAW DIAMOND
EMBEDDED IN ROCK

DIAMOND CUT IN FACETS

A diamond is the hardest substance known to man. And diamonds were formed by being "squeezed together".

This happened, according to scientists, about 100,000,000 years

HOW WERE DIAMONDS FORMED?

ago. At that time there existed beneath the ground a mass of hot liquid rock. The earth was in its early cooling stage, and in the process the mass of liquid rock was subjected to extreme heat and pressure. One of the results was that certain chemical combinations were formed. And one of these was highly crystallized carbon—what we call a "diamond".

Two of the most interesting things about diamonds are their hardness and their brilliance. A diamond is actually about five times as hard as corundum, the next hardest substance on earth.

And because a diamond is so hard, getting it ready for use in jewellery is quite a complicated and skilful process. First, a diamond is cleaved, or divided. This requires a great deal of study to make sure it will split along certain natural lines. A narrow notch is then cut with another diamond having a sharp point; an iron or steel edge is laid on this line, and a sharp blow is struck. If all has been done correctly, the diamond, the hardest substance in the world, splits instantly in two in exactly the direction desired!

Diamonds also have "facets", or little faces, cut into them. This is done on a high-speed iron wheel on the edge of which is diamond dust mixed in oil. The average brilliant diamond is cut with 58 facets! All this is done to make the diamond have the right shape and brilliance.

Did you know that the continents of the world rest on granite? It is the hard rock that forms much of the earth's outer crust.

The name "granite" comes from the Latin word *granum,* meaning "grain". The grains in granite are crystals

WHAT IS GRANITE? of quartz, feldspar, mica, and hornblende. Granite varies in colour. It may be greyish or pinkish, and it may also be coloured by impurities.

Granite is one of the "igneous", or fire-made rocks. It is formed, for the most part, at some depth in the earth. Granite was formed when hot rock or molten "magma" was slowly cooled in the earth. Magma is a dough-like rock.

Granite is usually formed under mountain folds where the rocks on the surface act like a blanket to prevent its rapid cooling. The only time it is found at the surface is when the rocks lying on top of it have been worn away by wind, water, or ice. It may also have been thrust upward by movements of the earth. When the surface rocks have weathered away, the great masses of harder granite are left. In the United Kingdom, Dartmoor, the rugged Cornish Coast, the Lake District, the Antrim Hills and the Isle of Skye are all granite outcrops.

When granite is exposed to the air, weathering begins at once. The feldspars break down first, changing to clay and salts. Only the quartz remains unchanged. In time, giant granite mountains are reduced to minerals. These minerals, with remains of plants and animals added, form the soil.

Granite is one of the strongest building stones. It is used for building exteriors, monuments, and gravestones. It must be highly polished to prevent weathering. The ancient Egyptians used granite to build temples, columns, and the pyramids.

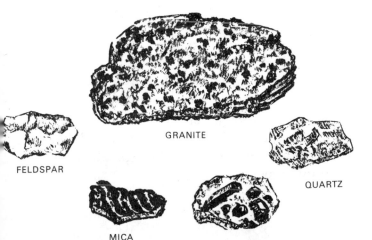

GRANITE

FELDSPAR

QUARTZ

MICA

HORNBLENDE

R.I.P.

Platinum is a metal—but what an amazing metal it is! It is greyish white in colour, and its name comes from the Spanish *plata* and means "little silver".

WHAT IS PLATINUM?

Platinum is harder than copper and almost as pliable as gold. You could take a single ounce of platinum and stretch it out into a fine wire that would reach across Western Europe from Cologne to Moscow. A cube of platinum measuring 30 centimetres each way would weigh more than half a tonne. Platinum is almost twice as heavy as lead.

Platinum is usually found in ores often mixed with the rare metals palladium, rhodium, iridium, and osmium, which are called "platinum metals". Occasionally, it is found with metals such as gold, copper, silver, iron, chromium, and nickel. It is found in the form of small grains, scales, or nuggets.

Large deposits of platinum were first discovered in South America in the eighteenth century. For a great many years it was considered quite useless, and so it was cheap. Then, when people began to find how useful this metal could be, and since it is quite rare, the price went up to the point where that cube of platinum mentioned above would have been worth over a million pounds.

What makes platinum especially useful is that it resists oxidation, acids, and heat. The melting point of platinum is about 1,843 degrees Centigrade. For most purposes, platinum is mixed (alloyed) with one of the other "platinum metals" or with silver, gold, copper, nickel, or tin.

While the chief use of platinum is for jewellery, it is also used for contact points where electrical circuits are opened or closed, in laboratory weights, in instruments for exact measurement of temperatures, and for fuses in delicate electrical instruments.

There are many different alcohols. One of the most common types is the kind found in alcoholic drinks. This is "ethyl alcohol", and is usually known as "grain alcohol".

WHAT IS ALCOHOL?

Grain alcohol is produced from starches and sugars, and can be made from most vegetables, grains, and fruits. When made from starch, the starch is first changed to sugar, and the sugar is then fermented to give alcohol.

Alcohol is generally made from corn, rye, barley and other materials. In Ireland the infamous "poteen" is made from potatoes, while most alcohol in the United States is made from Blackstrap molasses.

Did you know that ethyl alcohol is also valuable as a fuel? It can even be used in motor-cars as a substitute for petrol. When used for engines, it is often mixed with other chemicals to improve it. During World War II, various countries that lacked oil used alcoholic mixtures in place of petrol in cars.

Although alcohol is lighter than water, the two liquids mix easily and make a solution that has a lower freezing point than water. Such a solution is commonly used as an antifreeze mixture in motor-car radiators.

Because it dissolves so many substances, alcohol is often used as a solvent, as in making varnishes for wood and lacquers for metals. Alcohol is also used in the preparation of anaesthetics such as chloroform and ether, and in the manufacture of many substances, such as dyes, medicines, liniments, and vinegar.

Alcohol is an antiseptic, and is used in museums and hospitals to preserve specimens. When taken into the body in small amounts, it unites with oxygen to give heat.

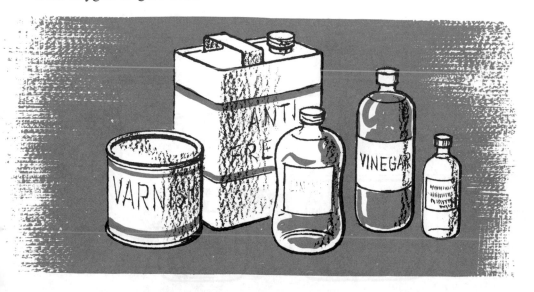

Aluminium is a silvery-white, lustrous metal that is only about one-third as heavy as iron. It can be drawn out into wires that are finer than the finest hairs, and hammered into sheets as thin as a sheet of newspaper.

WHAT IS ALUMINIUM?

It may surprise you to learn that it is the most abundant of all the metals in the world. Nearly 8 per cent of the earth's crust is aluminium.

But aluminium is never found free in nature. It is combined with various substances to form parts of many rocks and soils. Did you know that sapphires, rubies, garnets, and other beautiful gems are compounds of aluminium?

The problem was how to separate cheaply aluminium from the other substances. On February 23rd, 1886, a twenty-two-year-old chemist named Charles Martin Hall found a way to make this metal cheaply and in large quantities. In melted cryolite, which is a compound of aluminium and sodium with fluorine, he dissolved a small amount of aluminium oxide. Then he placed the mixture in a carbon vessel and passed a direct electric current through it. After about two hours, little "buttons" of metallic aluminium were found in the bottom of the vessel. This same general method is still used for the production of the world's entire supply of aluminium metal.

Cryolite is found only in Greenland, but can be manufactured if the mineral form is not available. Bauxite, an impure aluminium oxide, is found in many countries, but must be purified before it can be used to produce metal.

Aluminium is an almost perfect material for cooking utensils because it is a good conductor of heat, and is easily kept clean and bright. It is also used in motor-car engines, aeroplanes, and train engines.

Most of us know talc only in the forms of a body powder. But talc has many important uses.

Talc is a mineral—the softest mineral known to man. It can be scratched easily with the fingernail. It is made of tiny flakes, or scales, of magnesium. Talc may be silvery white or even a delicate green.

WHAT IS TALC?

When talc is in solid form it is called "soapstone". In this form it is usually greyish or greenish in colour, and is very soft and greasy to the touch. Often it has brown spots.

The best quality talc comes from Piedmont, Italy. There are also deposits in England, Canada, Germany, and Zimbabwe. In the United States, mainly along the Atlantic Coast, there is more talc than in all the rest of the world.

Because it resists ordinary heat so well and can be easily shaped, soapstone was used in the making of household articles. For this reason it was sometimes called "potstone". Cooking utensils and parts of stoves were sometimes made from it. Laundry tubs and sinks were also made from soapstone.

Soapstone hardens at high temperatures, and so is used for lining furnaces. Slabs of soapstone are used for acid tanks in laboratories, as it cannot easily be eaten away. It is a poor conductor of electricity, and for this reason can be used as a base for switchboards and electrical insulation.

Many primitive people have shaped this mineral into cooking utensils. And the ancient Egyptians carved talc into charms, which they coated with a coloured glaze.

About three-quarters of the talc processed in the Western World goes into the manufacture of paint, glazed tiles and other ceramic products, roofing, paper, and rubber.

Suppose you are in a ship crossing the ocean, or making your way across some huge desert that has no landmarks. How could you describe your exact location so that anyone in the world could find you? That is what latitude and longitude do. They provide the means for locating a place anywhere on the earth's surface.

WHAT IS LATITUDE AND LONGITUDE?

If we want to locate a place in terms of its position north or south, we refer to the latitude. We call the line running around the centre of the earth the Equator. It has zero latitude. As we go north of the Equator, we have north latitude, and as we go south of it, we have south latitude. Imagine lines drawn around the earth at certain regular distances north and south of the Equator. These lines are called "parallels", because they are all parallel to each other and to the Equator. The distance between each line is measured not in miles, but in degrees. A degree is $\frac{1}{360}$ of a circle.

Every 15 degrees we have another line of latitude. As we reach the North Pole we have 90 degrees latitude north, and at the South Pole we have 90 degrees south.

Now suppose we want to measure distance east and west. The lines we use are called longitude. But what should our starting point be? A long time ago it was decided to use a line that passed through Greenwich, England, as the zero line for longitude. Lines of longitude are called "meridians", so the line passing through Greenwich is the prime meridian. As we move east of this line, at distances of 15 degrees, we have east longitude, and as we move west, we have west longitude. To get even more exact measurement, a degree is divided into 60 minutes, and a minute into 60 seconds.

The antarctic region is the area around the South Pole. It includes the continent of Antarctica, which is the fifth largest continent. It is almost as large as Europe and the United States combined.

IS THERE ANY KIND OF LIFE IN THE ANTARCTIC? This region is the coldest and bleakest part of the earth. It is surrounded by the world's roughest seas. It has strong winds, blizzards, little rainfall, and such severe cold that the whole region is almost useless. There is never enough sunlight to warm the land, and there is a year-round covering of snow. The coldest temperature ever recorded in the world was in Antarctica, more than −38 degrees Centigrade. Because of the extreme cold, nothing seems to spoil, for there is no rot, rust, or bacteria.

What is to be found under the icy blanket of Antarctica? Not enough of it has been explored to really know. A few coal layers and small mineral veins have been seen by explorers. Probably other minerals do exist, but it would be so hard and expensive to get at them that they remain untouched.

The only plants that exist there are the simplest forms—a few mosses, lichens, fungi, and algae—which are of no value and furnish no food. Only birds and animals that can find food in the sea live in the region.

The most common birds are skua gulls, snowy petrels, and several species of penguins. The penguins live and nest near the edge of the continent. They have underdeveloped wings and cannot fly on land, but in the water they are good swimmers. There are several kinds of seal in antarctic waters. The only industry in Antarctica is whale hunting. But so many whales have been caught there that there is now an international control to limit whale hunting.

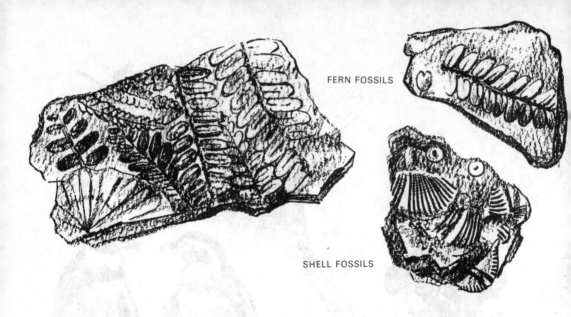

FERN FOSSILS

SHELL FOSSILS

A fossil is the remains of plants and animals preserved in rock. Sometimes they take the form of shells, bones, scales, or other hard parts of animals. Sometimes an entire animal is preserved. Or a fossil can be a film of carbon left by a decaying plant. It might be the track of animals walking across mud.

HOW ARE FOSSILS FORMED?

When a plant or animal dies, it gradually disappears. The soft parts decay. The hard parts are worn away by wind and rain. But if the body is covered by sand or other substances, parts of it may be preserved for a long time, and they may become fossils.

Most fossils are remains of plants and animals that lived and died in water. Their bodies became quickly covered by sand carried in the water. Gradually, more sand and mud covered the bodies, pressing down on the layers of sand underneath. The bottom layers hardened into rock, a form of rock called "sedimentary rock".

The sedimentary rocks built up very slowly, and the bodies of animals and plants buried in them gradually changed. Minerals from the water filled in the tiny pores in the bones, or the insides of shells. After the shell had crumbled away, a cast of the shell remained in the rock and so a mould of the outside of the shell remained in the rock. This process may take thousands of years.

On land, the bodies of plants and animals may be covered by blowing sand or perhaps ashes from a volcano. Insects and other small animals may be trapped in sticky sap. If this sap hardens into amber, it preserves the bodies of the animals inside. Larger animals may fall into tar pits or quicksand, and their bodies may be preserved for millions of years.

Archaeology gives us the story of the people who lived in the past. Archaeologists study the objects these early people left behind.

WHAT IS ARCHAEOLOGY?

There are two parts to archaeological work. Each part requires special training. The first part is "excavating", or digging up the places where early people lived or worked. This is a job that must be done slowly and carefully. It includes keeping records of the work done.

The second part is the studying of everything that is dug up, and of describing all these things so clearly that the information can be understood and used by anyone interested in the past. When both jobs are finished, the archaeologist can write the story of the people.

The story is never quite complete, for it is based only on the things left behind by a people. Most often these are the objects that were used each day. The remains of houses, tools, jewellery, dishes and other containers, and toys are often discovered; bones of animals used for food are also found.

Many of the things the early people threw away will not be found by archaeologists. For example, objects that were made of leather, wood, cloth, wool, or straw are not likely to remain. These materials decay. And we may never know if the people were artistic, because lovely weaving and handsome woodwork may also be lost.

Archaeology began when people became curious about what happened in earlier times. In the fifth century B.C., a Greek historian, Herodotus, visited Egypt and was interested in the ancient monuments. But after the time of the ancient Greeks, this kind of curiosity seemed to have died.

In the 1500's travellers to Greece and Italy began to take an interest in the ancient monuments they saw there. The Italians began to poke among the ruins. They found coins, vases, and other objects. Soon more and more people became interested in "digging up the past", and the science of archaeology was on its way.

Early man, living thousands of years ago, made caves and rock shelters his home. In fact, some of the earliest cave dwellers did not even look like people living today.

WHO WERE THE CAVE MEN?

These were the Neanderthal people. Their brains were as large as modern man's, but they had rugged faces with heavy ridges over their eyes. They were only a little over five feet in height and could not stand as straight as people do today.

These "cave men", or cave dwellers, were not good housekeepers. Anything they did not want, they left on the floor of the cave. Over thousands of years this mass of rubbish piled up and sometimes filled the caves.

The caves were large, dark, and frightening. The people lived in the mouth of the cave, where they were protected from wind, rain, and snow, without going into the darkness deep in the cave.

During the last part of the Ice Age, Cro-Magnon men, people who looked much like people living today, started to move into Europe. Like the Neanderthals before them, they lived in the mouths of caves.

But there were not enough caves for everyone, so some made tents and underground houses to live in. These are the men who made the famous cave paintings found in southern France and northwestern Spain.

These paintings are quite remarkable. They are full of life and power, and show many of the animals these cave dwellers hunted, such as the bison, the bear, the wild boar, the mammoth, and the rhinoceros.

CRO-MAGNON MAN

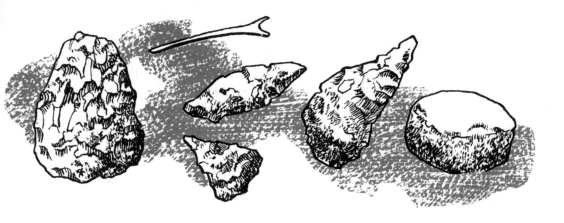

Far back in prehistory, before man could write, was a period of time known as the Stone Age. Man has lived on the earth for at least 500,000 years, but he did not begin to write until about 5,000 years ago. So pre-

WHAT WAS THE STONE AGE? history covers a very long time.

Because man learned to make stone tools during this time, it is called the Stone Age. The early part of it is known as the Old Stone Age.

The first type of stone tool that was made was probably a big stone chipped so that it had a sharp cutting edge all around. Scientists have called it a "hard axe". Chips struck off pieces of stone were also used as tools. The hand axe and the chips, or flakes, were all-purpose tools that man kept making and using for thousands of years.

Later, in the Ice Age, there were people living in Europe who are called Neanderthal by scientists. They had better tools than the people who had lived in the earliest days, and they hunted in groups instead of alone.

After the Neanderthals came the Cro-Magnon men, who were a more advanced people. They had all kinds of tools: spear points, harpoons, scrapers, and knives. They, too, lived by hunting.

About 6000 B.C., there came a great change in man's way of life. He learned to grow crops. This marked the beginning of the Neolithic, or New Stone Age.

He used animals as a source of food and the skins for clothing. He kept flocks of animals, built homes, and soon began to make new things that were not found in nature.

Clay could be moulded into dishes and bowls. When it was baked it could be used for cooking food. Wool and flax could be spun into yarn. When men worked together, villages and then cities grew. And from these beginnings all that we call civilization came into being.

The great Ice Age, or Glacial Period, was a time when a great mass of ice came down gradually from the north and covered parts of the world. It came down over North America, and a similar mass of ice came down

WHAT HAPPENED TO ANIMALS IN THE ICE AGE?

over northern Europe and western Siberia.

When did this happen? It is thought that it began nearly 1,000,000 years ago. When did it end? In the United Kingdom it may have ended only a few thousand years ago, and in some parts of the world it still has not really ended. The glacial period still remains in Antarctica and Greenland.

Millions of square miles of Central Europe were buried under a great creeping ice sheet which reached as far south as London, Rumania and the southern tip of Russia.

When the Ice Age came, animals from the Arctic migrated southward in front of the glaciers. Animals which could not stand the new, colder conditions were forced to migrate to warmer regions, or die out. Native wild animals now only found in America are merely a remnant of the many varieties of beasts known to have lived there before the Ice Age.

Man, of course, was able to adapt his life to the colder climate. This probably helped him gain in intelligence because more difficult living conditions made him use his mind and ingenuity in order to survive.

Plant life also moved south in front of the glaciers, and moved back again as the glaciers melted. But many kinds of plant simply died out.

In trying to learn how man developed, scientists study whatever remains of prehistoric man they can find. These include tools, cooking utensils, skeletons, and parts of the body.

WHO WAS NEANDERTHAL MAN?

In 1856, the remains of men were dug from a limestone cave in the Neander Gorge in Germany. These were the first complete skeletons ever found of prehistoric men, and this was because these people buried their dead.

Neanderthal people probably lived for about 70,000 years in central Asia, the Middle East, and many parts of Europe. This was in a period of about 150,000 to 30,000 years ago.

What was Neanderthal man like? He was heavy and stocky. His skull was flat. His face was long with a heavy jaw. He did not have much chin or forehead. Probably the earliest Neanderthal people lived when the climate was warm, between glacial periods. But then another ice age came and they began to live in caves and learned how to fight the cold.

There are many hearths in the caves that have been found which show that these people used fire to keep warm and protect themselves. They also may have cooked their meat.

Neanderthal man not only had hand axes but he also had "flake" tools. These are tools that were made of broad, thin flakes of flint with a good, sharp edge.

Some of the flake tools were points in the shape of rough triangles. They probably served as knives for skinning and cutting up animals. Neanderthal hunters may also have used pointed wooden spears.

Now here is one very curious thing about Neanderthal man: he had a larger brain than modern man has!

All over the world, there are people who are waging "conservation" campaigns. Conservation means many things to many people.

WHAT IS CONSERVATION?

To some it means preserving the wilderness in certain sections. To others it means preserving the wildlife. Conservation includes efforts to protect forests, as well as the wise use of all natural resources.

The problem of conservation has arisen because mankind is using the world's natural resources in greater quantity and variety than ever before. As the world's population grows, and as more people live at a higher standard, there is a greater demand for resources. These resources must be "conserved" to assure that there will be enough for the future.

What do we mean by "resources"? Well, they can be divided into three basic kinds. One is renewable resources. For example, water, farmland, forests, and grazing land, even while they are being used, can be improved and renewed through good management. This would include protection from erosion, irrigation, and fertilization.

A second group of resources is not renewable. These are mainly minerals. They are used up once they are taken from the earth. These include coal, oil, and natural gas.

There are some natural resources that cannot be used up. For example, solar energy, climate, and oceans cannot be increased, decreased, or damaged by man. Man can only destroy the beauty of scenery, or cause pollution of air, rivers and canals.

RENEWING FOREST

Deserts have come to symbolize for us places of extreme heat. The fact is, most of the famous deserts of the world are places where the thermometer goes bubbling away and where the sun beats down without mercy.

ARE DESERTS ALWAYS HOT? But this does not mean that a desert must be a place where it is always hot. Let us get a definition of a desert and we will see why this is so. A desert is a region where only special forms of life can exist because there is a shortage of moisture.

In a "hot" desert, there simply is not enough rainfall. So the definition holds true. But suppose there is a region where all water is frozen solid and cannot be used by plants. This satisfies the definition, too. Only it would make this a "cold" desert.

Did you know, for example, that much of the Arctic is really a desert? There is less than 40 centimetres of rainfall a year, and most of the water is frozen. So it is properly called a desert. The great Gobi Desert in the middle of Asia is bitterly cold in winter time.

Most of the dry, hot deserts with which we are familiar are found in two belts around the world, just north and south of the Equator. They are caused by high atmospheric pressures that exist in those areas and prevent rain from falling. Other deserts, which are found farther away from the Equator, are the result of being in "the rain shadow". This is the name for an effect that is caused by mountain barriers that catch rainfall on their seaward side and leave the interior region dry.

No great rivers originate in deserts. But a river may rise in moister areas and cross great deserts on its way to the sea. The Nile, for example, flows through the desert region of the Sahara and the Colorado River flows through a desert, too.

Did you know that nearly all the soil that exists in the world today was once rock? Nature has been at work for millions of years weathering and crumbling the rock into the tiny fragments we call soil.

WHAT IS SOIL? This is done in many ways. Alternate heat and cold cracks off surfaces of rock. Wind-blown sand wears away rock. Glaciers scrape rock surfaces. Running water carrying mud and sand rubs away rock surfaces. Waves beating against a shore pound rocks into smaller and smaller pieces. Certain bacteria give off acids which help crumble rocks.

One way to classify soil is according to the size and quantity of the rock particles in it. Sandy soil is composed chiefly of sand. Clay soil has very fine particles and tends to be heavy, cold, and damp. "Loam" is a kind of medium mixture of sand and clay. Stony soil contains a large proportion of rocks or pebbles. "Muck", or peat soil, has few rock particles and is made up chiefly of decayed vegetation.

The soil in which plants grow is made up of more than rock particles. It is a complex substance which also contains mineral salts, decayed organic material, and living organisms.

The value of a soil depends on its power to supply plant foods, air, and water to the roots of plants. If we sterilized soil and killed every living thing in it, the soil would no longer be "fertile".

But even if a soil contained all the necessary plant foods, nothing would grow in it without water to dissolve these foods. Water rises in soil just as water rises in a sponge placed in a saucer of water. The rising of this water keeps plants growing even when it does not rain for a long time.

If you have spent holidays by the sea, you must have noticed the difference between high and low tide. In some parts of the world there is as much as 12 metres between the height of high and low water.

ARE OCEAN TIDES USEFUL? Clearly, this movement of water is a great source of unused energy. If it were harnessed, as it is from waterfalls and rivers, the power could be enormous. The French have pioneered this form of tidal power in their huge hydro-electric project near St. Malo in Brittany. Nestling at the foot of the Cotentin peninsula between Dinard and St. Malo, it is able to take advantage of about half the estimated 56 million horse-power which is swept into the Channel by the Atlantic tide. The 24 separate power

stations, which are built into the dam, act simultaneously to produce 540 million KWH of electricity a year. This is less than some of the hydro-electric complexes built on the great rivers of Europe, but it is a great deal more reliable, as the rise and fall of the tide is unaffected by adverse weather conditions.

The outside of the earth is a crust of rock which is about 10 to 30 miles thick. When we go down into this crust, we find that it begins to get hotter and hotter.

WHY IS IT HOT INSIDE THE EARTH?

For about every 40 metres we go down, the temperature grows one degree higher. At two miles below the surface of the earth the temperature is high enough to boil water! If it were possible to dig down 30 miles, the temperature would be about 1,200 degrees Centigrade. This is hot enough to melt rocks. At the centre of the earth, scientists believe the temperature to be about 5,500 degrees Centigrade.

The crust of the earth has two layers. The upper layer, which makes the continents, is made up of granite. Under the layer of granite is a thick layer of very hard black rock called "basalt". This layer supports the continents and forms the basins that hold the oceans. At the centre of the earth, it is believed that there is a huge ball of molten iron, with a diameter of about 4,000 miles.

How did the centre of the earth get to be this way? According to most scientific theories, the earth and sun were once related in some way. Most scientists believe that the earth was once a hot, whirling mass of gas, liquid, or solid that began its regular trips around the sun. As years went by, it slowly cooled and the large mass grew smaller. As it whirled, it slowly took a ball-like shape. It was red-hot and held in its path by the attraction of the sun.

As the earth cooled, a hard crust formed on the surface. Nobody knows how long it took for the crust to form. But underneath that crust there remained the hot centre core of the earth, and it is still there today.

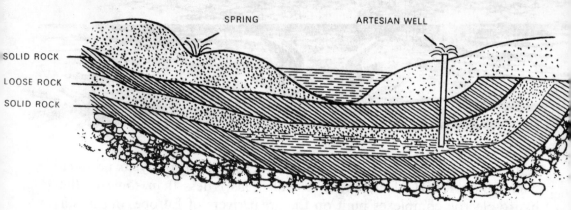

SPRING   ARTESIAN WELL

SOLID ROCK

LOOSE ROCK

SOLID ROCK

People who live in the city do not have to worry about wells or springs. The city supplies them with water. But out in the country and in some suburbs, obtaining a water supply may be quite a problem. Such water may come from a spring or a well.

WHAT'S THE DIFFERENCE BETWEEN A SPRING AND AN ARTESIAN WELL?

A spring is water that flows from a natural opening in the ground. During each rainfall, part of the water soaks into the soil and rocks through small spaces and cracks and is pulled down by gravity as far as the openings in the rocks will allow.

At different levels below the surface of the land there is a zone where all the openings in the rocks are completely filled with water. This is called "the underground zone". The upper surface of it is called "the water table".

In valleys or other low places in the land surface, below the water tables, springs occur where there are cracks in the rocks. In other words, the water that has been stored up there escapes as spring water.

Some springs flow all year because they receive water from deep within the ground-water zone. Other springs flow only in the rainy season, when the water table is at its highest level.

An artesian well is a well from which the water bubbles up naturally above the surface of the earth.

An artesian well is formed when a layer of loose rock, gravel, or sand is sandwiched between two layers of solid rock. The loose gravel or sand has spaces to hold the water. So we have three layers—solid rock above and below, and a porous layer that is like a pipe between them. These three layers are not horizontal, they lie at an angle. Water enters the middle layer at the top end. Farther down, if an opening is made, there is pressure that makes the water spurt out and we have an artesian well.

74

The Grand Canyon in Arizona is a natural wonder of the world. At some points it appears like a magic city of rock, with temples, towers, and castles of dazzling colours.

HOW WAS THE GRAND CANYON FORMED?

One of the most amazing things about it is that the Grand Canyon was made by a river. The waters of the Colorado River cut out this great gorge in the course of thousands of years. When you consider that it was cut out of solid rock in many places, you begin to appreciate the tremendous force of these waters. Even now, year by year, the rushing Colorado continues to cut deeper into the bottom of the gorge.

In certain places, the gorge of the Grand Canyon is more than a mile deep, and it is from 4 to 18 miles wide. As the river cut deep into the plateau to form the Canyon, it laid bare on the rock walls of the Canyon the story of hundreds of millions of years of the earth's history.

Down at the bottom of the gorge, beside the river, ancient crystalline rock is exposed. This is the buried remnant of an ancient mountain range which was folded back on itself and worn down by weather and water. The rise and fall of this mountain range millions of years ago is revealed only by the erosion of the Grand Canyon.

On the base of this buried mountain range rest beds of quartzite, sandstone, and limestone. They were formed over the years as ocean waters from the east and from the west flooded the section, and as whole mountain ranges rose and disappeared. Proof of the fact that great seas once rushed over these rocks is to be found in the fossils that turn up here. There are fossil remains of seaweed, sea shells, and fish.

You can get a pretty good idea of what causes an earthquake from thinking about what happens during an earthquake. During an earthquake, there is a trembling of the ground. It is this trembling of the earth which may cause buildings to fall.

HOW DOES AN EARTHQUAKE START?

So an earthquake is a trembling or vibration of the earth's surface. What makes it happen? Well, the rock of the earth's crust may have a "fault", a kind of break in the crust. The earth blocks shift. Sometimes the sides of the fault move up and down against each other. At other times, the sides of the fault shift lengthwise.

But when one rock mass has rubbed on another with great force and friction, we have a lot of energy being used. This vast energy that comes from the rubbing is changed to vibration in the rocks. The vibration is what we feel as an earthquake. And this vibration may travel thousands of miles.

The reason earthquakes take place in certain regions frequently and almost never in other regions, is that the faults in the earth's crust are located in these regions.

GLACIER

Glaciers are not a rarity today. The most common type are called "valley glaciers". In the Alps alone there are more than 1,200 valley glaciers, and in the high mountains of southern Alaska there are tens of thousands of them.

HOW DOES A GLACIER MOVE?

Valley glaciers creep downward like great rivers of ice from snowy mountains. The source of the large quantities of snow that form most valley glaciers is a valleyhead that is shaped like an amphitheatre with steep walls. Snow is blown into

ICEBERG

this area or slides down in avalanches. It does not melt during the summer but gets deeper year by year.

Eventually, the increasing pressure from above, together with some melting and refreezing, forces the air out of the lower part of the mass and changes it to solid ice. Further pressure from the weight of ice and snow above eventually squeezes this mass of ice until it begins to creep slowly out of the basin and down the valley.

When the glacier moves down below the region of snow, the front of it starts to melt. If the melting takes place as rapidly as the glacier moves, the front edge remains at the same position in the valley. But if melting takes place faster than the advance of the glacier, the front of the glacier retreats back up the valley. Where valley glaciers move into the sea they break off in huge blocks and we have icebergs.

In February, 1943, in the middle of a cornfield in Mexico, people saw a rare and amazing thing taking place. A volcano was being born! In three months it had formed a cone about 300 metres high. Two towns were destroyed and a wide area damaged by the falling ash and cinders.

HOW DOES A VOLCANO FORM?

What makes a volcano form? The temperature under the surface of the earth becomes higher and higher the deeper you go down. At a depth of about 20 miles, it is hot enough to melt most rocks.

When rock melts, it expands and needs more space. In certain areas of the world, mountains are being uplifted. The pressure becomes less under these rising mountain ranges, and a reservoir of melted rock (called "magma") may form under them.

This material rises along cracks formed by the uplift. When the pressure in the reservoir is greater than the roof of rock over it, it bursts forth as a volcano.

In eruption, hot gaseous liquid, or solid material is blown out. The material piles up around the opening, and a cone-shaped mound is formed. The "crater" is the depression at the top of the cone where the opening reaches the surface. The cone is the result of a volcano.

The material coming out of a volcano is mainly gaseous, but large quantities of "lava" and solid particles that look like cinders and ash are also thrown out.

Actually, lava is magma that has been thrown up by the volcano. When the magma comes near the surface, the temperature and the pressure drop, and a physical and chemical change takes place that changes the magma to lava.

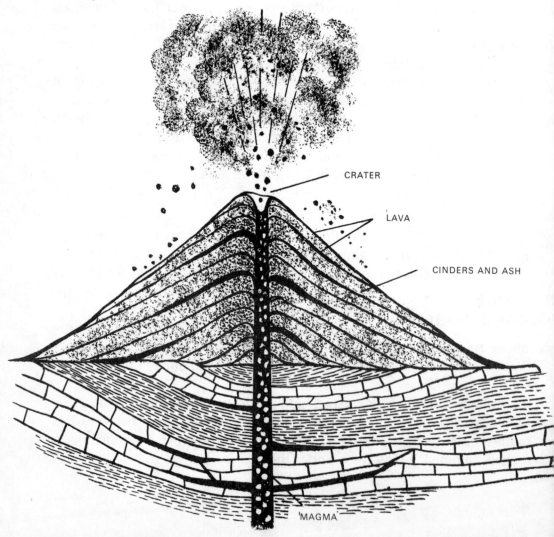

CRATER

LAVA

CINDERS AND ASH

'MAGMA'

There are many things about our own earth that still remain a mystery to us, and one of them is how the oceans were formed.

Actually, we do not even know for sure how old the oceans are.

HOW WERE THE OCEANS FORMED?

It seems certain that oceans did not exist in the first stage of the earth's growth. Perhaps they first came into being as clouds of vapour which turned into water as the earth grew cool. Estimates have been made of the ocean's age, based on the amount of mineral salt in the ocean today. These estimates range between 500,000,000, and 1,000,000,000 years.

Scientists are almost sure that most of the earth's land was covered by the sea at one time in the past. Some areas of the earth have been under water several times. But we do not know if any part of the deep ocean was ever land, or whether any land existing today was once beneath the deep ocean.

There is a great deal of evidence to show that certain parts of the land were once the bottom of shallow seas. For example, most of the limestone, sandstone, and shale found on land were deposited as sediment. The chalk that is found in Kent, Sussex and Wiltshire was deposited on the bed of a sea. It is made up of the shells of tiny creatures that sank to the ocean bed to form what we call chalk.

Today, the waters of all the oceans cover nearly three-quarters of the surface of the earth. While there are many great ocean areas where man has not yet explored the bottom or taken soundings, we have a good, rough idea of what the bottom is like. There are sections that are like mountain ranges, and there are plateaus and plains. But the ocean bottom is not as varied as the surface of the continents.

Rain and other water on the earth's surface is constantly being carried off. Rivers are the larger streams that accomplish this task. Streams smaller than rivers are brooks. And still smaller streams are rivulets.

HOW DO RIVERS FORM?

These flow together and join until the growing stream may become a large river.

Many rivers flow into the sea. But some rivers flow into inland lakes, and rivers that enter dry plains may even grow smaller and smaller until they disappear by evaporation or by sinking into the dry soil.

River water comes in part from rain water that flows along the ground into the stream channel. Or the river water may come from melting snow and ice, from springs, and from lakes.

Large rivers have many tributaries, or smaller streams, that flow into the main stream. The Ohio and Missouri—which are giant rivers themselves—are really tributaries of the still greater Mississippi. Each tributary has its own smaller tributaries, so that a great river system like the Mississippi is composed of thousands of rivers, creeks, brooks, and rivulets.

The land drained by a river system is called its "drainage basin", or "watershed". The Missouri-Mississippi, which is about 3,890 miles long, drains about 1,243,700 square miles. The Amazon River, some 3,900 miles long, has a watershed of over 2,722,000 square miles.

Rivers wear away the land and carry it, bit by bit, into the sea. During thousands of years, this can cause great erosion of the land. The Grand Canyon is the world's best example of how rivers can cut great valleys into the land.

The only reason a day has 24 hours in it is that man has decided he would like to work out time that way.

WHY IS THE DAY 24 HOURS?

Nothing occurs in nature or in the world that has anything to do with hours or minutes or seconds. These divisions of time were made up by man for his convenience.

But something does happen that has to do with what we call a "day". And that something is the rotation of the earth on its axis from west to east. Every time it goes around once, a specific amount of time has passed. We call that time a "day".

Scientists can measure that time exactly and they use the stars to do it. Observatories have what are called "sidereal" clocks. A sidereal day begins the instant that a given star crosses a meridian and lasts until the instant that it recrosses the same meridian.

Since man has broken up the day into hours, minutes, and seconds, we can say how long a sidereal day is. It is 23 hours 56 minutes and 4.09 seconds long, which means that there are 366 sidereal days in a year. We base our time (solar time) on the Earth's rotation relative to the Sun, which gives us a slightly longer day and $365\frac{1}{4}$ days in a year, hence we have a leap year every fourth year where there is one extra day, to make up.

To early people, a day meant simply the space between sunrise and sunset. The hours at night were not counted. The Greeks counted their day from sunset to sunset. For the Romans, it was from midnight to midnight.

Before clocks were invented, day and night were divided into 12 hours each. This division was not practical as the length of the two periods differs with the seasons. Today, most countries have a day which, by law, extends over the 24-hour period from midnight to midnight, following the Roman method.

When astronomers use the word "universe", they mean space and all the heavenly bodies contained in it. It is impossible for human imagination really to grasp what this involves.

DOES THE UNIVERSE EVER END?

Just to give you an idea, a light year equals about six billion miles. Our own galaxy, the Milky Way, is about 100,000 light years in length. There are millions of other galaxies, and one of the nearest to us is about 2,000,000 light years away. The most distant ones are billions of light years away. And all of this is only that part of the universe that we know about. There may be more that we have not detected yet!

In fact, astronomers believe that the part of the universe that is observable by any kind of instrument is only part of the whole universe. The question is then, how much more is there?

When astronomers try to answer a question like this, they become involved with the nature of space itself. According to the present theory,

81

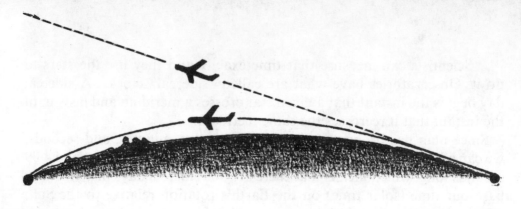

SAN FRANCISCO

SAN FRANCISCO   NEW YORK

space curves around on itself. This means that you can never get "outside" space, because your path will always curve around and lead you back again.

For example, when a plane flies from New York to San Francisco, it does not really fly in a straight line. Since the earth is curved, if the plane flew in a straight line, by the time it was over San Francisco it would be several thousand miles up in the air.

So in flying from New York to San Francisco, a plane follows a curved path. And if the plane continued in that same curved path, it would eventually come back to New York. Astronomers believe that space curves around in a special way—not as simple as earth's curving. A picture of it cannot be drawn on paper nor can a model be made of it. But it can be figured out by using complicated mathematics.

Nowadays we hear about "flying saucers", and people wonder if there are other worlds where some sort of living creature might exist. The reason people can even imagine such things is that we know that our solar

WHAT IS THE SOLAR SYSTEM?

system is only a tiny part of the whole immense universe. And scientists believe that there are probably millions of other "solar systems" that may be similar to our own.

A solar system is simply a sun and all the bodies around it that it controls by gravity. Our solar system is made up of all the planets, moons, asteroids, and comets that our sun controls by gravity. Our earth is simply one of the planets.

The planets vary greatly in size and distance from the sun. Mercury is the smallest planet and the nearest to the sun. It goes around the sun in only 88 days. Venus is about 68 million miles from the sun, and goes around it in 225 days. The earth is 93 million miles from the sun. Mars is about 142 million miles from the sun and goes around it in 687 days.

Jupiter, which is about 483 million miles from the sun, takes 12 years to make one trip around it. Saturn, 886 million miles from the sun, takes $29\frac{1}{2}$ years to make one orbit. Neptune takes 165 years. So you see, while these planets are part of our solar system, each one is quite different and exists under very different conditions.

NICHOLAS COPERNICUS

It is much harder for us to understand the universe as we know it today, than it was for ancient man to grasp his idea of the universe. Today we consider the universe to include not only the earth and our solar system,

HOW DID ANCIENT ASTRONOMERS PICTURE THE UNIVERSE?

but the galaxy to which this solar system belongs (called "the Milky Way"), and all the other galaxies as well. There are some 200,000,000,000 stars in just our own galaxy—and there are millions of other galaxies stretching out into the universe. Man's imagination just cannot grasp this vastness!

But in ancient times, they had a very simple picture of the universe. They thought that the sun, moon, stars, and planets were small objects moving around the earth. They believed that the universe was as it appeared to them—with a vast, flat, immovable earth in the centre and a great dome overhead, sprinkled with thousands of little shining lights.

The Greeks started the true science of astronomy. Most of the ancient Greeks thought that the earth stood still in the centre of the universe. Pythagoras, who lived in the sixth century B.C., seems to have been the first to suggest that the earth is a sphere. But he still thought it was the centre of the universe and did not move.

Aristarchus, who lived in the third century B.C., believed the earth was a sphere that rotated on its axis and revolved around a stationary sun. In the second century A.D., an astronomer named Ptolemy wrote a book called the *Almagest*. He thought the earth was the centre of the universe, and he tried to show how the planets, the sun, and the moon moved around the earth. His ideas were accepted for 14 centuries.

Copernicus, in 1543, suggested the sun as the centre of the universe. Then came the discovery of the telescope and man had a better means of finding out what the universe is really like. As more and more facts were gathered, our modern idea of the universe was gradually developed.

Meteors, also called "shooting stars", have long been a mystery to man.

Today, astronomers feel they have a pretty good idea of what meteors are. They believe them to be broken fragments of comets. When comets

WHAT ARE METEORS MADE OF?

break up, the millions of fragments continue to move through space as a meteor swarm or stream. The swarms move in regular orbits, or paths, through space. Some of the larger fragments may become detached and travel through space singly.

Most individual meteors are quite small, but occasionally there are some that weigh many tonnes. They are usually destroyed entirely by heat when they pass through the earth's atmosphere. Only the larger ones reach the earth.

When a piece of meteor reaches the earth it is called a "meteorite". The largest one found so far weighs between 60 and 70 tonnes and is still in its resting place in Africa.

There are two main kinds of meteorites. There are those composed chiefly of nickel and iron. These are called the "metallic" meteorites. Some are composed of minerals and look like a piece of igneous rock (rock formed by intense heat). These are called the "stony" meteorites or "aerolites". The outer surfaces of either kind usually have black crusts which are the result of the terrific heat experienced in passing through the atmosphere to earth.

In olden times, people trembled with fear when they saw a comet. They believed that comets were evil signs foretelling plagues, wars, and death. Of course we no longer believe this, but some people still wonder if a comet could cause harm on earth.

CAN A COMET EXPLODE? comet could cause harm on earth. Suppose a comet explodes?

As far as we know, comets do not explode. But they do break up. For example, there was a certain comet that had been observed several times, and then in 1846 it split in two, making a pair of comets. Finally, both parts broke up into bits too small to be seen. These pieces are thought to be the shower of meteors that we see regularly in late November. So it would seem that comets do eventually die. They do this by breaking up and then scattering along their orbits in the form of meteoric dust.

A comet is not a solid chunk of matter. Scientists think that comets are made of great swarms of bits of solid matter combined with gases. The brightest part of a comet is "the head". The centre of the head is made of the heaviest material and is called "the nucleus". Around the nucleus is a part known as "the coma". It is a hazy, cloudlike cover that may be 150,000 miles or more across. And the tail of a comet is made up of very thin gases and fine particles.

So even though a comet looks pretty solid when it glows across the sky, it is really mostly tiny particles and gases.

In 1610, Galileo, the man who first explored the heavens with a telescope, first noticed something strange about Saturn—it seemed to have things sticking out of its sides!

WHAT ARE THE RINGS AROUND SATURN?

In 1655, a man called Christian Huygens studied Saturn with a better telescope, and he saw something so strange he was afraid to tell anyone about it! So he set down his observations in a code, which, when translated, says: "It is girdled by a thin flat ring, nowhere touching, inclined to the ecliptic".

The rings of the planet Saturn, so startling to the first men who noticed them, still remain one of the great mysteries of our solar system. In fact, as far as is known, such rings exist nowhere else in the heavens.

Of course, aside from the rings, we do know certain things about the planet Saturn. It takes $29\frac{1}{2}$ years to go around the sun, it is second in size to Jupiter, and it has nine satellites that revolve around it. It has an atmosphere around it that we cannot penetrate, but what we do see is not solid matter. There may be some rocky metallic material at the core of the planet.

And it has those mysterious rings. There are three main rings all on the same plane (like three rings you might make on a flat dish), and they lie in the plane of Saturn's equator. The rings extend outward for about 170,000 miles.

The middle ring is the brightest. It is separated from the outer ring by a gap about 1,800 miles wide. The inner ring is very dim. Other faint outer rings have been detected by spacecraft and one may even extend from the inside ring almost down to the cloud tops of the planet.

The rings are not solid, but are composed of pieces of ice-coated rubble orbiting the planet like tiny "moonlets". They may be fragments of a moon which has never been formed.

The first telescope was invented in 1608 by a Dutch optician called Hans Lippershey. Before that, even as far back as the 13th century, scientists had been experimenting with magnifying lenses. Poor Lippershey was

WHAT IS A
RADIO TELESCOPE?

refused a patent for his invention, and the famous Italian astronomer, Galileo, hearing about this new idea, built his first telescope in 1609 and took all the credit for the wonderful new invention. It was a crude instrument; in fact, his most powerful telescope only magnified objects thirty-three times, and one could only see a small area (less than a quarter of the moon) at a time. Nevertheless, Galileo made some outstanding discoveries—he was the first to see the rings of Saturn, four of the satellites of Jupiter and the mountains and craters of the moon. Today, the principle behind Galileo's telescope is used for opera glasses, because it does not matter about their restricted vision and small magnification.

But telescopes have advanced beyond recognition since the time of Galileo and, with the coming of electronics, the radio telescope was invented. The radio telescope was developed after the Second World War—it is a sort of giant "eye" that sees by radio waves sent out from the stars, in just the same way as we see their light waves. The "mirror" of the telescope is a huge saucer-shaped radio reflector many feet in diameter, and it has enormous advantages over an ordinary telescope because it can tune in on stars and galaxies that give no light at all, or such a faint light that it is not visible to an optical telescope. The radio telescope can also penetrate clouds of cosmic dust and gas that fill vast regions of space and the great thing is that scientists can use it in all weathers because radio waves have no difficulty in travelling through the cloud of the earth's atmosphere.

The largest radio telescope that can be pointed anywhere in the sky is at Jodrell Bank in Cheshire. The bowl is 76 metres across, and you can get a good view of it from the London/Manchester train.

Every bright star is a sun, like our own sun.

This means that stars are huge globes of glowing gas. They are so hot that if a piece of steel were placed there, it would disappear in a puff

WHAT IS A STAR MADE OF? of gas! In many of the stars, the gases are very thin. This is because the particles, or atoms, of matter in the gas are so far apart.

But the stars do have matter in them. We know, for example, that the sun contains more than 60 of the chemical elements present in the earth. Among the elements in the sun are hydrogen, helium, iron, calcium, and magnesium.

In cooler stars, the matter may be more nearly liquid, somewhat like the boiling iron in a blast furnace. In some very old and cold stars, the matter may be so densely packed that a cubic inch of it would weigh a ton. Such stars are called "dead" or "dark" stars.

Astronomers can find out all this by using instruments called "spectroscopes". The spectroscope studies the light a star gives, and from this we can learn what kinds of matter it contains and how hot it is.

The different colours of the stars, white, blue, yellow, or red, indicate what chemical elements are present in them. Different temperatures of stars also cause differences in the light they give, in their "spectrum". In this way the temperature of a star can be determined.

"Countless as the stars at night." This is the impression we get of the sky when we look up at night and see the stars. But it may surprise you to know that only about 6,000 stars can be seen without a telescope.

HOW MANY STARS CAN WE SEE AT NIGHT? That does not mean a person can look up and count 6,000 stars. Because one-fourth of these 6,000 stars are too far south to be visible in Western Europe. And of the stars that can be seen from any one place on earth, only one-half are visible at one time as the others are below the horizon.

What's more, many of the stars near the horizon cannot be seen because of haze. So what do we end up with? If you started to count the stars that you could see, you would probably not be able to count many more than 1,000.

Photographs can be taken of the same sky by a camera attached to a telescope. Many more stars can be counted on a photograph of a particular spot in the sky than the unaided eye can see there. And with a time exposure, even more stars will be added.

Finally, by using a very powerful telescope, it would be possible to photograph more than 1,000,000,000 stars!

Once a star is noticed in the sky it must be given a name or an identification number. Long ago, people in many lands—the Arabs, the Greeks, the Romans, and the Chinese—gave names to the brightest stars and to other stars that were in some way remarkable. More than 100 stars were given names.

And man has wanted to have a catalogue of the stars that were known. The first known star catalogue listed 1,025 stars and dated from about A.D. 137. A modern catalogue of the stars lists more than 457,000 stars!

LEO THE LION

Sometimes we can measure something—and yet have no real understanding of what that measurement means. When it comes to distances in the universe, for example, we are able to measure them, but our minds cannot really grasp what that means in terms of our life.

WHAT ARE THE NEAREST STARS?

For distances in the universe, a special unit of measurement was set up, called "the light year". A light year is simply the distance a ray of light will travel in a year. Since light travels about 186,000 miles a second, in one year it will travel a distance of nearly 6,000,000,000,000 (six billion) miles!

The closest star to us is Proxima Centauri, and this is about four and a third light years away. That means a distance of 26 billion miles! This star can be seen from the Southern Hemisphere. The nearest star in the Northern Hemisphere is Sirius. It is eight light years away.

The farthest stars we can see with the naked eye are about 8,000,000 light years away. When we look through powerful telescopes, we can see stars a thousand times farther away. Through such telescopes, stars six thousand trillion miles away can be seen. The light from these stars started out a thousand million years ago on its way to the earth!

A star is a ball of very hot gas which shines by its own light. Planets, as you know, and our moon, too, shine only by light reflected from the sun. And planets shine with a steady light while stars appear to twinkle. This

WHAT MAKES THE STARS SHINE?

is caused by substances in the air between the star and the earth. The unsteady air bends the light from the star, and then it seems to twinkle.

Why does our sun shine? Because it is a star! And not a very big or bright star at that. Compared to all the other stars in the sky, it might be considered medium-sized and medium-bright. There are millions of stars that are smaller than our sun. And many stars are several hundred times larger than the sun. They look small only because they are so far away.

Ever since the days of the Greek astronomers, some 2,000 years ago, the stars have been divided into classes according to their "magnitude", or brightness. Another way of grouping stars is according to their spectra, or the kind of light that comes from the stars. By studying the differences in these spectra, the astronomer may learn about the colours, the temperature, and even the chemical composition of the stars.

When we look up at the sky, we do not see too many differences among the stars. Some look a bit bigger, some are brighter than others. But we really cannot get a good idea of the tremendous differences that exist among them.

WHY ARE SOME STARS BRIGHTER THAN OTHERS?

One way of classifying stars is by their spectra— a spectrum is a breakdown of the light given off. In this way, stars range from blue stars to red stars. Our sun is considered to be yellow, and is in the middle of the series.

The blue stars are large and hot and brilliant. Their surface temperatures may be as high as 27,750 degrees or more. The sun is medium-bright and has a surface temperature of about 6,000 degrees. Red stars are rather cool and have surface temperatures of 1,650 degrees or less. So you can see that some are very much brighter than others, but because of their great distance from the earth we are not aware of it.

The brightness of a star is called its "magnitude". A star of any given magnitude is about two and a half times fainter than a star of the magnitude above it. So magnitude is a sort of scale for measuring brightness. Stars fainter than the sixth magnitude cannot be seen without a telescope. Stars of the first magnitude are the brightest, and there are about 20 such stars we know of. But there are at least a thousand million stars that are only of the twentieth magnitude.

You've heard the expression: "As sure as the sun will rise tomorrow." The sun is for us a pretty steady and dependable thing. Whether we see it or not, we know it is always there, shining in the same old way.

DOES THE SUN SHINE THE SAME ALL THE TIME? And for all practical purposes, that is good enough. The sun is a star, and so it shines by its own light. Where does it get this energy? It is now believed that hydrogen atoms in the very hot interior of the sun combine to form helium. When this happens, it sets free energy which flows steadily to its surface. And the sun should be able to continue radiating this energy for many millions of years to come.

But if we examine the sun in a little more detail, we do not get quite the same "steady" picture. First of all, the sun is not a solid body like the earth, at least at its surface. In fact, different parts of the sun rotate at different rates. The sun's rate of rotation increases from 25 days at its equator to 34 days at its poles.

The outer layer of the sun, called "the corona", is composed of light, gaseous matter. The outer part of this corona is white, and it has streamers that extend out millions of miles from the edge of the sun. These may cause small, but definite differences in the way the sun shines.

Another layer of the sun, called "the chromosphere", is about 9,000 miles thick and is made up largely of hydrogen and helium gas. From this there project huge clouds called "prominences", which may rise to heights of 1,000,000 miles. These also are part of the "unsteady" way the sun shines.

Centuries ago, the Incas of Peru called themselves "Children of the Sun", and performed ceremonies in worship of the king of the heavenly bodies. They were wrong, of course, in thinking that the sun was a god; but they

WHAT IS THE ORIGIN OF THE SUN? were right in believing that there would be no life on earth if it were not for the sun. If the light from the sun were suddenly cut off, life on earth would be impossible.

But there is really nothing special about the sun. It is just a star. Not the biggest or the smallest, not the brightest or the dullest—just an ordinary star like millions of others in the universe. It happens to be the nearest star to us, and we are at just the right distance from it to make it possible for us to enjoy the benefits of its heat and energy.

Since the sun is a star, scientists cannot really know what its origin was—because they still do not know how the stars in the universe came into being. The invention of the spectroscope revolutionised the study of the sun, by making it possible for astronomers to discover a great many of the elements which go into its make-up. It is now known that nearly all these elements are found in the earth's crust, too.

It is rather hard for us to realize that our sun is merely just another star in the sky. This is probably because we think of the stars as looking so tiny. The sun looks larger than any star because it is only about 93

HOW HOT IS THE SUN? million miles from the earth. The nearest star is 25 billion miles away!

What is the temperature on the surface of the sun? Scientists believe that it is about 6,000 degrees Centigrade. To give you an idea of how hot this is, white-hot molten iron used in making steel reaches a temperature of about 1,430 degrees. So you see how much hotter the sun's surface is. And as for the interior of the sun, astronomers estimate it may be as hot as 20,000,000 degrees Centigrade.

Remember, scientists are only making a "guess" about this, because we know almost nothing about the interior of the sun. We do know something about the composition of this star. For example, it has been learned that the sun contains more than 60 of the chemical elements present in the earth. But it is hard to study the sun's interior because the sun is surrounded by four layers of gaseous matter.

How can we even think about the sun in this way? Won't the sun last for ever? The reason science can consider this question is that we know the sun is simply a star, and this means we can compare it with other

**HOW LONG WILL
THE SUN LAST?**
stars. And since other stars have gone through a process of change, science believes that the same will eventually happen to the sun.

At one time, in fact, it was believed that the sun was a body that was slowly cooling off. It was simply "burning". Now we know that if this were so, the sun could only have lasted several thousand years.

If it is not "burning", then what is going on in the sun? We now have evidence that indicates that the sun's radiant energy is the result of atomic transformations. The hydrogen atoms in the very hot interior of the sun combine to form helium. This sets free the energy which flows steadily from the inside of the sun to its surface.

How long can this go on? Well, let us suppose it goes on exactly as it is doing now for another 150 billion years. As a result of this process, the mass of the sun would be reduced by roughly 1 per cent! So it seems that the sun can continue to shine and supply the earth with energy for many billions and billions of years to come.

To get a picture of what happens during an eclipse, think of these three bodies: the earth, the sun, and the moon. The moon revolves around the earth. The sun shines out there beyond the moon. But sometimes, as the

**WHAT CAUSES AN
ECLIPSE OF THE SUN?**
moon goes around the earth, it passes directly between the earth and the sun. And that produces an eclipse of the sun.

An eclipse of the sun occurs only when the moon is new, for then the moon is on that side of the earth facing toward the sun. If its path lay directly in line with the orbit of the earth about the sun, an eclipse would take place at every new moon. But in its trip around the earth, which takes about $29\frac{1}{2}$ days, the moon passes sometimes above and sometimes below the path of the earth.

Astronomers can predict very accurately the exact time that an eclipse will take place and how many hours and minutes it will last. They

are also able to tell in advance whether an eclipse will be "total", "annular", or "partial".

If the moon hides the sun completely, the eclipse is total. The moon is not always the same distance from the earth, and often it is too far from the earth to hide the sun completely. Then, when an eclipse takes place, the moon is seen as a dark disc which covers the whole sun except a narrow ring around its edge. This thin circle of light is called "the annulus", meaning ring. This is an annular eclipse. An eclipse is partial whenever only part of the disc of the moon comes between the sun and the earth.

Every year there must be at least two eclipses of the sun, and there may be as many as five. At any one place on the earth's surface, a total eclipse of the sun will be visible only once in about 360 years. This is why astronomers have to travel great distances to "catch" a total eclipse of the sun.

In 1610, soon after the telescope was invented, Galileo became the first man to see spots on the sun. Through the telescope the sunspots look like dark holes in the sun's white disc.

WHAT ARE SUNSPOTS? Sunspots may be observed on almost any clear day. They vary greatly in size. Some appear like mere specks on the sun's surface. One very large spot was about 90,000 miles long and 60,000 miles wide. Groups of sunspots are known to measure 200,000 miles in length.

Astronomers are fairly sure that sunspots are electrical in nature because of certain effects they produce. One astronomer has shown that they are tremendous whirls of electrified matter that come bursting out from the interior of the sun in pairs like the ends of a U-shaped tunnel.

Sunspots, or their release of electrical energy, send beams of negatively charged electrons shooting into space. Some of these electrons enter the earth's atmosphere and produce certain electrical effects.

One of these effects is the "aurora borealis" (or Northern Lights). Electrical energy from sunspots also disturbs radio transmission. These electrons also seem to increase the amount of ozone in the upper atmosphere. This extra ozone may absorb more of the sun's heat than usual, so sunspots may have a bearing on our weather.

Most sunspots only last a few days, but some last two months or more. They increase in number, then diminish, in a regular cycle which runs about $21\frac{1}{5}$ years. Records of sunspots have now been kept for more than 100 years and we are still learning about what they are and how they affect us.

In ancient times, the moon was worshipped as a goddess who ruled the night. Since those ancient days, man has learned a great deal about the moon—and now, at last, human beings have landed there and explored

WHY DOES THE MOON SHINE? parts of its cratered surface thus solving many of its mysteries.

But there is no mystery at all as to why the moon shines. It is a satellite of the earth. That is, it is a small body that revolves around it, just as the earth revolves around the sun.

The only reason we can see the moon from earth, or that it "shines", is because light from the sun strikes its surface and is reflected to us. Strangely enough, we can only see one side of the moon from the earth. This is because the moon rotates on its axis in the same length of time it takes for it to make its journey around the earth. Of course, man has seen the other side from television pictures sent back by the various Apollo crews as they orbited the moon.

Since the moon has no atmosphere, or air, the light from the sun which hits it has rather interesting effects. For about 14 days, the surface of the moon is heated by the direct rays of the sun to a temperature above that of boiling water. The other half of the lunar month, it is exposed to the cold of a long, dark night, because there is no air to stop the heat from the sun radiating away again. The earth does reflect light back on to the moon (this is called "earthshine") but it does little to help raise the temperature of the lunar night which can fall to about -200 degrees Centigrade!

There is gravity on or in every single object that exists in the universe. For gravity is simply the force which pulls every object in the universe towards every other object in the universe.

IS THERE GRAVITY ON THE MOON? But the force of gravity depends on two things: the mass of the objects involved, and their distance from each other. For example, there is a force of attraction between you and the earth. But the earth is so enormous compared to you, that it pulls on you. The force of this pull is what you weigh at the earth's surface. But if you were twice as far from the centre of the earth as you are now (or 4,000 miles in the air), you would weigh only one-quarter of what you weigh here on earth.

The moon is a huge object but compared to the earth it is rather small. The moon weighs only $\frac{1}{81}$ as much as the earth. So its gravity, or pull, on its surface is much less than that of the earth. In fact, it is only one-sixth as strong as that of the earth.

So when a man is on the moon, his weight is only one-sixth of his weight on the earth. If he made a jump while standing on the moon, he could jump six times as high! And if he threw a ball, it would go up six times as far, because the pull of the moon's surface is so much weaker than that of the earth.

Since man first appeared on earth, the moon has been a mystery to him. In ancient times it was even worshipped as a goddess who ruled the night. Right now, we are living in the days when more is being found out about the moon than ever before in the whole history of mankind. Pictures of the other side of the moon have already been taken by the Americans and the Russians.

WHY CAN WE SEE ONLY ONE SIDE OF THE MOON?

The fact that we cannot see the other side of the moon from the earth is due to a simple fact. The moon is a satellite of the earth, a small body that revolves about it, just as the earth moves in an orbit about the sun.

This journey of the moon around the earth takes a certain definite period, about $29\frac{1}{2}$ days. The moon also rotates on its axis, but the time it takes for the moon to rotate is the same length of time it takes for it to go around the earth. So we see only one side of the moon.

If you want to get a picture of how this works, try this: hold your left hand in front of you and clench your fist. Imagine that is the earth. Now take an apple or orange and mark around it with a pencil to indicate two halves. Imagine that is the moon.

Now face one side of the "moon" towards the "earth". Keeping that same side facing the earth, make a complete circle around the earth. You will see that not only did the moon go around the earth, but it also made a complete rotation on its axis. And yet only one side ever faced the earth!

Not all clouds are up in the sky. Some are on the ground! What we call fog is simply a cloud that is next to the ground.

All air has some moisture in the form of water vapour in it. When warm, moist air cools, it often can no longer hold its moisture as water vapour. The extra moisture changes (condenses) into small drops of water which can be seen. So a cloud is a collection of moisture in the air.

HOW DO CLOUDS STAY UP IN THE SKY?

The air currents keep the cloud up in the sky. But if the cooling continues, more and more vapour is changed into drops. Gradually, the tiny droplets become larger and larger as they collect more moisture. When the drops become so large that they can no longer be held up by the air currents, they fall to the ground as rain.

Clouds can form at many different heights above the earth. In fact, clouds are divided into types according to their distance from the earth. The four main families of clouds are high clouds, middle clouds, low clouds, and clouds which may extend through all levels.

What is the weather anyway? It is simply what the air or atmosphere is like at any time. No matter what the air is—cold, cool, warm, hot, calm, breezy, windy, dry, moist, or wet—that's weather.

WHAT MAKES THE WEATHER?

Weather may be any combination of different amounts of heat, moisture, and motion in the air. And it changes from hour to hour, day to day, season to season, and even from year to year.

The daily changes are caused by storms and fair weather moving over the earth. The seasonal changes are due to the turning of the earth around the sun. Why weather changes from year to year is still not known, however.

The most important "cause" of weather is the heating and cooling of the air. Heat causes the winds as well as the different way in which water vapour appears in the atmosphere.

Humidity, the amount of water vapour in the air, combined with the temperature, causes many weather conditions. Clouds are a kind of weather condition, and they are formed when water vapour condenses high above the ground.

When the cloud droplets grow larger and become too heavy to be held up by the air currents, they fall to the ground and we have the weather known as rain. If the raindrops fall through a layer of air which is below freezing, the drops freeze and our weather is snow.

One of the ways the weather forecaster studies the weather is to look at the "fronts" that exist. Fronts are boundary lines between the cold air moving southwards from the north, and the warm air moving from the tropics. Most of the severe storms which cause rain, snow, and other bad weather are in some way related to these fronts.

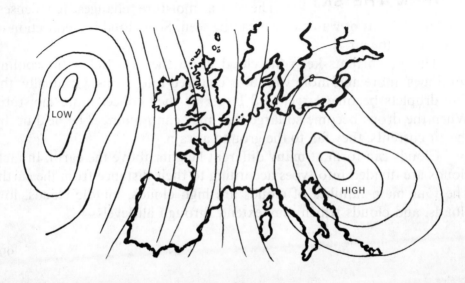

Sometimes when we are outdoors, a sudden and mysterious thing takes place. A wind begins to blow. We cannot see it, but we feel it, and we have no idea what started it.

WHAT MAKES A WIND? A wind is simply the motion of air over the earth. What causes the air to move? All winds are caused by one thing—a change in temperature. Whenever air is heated it expands. This makes it lighter, and lighter air rises. As the warm air rises, cooler air flows in to take its place. And this movement of air is wind!

There are two kinds of winds, those that are part of a world-wide system of winds, and local winds. The major wind systems of the world begin at the Equator, where the sun's heat is greatest.

Here the heat rises to high altitudes and is pushed off towards the North and South Poles. When it had journeyed about one-third of the distances to the poles, it has cooled and begins to fall back to earth. Some of this air returns to the equator to be heated again, and some continues on to the poles.

These types of winds, which tend to blow in the same general direction all the year round, are called "prevailing winds". But these global winds are often broken up by local winds which blow from different directions.

Local winds may be caused by the coming of cold air masses with high pressure, or warmer air masses with low pressure. Local winds usually do not last long. After a few hours, or at most a few days, the prevailing wind pattern is present again.

Other local winds are caused by the daily heating and cooling of the ground. Land and sea breezes are examples of this kind of wind. In the daytime, the cool air over the ocean moves inland as the sea breeze. At night, the ocean is warmer than the ground, so the cooler air moves out to sea as the land breeze.

Of course, we are all quite accustomed to thunderstorms. These are usually local storms. But there are certain kinds of storms that may cover thousands of square miles. One such type is called a "cyclonic storm" or

HOW DO TORNADOES START? "cyclone". In a cyclone, the winds blow towards the centre of an area of very low pressure.

A curious thing about them is that the winds blow in spiral fashion. In the Northern Hemisphere such storms turn anti-clockwise, in the Southern Hemisphere they turn clockwise!

A tornado is simply a special kind of cyclone. A tornado arises when the conditions that cause ordinary thunderstorms are unusually violent. There is an updraft of air. There are winds blowing in opposite directions around this rising air. This starts a whirling effect that is narrow and very violent. When this happens, centrifugal force throws the air away from the centre. And this leaves a core of low pressure at the centre.

This low-pressure core acts like a powerful vacuum on everything it passes. This is one of the destructive things about a tornado. It can actually suck the walls of a house outwards in such a way that the house will collapse. The other destructive thing about a tornado is the high winds that may blow around the edges of a whirl. These winds can reach 300 miles per hour and nothing is safe against them.

Storms are given many different names, depending on their nature and where they take place. But all storms are alike in that a storm is simply air that is moving rapidly from one place to another.

WHAT'S THE DIFFERENCE BETWEEN A HURRICANE AND A TORNADO?

If it is air alone, it is called a "windstorm". If it has picked up dust along the way, it is called a "dust storm". Most storms, however, include water in some form. Water may come with a storm as rain. The most violent and dangerous storms of all are hurricanes and tornadoes.

Hurricanes are storms that start in the Tropics. They strike the United States for example, mainly in the Gulf of Mexico area and also all along the eastern coast. Now a strange thing is that exactly the same kind of storm, when it takes place in the East Indies and the China Sea, is called a "typhoon". A general name for both is "tropical storms".

In a hurricane, the storm area is usually from 100 to 400 miles in diameter, and winds around the hurricane may reach speeds of 75 to 125 miles per hour. A special feature of the hurricane is the calm, central part of the storm, which is called the "eye" of the storm. This eye is about 5 to 15 miles in diameter. As it moves over an area, the winds become almost calm. This sometimes leads people to believe that the storm is over. However, after the eye passes, the winds begin to blow with equal violence from the opposite direction, since a hurricane is a circular storm. The winds move in a kind of circle as the storm itself moves.

Another type of circular storm is the tornado, but it is different from a hurricane because it is usually only up to about 1,500 metres in diameter. Tornadoes are formed most often in the central Mississippi Valley of the United States. A tornado begins as a black, funnel-shaped cloud in a larger thunderstorm area. The path of a tornado may only be a few kilometres long and a few hundred metres wide—but it can destroy everything in its path.

The word "monsoon" comes from an Arab word meaning "season". It has to do with a type of climate in which winds blow from sea to land (onshore) during the warm season, and from land to sea (offshore)

WHAT IS A MONSOON?

during the cool season. The warm season of onshore winds is often very rainy, while the cool season of offshore winds may be dry.

What causes this seasonal change in winds and rainfall? It is due to the fact that large continents or land masses heat and cool more rapidly than the surrounding oceans. Central and Southern Asia grow warm rapidly in the spring, and during the summer they are much warmer than the Indian Ocean on the south, or the Pacific Ocean on the east.

The warmer temperatures inland create lower atmospheric pressures, and therefore the wind blows inland from the surrounding seas. This is the onshore or summer monsoon.

In the autumn, interior Asia cools rapidly and during the winter it has much lower temperatures than the surrounding oceans. These lower temperatures create high atmospheric pressures, and therefore the winter monsoon winds blow outward from the dry interior regions toward the sea.

Southern and Eastern Asia have the strongest development of monsoon climate because of the vast size of that continent.

Over many parts of the oceans, sailors have used the change-about of the monsoon winds in their going back and forth to India. They go from India to Africa during the winter and return in the summer, because the winds blow that way.

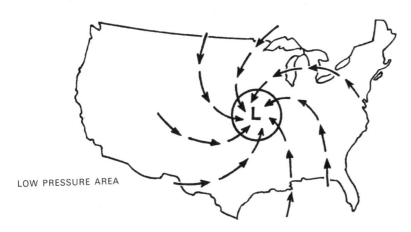

LOW PRESSURE AREA

A cyclone is a kind of storm, and a storm is simply air that is moving rapidly from one place to another.

WHAT IS A CYCLONE? A storm starts when warm, moist air from the Equator moves northwards into the Northern Hemisphere and meets a mass of cold, dry air moving southwards from the Arctic region.

These two kinds of air masses do not mix. The sharp boundary that is formed where they meet is called a "front". As the air masses continue to move, the lighter, warm air climbs up over the cold air. As it is forced upwards, the warm, moist air is cooled. The moisture then condenses, forming clouds.

While all this is going on, the air pressure begins to fall at the centre of the storm. The winds begin to blow around the low-pressure area in an anti-clockwise direction. Thus, the warm, moist air moves northwards around the eastern side of the storm, while the cold air moves southwards around the western side.

A low pressure area is known as a "cyclone". The mass of air in such an area could vary in diameter from 400 to 1,000 miles. A tornado is also a circular storm, and it is sometimes confused with a cyclone. But a tornado may be only 30 to 1,600 metres in diameter.

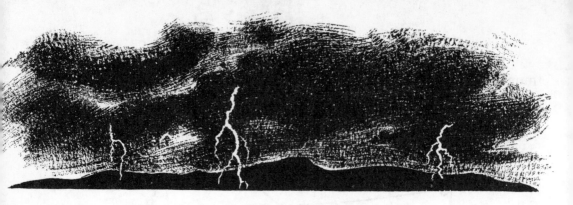

There are many people who actually tremble with fear at the sound of a clap of thunder during a thunderstorm. There is absolutely no reason to have any fear of thunder. By the time the sound of thunder reaches you,

IS THUNDER DANGEROUS? the bolt of electricity which caused it has already done its work. You hear the thunder after the lightning flash simply because sound travels much more slowly than light.

Should you be afraid of lightning? Well, there is no question that lightning can cause damage, and in some rare cases it has even been known to kill people. But your chances of being struck by lightning are extremely slight.

Lightning, of course, is a form of electricity, and this is what can make it dangerous. It is a giant spark of electricity that we see as a bright flash of light. It may jump across the space between two clouds, or from cloud to earth, or even from earth to cloud!

During a storm, different electrical charges (positive or negative) are built up by the clouds and the earth. When the difference between the charges becomes great enough, a spark—which is lightning—jumps the space between.

During and after an electrical discharge, currents of air expand and contract. The expanding and contracting currents violently collide, and produce the noise we call "thunder".

Condensation is the opposite of evaporation. In evaporation, a liquid changes into a gas or vapour. In condensation, a gas or vapour turns into liquid or solid form. This happens when it is cooled or compressed.

WHAT IS CONDENSATION? There are two important changes that take place when a gas condenses. The first is that the volume of the gas decreases when it turns into a liquid state. The second is that heat is given off, which is called

106

"heat of condensation". When steam condenses to water, for every gram of water formed, 540 calories are released.

Condensation is important in many ways in the world around us. When water vapour in the air is condensed, we have clouds. Dew is formed when moisture-filled air comes in contact with a surface cooled to the right temperature. The moisture in the air condenses on the surface.

You have probably noticed condensation taking place in front of your eyes when you looked at a glass of iced water in humid weather. There was warm, moist air and as it struck the surface of the cold water the moisture in the air condensed on the outside of the glass.

Sometimes vapour in the air can condense directly into solid form. For example, in below freezing temperatures, vapour condenses into frost on the cold pipes of a refrigerator.

Nature carries on a continuous process of evaporation and condensation. Millions of tons of water are evaporated every year from oceans and lakes and then are condensed as rain or snow.

Snow is really nothing more than frozen water. Then why doesn't it look like ice?

There are a large number of ice crystals in each snowflake, and the reflection of light from all the surfaces of the crystals makes it look white.

WHAT IS SNOW?

Snow begins to be formed when water vapour in the atmosphere freezes. Tiny crystals are formed that are clear and transparent. Since there are currents in the air, these tiny crystals are carried up and down in the atmosphere. They fall and rise as different air currents move them along.

While this is happening, the crystals begin to gather around a nucleus, so that in time there may be a hundred or more gathered together. When this group of ice crystals is big enough, it floats down towards the ground. We call this collection of ice crystals a "snowflake".

Some crystals are flat and some are like a column of needles. But regardless of the shape, snow crystals always have six sides or angles. The branches of any single snowflake are always identical, but the arrangement of the branches is different in every case. No two snowflakes are ever exactly alike.

Did you know that snow is not always white? In many parts of the world red, green, blue, and even black snow has been seen! The reason for the different colours is that sometimes there are tiny fungi in the air, or dust is floating about, and this is collected by the snow as it falls.

Because snow contains so much air, it is a poor conductor of heat. That is why a "blanket" of snow can protect dormant vegetation in the ground and why igloos and snow huts can be made of blocks of snow and keep people inside quite warm.

One of the most unusual weather conditions we can experience is a hailstorm. It is quite a thing to see and hear hailstones coming down, sometimes with such force that great damage is done. Animals, and even men, have been killed by hail!

WHAT CAUSES HAIL?

A hailstorm usually occurs during the warm weather and is accompanied in many cases by thunder, lightning, and rain. Hail is formed when raindrops freeze while passing through a belt of cold air on their way to earth.

Single raindrops form very small hailstones. But an interesting thing can happen to such a raindrop. As it falls as a hailstone, it may meet a strong rising current of air. So it is carried up again to the level where raindrops are falling. New drops begin to cling to the hailstone. And as it falls once more through the cold belt, these new drops spread into a layer around it and freeze, and now we have larger hailstones.

This rising and falling of the hailstone may be repeated time after time until it has added so many layers that its weight is heavy enough to overcome the force of the rising current of air. Now it falls to the ground.

In this way hailstones measuring 8 to 10 centimetres in diameter and weighing as much as 450 grams are sometimes built up. Snow, too, freezes around hailstones when they are carried into regions where it is forming. So the hailstones are frequently made up of layers of ice and snow.

Frozen rain is sometimes called hail, but it is really "sleet"! And soft hail which sometimes falls in winter is only a form of snow.

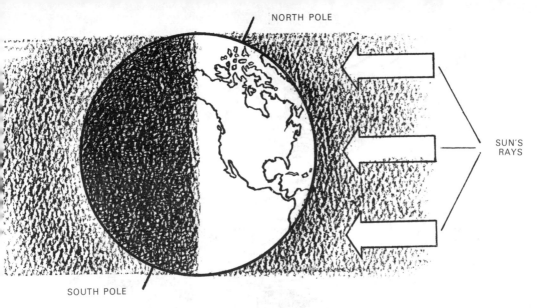

NORTH POLE

SUN'S RAYS

SOUTH POLE

Oddly enough the earth is about 3,000,000 miles nearer to the sun in our northern winter than it is in summer. Yet it is much warmer in summer.

WHY IS IT WARMER IN SUMMER?

The reasons are not caused by different distances from the sun, but by the slant of the earth's axis as it moves around the sun. Scientists have learned that the Equator of the earth is tilted $23\frac{1}{2}$ degrees to the path of the earth around the sun.

As the earth moves around the sun, the earth's axis always points in the same direction, towards the North Star. For this reason, during part of the year the North Pole tilts towards the sun and part of the year away from it. When the North Pole is inclined towards the sun, the Northern Hemisphere has its summer. When the North Pole is inclined away from the sun, the Northern Hemisphere has its winter. In the Southern Hemisphere these seasons are reversed.

The difference in weather with the seasons occurs because the sun's rays are more slanting in winter and less slanting in summer. Slanting rays produce less heat for two reasons. One is that they scatter their heat over a larger area of the earth's surface. The other is that they lose more of their heat in passing through the atmosphere.

Other factors, primarily water, land, and altitude, help regulate the climate. Water has a stabilizing effect and helps prevent great changes in temperature. Land does not store up heat (the way the ocean does), so big temperature changes can take place over large land areas. Air grows less dense with altitude and cannot absorb as much heat as at sea level. So the higher the altitude, the lower the temperature.

The story of how St. George, the patron saint of England, overcame the monstrous dragon is known to everyone, but no one is quite sure how he came to be adopted as our patron saint, or even whether he ever existed! It has been suggested that we,

WHO WAS ST. GEORGE? as a "nation of shopkeepers", instinctively adopted a man as our patron saint who is supposed to have made a huge fortune selling bacon to the Roman army!

We do know that there was a man called George who was venerated as a saint in Palestine in the early days of the church; but, apart from the legend that he held a high position in the Roman army and served in Britain for a short time, none of the details of his life can be proved.

But probably the only historical fact that we can find about St. George is that, in the year 303 A.D., he was martyred during the furious persecution of Christians by the Emperor Diocletian. The Golden Legend —a collection of the lives of the saints, compiled by Jacobus de Voragine, Archbishop of Genoa—tells us that St. George, after slaying the dragon, took off his knightly clothes and gave everything he had to the poor. He taught about Jesus Christ until he finally died a martyr in the year 303.

St. George was adopted as our patron saint during the time of the Norman kings of England. In 1346, the Order of the Garter was founded by Edward III. In the insignia, the George, which represents St. George and the dragon, is suspended from the collar. Some years later, the magnificent St. George's Chapel was built by Edward IV at Windsor. It was here, during the reign of Henry V, that a heart, thought to be St. George's heart, was placed as a precious relic.

We celebrate St. George's day on April 23rd when his red and white flag is flown from every Anglican church in the country—but we cannot be too possessive because he is also the patron saint of Portugal!

Everybody knows that Columbus "discovered America". Then why wasn't it named after him?

The reason for this might be considered an accident of fate. When

WHY IS AMERICA SO CALLED? Columbus made his first journey, he sighted land early in the morning of October 12, 1492. Columbus went ashore, took possession in the names of King Ferdinand and Queen Isabella of Spain, and named the land San Salvador. That land however, was not the mainland of the continent. It is what we now call Watling Island, in the Bahamas. Columbus actually thought he had reached India (which was his goal), so he called the natives Indians.

Columbus cruised on, looking for Japan. Instead he discovered Cuba and Hispaniola (Haiti and the Dominican Republic today). On March 14, 1493, Columbus returned to Spain.

On his second voyage, which started on September 24, 1493, Columbus discovered several of the Virgin Islands, Puerto Rico, and Jamaica. But he was still determined to find India. On his third voyage, in 1498, he discovered Trinidad and touched South America. But he thought he had found a series of islands.

Another explorer, Amerigo Vespucci, meanwhile was claiming that he had been the first to reach the mainland of South America. This was on June 16, 1497. (Many experts believe that Vespucci did not really make his voyage until 1499.)

On a trip in 1501, Vespucci sailed along the coast of South America and wrote letters saying he had found a new continent. His information was used by a German map-maker—and in his maps he used the name "America" (after Amerigo Vespucci) for the new continent. And that name has been used ever since!

Suppose there were somebody in your town who cheated every time he sold you something. If you and your friends got together and decided not to buy from him anymore, you would be conducting a boycott!

WHAT IS A BOYCOTT? The word "boycott" had a very interesting origin. In the days when many Irish landlords lived in England, their estates in Ireland were managed by land agents. It was the job of these agents to collect as much money as possible, quite often regardless of whether the tenants could afford to pay.

One of these agents was Captain Charles Cunningham Boycott. In 1880, he refused to let the Irish tenant farmers decide how much rent they should pay and evicted them from their homes. As a result, the tenants chased away his servants, tore down his fences, and cut off his mail and his food supplies. Other tenants began to treat other land agents in the same way. When it happened to other land agents, it was said they had been "boycotted". Today it is applied to any organized refusal to trade or associate with a country, a business concern, or an individual.

When trade unions developed in the United Kingdom, they often used the boycott against employers. There were two kinds of boycotts. A primary boycott was when a body of workers refused to work for an employer or to buy his products. A secondary boycott was when these workers persuaded or forced other groups not to have any dealings with the employer.

In courts of law, the primary boycott has generally been held legal. But decisions by many courts have held the secondary boycott to be illegal because they affected the rights of third parties.

Very few people who study Latin today expect to speak it or even to read it. It is used mostly by scholars. We now consider Latin a "dead language" for this reason. But Latin was once a living language.

DID PEOPLE EVER SPEAK LATIN? After Rome was founded in 753 B.C., the small town began to grow. Within a limited area around the town, Latin was a common language spoken by the people. This language was named after the Latini, one of the tribes living in the Tiber Valley. This early Latin was a combination of the tongues spoken by all the people in the neighbourhood of Rome. It was heavy and unwieldy, not a graceful language at all, and very few traces of this early Latin remain.

At this time Latin had no literature. By the year 240 B.C., Rome had conquered Greece, and Greek literature provided an example to the Romans.

The common people who could neither read nor write were greatly interested in the theatre, so Latin writers created plays for their amusement. By this time Latin had developed in many ways. There was a written Latin with regular rules for spelling and grammar, and there were records of both the common and refined way of speaking. In other words, the foundation was laid for later writers who made Latin a truly beautiful and expressive language.

While the literary language of Latin was developing, the true speech of Rome was Vulgar Latin. It was quite different from the written language. Most of the people of Rome could not use the polished written language. It was used mostly by highly educated literary men. The Vulgar Latin of the people was an everyday language, easily understood and not always grammatically correct.

Stamp collecting, or philately, has been a hobby of millions of people all over the world for more than 100 years and the General Post Office has even established a special department to help stamp collectors!

WHY DO PEOPLE COLLECT STAMPS?

Of course many people collect stamps to make money. But you have to know a great deal about stamps to make big profits this way. In fact, many "collectors" never make money on stamps because they have mistaken ideas about them. They may think age alone makes a stamp valuable. Or they may see a strange stamp and think it is scarce and, therefore, valuable.

Of course, the most valuable stamp is the rarest one, but age alone does not make it valuable. The famous Cape Triangle is a case in point. In 1861, the South African Post Office found that they were running out of stamps and there was no sign of the new supplies, so they arranged for a local firm to print enough stamps to last until they arrived. There was a mistake in the colour printing and the result was the One Penny Blue which should have been red and the Four Penny Red which should have been blue! Later, when the story came out, these stamps were discovered to be extremely rare and worth a small fortune.

The Cape Triangle was the result of a printing mistake—sometimes the scarcity is man-made. A famous dealer in the 1870's decided to buy up enormous quantities of certain varieties and destroy them. Today, these stamps are worth two or three times as much as other common stamps of the period.

When faced with the obviously powerful social force of many pagan customs, the early Christian church thought it wiser to adapt them to suitable Christian rituals than to destroy them. Many of our beliefs and

HOW OLD ARE ENGLISH FOLKLORE AND CUSTOMS?

rituals that still exist today are more than 2,000 years old. Some of the ancient rituals designed to increase fertility and fend off evil persist today in traditional customs, though in altered forms. Other customs celebrate the memory of past heroes or historical events. Still others derive from what were once necessities.

Boundary customs, for example, defined and protected communal boundaries in the days when maps were not available to the majority of people.

Morris dances, a relic of pre-Christian fertility rites, are much the same as they were, but today they are danced for fun.

Original legends concerning folk heroes were elaborated in the absence of written records. The Celtic imagination has produced many folk heroes, including King Arthur—Robin Hood is the only major English figure in our folklore!

Many of our customs and traditions are connected with national festivals, such as Christmas, Shrovetide, Easter and May Day. These customs, of course, are observed all over the country, though some of them have local variations.

Many customs that flourished for hundreds of years to within living memory have gradually disappeared as a result of the shifting population and the effects of the social upheavals of two World Wars. The surviving customs and traditions are direct, living links with our history.

The taking of a census by a government is as old as the custom of collecting taxes and raising armies. In early times, the ruler's only object in taking a census was to discover how many people he could send to the wars or

WHY IS THE CENSUS TAKEN?

how much money he could get. Since the people suffered from the census, they did all in their power to make it incorrect.

In most countries, fairly simple questions are asked in a census—the age of the people living in a house, the relationship of these people, their birthplaces and nationality, their jobs and for whom they work. Some questions ask about date of marriage and number of children. Figures about agriculture may also be included, such as acres of land and kinds of livestock owned.

After all the information is gathered, the figures are totalled and separated according to sections or classes. They then become available and helpful to the government. For example, a total of age groups can be useful to the government for planning how many schools will be needed at a certain time, or in estimating future costs of pensions.

The census shows whether the population is increasing or decreasing. It shows the movement of population to the city or the country. It reveals whether social conditions are improving or growing worse. It tells which industries are advancing and which are slowing up.

Where politicians are elected on the basis of population, a census helps decide the number of representatives from each section. It helps the government in making laws, and it helps business, social, and economic interests in conducting their affairs and making their plans.

"Whig" is a strange word. It comes from the old Scottish "Whiggamore", the name given to hungry, discontented farmers who spasmodically fought against the English in Scotland. By the end of the reign of Charles

WHAT IS A WHIG?
II, Whig had become the name of the basically Protestant, anti-court party in Parliament.

Up until 1660, when Charles II returned to England to take his throne, Parliament was made up of Members who acted as individuals. After 1660, the terms of the Restoration meant that the King had less power, and Parliament began to move towards the Party system that we have today.

The last part of the seventeenth and the beginning of the eighteenth centuries was a time of great social change in England. The Dutch, who had had the monopoly of trade with the New World and India, were beginning to lose their grip because they were fighting for survival at home, against the Sun King, Louis XIV of France. So the English, with their tradition of seamanship, stepped in. This meant that huge fortunes were being made from trade by men who had never had money before, because wealth had been in the hands of the old land-owning families of England. Of course, there were jealousies, rivalries, and basic differences of political thinking between these two parties, and this was reflected in Parliament. The merchant party, who wanted to protect their trade with a peaceful foreign policy and a stable currency, became known as Whigs. The land-owning families, who were at court near the King, loyal to the Stuarts, more tolerant of Catholics and less committed to the expansion of world trade, became known as Tories.

David Livingstone was born in 1813 at Blantyre, in Scotland. At the age of ten he started work in a cotton mill, and with his first earnings bought a Latin primer. Although his work was arduous, he attended night school and studied at home.

WHO WAS DAVID LIVINGSTONE?

When he was 20 years old, he was thrilled by reading an account of a missionary's labours in Asia, and resolved to devote his life to the alleviation of human misery. Then followed college classes in Glasgow, examination and acceptance by the London Missionary Society, and the completion of his medical studies in London. He also studied theology, botany, zoology, and astronomy—all with his future life-work in mind.

In 1841, he arrived at Cape Town, and for thirty years Dr. Livingstone travelled all over Africa. He discovered the mighty Victoria Falls and the upper course of the Zaire (the Congo), among other things.

His meagre salary and money from his books all went to equip and finance new expeditions. During the last fifteen years of his life he held a roving commission from the British Government as Consul.

His last expedition ran into trouble. He was weakened by fever, and some of his native carriers deserted with supplies and his precious medicine chest. A relief expedition sent by the *New York Herald*, under the command of H. M. Stanley, found him at Ujiji. Stanley tried to persuade Dr. Livingstone to return to civilization, but he refused and set out westward to seek the sources of the Nile.

Dysentery, with complications, attacked him and he grew steadily worse, until, on the morning of May 1st, 1873, he died. His faithful native attendants preserved his body as well as they could and carried it halfway across Africa. His body was taken to England, where it was buried at Westminster Abbey.

The Alamo is a building in San Antonio, Texas. It is actually the chapel of the Mission San Antonio de Valero, which was founded by Franciscans in 1718. A popular name for it became "the Alamo mission", because

WHAT WAS THE ALAMO? it stood in a grove of cottonwood trees and the Spanish name for this type of tree is *alamo*.

The mission originally consisted of the chapel, a convent yard, convent and hospital building, and a plaza, all surrounded by a strong wall. When the Indians disappeared from this region, the mission was abandoned, and after 1793, it was sometimes used as a fort.

In 1835, a group of United States settlers in Texas revolted against Mexico. Texas at that time was part of one of the Mexican states. Many Americans from other parts of the United States came to help these men in their fight. Among them was a man called Davy Crockett.

Late in 1835, the Texans captured San Antonio and began to use the Alamo as a fort. The Mexican general, Antonio López de Santa Anna, marched on San Antonio with about 4,000 men. In the Alamo were about 180 men. They were led by Col. William Travis and Col. James Bowie.

On February 23, 1836, the Mexicans surrounded the fort but were held off for 13 days. On March 6, 1836, they finally blasted a hole in the wall of the Alamo. As Mexican troops poured into the mission, the Texans continued to fight with knives and bayonets.

More than 500 Mexicans were killed, but the battle was soon over. There were not enough Texans to hold the fort. Five men were taken prisoner and later shot. "Remember the Alamo!" became the battle cry of the Texas army. Six weeks after the fall of the Alamo the Texans, under Sam Houston, defeated Santa Anna's army and captured him in the Battle of San Jacinto.

When a question on an important issue is due to come before the House of Commons, the attention of all is focused on the group of men who occupy the front benches to the right of the Speaker of the House. These

WHAT IS THE CABINET? men, as leaders of the majority party in the House of Commons, will propose the government policy.

The Cabinet has been defined by Walter Bagehot as "the link that binds together the legislative and the executive branches".

Briefly, the Cabinet consists of the Prime Minister and a group of senior Ministers who take collective responsibility for the Government's actions and proposals. It is really a steering committee of the Government party. The Ministers of the Crown Act 1937 established that seventeen senior Ministers should form the Cabinet, and that, of these seventeen, not more than fifteen should be members of the House of Commons. Although the figures often vary, the principle remains unchanged.

Under the modern system of government it is to the Prime Minister and the Cabinet, rather than to the monarch, that the people of the country look for guidance and direction. The Queen may do very little without the approval of her ministers; her role in government is largely nominal.

The British system of responsible Cabinet government has been adopted by Canada, Australia and New Zealand, and also by many European countries. In the United States, there are twelve cabinet departments in the executive branch of the government. Each has a secretary, who is appointed by the President, with the approval of the Senate. The secretaries are mainly responsible to the president, who may appoint or remove anyone he wishes, subject to Senate approval. The president's cabinet of secretaries acts as his advisers on matters that concern their respective departments.

The way we live in our society is to divide ourselves into families. Our immediate family and our relatives are our "group". But there are many primitive groups of people who divide themselves differently.

WHAT IS A TOTEM POLE? Among such people there are "tribes", and all members of a tribe are considered to be related. This relationship may be real, or they may just decide to call themselves related.

These groups usually have an "ancestor", who may be a kind of mythical human being, and the deeds of this ancestor are glorified through the ages. Or this "ancestor" may be an animal or even a plant or natural object!

Usually, the tribe is descended either from an ancestor who had a special relationship with a certain animal, or from the animal itself. In such cases, the group takes its name from the animal, and its symbol becomes the badge or "totem" of the group. The animal is called "the totem animal". Such a group is known as a "totemic tribe".

Many of the tribes have carved and painted totem poles. They may show the totem animal or ancestor and other beings important in the story of the tribe. The totem pole is usually set up in the village to give the tribe prestige and to show their pride in their ancestor.

People who live in such totemic tribes have different practices in different parts of the world. As a rule, members of the same tribe are not allowed to marry. The children belong to the mother's tribe, and not the father's.

120

Ever since the time of ancient Greece, stories have been told about the lost island, or continent, of Atlantis. It was thought to be a very large island in the Atlantic Ocean, just west of the Rock of Gibraltar. It was

WHAT WAS THE LOST CONTINENT OF ATLANTIS?

believed to be a perfect place—a kind of paradise.

According to legends, Atlantis was a powerful kingdom whose people conquered all South Western Europe and North Western Africa. They were finally defeated by the Athenians from Greece.

The people of Atlantis then became wicked. As a punishment, the island was swallowed up by the ocean. This legend is told in the *Timaeus*, written in the 300's B.C. by the Greek philosopher Plato. The island was supposed to have been lost more than 9,000 years before Plato's time.

During the Middle Ages, the stories about Atlantis were believed to be true. In the fourteenth and fifteenth centuries, many voyages were made to try to find Atlantis. The stories may have come from some true happenings. Perhaps a traveller brought back tales of his discovery of a new and strange land, and in time these tales became part of the legend of Atlantis.

Even today there are people who firmly believe there was such a place. According to the man who is considered the greatest expert on Atlantis by these believers, Atlantis was a place where man first became civilized. He also believes many of the gods worshipped by ancient peoples were really the kings and queens of Atlantis, and that the Atlanteans were the first to manufacture iron and have an alphabet.

This is certainly a strange name for a mass of water—but no other sea in the world has had such a variety of names!

It was first called "dead sea" by ancient Greek writers. The Hebrews

WHAT IS THE DEAD SEA? called it "the salt sea", among other names. Arab writers called it "the stinking sea".

What is so strange about this sea? It is really a large, narrow salt lake that lies between Jordan and Israel. It lies in a deep trough, or "rift", which is a deep depression in this area.

The Dead Sea is about 48 miles long, and ranges from 3 to 11 miles in width. Now comes the amazing part. The Dead Sea is the lowest area of water in the world. The surface of this sea is about 400 metres below sea level. The southern part of the sea is very shallow, but in the north the depth is about 400 metres.

There are no rivers flowing out of the Dead Sea. But into it drain the River Jordan from the north and many small streams from the surrounding slopes. There is only one way that surplus water can be carried away—by evaporation. This leaves a large concentration of minerals, such as salt, potash, magnesium chloride, and bromine behind in the water.

The Dead Sea is the world's saltiest area of water. The water is about six times as salty as that of the ocean! There are so many minerals concentrated in this sea, that a man swimming in it will float with his head and shoulders out of the water at all times! These minerals can be valuable to man. In fact, it is estimated that dissolved in this water are about two million tons of potash, which is used in making artificial fertilizers.

The Dead Sea is one of the strangest areas of water to be found on the earth. Millions of years ago, the Dead Sea was about 420 metres higher than it is today, and so it was on a higher level than the Mediterranean.

IS THERE ANY LIFE IN THE DEAD SEA? At that time, life did exist in it. But then a great dry period came, and so much of it evaporated that the sea gradually shrank in size to its present state.

One of the most amazing things about the Dead Sea is the amount of salt it contains. Normal ocean water contains about 4 to 6 per cent of salts. The Dead Sea contains 23 to 25 per cent of salts! If you taste this water, it is not only salty, but it may make you feel sick because of the magnesium chloride in it. The water also has a smooth, oily feeling because of the calcium chloride in it.

No animal life can exist in the Dead Sea. The River Jordan flows into it, bringing fish along with it. But the fish die, furnishing food for the sea birds.

If you ever make a trip to Italy, one of the most fascinating sights to see is Pompeii. For here is a city, almost 2,000 years old, that you will be able to see and study in greater detail, and better preserved, than almost any other ancient city.

WHAT WAS POMPEII?

Why is this so? On August 24th, in the year A.D. 79, there was a great eruption of Mount Vesuvius, a volcano in southern Italy. The lava, stones, and ashes thrown up by the volcano completely buried two nearby towns.

The town of Herculaneum, about two miles away, was deeply covered by a stream of mud which flowed down the slope of the mountain. Pompeii, farther along the coast, was buried by the rain of ashes and pebbles of light pumice stone. These fell over Pompeii in a dry state, and the mass which covered the city was from 5 to 6 metres thick.

When water came down on top of this, the material became like clay or plaster of Paris. As a result, objects that were caught in it made moulds of the material, and the two towns were remarkably preserved underneath!

Survivors of this disaster returned to the towns, and by digging down and tunnelling were able to remove most of the valuable objects, including slabs of marble that were on the large buildings.

In the Middle Ages, this place and everything about it was forgotten. In 1594, an underground aqueduct was started here, and the ruins were rediscovered. But it took until 1763 before any real excavating was done, and it has been carried on ever since. But a substantial part of Pompeii is still buried!

When we try to learn of the accomplishments of ancient man, we usually have to search or dig for evidence. But there is a case where ancient man has left all the evidence standing in a huge structure, and we still cannot understand what it is, what it was used for, and who built it!

WHAT IS STONEHENGE?

This is Stonehenge. It consists of large, standing stones in a circular setting, surrounded by an earthwork, and located near Salisbury, England. As long ago as the year 1136, it was written that the stones were magically transported from Ireland by Merlin. Of course, this was only a legend. More recently, it was believed that Stonehenge was put up by the Druids, who were priests in ancient Britain. But there is actually no reason to believe that this is so.

Stonehenge has a somewhat complicated structure. On the outside is a circular ditch, with an entrance gap. Then there is a bank of earth. Inside the bank is a ring of 56 pits. Between these and the stones in the centre, are two more rings of pits.

The stone setting consists of two circles and two horseshoes of upright stones. Then there are separate stones which have been given names, such as the Altar stone, the Slaughter stone, two Station stones, and the Hele stone.

In most of the holes that have been excavated, cremated human bones have been found. By studying the pottery and objects found, and by making radioactive-carbon tests, it has been estimated that parts of Stonehenge date back to about 1848 B.C., and possibly 275 years earlier or later than this date.

Part of Stonehenge is aligned so that the rising sun in midsummer is seen at a certain point, but nobody is sure if this was intentional.

So this huge and remarkable structure, which may be 4,000 years old, still remains a fascinating mystery!

The words "Anglo-Saxon" have come to mean anyone who is English or of English descent. But the Anglo-Saxons were actually a people who lived long ago.

WHO WERE THE ANGLO-SAXONS? The Romans had conquered Britain and occupied it for about 400 years. Then the Roman soldiers were called back to Italy. Britain was left undefended—at first, the Britons managed to carry on the Roman way of life, but by 450 A.D., wandering tribes began to settle in the part of England we now call East Anglia.

The Britons found that the newcomers were merciless people, whose songs were all songs of war. They belonged chiefly to three German tribes, the Angles, the Saxons, and the Jutes. All of them lived on or near the shores of the North Sea and the Baltic.

These newcomers were fair-haired, tall, and very courageous. Before the end of the sixth century, they had destroyed the Roman power in Britain and had founded seven kingdoms here.

At first each of these kingdoms had its own ruler, but in 829 they were united under an overlord. One of his successors was Alfred the Great, who reigned from 871 to 900. In 1066, the rule of the Anglo-Saxon kings in Britain was brought to an end by the Norman conquest.

Old English, or Anglo-Saxon, the language they spoke, was a mixture of the tongues spoken by the Angles, the Jutes, and the Saxons. Present-day English grew out of Anglo-Saxon, but there is little resemblance between them, except to language experts. Anglo-Saxon must be studied like any foreign language.

To us, cannibalism, or the eating of human flesh, is a horrible thing to think about. Yet it has existed as a practice among certain people and may still exist among some primitive tribes.

WHY DO CANNIBALS EAT PEOPLE? The first thing we must understand is that cannibals did not eat human flesh because they liked it. They ate it because it was part of a sacred rite, a kind of religious observance.

For example, among certain people of East India a long time ago, it was the custom to eat one's parents—because they respected and honoured them! Many primitive tribes believe that a man acquires the spirit of whatever he eats. If he eats a lion, he will be lionhearted; if he eats a deer, he will be able to run fast; if he eats a fox, he will be cunning. So the more one of these men respected his father, the more anxious he was to eat him.

Among other primitive peoples it was the custom to eat a criminal who had been condemned to death, but not a person who had died a natural death. The reason for this was that they believed that a criminal had offended the gods. Therefore he had to be sacrificed to the gods to satisfy them. And since it was the practice to eat or taste sacrifices to the gods, this had to be done even if the sacrifice was human.

Our word "cannibal" comes from Caniba, or Carib, the name of the West Indian tribe among whom the Spaniards first noticed the practice of eating human flesh. Some of the early North American Indians also practised cannibalism as part of their religion.

Nobody is quite sure how many cannibal tribes still exist. Some authorities think there are none, while others believe there are some in the interior of New Guinea.

Man has followed a path towards what we consider to be "civilization". At first, of course, in the earliest stages, man lived somewhat like the animals. He had no language, ate food where he found it, and had no home. Then, at the first stage of savagery, he learned to make fire and to eat fish.

WHAT IS CIVILIZATION?

He later learned to make crude tools and to hunt and protect himself, and the families joined into tribes. Then even later, he learned how to make pottery to cook and carry food. But he was still in the age of savagery.

The next step was what is called barbarism. Man learned how to plant seeds to raise his food, and he began to tame animals for his use. Then, later he learned how to use metals such as copper and iron, so he could make weapons and hunt better. And he also began to build houses.

Man was in the final or last stages of barbarism when he invented the most important thing to bring him to civilization. This was writing. At that time, his first kind of writing was writing in pictures, but in time this developed into writing with an alphabet.

The reason that the invention of writing really marked the beginning of civilization is that it enabled man to keep records of past happenings —and so man could read of and profit by the experience of others.

During all this time, man was also learning how to live by certain rules—in other words, by government. And with that came ideas of right and wrong, so that man lived by certain morals.

When did all this take place? It started with the very first days of man's life on earth and led up to the first stages of civilization about 5,000 or 6,000 years ago.

It is practically impossible to turn anywhere in our modern world and not see a form of art. Your furniture, your rug, the dishes in the kitchen, the car, your watch, even your clothes—all represent art in some form.

WHAT ARE THE FINE ARTS? The reason is that somebody designed each thing, chose colours, and tried to make it attractive. But there is an important purpose behind this kind of art—and that purpose is to have things used. What we call "the fine arts" have a different purpose—and that is beauty.

The fine arts are considered to be painting, sculpture, literature, drama, music, dancing, and architecture. Of these, the only one which is also involved in "use" is architecture. Architects have to think about the usefulness of their buildings as well as about their beauty.

But in the fine arts, the end result of a lot of hard work by the artist may have absolutely no use at all. It was created to provide certain satisfactions we get from beauty, and that is all. So a statue, a melody, a picture, a play, a book, and a dance are all examples of the product of the fine arts.

Today, many curious experiments are being made in all the fine arts. But the traditional methods and products of the fine arts all have things in common. For one thing they have "design". Design can be with sounds, with stone, with words, with building materials, with lines, and paint. A work of fine art is designed. And within that design, the creator uses "rhythm", "balance", and "harmony".

Rhythm comes from the more or less regular repetition of similar sounds, colours, shapes, and movements. Balance is the arrangement of what the artist works with so that the result seems right to us. And harmony is putting things together that seem to belong together. These, of course, are only rough ideas of what a creator in the fine arts tries to do.

Students who graduate from a college or university receive a "bachelor's" degree. This has nothing to do with being unmarried, and nobody knows exactly how this word came to be associated with the degree. If the

WHAT IS A BACHELOR'S DEGREE? student has done work in cultural subjects, generally called the arts, he gets a B.A. degree which means Bachelor of Arts. A student who specialized in scientific subjects is awarded a B.Sc. degree (Bachelor of Science).

Many people do not stop their studies at this point but go on for postgraduate studies. The degrees they get are called M.A. (Master of Arts) and M.Sc. (Master of Science). Then there are some who continue from there, and when they complete a few more years of postgraduate study and publish a "thesis" which shows they have the ability to carry out independent research, they get a degree of Ph.D. (Doctor of Philosophy).

Other kinds of degrees are given to people who have completed professional courses—such as to be a doctor or a lawyer, but they often have to pass other exams before they can go into practice.

Our system of education is now so specialized, that colleges and universities give degrees for studies in agriculture, forestry, pharmacy, dentistry, nursing, engineering, architecture, and many other professions.

One does not get a degree for the honour of having it, though, it is an achievement. In many cases, only those who have a university degree can enter certain occupations and professions, such as medicine, law, and so on.

The Queen's London home is by no means the oldest or the most magnificent royal palace in the world. It stands, however, in a lovely situation, between St. James's Park and Green Park, and has extensive, beautifully tended gardens of its own.

WHEN WAS BUCKINGHAM PALACE BUILT?

The first house to be built where the palace now stands was Goring House; later called Arlington House when it became the town residence of the Earl of Arlington, a statesman during the reign of Charles II. This house was pulled down in 1703, and another built in its place by the Duke of Buckingham and Normanby; hence its name today.

Soon after his marriage, in 1761, George III bought the house, and ever since then it has been a royal residence. In each succeeding reign it has been built on to and improved. The present facade was added in 1913.

Buckingham Palace is full of art treasures and antiques. Guided tours of the State Rooms have been given via television, and, at the Queen's Gallery in Buckingham Palace, there is always a selection of her treasures on view.

During the summer, particularly, the pavement in front of the palace is thronged with visitors, from both home and abroad, watching the Changing of the Guard, and perhaps hoping to catch a glimpse of the Queen as she leaves for one of her many engagements. When the Queen is in residence her royal standard is always seen flying from its mast above the Palace.

Maybe you did not even know the Nile River had a "riddle". Well, it is something that has puzzled people for thousands of years, and it has to do with a very curious event.

WHAT IS "THE RIDDLE OF THE NILE"?

Every year in Egypt, the Nile River starts to rise in July and continues to rise until October, when its level is about 7.5 metres above the level in May. During the high-water season, the Nile spills over its banks and deposits fertile silt on the fields along its course.

What makes this rising of the river mysterious is that there is practically no rainfall in Egypt! So for hundreds of years people have wondered what makes the Nile rise so regularly each year. This "riddle of the Nile" was not solved until late in the nineteenth century.

The Nile is the longest river in the world. It flows over 4,000 miles from south to north in the north-eastern part of Africa, mainly in the Sudan and Egypt. The yearly flooding of the Nile has made its valley a fertile ribbon in a hot, dry, barren wasteland, and people have lived here for thousands of years.

There are two great principal sources of the River Nile—the White Nile and the Blue Nile. The White Nile has its origin at Lake Victoria in Uganda. It has a fairly even flow throughout the year, so it cannot cause the annual rise of the Nile River. During April and May, when the water in the lower Nile is at its lowest, 85 per cent of the water is coming from the White Nile.

But what about the Blue Nile? It rises in Ethiopia. In the Ethiopian Mountains there are heavy rains and melting snows. And when these come down every year, they cause the Nile River to rise and overflow. And that is the answer to "the riddle of the Nile"!

When we say "country", we usually mean an independent state that has a distinct territory and its own government.

WHAT IS THE SMALLEST COUNTRY IN THE WORLD?

The world's smallest independent state is Vatican City. It lies in the midst of Rome, Italy, and has a total area of only 0·17 square miles! It is the place of government of the Catholic Church.

The Pope, the head of Vatican City, rules through a civil governor. Vatican City has its own flag, post office, railway station, and money. It also has a telephone system and radio broadcasting station. Support comes chiefly from contributions made by Catholics throughout the world.

Within Vatican City there is the Vatican Palace (the Pope's residence), the gardens, and the large St. Peter's Basilica. In the Palace are art museums and libraries. The Vatican Library, in a separate wing, is one of the greatest in the world.

Vatican City has diplomatic relations with other countries and receives representatives from many nations.

Over the years, political control was gained by the popes over a large territory in central Italy. In 1859, this land, called the "Papal States", covered about 16,000 square miles.

In 1870, Rome was made the national capital of Italy. Against the objections of the Pope, the Papal States were made part of the kingdom of Italy.

In 1929, an agreement was reached between the Pope and the Italian government and the Vatican City was set up.

The famous cathedral of St. Paul, dominating the City of London from its position on the top of Ludgate Hill, raises its huge dome far above most of the surrounding buildings. Long before Christianity came to this country, a temple dedicated to Diana is supposed to have stood on the site now occupied by the Cathedral. Ethelbert, the king of Kent, is known to have built a great Christian Church there, at some time during the seventh century, but this was destroyed soon after the Norman Conquest of 1066, to make room for "Old St. Paul's". This building is said to have been longer and higher than the present building; but "Old St. Paul's" was destroyed in the Great Fire of 1666.

WHO DESIGNED ST. PAUL'S CATHEDRAL?

For Sir Christopher Wren, the tragic Great Fire provided a great opportunity. Four months before the disaster, he had submitted designs for the remodelling of the old cathedral, but as the great church had been almost totally destroyed, he was asked to design a new cathedral. His own favourite design, however, was very different from the one eventually adopted.

The most imposing feature of the cathedral, which took thirty-five years to complete, is the dome. It consists of a large outer dome and a much lower inner dome. Between these two domes, a hollow cone of brickwork supports the lantern, ball and cross. The cross is 111 metres above the ground. In the Whispering Gallery, which runs around the inside of the dome, a whisper near the wall at one side can be distinctly heard on the other side, over thirty metres away. The hollow golden ball, beneath the cross, is nearly two metres across and can hold ten people.

The tombs of many famous men, including Nelson, Wellington and Wren himself are honoured there.

It is quite an amazing experience to be in a city where most of the "highways" are canals! But unlike most cities, Venice's highways, the canals, were there before the city was built!

WHY DOES VENICE HAVE CANALS? Venice is built on a group of mud banks that formed over 100 small islands at the head of the Adriatic Sea. All buildings are erected on pilings driven into this mud. In between the mud banks are strips of the sea, and these are the famous canals of Venice!

In this city, transportation is either by boat or on foot. There are no cars or carts allowed inside the old town. There are numerous narrow alleys and little bridges which span the canals. And everywhere one sees that small boat known as "the gondola". The gondolier, the driver of the boat, stands on a platform in the rear of the boat and propels it with a long pole.

Venice is a very old city. Long before the Huns swept down through Italy in about the middle of the fifth century, there were people already living on the little islands of the lagoon. After a while, 12 lagoon townships were formed. This was the beginning of the state of Venice, within which developed gradually the city now known as Venice.

In 1450, Venice was the head of a huge colonial empire and was the chief sea power in the world. Beginning with the sixteenth century, new trade routes were discovered and the trade of Venice began to decline.

In the following years, Venice was involved in many wars, lost its empire, and was practically destroyed by its enemies. In 1866, Venice voted to become part of the kingdom of Italy.

Today, Venice is one of the great artistic centres of Europe and is beginning to regain its position as a great port.

When people settle down in a community or a country, they tend to become like the people already living there. But those who wander around are likely to continue following their own ways wherever they go.

WHY DO GIPSIES KEEP THEIR OWN CUSTOMS? The gipsies are a wandering people. Often there are adult gipsies who have lived in as many as six different countries and speak several languages. Although European gipsies may settle in a town or city for a time, they soon are on the road again.

Because the gipsies seemed strange and different, the other peoples of Europe disliked and feared them. This, of course, would not exactly encourage the gipsies to give up their own customs and adopt those of the people who made life difficult for them.

There are two groups of gipsies who are more likely to settle down and live in one place than others, and these are the Hungarian gipsies, called *tziganes*, and Spanish gipsies called *gitanos*. When gipsies have lived a long time in a country, they usually adopt the religion of the country, but add a great many primitive customs and traditions of their own.

Nobody knows where the gipsies originated, but they are believed to have come from India in the tenth century and migrated to Persia. They reached the Balkans and Greece in the fourteenth century, then moved westwards. They reached England by the sixteenth century.

The English thought they came from Egypt, so they called them "gipsies". But the gipsies call themselves "Rom", and their language is called "Romany".

Mermaids are creatures who never existed in actual life, but who exist in the folklore of almost every people. They are supposed to be beautiful creatures who live in the sea, half human and half fish.

WHAT ARE MERMAIDS? In ancient Greek mythology, the mermaids are the sirens who entice sailors to their deaths. In German folk tales, mermaids are called Rhine maidens and live in a castle at the bottom of a river. Even the Red Indians had a legendary tale about a mermaid!

Mermaids are usually represented as having human bodies as far as the waist, but fishlike tails from the waist down. In addition to mermaids, there were also supposed to be mermen. They often fell in love with mortal maidens whom they captured or lured away in the ancient stories.

It is hard to say where the idea of mermaids and mermen originated. It may have begun when the earliest explorers and traders went sailing over the ocean. Primitive people, who had never seen boats before, may

136

have thought the sailors came up from the depths of the sea and were therefore half-fish.

It is also possible that the legends were started by glimpses of sea creatures who vaguely resembled human beings. Manatees, seals, and walruses are thought to have been mistaken at times for half-human creatures.

There are several stories told about mermaids in all countries. Mermaids are supposed to reveal things that are about to happen. It is said that a mermaid imparts supernatural powers to a human being. There is a story of a mermaid who falls in love with a human being, lives with him for a time, and then because some promise is broken, returns to her true home in the sea. In another legend, a mermaid falls in love with a man and entices him to go and live with her below the sea.

Mankind has many myths about giants and races of super-human creatures. There is also a famous legend about an amazing race of women, the Amazons.

WHO WERE THE AMAZONS?

The Amazons were believed to be a race of bold, warlike women. They were supposed to have come from the Caucasus Mountains and settled in Asia Minor. They were governed by a queen, and the entire state was run by women. They even fought their own wars and established their own cities!

According to legend, the Amazons either drove away or killed all the men who came among them. But when they tried to invade Athens, they were finally overcome and their entire army was wiped out.

The ancient Greeks, whose own women lived a quiet life at home, were fascinated by the tales of these wild, brave women, and made them a favourite subject of Greek art. They were usually shown mounted on horseback, armed with a lance and bow, and carrying a shield.

In the year 1541, an explorer named Francisco de Orellana was the first white man to travel the full length of a certain great river that flows through Peru and Brazil. On his journey he discovered long-haired Indian warriors. Because of their long hair, he thought they were women. So he called the river "the Amazon", naming it after the women of the early Greek legends.

On Easter Day in 1722, a Dutch admiral called Jacob Roggeveen landed on a grass-covered island in the South Pacific. He named it Easter Island and discovered it to be a very strange place indeed.

WHAT ARE THE EASTER ISLAND STATUES? The island was more than 1,000 miles from the nearest inhabited land. There were over 2,000 natives living on the island, and they were a dark Polynesian people. But the most curious thing of all was what this explorer saw on the island.

All along the coast he found large, stone heads. They had long faces and exceptionally long ears. Some of these statues had hands and some wore hats that were made of red lava. He soon discovered that these statues not only appeared along the coast, but they were at scattered points inland. Many were found partially finished in the quarries where they had been carved.

Primitive peoples all over the world have various art forms, usually connected with their religion, but nothing like these statues had ever been found anywhere else! And the truth is, they still remain a mystery. How could these heavy figures, some of which weigh about 50 tonnes, be moved from the quarries to their places? What form of transportation could the primitive people have developed?

No one knows! It is believed that the statues were probably connected with primitive religious practices and burial customs of the people.

And many of the statues were purposely broken during native wars that took place on the island during and after the eighteenth century. But even the natives living on the island today cannot explain the meaning of the huge statues!

Today the island is governed by Chile. Except for a small section reserved for the natives, the entire island is used for grazing cattle and sheep. The island is about 13 miles long and 7 miles wide at its broadest point.

Actually, we know very little about the Druids—they never wrote anything down so that when the order died out, everything they taught and had learnt passed away with them.

WHO WERE THE DRUIDS?

Many of the popular misconceptions about them date from the fertile imagination of John Aubrey, an historian of the late seventeenth century. Aubrey was fascinated by Stonehenge and he believed that it was the Druids who built it and worshipped there. As very little was known about them at the time and Aubrey had no scientific aids to help him date Stonehenge, it seemed the obvious answer to the mystery. The Order of Druids was started up again, and special ceremonies were invented to be performed at Stonehenge on Midsummer Day.

We do know, from the Roman historian Pliny, and from Julius Caesar's account of the Gallic Wars, that, as early as 200 B.C., the Druids were very influential in Celtic society—their authority was unquestioned in matters of law and religion, history and natural sciences. Pliny tells us of the religious significance of mistletoe and the importance of the oak tree. Julius Caesar, who was thoroughly aware of their influence in Britain, naturally enough, was anxious to discredit them: so he is more inclined to tell us of their practice of human sacrifice in times of great disaster and little of their wisdom and learning.

Under Roman rule, the Druids were forced to fly farther and farther west, until they finally settled on the Island of Anglesey. Here, they worshipped and taught until, with the coming of Christianity, the old religion finally died out—but not quite, because we still pick mistletoe at Christmas!

The most brutal sport that has ever existed in the history of the world was the fights of the gladiators in ancient Rome. They had their roots in an old custom among the Etruscan people of setting slaves to fight each other when a big funeral was being held. The Romans adopted this idea in the year 264 B.C. At first the fights were confined only to funeral ceremonies, but gradually they became the chief amusement of the Roman people and were held in huge arenas.

WHAT IS A GLADIATOR?

In the beginning, the contestants were slaves and condemned criminals. Later on, schools were formed to train the gladiators, and all kinds of citizens became gladiators, hoping to win fame and fortune. Great amphitheatres were built especially for this purpose.

The spectacle usually began with a parade of the gladiators, who often wore splendid armour of gold or silver. After the parade, there was a mock battle with wooden weapons to build up the appetite of the spectators. Then the trumpets sounded a signal, the men threw aside their harmless weapons for real ones, they separated into pairs, and the bloody battles began.

They used a variety of weapons. The gladiators fought in pairs, and when one fell wounded, it was the rule for the people in the stands to decide his fate. If they wanted to spare his life, they waved their handkerchiefs in the air. If they held their thumbs down, the victim had to be slain.

In time, the Romans grew bored with even these bloody battles and invented new spectacles. They set gladiators to battle with lions, tigers, and other wild beasts.

There were many efforts to stop these bloodthirsty spectacles, but they did not end until the year A.D. 500, when the Emperor Theodoric suppressed them.

There are two great poems, called the *Iliad* and the *Odyssey*, which are the greatest works of ancient Greek literature. Many people consider them to be the greatest poems ever written in any language.

WHO WAS HOMER? For a long time it was believed that they were written by a man called Homer. He was supposed to be blind and to have lived in Chios in Asia Minor. But today, most experts on the subject doubt that Homer, or any other one man, made up the poems by himself.

Nobody knows for sure how they were written, but this is what the experts believe. In ancient Greece there were many poets who travelled from town to town telling stories. They entertained kings, noblemen, and commoners by reciting poems made up by themselves or by others.

One of the favourite subjects of these storytellers was the Trojan War. Each poet had his own version of that great event and made up his own way of telling it. But at that time, writing was probably unknown. So poems were learned by heart and passed on by word of mouth.

Then, about 800 B.C., a very great poet came along. Perhaps his name was Homer, and perhaps it was not. He put together many of the older poetic stories of the Trojan War and made them into one great poem. It was called the *Iliad*, which comes from Ilion, another name for Troy.

A little later the *Odyssey* was put together in the same way. This was done either by Homer or another great poet. The *Iliad* and the *Odyssey* were so much better than the other versions of the Trojan War story, that almost all of the travelling poets learned them and recited them all over Greece.

At one time, people believed that there lived on this earth with us all kinds of strange beings who had magical powers. Sometimes they were called fairies, and sometimes they had special names, depending on their power or on the country where they were supposed to live.

WHAT IS A LEPRECHAUN?

Leprechauns were the fairy shoemakers of Ireland. They were little old wrinkled men, not even as big as a new-born child. In Scotland, fairies about 60 centimetres high, were called brownies. A brownie chose some house to serve and, coming at night, scrubbed and cleaned and did all sorts of work. All he would take in payment was a bowl of cream and a bit of white bread.

In England, the very smallest fairies were called pixies. They would wear green jackets and red caps and dance to the music of crickets and grasshoppers. In France, they were called fées and in Scandinavia, white elves. They lived in the woods and fields and a mortal could find his way to their home only on one of the four magical nights of the year—Midsummer Eve, May Eve, Christmas Eve, or Hallowe'en.

Fairies that were bigger in size had different names. For instance, if they were from 45 centimetres to the size of children, they were called goblins. In Germany they were called gnomes and dwarfs. And in Scandinavia they were called trolls.

Sometimes there were human-sized fairies, and they were hard to tell from mortals. In Germany, if you met a man with green teeth he was a nix, or water spirit. When nixes ventured on land, some bit of their clothing was always wet.

Of course it was considered very difficult to know the real size of a fairy because they were so seldom seen.

Sometimes a man, or a thing he does, captures the imagination of a country. His deed may not be decisive in his country's history, but he becomes a kind of national hero. Such a man was George Armstrong Custer.

WHAT WAS CUSTER'S LAST STAND?

Custer graduated from the United States Military Academy in 1861, and joined the Union forces in the Civil War. He became one of the most daring cavalry leaders in the Union Army. When the war ended, Custer was made a lieutenant colonel in the regular army and went to Kansas to fight the Indians.

In 1876, Sioux Indians were attacking the Western settlements. A large United States force was sent against them. Custer, with about 600 men, was sent on a scouting expedition. On June 24th, 1876, he was told that Indians, under the leadership of Sitting Bull, were encamped on the Little Big Horn River in Montana. Custer's scouts reported only a few hundred Indians, but the number turned out to be more than 2,500.

Custer then made the mistake of dividing his small force in hopes of surrounding the enemy. One unit attacked and then retreated when it saw the size of the Indian force. A second never got into the fight. With about 225 men, Custer attacked the Indians. In hand-to-hand fighting all of his little band was killed. This desperate fight they made became known as "Custer's Last Stand".

The tragedy stunned the country. Today, a monument and national cemetery mark the site of this battle. Custer himself is buried at West Point.

More than 1,500 years ago there was an Indian tribe in America who lived in homes dug in the walls of cliffs. They were the Anasazi Indians, and their homeland was "the Four Corners" region, where the present

WHO WERE THE CLIFF-DWELLERS? states of Utah, Colorado, Arizona, and New Mexico come together. Anasazi is a Navaho word which means "old peoples". They were the ancestors of the Pueblo Indians who live in the Southwest today.

These early Indians were hunters, food gatherers, and farmers. They lived in small villages in groups of 30 to 60 persons, all of whom were related. Later they built large houses with rooms joined in straight or curved lines. Such villages are called "pueblos", from a Spanish word which means "village".

Many of the villages were made up of caves high up on the sides of the canyons. The cliffs were chosen so that they faced the south, and thus were warm and sunny during the winter.

At some time between the years 1050 and 1300, the small villages grew into large towns. These towns were made up of large apartment buildings, sometimes numbering several hundred rows of rooms. They were one to four stories tall, with terraces on each floor.

The back wall of a cave was one end of the room. The ceilings were low and held up by poles. The doorways were also low, facing out on the canyon. Every apartment village had a number of meeting rooms, called "kivas", where the men held their social gatherings and their secret religious meetings. These kivas were underground.

Placed up high on the cliffs were watchtowers with loopholes. Watchers could call out a warning and men working below could scramble up the cliff, pulling their ladders after them. Without ladders the enemy could not hope to conquer even the smaller villages.

Besides growing corn, beans, and pumpkins, the Anasazi raised cotton, which they wove into ponchos, bags, and blankets. About the year 1300, they suddenly left their cliff homes and moved southwards. Nobody knows to this day what caused this move!

The present-day division of England, Wales, Scotland and Ireland into counties is derived from a long, continuous process of historical, legal, economic and social change over a period of more than a thousand years.

WHY DO WE HAVE COUNTIES?

The county structure of local government began in the "shires" of Anglo-Saxon England.

The shires were formulated as regions of administration and defence. The Norman invaders of 1066 took over the county structure of local government; it was amended and improved by their successors, and gradually reached the disorderly, uncivilized border areas of Wales and Scotland.

In Wales, there has been little change to the county map since the time of the part-Welsh Tudors. In Scotland, a system of sheriffdoms that closely resembled the English county system existed for hundreds of years. In Ireland, division into counties was established by the barons of Henry II and refined by Oliver Cromwell five hundred years later. In more recent times, British county history has been mainly a record of gradual change, reflecting the changing pattern of our society. An important factor in changes in the past hundred or so years has been the shift in population; especially the vast migrations from country to town, a result of the Industrial Revolution.

Large urban areas that had grown to contain more people than the entire surrounding county were detached from the county system in 1929 and reconstituted as separate administrative units. One county even swallowed up another! The creation of the administrative area of Greater London, in 1965, resulted in the former county of Middlesex becoming nothing more than a postal district.

In some cases, there are now two county towns; one, the historic county and market town; the other, the administrative headquarters.

The Inca civilization was at least 400 years old at the time Columbus discovered America.

WHO WERE THE INCAS?

The land of the Incas included what is now Bolivia, Peru, Ecuador, and part of Argentina and Chile. In the centre of the Inca Empire was Cuzco, the capital, the Sacred City of the Sun. It was the centre of the only world these people knew, and to this city came caravans from every part of the empire with grain, gold and silver, fine cloth, and fresh, green coca leaves.

The Incas were stern but just rulers. They allowed the people they conquered to follow their own customs. The family was the centre of government. Each group of ten families had a leader. He reported to a captain who had 50 families under him, and so on up to the Inca, who ruled the empire.

Everyone in the Inca Empire worked, except the very young and the old. Each family had a certain amount of land to farm. The people wove their own clothing, made their own shoes or sandals, their own dishes of pottery, and objects of gold and silver.

The people had no personal freedom: the Inca decided what clothes they wore, what food they ate, what work they did. The sick, poor, and old were cared for. The Incas were wonderful farmers and grew excellent crops. They built great aqueducts to bring mountain streams down to water their fields.

Many of the buildings which the Incas erected still stand. And they built unusual bridges made of vines and willow branches braided into huge ropes. The people were very skilful at weaving and pottery. They made cotton cloth so fine that the Spaniards thought it was silk, and they made fine clothing of wool.

After many centuries of prosperity, the Inca Empire was divided between two half-brothers who began to fight each other. When the Spaniards came, they found it easy to conquer them and destroy the empire.

RUINS OF INCA CITY

AZTEC WARRIOR

One of the most important peoples of ancient America were the Aztecs, who lived in the valley which now contains Mexico City. Long before the Europeans came from across the sea, these American Indians were making history.

WHO WERE THE AZTECS?

They had developed a way of life almost the equal of many of the European peoples. They carved their history in stone. They built temples and towers and homes of solid masonry. They were quite skilled in astronomy, law, and government, and were expert in many arts and crafts. They were in some ways a kind and gentle people. They were lovers of nature, especially birds and flowers. They also were fond of music, dancing, plays, and literature.

The Aztecs, however, had also risen to power through military abilities, and warfare was often carried on for the purpose of capturing enemies for sacrifice to their war god. The custom of sacrificing human life was shocking to the Europeans, but this developed naturally among the Aztecs because they combined religion and warfare.

The Aztecs were also called Mexica. From this, or from one of their gods, comes the word for Mexico. In 1325, 167 years before Columbus ever saw an Indian, the Aztecs, according to tradition, started to build their capital which they called Tenochtitlán. This city was later to become the capital of the Spanish and finally of the Mexican republic.

No one knows exactly where the Aztecs came from. The legends about them indicate that they came from the north. They probably arrived in the Valley of Mexico in the twelfth or thirteenth century. In these early times they were known as Tenochcas. The Toltecs, who already lived in the valley and were quite cultured, considered the Aztecs barbaric newcomers. Because of this the Aztecs had a difficult time settling in the valley. But in time they rose to great power and ruled over the peoples of the Valley of Mexico.

The first "Americans" went to America so long ago that we cannot really know as much as we would like to know about their earliest history. But this is what most authorities think happened.

WHERE DID THE AMERICAN INDIANS COME FROM?

About 12,000 years ago, bands of hunters on foot wandered into a strange new land, following herds of elk and caribou. The land these early hunters came from was probably Siberia. They crossed over to Alaska where the continents of Asia and North America are closest together at the narrow strip of water now called Bering Strait.

For thousands of years more hunters went to North America. They did not all go at once, but went in small family groups. Although they came from the same homeland and were originally alike, they went over a period of thousands of years and thus the groups differed in many ways. They differed in language, in appearance, in customs, in ways of making a living, and in the way they adapted themselves to life in the new land.

They all had straight, black hair and high cheekbones. They were all dark-skinned, but their shadings varied. The skins of some had a reddish tinge and so these people were often called "red men".

They used the same sort of weapons and tools, and methods to provide themselves with their food, clothing, and shelter. But they used different materials to satisfy these needs.

The biggest differences that developed among these people were a result of where they settled to live. There were five main living centres where these people settled: the Northwest Coast, the California region, the Southwest, the Eastern Woodlands, and the Plains. The tribes that developed in each of these centres were quite different from each other —though they were all what came to be known as "Indians".

Everybody knows Hercules was a "strong man". But to the ancient Greeks he was much more than that. They worshipped him as a god.

According to legend, Hercules was the son of Zeus and Alcmene, a mortal princess. Hera, the divine wife of Zeus, hated Hercules. While he was still in his cradle, she sent two serpents to kill him, but the infant strangled them. Hercules married Megara, but Hera caused him to be seized with a fit of madness. During the seizure, he killed his wife and children.

WHO WAS HERCULES?

To make up for this terrible deed, the oracle at Delphi ordered Hercules to offer his services to King Eurystheus, who gave him twelve labours to do. It is these twelve labours which Hercules undertook that make up most of the legend about him.

First he strangled a fierce lion. Then he was sent to kill the Hydra, a monster with nine heads, eight of which were mortal and one immortal. Every time Hercules struck off a mortal head, two more grew in its place. But Hercules finally killed the Hydra. His third labour was to capture a particularly fierce wild boar. His fourth was to kill the golden-horned hind. His fifth labour was to clean the stables of 3,000 oxen belonging to King Augeas. They had not been cleaned for 30 years. Hercules directed the courses of two rivers into the stables and cleaned them in a day.

His sixth labour was to kill the birds of Stymphalus; his seventh to capture the Cretan bull. His eighth task was to capture the wild horses of Diomedes, which fed on human flesh. For his ninth labour he brought back the belt of Hippolyta, the queen of the Amazons. For his tenth, he brought back the oxen of Geryon from a far-western island. On his way he split apart a mountain to form the Strait of Gibraltar. His eleventh labour was to secure three golden apples from Hesperides. His twelfth was to bring to Eurystheus the watchdog of Hades, Cerberus.

Ancient Greece produced many great men, and one of the most interesting of them was a man called Pythagoras, who lived in the sixth century B.C.

WHO WAS PYTHAGORAS? Pythagoras was a religious teacher, a mathematician, and a philosopher. But because of his ideas and beliefs, he had to leave Greece and settle in Southern Italy.

What were some of those unusual beliefs he had? Pythagoras believed in immortality and the "transmigration of the soul". This meant that after death, any soul which did not go to heaven then occupied the body of another man, or even an animal. Because he believed this, he prohibited his followers from eating or sacrificing animals.

The followers of Pythagoras were called "Pythagoreans", and they observed many other strict rules of conduct. For instance, they had to observe silence and they could drink no wine.

Of course, we may think that some of his ideas were rather foolish, but Pythagoras also made many important contributions to knowledge. He discovered that the length of a musical string is in exact numerical relation to the pitch of its tone. From this he developed a theory of harmony and the belief that number was the first principle of the whole universe.

Pythagoreans also had a theory of the solar system which was nearly correct. They believed the earth was a sphere revolving around a central fire. Pythagoras also taught the theorem that "the square of the hypotenuse of a right-angled triangle equals the sum of the square of the other two sides".

Practically everybody has heard of or read stories about King Arthur and his Knights of the Round Table. They are not considered to be true stories, but legends. What are they based on?

DID KING ARTHUR EVER EXIST? Well, no one knows who King Arthur really was. Most writers of history believe that there was a great chief of one of the tribes in Britain around the year A.D. 500, and the legends have grown up about this man.

King Arthur may have been part Roman and part British, for the

Romans had ruled England for nearly 400 years. Arthur probably led a large army against the Saxon invaders.

In both Wales and Brittany, Arthur was remembered and admired. Stories about him were passed from one generation to another. Each story was more wonderful than the last. Finally, Arthur became one of the greatest heroes who ever lived. He killed horrible monsters, had great magical powers, and became a great and good king.

Nobody knows for sure just where Arthur had his castle. There are about six different places in England that claim to be the location of Camelot, his home.

The first writer to mention Arthur was an early Welsh historian who lived about the eighth century. After that first mention of Arthur, nothing was written about him for about 400 years. Then in the twelfth century, stories about King Arthur became quite common. The earliest were written in Latin, and then French and English poets began to write about him.

In the fifteenth century, Sir Thomas Malory wrote down many of the stories about Arthur in a book called *Morte d'Arthur (Death of Arthur)*.

About 1,200 years ago there was a group of people, the Norsemen, who came from the coastal regions of Norway, Sweden, and Denmark. Their name "viking" was probably taken from the *viks*, or sounds, of their home region. The vikings were great sailors and adventurers.

WHO WERE THE VIKINGS?

They were strong and sturdy, often with blue eyes and fair hair. At a time when the rest of Europe was terrified to sail the sea, the vikings were great explorers and traders. They preferred conquest and adventures to a life of quiet safety.

In A.D. 793, the vikings made their first attack on the English coast. From that time and through to the eleventh century, they raided the coasts of Western and Eastern Europe. They plundered England, Ireland, France and Spain. They even journeyed as far south as Algiers.

Vikings discovered islands to the west of Greenland and a portion of the North American continent, which they called Vinland. A colony was attempted at Vinland and settlers remained on the continent for three years.

The Norsemen had a civilization of their own. Viking ships, carriages, household dishes, and ornaments have been discovered in their graves. There were many iron deposits in viking lands and the Norsemen became skilled workers in this metal.

The vikings were originally pagans. Odin and Thor were their chief gods. According to viking beliefs, the gods lived in a place called Valhalla, and heroes who died in battle were welcomed there. They also had a literature of "sagas", or stories, which were about life among the kings, chieftains, and common people.

The Norsemen had a good system of law based on fairness and sportsmanship. It is even believed that the jury system we have today can be traced back to the ancient Norsemen.

Horatio, Lord Nelson, was the most famous commander in the history of the British Navy. Born in 1758, he was so frail and weak in early childhood that no one expected him to live! His father was a clergyman, and

WHO WAS LORD NELSON? the family had very little money, so Horatio had to leave home when he was twelve, and join the Navy as a midshipman to make his own career.

When he was twenty-one, he was made Captain of a frigate and, with his new authority, he set about reforming discipline on his ship, saying that cruelty made cowards of his men.

Nelson's rise to fame began in 1793, when he was put in command of the Agamemnon, during the revolutionary war with France. For the next three years he repeatedly distinguished himself by his calm, bravery and judgement. It was at this period that he lost his right eye at the battle of Calvi, and soon after, in the Canary Islands, he lost his right arm.

His heroism, however, was rewarded when peace was declared, by a pension, a knighthood and promotion to the rank of rear-admiral. Soon afterwards, Napoleon came to power and the peace was broken.

Nelson was charged to find and destroy Napoleon's fleet which planned to attack the overland route to India and Egypt. The result of the encounter was a rousing victory for Nelson and he became the idol of England.

The end of his brave life came suddenly on October 21st, 1805. Lord Nelson had been recalled from his retirement to take the sole command of the Mediterranean fleet and defend England from the very real threat of Napoleonic invasion. During the battle with the French and Spanish fleets off Cape Trafalgar, Nelson was fatally wounded by a musket-shot from one of the French ships, and he died a few hours later in his cabin at the very moment of victory.

Sometimes a man comes along who changes our whole way of looking at life and the universe around us. Such a man was Nicolaus Copernicus, a Polish astronomer who lived from 1473 to 1543.

WHO WAS COPERNICUS?

Astronomers used to believe that the earth was the centre of the universe. Among these astronomers was Ptolemy, an Egyptian who lived in the second century and who wrote a book that was accepted as true for hundreds of years.

Ptolemy said that the earth stayed fixed in a permanent place, while the great hollow spheres called the heavens revolved around it. But Copernicus realized a new truth in the science of the heavens. He decided that Ptolemy had believed the earth was fixed and the sun moved around it for one chief reason—Ptolemy had observed the Great Dipper moving slowly, night after night, around the North Star.

Copernicus understood that it was the earth's turning on its own axis that gave this effect of movement to the sun. Copernicus concluded that the earth, itself a tiny part of the whole universe, not only rotated on its axis, but also revolved around the sun in the company of other planets.

Copernicus' theory was startling in the sixteenth century. He knew he would face opposition from the scientists and churchmen who taught that the earth was the centre of the universe. His writings were finally published near the end of his life, with a statement that it did not claim to be true fact but was only one man's idea. Today that theory is the foundation of the whole science of astronomy.

If a person has some way in which he can be hurt, or some spot in which he can be wounded, he is said to have an Achilles heel.

WHO WAS ACHILLES? This expression goes back to one of the greatest heroes of Greek legends, Achilles. When Achilles was born, the Fates, the goddesses that controlled man's destiny, foretold that the infant would die young. Achilles' mother, Thetis, wanted to avoid this fate for her son, so she dipped him in the water of the River Styx. This was supposed to make him invulnerable and protect him from deadly wounds.

Every part of Achilles was thus made safe against injury, except one part—the heel by which his mother held him! And later on, he was to die from a wound in the heel.

Achilles grew to be a handsome young man, swiftest of mortals in the race, and the joy of all who beheld him. Eventually Achilles became famous as the greatest of the Greek warriors during the Trojan War.

In the tenth year of the struggle, he captured a girl named Briseis. But the leader of the Greeks, Agamemnon, took the girl away from him. Achilles was furious and decided not to fight any more. The Greeks were helpless without their great hero. So they persuaded Achilles to lend his armour and his men to his friend, Patroclus.

But Patroclus was slain by the Trojan hero Hector, and the armour was captured. Then Achilles decided to obtain revenge. He became friends again with Agamemnon, and put on armour and a shield. He took to the field and killed Hector. And in revenge he dragged Hector's body around the tomb of his slain friend.

Later, Hector's brother, Paris, shot a poisoned arrow at Achilles. It entered his heel, the one part of his body that had not been dipped in the Styx, and Achilles died from the wound.

Socrates has come to stand for the ideal of a wise man, yet one of his principles was that it is wise to know that your wisdom is worth nothing!

He was born in Athens, Greece, about 470 B.C. Little is known of

WHO WAS SOCRATES?

his parents or childhood. He left no writings. His disciple, the great philosopher Plato, wrote down, in the form of dialogues, Socrates' teachings and ideas, together with many scenes from his life.

According to Plato, Socrates spent his time in the market place of Athens talking to anybody who would listen. He liked especially to find someone with firm ideas on a subject. Socrates would draw him out with leading questions and show him he was ignorant of the subject he had been so sure about. Hence, the method of arguing by asking questions is called Socratic. His fundamental principle was "Know thyself".

The Athenians disliked him because he upset all their former ideas. Therefore they said to him that he did not believe in the gods, or in truth, or in justice.

In the year 399 B.C., his enemies brought him to trial on the charge of having corrupted the youth of Athens and of neglecting his religious duties. No one believed the accusations and Socrates realized this. The defence he made, known as "the Apology of Socrates", was afterwards written out by Plato. It was mocking and courageous. Although Socrates knew that he would be condemned to death, he said he must go on leading the same life, devoting himself to the search for truth.

In prison, Socrates passed his last day discussing with his friends the immortality of the soul. He took the cup of hemlock, the poison which was given him, without trembling and drank it. His friends burst into tears, but he begged them to be silent. He died with a smile on his lips.

SOCRATES

It is not often that we make a hero of a robber, but Robin Hood somehow seems to be different. Everybody knows it is wrong to steal, yet Robin Hood is admired. The reason for this, of course, is that he stole from the rich and gave to the poor.

WHO WAS ROBIN HOOD?

Did Robin Hood ever actually exist? We know that he was a favourite figure in the ballads and stories of England in the fourteenth and fifteenth centuries. He was supposed to have lived in the twelfth century. In a Latin history which appeared in the year 1521, this is what was written about Robin Hood:

"About the time of Richard I, Robin Hood and Little John, the most famous of robbers, were lurking in the woods and stealing only from rich men; they killed none except those who resisted them or came to attack them. Robin kept 100 archers on the proceeds of these robberies, well trained for fighting, and not even 400 men dared to come against them.

"All England sings of the deeds of this Robin; he would not allow any woman to be hurt, nor did he ever take the goods from the poor; indeed he kept them richly supplied with the goods he stole from the abbots."

One can see how such a character must have captured the imagination of the people of that period, because they loved chivalry and archery. Robin pleased them and they built around his name one legend after another. They made him a great sportsman, a wonderful archer, and a lover of the green woods where he lived.

There are many theories about Robin Hood. One of these suggests that he was a Saxon, and among the last of those who held out against the Normans when they conquered England. It seems certain that a Robin Hood really did exist. But it is also pretty certain that many of the stories that existed in other legends came to be told about Robin Hood.

Chapter 2

Animal Life

In the folklore and legends of countries all over the world, there are tales of great and horrible dragons.

DID DRAGONS EVER EXIST? They were pictured as huge, snake-like monsters frightful to behold. They had bulging eyes, their nostrils spouted flames, and their roar was so great they caused the earth to tremble.

One of the most famous of these ancient dragons was the Hydra, which had nine heads! It devoured many beautiful young girls before it was slain by Hercules. Another famous dragon was the Chimera, a fire-breathing monster that met its death at the hands of a young warrior, Bellerophon, who was helped by his winged steed, Pegasus.

Many dragons were supposed to be guarding great treasures. The Golden Fleece was guarded by a dragon with a hundred eyes! In other cases, great heroes always fought battles with dragons.

Although the dragon usually represents the spirit of evil, it has also been used as a symbol of protection. The early warriors painted fierce dragons on their shields to frighten away enemies.

At one time people actually did believe that dragons existed. For example, before the time of Columbus, sailors used to be afraid to venture into unknown seas because they believed huge dragons would swallow up the ships and men.

Of course, dragons never existed except in legends, myths, and fairy tales. Then why did the belief in them arise? In prehistoric times, all kinds of huge reptiles roamed the earth. The most terrifying of these beasts, the dinosaur, lived long before man appeared on the earth. But it is possible that during the time of the cavemen some reptiles of great size still survived, and from this came the legends of the dragons.

BRONTOSAURUS

About 180 million years ago the reptiles ruled the earth. In fact, there were so many of them and they were so powerful, that this period is known as the Era of Reptiles. The scientific name for this period is Mesozoic Era.

WHY DID DINOSAURS BECOME EXTINCT?

The largest of all the reptiles were the dinosaurs. And the largest dinosaurs were probably the biggest animals that ever walked the earth! Yet about 60 million years ago the dinosaurs died out because changing conditions made life impossible for them.

The first dinosaurs were probably no bigger than a turkey, and, like a turkey, they walked on their hind legs. In time, some of them grew heavier and longer, and finally became so heavy that their legs would not support them on land. So they had to spend most of their lives in rivers and swamps, where water could keep their huge bodies afloat!

One of these giants was called "Brontosaurus". This dinosaur was 20 to 25 metres long and weighed about 38 tonnes. Other kinds of dinosaurs remained on land. For instance, "the Tyrannosaurus" was a monster about 14 metres long and 6 metres high. The Tyrannosaurus was probably the most ferocious animal that ever lived.

Dinosaurs developed in many different ways, but none of them ever developed a good brain. One reason dinosaurs disappeared may be that they were just not bright enough to know how to survive and escape from all their natural enemies.

Most scientists believe that changes in the earth and in climate killed off the dinosaurs. Swamps dried up, mountains appeared, and certain dinosaurs could not live on dry land. Also, changes in climate produced changes in vegetation, and since many dinosaurs were plant eaters, their food supply disappeared! And finally, as the earth began to have seasons, shifting from hot summers to snowy winters, dinosaurs could not fit themselves to these changes and gradually died out.

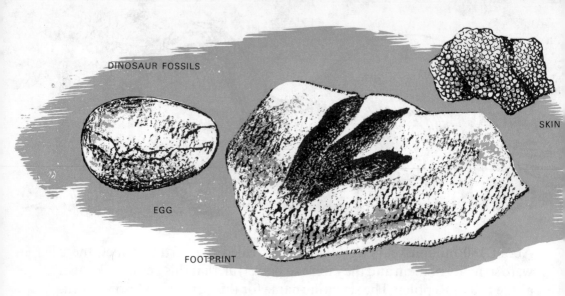

DINOSAUR FOSSILS

SKIN

EGG

FOOTPRINT

Scientists believe that dinosaurs first appeared on the earth about 180 million years ago, and died out about 60 million years ago. This is long before human beings appeared on earth, and also before such animals as

HOW DO WE KNOW WHAT DINOSAURS WERE LIKE?

dogs, rabbits, horses, monkeys, or elephants. Then how can we possibly know anything about these giant creatures?

Everything we know about dinosaurs— and everything we will ever know—comes from fossils. These are remains which these creatures left in the earth. But there are many different kinds of fossils.

The most common fossils are petrified remains of what were the hard parts of their bodies—bones, teeth, and claws. Scientists can study these remains and from them reconstruct how the whole body of the dinosaur was built!

Sometimes, petrified tendons and skin are found, and this provides even more clues. Fossils can also be trails or footprints that were made in wet sand or mud that hardened into stone over the ages. From these, it is possible to tell how the dinosaurs walked and whether it was on two legs or four. And the rarest fossils of all from this time are dinosaur eggs.

In this way we can tell that the Brontosaurus was a monster from 20 to 25 metres long and weighed about 38 tonnes. We know it lived in swamps and was a plant-eater. And we also know that a dinosaur called Allosaurus had sharp teeth and powerful claws and it fed upon Brontosaurus and other plant-eaters. You see, scientists have found, among the broken and deeply scratched bones of Brontosaurus—fossil teeth of the Allosaurus!

To begin with, there are many kinds of deserts. Some are the familiar deserts of bare rock and shifting sand, upon which the hot sun beats down. But some deserts, such as the Gobi, have bitterly cold winters. So a desert

HOW DO PLANTS AND ANIMALS LIVE IN THE DESERT?

is really a region where only special forms of life can exist. And the form of life is the kind that has managed to adapt itself to the particular conditions of the particular desert.

For example, cacti are well-known desert plants. They have thick, fleshy stems without true leaves. Desert shrubs that have leaves usually have small ones. Little or no leaf surface prevents too much evaporation of water from the plant.

Many desert plants have thorns, spines, or a disagreeable taste or smell. This discourages animals that might eat them and so helps them survive. Desert plants usually lie dormant during the dry or cool season, or drop seeds that can survive such a period.

RICAN
CTUS

When the period for growth arrives, the seeds germinate and give rise to plants that rapidly flower and drop more seeds. Within a few weeks or months, the plants are ready again for the long season of dormancy.

When it comes to animals, they must be able to do without water for long periods, or be able to reach water holes at great distances. The camel, for example, is highly adapted to desert life. It has padded feet to walk on sand, a water-storing stomach, humps of fat as a reserve supply of energy, and nostrils that can be closed to keep out sand during windstorms.

Many of the smaller desert creatures need to drink no water at all. They get what liquid they need from the sap of food plants and from night dew on leaves or stones.

161

Suppose you lived in a country long ago and had never seen a horse. Then suddenly you saw men riding on horseback, jumping ditches and running with the horse, staying on its back no matter what? You might think the horse and the man were one crea-

WHAT WERE CENTAURS?

ture! Some Indians in America actually thought that when they saw the first Spaniards on horseback.

In ancient times, in the mountains of Thessaly in Greece, there lived a group of people who used to hunt bulls on horseback. They were such excellent riders, that people in the surrounding areas began to believe these were not really men on horses—but creatures that were half men, half horse. It is believed that the myth about the centaurs may have started this way.

The centaurs, in Greek mythology, were a race of beings, part horse, part man, who lived in the mountains of Thessaly and Arcadia. They were supposed to lead a wild and savage life, and Homer, the great poet, calls them "savage-beasts".

Characters in Greek myths always seem to have interesting adventures, and the centaurs were no exception. One such story concerns a king called Pirithous. He was celebrating his marriage to a woman called Deidamia. In the midst of the celebration, a drunken centaur called Eurytion carried her off. This started a great battle between the centaurs and the king's people. The centaurs were defeated.

But that kind of behaviour is what seems to have been expected of the centaurs. In later times, statues and paintings of centaurs often showed them pulling the cart of Dionysus, who was the god of wine, or being ridden by Eros, who was the god of love.

The idea of the centaurs, and the battles that were supposed to take place with them, had a symbolic meaning. It was supposed to suggest the struggle between civilization and barbarism.

Long ago, voyages to distant lands were lengthy and dangerous undertakings. Travellers who dared make these trips brought back strange tales of the wonderful sights they had seen. Often they told of mythical animals,

WHAT WAS A UNICORN? which were both strange and horrible. These tales grew more marvellous each time they were told.

Sailors told of seeing sea-serpents, fearful man-eating creatures which were 60 metres long, 6 metres thick, and had bright blue eyes. Mermaids with long, green hair and shiny, scaly tails were supposed to haunt the seas and lure sailors to destruction.

Travellers said that in the countries they had visited they had seen unicorns. These were animals with the head and the body of a horse, the hind legs of an antelope, the tail of a lion, and the beard of a goat. Each unicorn had a single, long, twisted horn set in the middle of its forehead. The horn was supposed to have the magic power to detect poison and was much sought after for drinking cups.

But the unicorn was a mythical animal that never existed, even though many people believed it did. Other mythical animals that people thought really existed included griffins, animals that were a cross between a lion and an eagle. The Greeks told stories of centaurs, creatures which were half man and half horse. Almost everyone believed in dragons, huge winged serpents that breathed forth fire.

Although modern scientists have tried to explain what some of these mythical creatures really were, no one can explain where people got the idea that unicorns, centaurs, or griffins existed. A unicorn, by the way, is still on our English coat of arms!

The craving for salt, both by animals and human beings, is one of the most interesting mysteries of nature.

We know that for thousands of years salt has been used and valued by man. Our word "salary" comes from the Latin word for salt. In ancient Mexico, salt was so important that a beautiful maiden was sacrificed to the salt god every year. And we know that today, when a prisoner in jail is deprived of all salted food, he practically goes crazy with desire for it.

WHY DO ANIMALS LIKE SALT?

The fluid in our body, the liquid part of it, is a salt solution. And since our body continuously eliminates liquid in many ways, including perspiration, it must make up for this loss of salt.

Now while there is enough salt in the oceans to cover the whole surface of the earth, the land part of the world is poor in salt. Plants do not contain much salt, and most of the salt in the land itself is washed off by rain water into rivers and oceans.

Land animals, however, are descended from creatures that used to live in the sea. Their body fluid is still what it used to be before they moved to dry land. This means that their body fluid is still like sea water! And since neither plants nor the land can give them enough salt, they keep craving for more and love to eat salt.

Carnivores, or animals who eat meat, do not crave salt. This is because they obtain it from the body fluid of their victims. But herbivores, or animals who live on vegetable matter, need more salt and love to eat it.

Remember the trained seal at the circus who could answer questions in arithmetic by blowing on a horn? Or the horse who would tap his foot the right number of times when his trainer asks him to count?

CAN ANIMALS COUNT?

The truth is that these animals were not really counting! What happened was the seal or the horse would notice a sign from the trainer—it might be a movement of the head or lips or eyes—and this sign would tell him when to stop blowing the horn or tapping his foot.

Of course, many animals can tell a larger quantity from a smaller quantity. For instance, many animals can pick a pile with six pieces of food instead of a pile with five pieces of food. Children who have not

learned how to count yet, can do the same thing. But being able to notice differences in quantity is not the same thing as counting.

Scientists now believe that certain birds and animals can actually count. In one experiment, a pigeon was offered one grain at a time. All the grains were good to eat, but the seventh grain was always stuck to the dish. After a while, the pigeon learned to count to six grains, and when the seventh grain was offered it refused to peck at it. This was real counting!

In another experiment, a chimpanzee was taught to pick up one, two, three, four, or five straws and hand over the exact number of straws that was asked for. But this was as far as this chimpanzee could count. It always made mistakes above five.

There is a very good reason why animals cannot learn to talk as human beings do, that is, use words to express ideas.

WHY CAN'T ANIMALS LEARN TO TALK?

Most of the intelligent things animals do is a result of inheriting certain patterns of behaviour. This works in special situations, but when you change the situation the animal usually does not know how to deal with it. The other reason animals behave "intelligently" is that they go through a trial-and-error method of learning.

Neither of these two ways of "thinking" can ever lead to talking. Talking means the use of words as symbols. The word stands for an idea or a thing—it is a symbol of it. And animals do not have the ability to deal with symbols. Their minds cannot use combinations of symbols the way human beings do.

When we study how a child learns to say "Mama", we can see how complicated learning to talk really is. First the baby learns to recognize mother by seeing her again and again. As soon as the child recognizes her, the mother keeps pointing to herself and saying "Mama" at the same time. Gradually the infant hears the sound "Mama". After a while, the baby remembers this sound, and now it understands the word "Mama".

Later on, the child makes a connection between the appearance of mother and the sound "Mama", and it identifies her. Now the mother shows the child how to say the word with its mouth. The baby imitates her and reaches the stage of word formation. It keeps on trying to say the word until certain muscles begin to work.

Finally the day comes when everything is ready for talking. The baby sees the mother, recognizes her, remembers the word, forms the word, starts the right muscles working, and says "Mama"!

The animal that most closely resembles man is the ape. Not only does the ape have a skeleton structure like man's, but he also has an "opposable" thumb. This means the thumb can be made to meet the finger tips,

WHICH ANIMAL RESEMBLES MAN THE MOST?

enabling the ape to use his hands to grasp things and to climb trees. Man's opposable thumb makes it possible for him to use tools.

Some people imagine that the ape is the ancestor of man, but this is not so. The theory of evolution holds that the apes and man may have had a common ancestor long ago, the so-called "missing link". But they evolved along different lines.

There are four kinds of "anthropoid", or "manlike" apes. The biggest and most powerful of these is the gorilla. Next in size is the orang-utan. Then comes the chimpanzee. Finally, smallest of all is the gibbon.

The gibbon is the least known of the apes, but he resembles man the most. The gibbon can stand up straight on his hind legs and he can walk like a man instead of half-stooping. But the gibbon does very little walking because he spends most of his life in trees. He swings from branch to branch with his long arms, stopping to pick leaves and fruit.

When a gibbon eats, he is likely to sit erect like a man, even though his diet may include spiders, birds, and eggs. The family life of the gibbon is closely knit. His mate and their children stay with him night and day. And since a young gibbon will stay with the parents until about the age of six, a gibbon family may have as many as eight or nine members. In the wilds of the jungle, a gibbon may live to the ripe old age of thirty!

All animals must learn to do some things. This is true even of those animals that function almost entirely by instinct. But the process of learning is not always the same.

CAN ANY ANIMALS USE REASON? In many cases when we think an animal is "learning" something, all that is really happening is that an instinct it was born with is developing or ripening. For example, birds fly rather clumsily when they first leave the nest. Their "learning" to fly is really the gradual development of their instinct.

The most common way in which animals learn, in the true sense of learning, is by making mistakes and remembering to avoid them in the future. This is the way dogs learn to "behave", or to do tricks, and the way horses are broken in and trained.

Animals very seldom learn by imitating. If one dog knows a certain trick, another dog cannot learn that same trick by watching the first and imitating it.

Then what about using reason? This means finding a solution to a problem or difficulty which they have never met before, and which they do not know how to solve from some inborn instinct. Experiments have shown that apes and monkeys are able to reason to a certain extent.

In one experiment, a monkey was brought into a room where a banana was hanging that it could not reach. There were two small boxes in the room. The monkey sat and looked at the banana and the boxes. Then it suddenly got up, placed one box on top of the other, climbed up and got the banana! The monkey had actually thought out how to do it— it had used reason.

Scientists believe that dogs, cats, and even some wild animals can probably reason to a certain extent, but it is hard to prove this is so.

All of us have seen the eyes of some animal glowing at us in the dark as we drive by at night, so it is natural to think that the eyes themselves are glowing.

DO ANIMALS' EYES SHINE IN THE DARK?

The truth is that the glow is only the reflection of light from some other source! It is probably caused by our car headlights, or it may be caused by a flashlight. The reason that reflection takes place is that there is a layer of crystalline substance in the eyes of many animals. This substance has the ability to reflect light. Man has almost none of this substance in his eyes.

This reflecting layer also helps the animals see in the dark, which is why they can see better at night than man can. The differences in colour of the light reflected from the eyes of animals is due to the different number of blood vessels in their eyes. An animal that has many blood vessels in its eyes will reflect a reddish glow. If it has fewer blood vessels, it will have a whiter glow.

When an animal sheds its skin or feathers and replaces it, we call that "moulting". Amphibians, reptiles, birds, and even insects moult.

Birds grow a whole series of feathers during their lifetime. When

WHAT IS MOULTING? they reach the adult stage, they have the plumage that is typical of their kind of

bird. Then adult birds change this plumage from time to time as old worn feathers moult (drop out) and new ones grow in their place.

If a feather is pulled out, it begins to replace itself at once. In addition, some birds grow bright, new feathers for the breeding season by moulting. So most birds moult twice a year, once before and once after the breeding season.

Since most birds do not shed many of their flight feathers at the same time, they are able to fly all through the moulting period. Also, flight feathers are often shed in pairs, one from the right and one from the left wing, so the flying balance is not upset. Ducks, swans, and geese are exceptions to this. They lose all their flight feathers when they moult, so they cannot fly. But since they are water birds they do not have to fly to escape from danger. They just take to the water.

During the moulting season the brightly coloured males often take on a drab-coloured set of feathers. This gives them the added protection of camouflage and makes it easier for them to hide.

Snakes have an interesting way of shedding their skin. A snake does not shed its entire skin, just the thin outermost part. The snake rubs its snout against something rough to loosen the old skin around the lips. Next it manages to get the loose parts caught on a rock or twig. Then the snake crawls out through the mouth opening of the old skin. It leaves the old skin in a single piece and wrong side out.

169

SPIDER MONKEY

GIBBON

HANUMAN MONKEY

The chimpanzee is a monkey, but it is a special kind of monkey. It is the most intelligent one of all!

Monkeys belong to the highest order of mammals called "primates", which includes man. All monkeys are covered with hair, usually live in trees, and have nails instead of claws on each of their five fingers and toes.

IS THE CHIMPANZEE A MONKEY?

Monkeys may be divided into four general groups: the lemurs; the Old World monkeys, including baboons, leaf monkeys, and others; the New World monkeys, including the spiders, howlers, and others; and the apes, including the gorilla, orang-utan, chimpanzee, and gibbon.

Of the three manlike apes, the orang-utan, the chimpanzee, and the gorilla, the one that is most like man is the chimpanzee. This ape is smaller than either the gorilla or the orang-utan, and it is more intelligent than either of the others.

170

CHIMPANZEES

The body of the chimpanzee, which has no tail, is similar to that of man, except that the chimpanzee has 13 pairs of ribs and man usually has only 12 pairs. Its flesh-coloured skin is covered with coarse, black hair, except on the hands and face. As it grows older, grey hairs appear about the mouth and the skin becomes dusky or black.

Chimpanzees live in small bands in central African forests, from Sierra Leone eastwards to Lake Victoria. They are captured quite easily, and live quite well in zoos. Sometimes they become so attached to favourite keepers in zoos that they will cry for them when sick!

Scientists who have studied them say there are at least 20 separate sounds that might be called a "chimpanzee language". On the ground they walk and run on all fours, and use their knuckles to support the weight of their trunk.

A male chimpanzee may weigh as much as 70 kilograms and be about 1.5 metres tall, though most of them are somewhat smaller.

WELSH TERRIER

POMERANIAN

FOXHOUND

Dogs have been domesticated longer than any other animal. During this time, men have developed more than 200 breeds of dogs.

HOW WERE DIFFERENT BREEDS OF DOGS STARTED?

In some cases, dogs were bred for special needs or uses. When dogs were taken into new countries, they tended to mate with the wild dogs of that country, or they would change in order to fit themselves to a new climate. Differences in climate is one reason for such dogs as the hairless breeds of Mexico and the heavily coated breeds of the far north.

It is hard to classify breeds, and it is just as hard to trace their ancestry. Today, dogs are generally classified into six groups, according to their use. These are: sporting dogs, which hunt by scent in the air; hounds, which hunt by ground scent; terriers, which hunt by digging into the earth; working dogs; toy dogs for companions; and miscellaneous, or non-sporting, dogs.

There are some theories about how some of the breeds of dogs started. The pointers are probably descendants of the foxhounds. They "point" at the game. Most hounds are probably descendants of the dog which used to be known in France as "the St. Hubert".

The foxhounds, which are the fastest of the hounds, are thought to be a cross between the keen-scented hounds and the swift coursing hounds. An unusual American breed of dog is the coonhound, which was developed by the pioneers.

Newfoundland dogs seem to be a cross between English retrievers and certain sheep dogs. The St. Bernard has three different types of dogs for its ancestors. The Great Dane is a breed which seems to be a cross between the mastiff and the greyhound. The Pomeranian is related to the chow and was developed in Germany. Bulldogs were bred in the Middle Ages and are related to the mastiff.

Dogs have been friends of man longer than other domestic animals. Hundreds of thousands of years ago, when giant, woolly mammoths still roamed the earth and men lived in caves, the dog first became man's friend.

WHY DO DOGS BURY BONES?

Despite the long history of being domesticated animals, the habits of dogs today can only be explained by going back to their ancestry before man tamed them. Strangely enough, scientists are not able to trace the origin of the dog as clearly as they can trace the history of the horse, for example. Some believe that dogs are the result of the mating of wolves and jackals a long time ago. Other scientists say that some dogs are descended from wolves, other dogs from jackals, others from coyotes, and some from foxes. The best theory seems to be that the wolf and our modern dog are descended from a very remote, common ancestor.

It so happens that many animals have instinctive habits today that are quite useless, but which their ancestors found necessary to life. These habits or instincts do not die out even though hundreds of thousands of years have passed. So if we recall that our dogs are descended from beasts which lived in a wild state a long time ago, we can explain some of their habits.

When a dog buries a bone today, it may be because his ancestors were not fed regularly by man, and had to store food away for future use. When a dog turns around three times before he settles down to sleep, it may be that he is doing it because his remote ancestors had to beat down a nest among the forest leaves or jungle grasses. When a dog bays, it is probably a reminder of the time when all dogs used to run in packs like wolves.

If you have a dog you love as a pet, you share some of your life with it. The dog lives in your home, keeps you company, and goes on trips with you. So it is hard to believe that the world your dog sees is quite different from your own. For dogs cannot see any colours.

CAN DOGS SEE COLOURS?

Test after test has been made to find out if dogs can be made to respond to different colours in any way. Usually this has been done with food. One colour would be a signal for food, the other colours were not. A dog was never able to distinguish colours from one another. Dogs rely on their remarkable sense of smell to tell things apart.

What about cats? The same kinds of tests were made. It was impossible to train a cat to come for its food in response to signals of different colours. It seemed that all the colours were like grey to a cat.

Is there any animal that is able to see colours? As far as tests so far have been able to prove, the only animal other than man that is able to distinguish colours is the monkey. Monkeys and apes have been trained to open a door of a particular colour in order to obtain food.

Actually, the colour blindness of animals is quite understandable. Most wild animals hunt at night or graze in the evening when colours are dim. Most animals have coats that are rather dull-coloured. Being able to see colours is not really that important to them in order to survive.

And most of them have developed their other senses to such a point that they can get along quite well in their own world.

We think of a dog as man's best friend. Yet sometimes even the friendliest dog can become a creature that brings death with its bite! Not because it has changed its character, but because it has become infected with a terrible disease.

WHAT MAKES DOGS GO MAD?

This disease is called "rabies". It infects the brain and the spinal cord, and these are both vital to life. The infection is caused by a virus; an organism which is too small to be seen with the ordinary microscope.

Now we usually think of this disease in connection with dogs, and that is because man most often receives the disease from a dog infected with the virus. But rabies can infect all warm-blooded animals, including wolves, foxes, skunks, cows, cats, and even bats. Most of these other creatures, however, seldom pass on the disease to man.

174

A dog may become infected with rabies and its owner may not know it for some time. This is because the disease may take four to six weeks to show up. The first signs are when the dog becomes quiet, has fever, and is not interested in food. Then it becomes excited. Saliva froths from the mouth. It growls and barks, and is likely to bite. After such symptoms appear, a dog is likely to die within three to five days. Since the virus is in the saliva, the disease is passed on by biting.

The horrible thing about this disease is that once it appears in man or animals, death is almost certain. That is why it is important to prevent the disease, and go to a doctor at once if one has been bitten by a dog. There is a serum that acts against the virus before it can spread, but it must be taken within three days of being bitten.

When something tastes good, or you feel pleased about something, you might make a sound like "Mmmm—mm!" When a cat wants to express contentment, it purrs!

DO ALL CATS PURR?

The purring sound is caused by the vibration of the cat's vocal cords. When a cat takes air into its lungs, the air passes through the voice box that contains the vocal cords. If the cat then wants to express its satisfaction about something, it will allow the vocal cords to vibrate as the air passes in and out of the lungs during breathing. When it chooses not to purr, the passing air does not affect the vocal cords—and no purr!

Of course when we think of "cat", we usually mean only the domesticated cat. But there are many other members of the cat family. Did you know that the lion, tiger, leopard, cougar, jaguar, ocelot, and lynx are also members of the cat family?

When it comes to making sounds, our own domesticated cat not only purrs, it can also meow, howl, and scream. The other kinds of cats make different sounds. The lion and tiger can roar. The jaguar and leopard make a sound that is described as a hoarse cough or bark.

But an interesting thing about the lion, tiger, jaguar, and leopard is that because of a difference in the formation of certain bones in the throat, they cannot purr!

But all cats, large or small, have the same general proportions of the body. If you blew up a picture of a cat to a very large size, you would see that it looks very much like a tiger.

People seem to think that goats will eat practically anything. And the truth is, that's just what they do!

A goat's instincts will prevent it from eating things that will do it

WHAT DO GOATS EAT? harm, but it will try to eat things most other animals reject. The reason for this seems to be that goats are rarely given the food and care bestowed on other domestic animals. The goat has been called the most optimistic of animals. Since it usually is not fed well, it will try to eat anything in the hope that it may be good.

The goat has always had a rather curious relationship with man. It is one of the most useful of animals. Since ancient times it has supplied man with healthy milk and satisfying meat. Its skin has been made into leather. Its wool has been woven into soft, warm cloth.

In spite of its usefulness, however, the goat has always had a bad reputation. This is probably due to its bad temper and the unpleasant odour of the males.

The goat contributes more to man in comparison to its size than any other animal. Goat's milk, for example, is considered by some to be better and healthier than cow's milk. It is often given to babies and invalids because it is easier to digest than cow's milk.

A few goats are raised for their flesh or are used as beasts of burden. Some are grown for their skins, which are made into goatskin, kidskin, and morocco leather. Other goats, such as the Angora and the Cashmere, are raised for their wool.

Goats were probably domesticated in Persia, but are now raised all over the world. There are about ten breeds of wild goats found in Europe, Africa, and Asia. They are sure-footed, active animals which generally prefer mountainous homes.

SOMALI ASS   NUBIAN ASS

Three names for the same animal are: donkey, ass, burro. But what is a jackass? It is simply the name for a male donkey, the female is known as a "jennet".

ARE A DONKEY AND JACKASS THE SAME?

The donkey is one of the oldest of all domesticated animals. It was domesticated more than 5,000 years ago by the Egyptians.

Because it is such a useful animal to man, it has spread around the world, and there are many different kinds of donkeys. For example, the Somali wild ass, which is found in Somalia and other parts of Africa, is a shy animal that lives in groups of from 5 to 20. It eats the dry grass and shrubs of the desert. Some natives do not hunt it, but others hunt it for food, for its hide, or to export it alive. Today it is a rare animal.

There are wild asses that live in Asia. One type, the Syrian ass, once lived in Syria and other parts of the Middle East, but is now probably extinct. The ass is strictly a desert animal, and can go for some time without water. Just before the young are born they gather into great herds, but soon break up into small groups, and scatter over the country.

The donkey of today is a descendant of the Nubian wild ass of North-Eastern Africa, where it once lived from the Nile to the Red Sea. Most of the wild types that existed in various parts of the world have been killed off. Today, man is trying to protect some of the few kinds that are left.

In many parts of Mexico and Central America, the ass, or burro, is a common means of transportation, instead of the horse or motor-car.

Over the years, strange ideas about certain animals spring up and in time many people come to believe them. One of these "legends" is that an elephant never forgets.

DO ELEPHANTS EVER FORGET?

The truth is that elephants do have good memories, probably better than most animals. There are many cases, for instance, where an elephant had some injury inflicted on it by a man and years later attacked the man who had done it harm.

But elephants certainly do forget. Just think of what it takes to tame and then train a wild elephant. The trainer has to be quite tough, often striking it and forcing it to do things against its will. If an elephant "never forgot", it would never allow itself to be tamed because it would always be attacking its trainer!

You have probably heard the expression: "He has a white elephant on his hands." People say this to mean that someone has an object, usually quite expensive, that he cannot sell or get rid of.

ARE THERE ANY WHITE ELEPHANTS?

The curious fact is that no one has ever seen a white elephant! That name is sometimes given to elephants that are very light in colour. In ancient times, these lighter coloured, or "white", elephants were considered sacred. They were even worshipped in certain parts of the world.

They were held to be so valuable that only a king was worthy to own one! There was good reason for this. Since these white elephants had to be treated with great care, they were provided with costly luxuries. They never worked, and they lived in special quarters. They had special servants whose job it was to care for them, and in some cases their food was served in troughs made of silver, or on special white cloths.

You can see how our expression about a white elephant came into being. It involved having something very expensive to keep up, and getting nothing in return!

Because the elephant is such a huge creature, it amuses us to think that a little mouse can frighten it. The reason many people believe a mouse can frighten an elephant is the idea that a mouse could get into the end of the elephant's trunk. They imagine this might suffocate the elephant.

ARE ELEPHANTS AFRAID OF MICE?

The truth is, however, that elephants show absolutely no fear of mice! One can often see little mice running about in an elephant's stall, and the big beast seems to disregard them completely. And since the elephant has a very keen sense of smell, we cannot believe that it does not know the mouse is there.

Even if a mouse did have the courage to crawl into the opening of the elephant's trunk, the elephant could probably take a breath and blow it right out of the cage!

When we look at most animals they do not seem especially strange to us. But when we look at a giraffe we feel it has a peculiar appearance. The reason for this is probably that long, long neck.

HOW TALL IS A GIRAFFE? The giraffe is the tallest animal in the world and often reaches a height of 5.5 metres. The giraffe also has long legs. Although its legs are about of equal length, very strong muscles have developed at the base of the neck so that its back slopes downwards from shoulder to tail.

The head is small and narrow, and the eyes, which are dark and soft, give this huge animal an expression of gentleness. The ears of the giraffe, which are quite large, are sensitive to the faintest sounds. As a matter of fact, that remarkable sense of hearing and a keen sense of smell are very important to the giraffe in detecting danger.

Another curious thing about it is the tongue, which is often 46 centimetres long. The giraffe can use its tongue so skilfully that it can pick the smallest leaves off thorny plants without being pricked.

When you see a giraffe moving, you notice that it ambles rather than walks. Despite this, it can gallop at more than 30 miles an hour when pursued and it can outrun the fastest horse!

While the giraffe is a gentle animal, it can put up a good fight when attacked. It kicks out its hind legs or uses its head like a sledge hammer. Even a lion is pretty careful when attacking a giraffe.

When you think of a giraffe, the first thing you probably think of is its long neck. But there is another rather remarkable thing about this strange animal—it has practically no voice!

DOES THE GIRAFFE HAVE A VOICE?
The reason we said "practically" is that certain giraffes, which have been observed, in zoological parks, have made certain types of noises. For example, female giraffes have been heard to moo softly, especially when they seem worried about something. And certain young giraffes, when hungry, have sometimes made sounds like those of a calf.

But in a giraffe, the voice box, or larynx, is almost completely undeveloped, so that we can say that most giraffes do not have a voice! But since all animals have some means for protecting themselves against enemies, the giraffe has other ways to make up for its lack of voice. One is the development of its senses of hearing and smell. A giraffe's ears are sensitive to the faintest sounds, which help it detect any danger. And its sense of smell is so good that it can "smell trouble" even when it is far away!

Another protection the giraffe has is its ability to move around. The giraffe can gallop at more than 30 miles an hour when pursued, and can run faster than the fastest horse!

Still another protection for the giraffe is its colouring. It blends in so well with its surroundings that, despite its enormous size, it is often very difficult to spot a giraffe when it is standing in a forest.

The camel is called "the ship of the desert", and there is good reason for it. Just as a ship is constructed to deal with all the problems that arise from being in the water, so a camel is "constructed" to live and travel and survive in the desert.

WHY DOES THE CAMEL HAVE A HUMP?
Where other animals would die from lack of food and water, the camel gets along very nicely. It carries its food and water with it! For days before it starts on a journey, a camel does nothing but eat and drink. It eats so much that a hump of fat, maybe weighing as much as 45 kilograms, rises on its back. So the camel's hump is a storage place for fat, which the camel's body will use up during the journey.

The camel also has little flask-shaped bags-which line the walls of its stomach. This is where it stores water. With such provisions, a camel is able to travel several days between water holes without drinking, and for an even longer time with no nourishment except what it draws from the fat of its hump.

At the end of a long journey, the hump will have lost its firm shape and will flop to one side in flabby folds. The camel will then have to rest for a long time to recover its strength.

Did you know that the camel is one of man's oldest servants and has been used by man in Egypt for more than 3,000 years?

The guinea pig is not a pig, and it has nothing to do with Guinea. It is related to the hares and rabbits and its real name is "cavy". In other words, it is really a rodent.

WHAT ARE GUINEA PIGS?

Long before the Spaniards came to the New World, the Incas of Peru, Ecuador, and Colombia had domesticated this rodent. They used it for food, and considered it a great delicacy. As a matter of fact, soon after the discovery of America the guinea pig was introduced into Europe for the same purpose, and was eaten by people everywhere. Nowadays, the only people who eat guinea pigs are some natives of Peru, but they are still kept as pets by many people in South America and all over the world.

They are about 25 centimetres long and weigh about 1 kilogram. They have no tail but have small, naked, rounded ears. The fore feet have four toes, the hind feet only three, and all the toes have broad claws.

They live wholly on vegetable food. While feeding they generally sit on their hind feet. When free they live in burrows and feed at dusk and on dark days. When they get plenty of green vegetation, they can get along without water. In captivity they may be kept on rabbit or rat food, but then they need water.

Guinea pigs have litters of two to eight or more, twice or three times a year. A few hours after they are born they can run about. They are gentle and easy to handle, and as pets they can live as long as eight years. There are many different coloured varieties with long or short coats available in pet shops.

SUMMER   WINTER

We think of ermine as a "royal" fur, and there is a reason for it. At one time, only members of the royal family were allowed to wear ermine. Later, nobles and government officials were allowed to wear this valuable fur. Their rank was shown by the arrangement of the black tail tips.

HOW DO WE GET ERMINE FROM A STOAT?

Ermine comes from the stoat. It is the white winter coat that certain species of stoat develop. This happens to stoats only in cold regions, such as Canada, Lapland, and Siberia. Here the fur changes to pure white in winter. In milder climates, the fur changes only slightly from the summer colouring of reddish brown on the back and yellowish white on the underneath.

Stoats are closely related to weasels, minks, and martens. All of the species have slender bodies, short legs, sharp-clawed feet, and quite long necks. In the United States and Canada, the commonest species is the long-tailed weasel. The males are about 40 centimetres long and the females about 33 centimetres. Both have tails about 10 centimetres long.

The short-tailed weasel is about 5 centimetres shorter than the long-tailed species. It is also lighter in colouring, and the tail is only about 5 centimetres long. An even smaller weasel is found in Alaska and northern Canada. This is called a "least" weasel. There is a large species in the southern part of the United States that keeps the same colouring all year.

Generally speaking, the weasel can be considered a friend of man. Weasels are tireless hunters and they destroy vermin, rats, mice, rabbits, and certain birds. But many a farmer will tell you the weasel is quite an enemy, too, because weasels love to rob poultry houses. A single weasel has been known to kill 40 hens in one night!

A beaver is a large rodent, or gnawing animal. Like all other rodents, the beaver has four chisel-shaped front teeth called "incisors". It is with these teeth that it cuts trees and bushes for food and for building dams. The

WHAT DO BEAVERS EAT?

beaver lives on wood, branches, saplings, and the roots of water plants.

Why do beavers build dams? The beaver lives in the water and it remains active all winter. Therefore, it needs a pool of water deep enough not to freeze quite to the bottom during the winter. So it builds a dam to raise the water level of the pond or stream in which it lives!

To build a dam, beavers place willow, alder, or other brush on the bottom of the stream. This is held in place with mud and stones. As the dam grows in height, sticks and branches may be placed in any position. Often the twigs take root and wind together and help to make the dam strong.

To cut a tree, the beaver gnaws two notches, one above the other. It pries out the wood between the notches with its teeth. Only one or two bites are needed to cut a stick 2 centimetres thick. Trees about 25 centimetres thick are used. A tree this size may be cut in one night. Generally trees with soft wood are used, such as the poplar, cottonwood, alder, willow, or birch.

Since beavers eat only the inner bark of trees and bushes, they may use the peeled sticks and logs to strengthen the dam. A dam is usually not more than two metres high, but it may be extremely long!

The home of the beaver is called a "lodge". It may be a stick-covered shelter in the stream bank or a house of sticks and logs built in a shallow part of the pond. The floor of the room is just above the water line and is covered with weeds or shredded wood. The entrances are all under water.

In late summer and autumn, the beaver collects food for the winter. So brush, branches, and logs are cut and stored under water near the lodge. These food supplies are sometimes over 1 metre high and contain hundreds of branches and saplings.

There are many things about the opossum that make it a strange and interesting animal. To begin with, did you know that opossums belong to a group of animals called "marsupial"? The females of this group have pouches on the underside of the body in which the young develop. The kangaroos of Australia are probably the best known of this group.

WHY DOES AN OPOSSUM HANG BY ITS TAIL?

Opossums are from 23 to 50 centimetres long with tails of 23 to 33 centimetres long. Their fur is greyish white in colour. Their round ears, long, narrow tails, and the palms of their feet are hairless.

The inside toe on the hind foot can be bent like a thumb to meet any of the other toes. The opossum uses his hind feet as hands. They help him climb trees. His long, flexible tail is also used in tree climbing.

Opossums spend a lot of time in trees, hunting and eating. Since they can use their hind feet like hands, they like to hang upside down when they eat, to give them more hands, as it were, to grasp their food. To do this, they wrap their tails around a branch, hang down and gather their food with their feet.

And what a variety of food they eat! Their diet includes small mammals, insects, small birds, eggs, poultry, lizards, crayfish, snails, fruit of all kinds, corn on the cob, mushrooms, and worms. At night, opossums invade orchards for fruit and hen houses for poultry and eggs.

For some reason, Nature allows most insects to live only a short time compared to other living things on earth.

But there is one insect that enjoys a longer life span than many

WHICH INSECT HAS THE LONGEST LIFE?

members of the animal kingdom. There is a species of the cicada that actually lives for 17 years! No other insect comes anywhere near it in length of life, except perhaps a termite queen.

The cicada's "life", however, is not exactly one that other insects should envy. It sleeps in the ground for those entire 17 years, comes out to enjoy only five weeks of life in the sun, and then dies!

Why does it take 17 long years for nature to develop this little insect? No one knows the answer. All we know is that a female cicada lays eggs on the twigs of trees. When the young are hatched from those eggs they drop down, burrow into the ground, and attach themselves to roots. And these young cicadas, which are called "nymphs", remain there motionless for 17 years, sucking the sap of the roots!

Then some kind of mysterious instinct makes them decide to go out into the light. They climb the trunk of a tree, their skins split open, and the mature cicada emerges.

The male cicada is the one who makes that shrill sound you hear in the countryside. Scientists say that the noise-making instrument of the cicada is the most complicated musical organ to be found in nature. The male cicada has little drumlike plates which are constantly kept vibrating by muscles that never seem to get tired.

There are more than 800 species, or kinds, of cicadas, and 100 of these are found in North America. But the 17-year cicada is found only in the United States. Most species of cicadas live only two years.

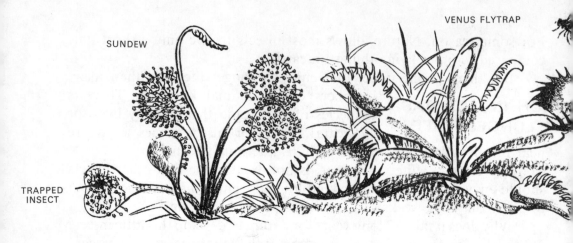

SUNDEW

VENUS FLYTRAP

TRAPPED INSECT

If you have never raised plants or flowers of your own, you probably have thought how delicate and harmless they are.

CAN PLANTS EAT INSECTS?

But there are at least three different plants that feed on insects, and each one seems to be as clever and as cruel as any animal that goes hunting for its food.

The best known of these is the Pitcher plant, which grows in Borneo and tropical Asia. The Pitcher plant gives out a sweet juice that attracts insects. To make doubly sure of luring victims, this plant has a red-coloured rim and cover. The insect comes over to take a look and to drink the nectar. It climbs over the rim of the plant, which is shaped like a pitcher. The inside of the pitcher is so smooth that the insect slides down and cannot stop itself. At the bottom, there is a bath of powerful liquid waiting for it. The insect is drowned and the liquid goes to work and digests the insect, thus providing food for the plant.

The Sundew is another tricky insect-eating plant. The upper part of each leaf is covered with little hairlike projections which give out a sticky fluid that attracts insects. This sticky fluid looks like dewdrops, which gives the plant its name. The moment an insect touches one of these hairs, it is stuck. Then all the other hairs start to bend towards the centre of the leaf until they have wrapped up the insect in a neat package. The fluid that surrounds the poor victim starts digesting him. After about two days the job is done and the hairlike tentacles open up again.

In parts of North and South Carolina, we find a plant called the Venus flytrap. This plant is the most business-like insect eater of all. It sits there with leaves spread open like hungry jaws. When a fly touches the hairs that grow along the leaf, the plant snaps it shut like a trap. After the fly is digested by juices in the plant, it opens up again.

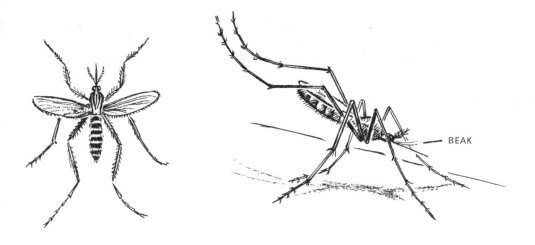

BEAK

Imagine yourself sitting or playing outdoors on a pleasant summer day. You hear a humming noise. Soon you feel a sting on your leg or arm. You slap hard. You look down and see a tiny speck of blood.

WHY WAS THE MOSQUITO MAN'S GREAT ENEMY?

You have just been engaged in a battle with one of the great enemies of mankind. To most of us, the mosquito is just an annoying pest. The humming noise about our heads (especially when we try to sleep) irritates us. The mosquito bite and the itching feeling afterwards is a nuisance.

But this little insect is much more than a pest. The mosquito, by spreading such diseases as malaria and yellow fever, played a part in the fall of the ancient Greek and Roman civilizations. It killed many of our pioneer ancestors when they opened up our Empire. It prevented countries along tropical coasts and in hot climates from being settled and developing as they should. Fortunately, we have learned how to deal with the diseases that this "pest" used to spread throughout the world.

The male mosquito feeds only on plant juices, but the female prefers blood! So the female is the one that bites you. And what equipment she has for doing an expert job! The "beak" of the female mosquito holds daggers with sawlike tips, plus a tube for injecting and a tube for sucking. As soon as she settles on your skin, she starts sawing. Into the tiny hole she injects a chemical so that your blood will not coagulate, or form a dry clot. Then she sucks up the blood she has prepared and flies off.

The itching you feel is not caused by the "bite". It is caused by the liquid she has injected. So if you kill her before she can suck back that irritating liquid, your itching will be worse!

For some reason we tend to think that certain creatures do not hear, see, or sleep—just because they look so strange to us. It is true that the grasshopper is a very strange creature indeed, but it has ears and it can hear!

CAN GRASSHOPPERS HEAR?

There are many varieties of grasshoppers, but in general appearance they are much alike. They all have strong jaws and three pairs of legs, and they usually have two pairs of wings. The first pair is leathery and straight. The second pair of wings is membranous and folds underneath the first pair. The hind pair of legs, which is used for jumping, is unusually long and well developed.

Grasshoppers are divided into two general groups depending on the length of their antennae, or horns: the long-horned and the short-horned grasshoppers. The short-horned grasshoppers are sometimes known as "locusts". The common brown field grasshoppers are also part of this group. This type of grasshopper "sings" by rubbing its hind legs across its fore wings. And it has "ears" for hearing on its abdomen at the base of the hind legs.

The long-horned grasshoppers, which include the green meadow grasshoppers and the katydids, have antennae which are much longer than their whole bodies. Only the males "sing", producing the sound by rubbing the bases of the fore wings together. Their "ears" are located on the first pair of legs. So although grasshoppers can hear, they have unusual kinds of ears located in strange places.

One of the most interesting insects in the world is the praying mantis. Sometimes people call it "the Sooth-sayer", "Rearhorse", or "Mule-Killer". The name Mule-Killer comes from the belief that the saliva of this insect can poison mules.

WHAT IS A PRAYING MANTIS?

The mantis is a long, slender insect that seems to be praying when it is standing still. The large front legs are held up in such a way that it gives the impression of being in prayer.

But the mantis is not "praying" at all—it is really "preying". In fact, it is one of the most bloodthirsty creatures known, and might be called a murderer and a cannibal.

The mantis lives on other insects. It captures them by sitting still with its traplike front feet ready to snap at the first insect that comes by. That is why the front legs are held up—to be always ready. On the inside of those legs are sharp claws to hold the victim.

The praying mantis moves about by walking on its four hind legs or by flying. The mantis is also said to be the only insect that can turn its head around and look over its shoulders. When another insect, such as a fly, comes along, the mantis shoots those front legs out, catches it, holds it firmly, and slowly eats it.

The mantis family has about 800 species. About 20 species are found in North America, all of which have brown or green wings and are about five centimetres long.

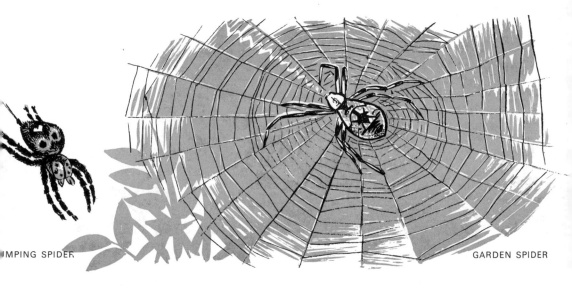

JMPING SPIDER   GARDEN SPIDER

Most of us think that spiders use silk only to spin a web. Actually, no other animal uses silk in as many ways as spiders do. They make it into houses, life lines, diving bells, cocoons, "aeroplanes", lassos, spring traps and the web we all know.

HOW DO SPIDERS SPIN THEIR WEBS?

Spiders are not insects, but belong to a species called "arachnid". Unlike insects, they have eight legs, eight eyes in most cases, no wings, and only two parts to their bodies.

Spiders are found in practically every kind of climate. They can run on the ground, climb plants, run on water, and even live in water.

The spider manufactures its silk in certain glands found in the abdomen, or belly. At the tip of the abdomen there are spinning organs which contain many tiny holes. The silk is forced through these tiny holes. When the silk comes out it is a liquid. As soon as it comes into contact with the air, it becomes solid.

The spider makes many different kinds of silk. It makes a sticky kind that is used for the web, because this catches insects. For the spokes of the web it makes a stronger silk, which is not sticky. And it makes a still different kind of silk for the cocoon.

Even the webs that spiders spin are of many different kinds. The wheel-like web is the one we see most often. There are also "sheet" webs, which are flat and shaped like funnels or domes. And the trap-door spiders make a burrow out of their web with a lidlike opening at the top to catch and hold their prey. Other spiders build a bell-shaped home of silk which is entirely under water!

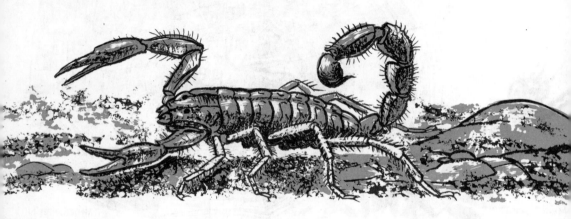

The very mention of the name "scorpion" makes us think of danger and poison. And the fact is that a scorpion can be a rather unpleasant creature to meet.

WHAT IS A SCORPION? In the United States, scorpions have actually caused deaths in only one place—Arizona. The Arizona scorpion is related to the Durango scorpion that lives in Mexico. The Durango scorpion's bite can kill a man within an hour, and over a period of 35 years it has caused the deaths of about 1,600 people.

Scorpions are related to the spider. A scorpion has four pairs of walking legs and a pair of strong pincers which it uses to grasp its prey. It also has a long, thin, jointed tail which ends in a curved, pointed stinger. This stinger is connected to poison glands.

When the scorpion walks, it carries its tail arched over its body.

When it grasps its prey in its pincers, it bends its stinger over its head and plunges it into the victim. The poison will kill or paralyse the insects, spiders, and other creatures on which the scorpion feeds.

Scorpions are mainly active at night. During the day they hid in dark places, such as beneath a stone, in bark, or in the dark corners of buildings. Adult scorpions always live and travel alone.

Young scorpions are born alive and cling to the mother's back. She does not feed them and after several days they go off on their own.

Scorpions are found mainly in warm climates. Of the roughly 500 species, 30 are found in the United States. Scorpions vary in size from 1 centimetre to about 17 centimetres. The largest are found in the tropics.

DO ANTS ALWAYS LIVE IN COLONIES?

Not only do ants always live in colonies, but the way they organize these colonies is one of the most fascinating things about them. They may live in colonies of several hundred thousand or in colonies with as few as 12 members. They may have their homes entirely underground, or in wood, or in a high mound, or in an acorn.

About 20 of the 2,000-odd species of this amazing little insect are found in Great Britain. The most common are the red and black ants.

All ants are social insects. Their communities are like little nations, with their queens, winged males and females, and wingless workers. The mound-building ants, such as big wood-ants common in some countries, build structures often to a height of 1 metre and a width of 30 centimetres.

Some kinds keep slaves. They go out on great war-like expeditions against smaller species, drive them out of their nests, and plunder their eggs, larvae, pupae and stores of food to take back to their own nests. The captured eggs, larvae and pupae are carefully looked after until they are grown to maturity, when they are made to serve their captors.

In Central Africa, South America and Southern Asia, there are species which are carnivorous. These are sometimes called "driver ants", and they are greatly feared, for they march relentlessly in long columns in search of living flesh. The biggest and fiercest of animals are helpless in the face of an army of driver ants, and are driven frantic by the millions of bites unless they can reach water and drown their tormentors. Nothing can withstand the remorseless savagery of driver ants on the march.

SOLDIER

QUEEN

WORKERS

Many people confuse termites with white ants. Although termites are social insects like ants, they are quite different. Termites have thick waists, are usually light in colour, and have evenly curved feelers, or antennae.

WHERE DO TERMITES LIVE?

Termites are found in every state in the United States and in Southern Canada. In Europe, they are found as far north as Paris and Vienna. The greatest number are to be found in the rainy tropical regions around the world.

Common termites burrow in wood and eat out the wood in which the colony lives. They form rooms which they may line with claylike material. This keeps the inner air moist.

In the tropics, many kinds of termites build nests. Some are mounds on the ground and may be 9 metres high and 15 metres across. Others are tree nests of various shapes and are usually about the size of a basketball. These nests protect the colonies from birds, lizards, spiders, and ants. Some African termite nests have umbrella-like caps to shed the rain. Others are built so they control the temperature within them.

The building of nests by termites is an example of working through instinct alone. The nest is built by the new workers born in the colony. These workers have never lived in the nest their parents came from and they have no way of learning from other termites. Yet when the nest is finished, it is like the one in the old colony from which the king and queen of the new nest came.

In the United States, termites fall into three groups: those that burrow under stones; those that burrow in wood; and those that burrow through the ground until they reach wood.

The battle between man and the insect world is constantly going on all about us. Some insects are merely pests. Some spread disease. And some spend a lifetime destroying the things man tries to grow or create.

WHAT IS A WEEVIL?

If there is any family of insects that man could certainly do without, it is the weevil. While the weevils are only a sub-division of the beetle group of insects, the weevils are themselves the largest natural family in the entire animal kingdom! They include over 35,000 known species, and there are probably several times that number that man has yet to discover and classify!

Weevils vary greatly in size, shape, and colour. They are usually small and are recognized by the trunk-like or knife-like projections on their heads. At the end of these projections there is a mouth. These snouts are used by the females for drilling holes for their eggs. Weevil larvae are usually fat, white grubs, and both the larvae and the adults have good appetites and are vegetable eaters.

But the reason why they are so destructive is not because of their large numbers or enormous appetites. It is because they attack the most vital and delicate parts of the plant—the buds, fruits, seeds, growing tips, and living tissues under the bark. When they get finished, the plant is apt to be dead.

The granary weevil destroys the grains of corn, wheat, and barley. This is one of the most destructive weevils of all. The rice weevil destroys not only rice, but a great many other dry food products.

The cotton boll weevil is the most serious enemy of the cotton crops of the world. It can ruin entire cotton crops.

With more than 2,500 different weevils to be found in North America alone, you can see what an enemy of man this insect is.

COTTON BOLL WEEVIL

Everybody knows that birds migrate. This means that during certain seasons they travel over special routes. But few people realize that many butterflies, and some moths, also migrate.

DO BUTTERFLIES MIGRATE?

One example of this is the painted-lady butterfly. Each spring it travels from Mexico to California. In Europe, the same kind of butterfly crosses the Mediterranean in the spring, going from northern Africa to Europe. When there is a butterfly migration, thousands, and even millions, travel together across the sky.

The best known of all migrating butterflies is the monarch. It spends the winter along the Gulf of Mexico and other southern areas. In spring, the young female lays her eggs on the milkweed plants that have begun to grow. The caterpillars that hatch from the eggs feed on the milkweed leaves.

When the adult butterflies develop, they fly some distance north. There they mate and lay eggs on the milkweed that has just begun to grow with the advance of spring.

Now this is an interesting kind of migration. Because it means that within a few months time several generations of monarch butterflies travel farther and farther north in search of milkweed. By the time it is late summer and the monarch butterflies reach Canada, they are not the original ones that started out—but descendants of them!

When autumn approaches and cooler weather appears, those monarchs that have survived fly back in great numbers. They make a huge swarm of butterflies in the sky, and people have seen them spread out in a swarm 20 miles wide!

Such masses of butterflies migrate like this year after year, and they always follow the same routes.

MIGRATION OF MONARCHS

Do you know how many different kinds of insects there are? There are somewhere between 2,000,000 and 4,000,000 different kinds of insects! Scientists have actually described in scientific language as many as 625,000 different kinds. They practically have no hope of ever being able to classify every single type of insect that exists. There is no other class of animals on earth that even comes close to having as many types as insects do.

HOW MANY KINDS OF INSECTS ARE THERE?

When it comes to trying to estimate how many insects are living in the world today—the number is so vast that the human mind cannot even imagine it! The only way scientists can even begin to count the insect population in any one area is to count all the insects that can be found in and on a square metre of rich, moist soil. That can be anywhere from 500 to 2,000. So it can be said that about 4,000,000 insects live in a single acre of good soil.

The majority of insects that exist are below the size that would attract the human eye. Many are microscopic. And there are only a few thousand insects of all those that exist which become annoying enough to man for him to try to control them.

When you think of it this way, you realize that man really moves about in a world of insects—but he has no idea that most of them exist or how many there are!

There are two things that most insects have in common: their body is divided into three parts; and they usually have six legs. This is true of most, not all of them.

Another name for the insects known as "aphids" is "plant lice". They are green or brownish in colour, and the largest ones are not more than six millimetres long.

WHAT IS AN APHID? Aphids reproduce so rapidly that if they were not destroyed by their natural enemies, they would eat up nearly all the vegetation in the world!

Aphids may be found on the leaves, roots, and young stems of many kinds of plants. They often do serious damage to fruit trees, flowers, vegetables, and field crops. They have unusually strong mouths, or beaks, which stick out from their tiny heads. With these beaks they puncture the surface of the leaf and suck out its juices, thus causing the plant to wither and possibly die.

One of the most curious things about the aphids is that they serve as "ants' cows". Ants can actually "milk" them as if they were a sort of cow. What happens is that the aphids produce in their bodies a sweet liquid called "honeydew". Ants love to drink this liquid.

So ants capture aphids and take care of them, just as a farmer might take care of his cows. The ants carry the aphid to the ant nest, supply it with plenty of green plants on which to feed, and protect it carefully from danger. When an ant wants to milk its cow, it strokes the aphid's sides gently with its long feelers. Then, as the tiny drops of honeydew flow from the rear of the aphid, the ant drinks the liquid!

Man, however, has no interest in protecting these insects, so plants are often sprayed with chemicals to destroy them.

As you know, a butterfly goes through a life cycle. First it is an egg, then it becomes a caterpillar, then a pupa (during which it sleeps through the winter), and finally it emerges as a butterfly.

WHAT DOES A BUTTERFLY EAT? There is one period during that life cycle when this creature does most of its eating, and that is when it is a caterpillar. In some kinds of butterflies, the only time in its life when it will ever eat anything is during that caterpillar stage. It feeds and grows until it bursts its skin and sheds it for a new one. It may repeat this process many times, and in a few weeks it can be many, many times as large as when it hatched.

But butterflies are equipped to eat. A butterfly has a head, a thorax, and an abdomen. Those butterflies which do eat have a tube instead of the usual insect mouth. This tube, when not in use, is coiled up like a watch spring. It can be thrust deep into the hearts of flowers to suck up their nectar.

In moths, which belong to the same insect order as butterflies, this tube can be 15 to 30 centimetres long, so it can reach into large, tubular flowers. Some moths have sawlike teeth at the tip of the tube with which they can cut through the skins of fruit in order to drink their juices!

Did you know that the antennae of moths and butterflies are really more than just feelers? They use these antennae not only to feel but also to smell and perhaps hear.

The ordinary housefly can manage to find enough food to live on almost anywhere. This is because of its tiny size and weight. A thousand adult flies weigh only about 25 to 30 grams.

WHAT DOES A FLY EAT?

Houseflies do not eat solid food, because they have no equipment for biting. The mouth parts of the fly are made for sucking up liquid food. What looks like the fly's "tongue" is really a snout like the elephant's trunk. It has two lobes at the end which act as funnels for drawing in its liquid food. When a fly lands on a lump of sugar (or other soluble food) it spreads saliva on the sugar which makes it liquid.

But don't houseflies bite people before a storm? This popular idea is incorrect. What happens is that other types of flies, sand flies or stable flies, are mistaken for houseflies. These flies are bloodsucking and so they do bite people.

If the housefly does not bite, why is it considered so dangerous to man? The claws, padded feet, and body are covered with bristling hairs, and its tongue is coated with sticky glue. This means dust and dirt will cling to the fly. And since the housefly will look for its food anywhere, including garbage and sewage, the bacteria of various diseases may be in the dirt and dust that sticks to the fly. Then, if the fly touches the food we eat, these disease bacteria will enter our body.

We all know that flies carry disease. The fly is born and may spend most of its life around rubbish and germ-breeding areas. The housefly actually chooses moist decaying matter as a place to breed.

HOW ARE FLIES BORN?

The female lays the eggs, which are white and about 1.2 millimetres long. From each egg comes a slender, wormlike maggot. This is the feeding stage, or "larva", of the fly.

After five or six days, the maggot's skin thickens and becomes brownish. This begins "the pupal", or resting, stage. Five or six days later, the full-grown fly bursts out of the pupal skin. The fly is then as big as it will ever be, for big flies do not grow from small flies. About ten days later, the fly mates, and soon after the female lays from 100 to 150 eggs!

Not all flies breed like the housefly. Many kinds hatch their eggs in their bodies, giving birth to living larvae. Some kinds lay eggs that are already at the pupal stage.

Man is waging a constant battle against the fly because it spreads disease germs. The best time to kill the housefly is in the winter and the early spring. During the cold weather, the fly hides away in dark, warm corners of buildings. When flies are seen during the winter in well-heated buildings, they should be killed. At that time, flies are easy to catch because they are very hungry.

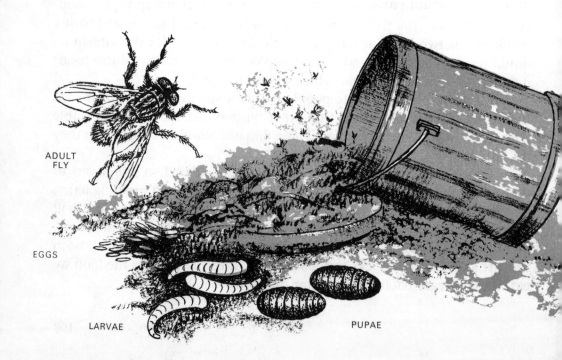

ADULT
FLY

EGGS

LARVAE

PUPAE

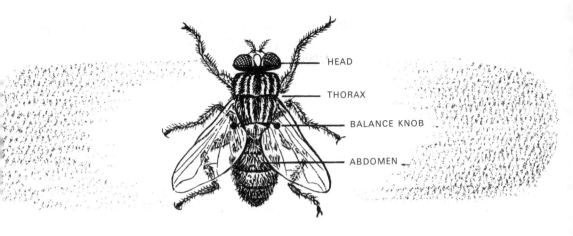

HEAD

THORAX

BALANCE KNOB

ABDOMEN

The fly is an amazing and deadly creature. The fly spreads more death and suffering than an invading army. It does harm by spreading disease with its hairy feet and legs from the filth on which it feeds and in which it breeds.

HOW CAN A FLY WALK ON THE CEILING?

This little insect is wonderfully made. The housefly has two big brown eyes and each eye is made up of thousands of lenses. These two big eyes are called "compound eyes". The fly also has, on top of the head, looking straight up, three "simple eyes" that can be seen only through a magnifying glass.

The feelers, or antennae, of the housefly are used as organs of smell, not of feeling. These antennae can detect odours at great distances. The mouth is made up of an organ that people call a tongue, but it is really all the mouth parts of an insect combined in one. This tongue is really a long tube through which the fly sucks juices.

The body of the housefly is divided into three parts: the head, the middle section, or thorax, and the abdomen. Behind the two transparent wings are two small knobs that help the fly balance itself in flight. The thorax is striped and has three pairs of legs attached to it. The legs are divided into five parts, of which the last is the foot.

The fly walks tiptoe on two claws that are attached to the underpart of the foot. Sticky pads under the claws allow the fly to walk upside down on the ceiling or anywhere else with the greatest of ease! It is because of these sticky pads and the hairs on the legs that the fly is such a carrier of disease germs.

Did you know that the entire life of a housefly is spent within about one hundred metres of the area where it was born?

There are thousands of different species, or kinds, of bees. So their habits and ways of life differ quite a lot. But probably the two things that we find most interesting about bees is how they produce honey, and how the "social" bees have organized their life.

WHAT HAPPENS TO BEES IN WINTER?

In producing honey, a bee visits flowers, drinks the nectar, and carries it home in its honey sac. This is a baglike enlargement of the digestive tract just in front of, but separate from, the bee's stomach. The sugars found in nectar undergo chemical changes while in the bee's honey sac as the first step in changing nectar into honey. Before nectar becomes honey, the honeybees remove a large part of the water by evaporation processes. Honey stored by bumblebees in cells called "honeypots" is almost as thin as nectar and will sour in a short time. Honey stored in the honeycombs by honeybees has so much water removed from the original nectar that it will keep almost for ever.

What about the winter? In temperate regions, the young queen bumblebees pass the winter in holes they dig in well-drained sandbanks or in other suitable places. They are the only members of the colony that live through the winter! In the spring, each surviving queen starts a new colony.

The honeybees are luckier. They can adapt themselves to all extremes of climate. They have a social organization that is so very efficient and complicated that it has been compared to that of man.

In the hive where they live, worker bees regulate the temperature with great exactness. They keep it at 34 degrees Centigrade where the young bees are being developed. During the winter, they do not let the colony temperature fall below 7 degrees. Honey stored in the hive is used as fuel by the bees. They have an efficient way of preventing the loss of more than a very small part of the heat they produce by consuming honey.

HONEY
SAC

HONEY BEES IN HIVE

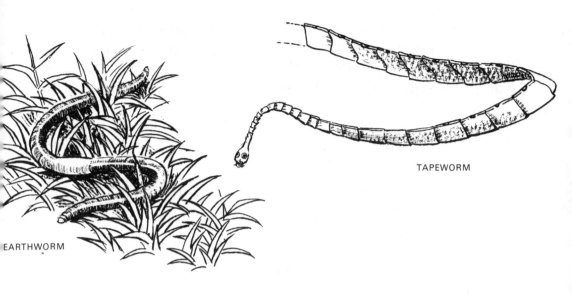

TAPEWORM

EARTHWORM

Scientists find it difficult to define exactly what worms are. They may best be described as elongated, boneless animals, having an undersurface fitted for crawling, and a more or less definite head end. One other im-

TO WHAT FAMILY DO WORMS BELONG?

portant feature of worms is that they can be divided into two similar portions, their right and left sides. So when you have something that fits this description, you have a worm.

Worms vary in size from microscopic to about 12 metres long. They vary in colour from transparency to dark brown, green, and red.

Worms form several distinct primary groups of animals. The most important of these are the flatworms; a group that includes the threadworms, roundworms, and hookworms; and the segmented worms.

The flatworms have flattened bodies. Each one contains both sexes within itself. Some of them are free living, others are parasites.

Among the parasitic flatworms is the tapeworm. It usually lives in the intestines of backboned animals, such as man and dogs.

The threadworms are a large group of threadlike worms, varying in size from hardly visible species to others a few metres long.

Among the most dangerous worms are the pinworm, trichina, Guinea worm, and the common roundworm. They cause serious illness to man and several animals.

The earthworms, with which we are most familiar, are among man's best friends. By burrowing into the soil, they loosen it for more effective growing of crops.

There is no other animal that man has fought with such energy for so long in so many places as the rat! There are many species of animals called rats, and most of them are harmless and interesting animals. But there

ARE RATS A PEST? are two common rats, the black rat and the brown rat, that have given rats a bad name.

Why does man fight the rat? Each year rats ruin hundreds of millions of pounds worth of grain. They destroy eggs, poultry, song birds, and spoil food in homes and on ships. Fires are caused by rats gnawing matches, gas pipes, and insulated electric wires. Houses may be flooded when they gnaw through water pipes. They damage floors and furnishings. Finally, they spread diseases such as the fortunately rare bubonic plague.

There are probably as many rats as people in the cities of the world. In the country, they actually outnumber human beings by three or four to one! They climb and burrow and live indoors or outdoors, in dry places or wet. They like vegetables best, but they will eat almost anything.

And since they can live almost anywhere and increase so rapidly, they are hard to control. A female rat may have ten litters of young in a year, and the young are ready to produce more young in only four months!

The black rat was originally a native of Asia Minor and the Orient but reached Europe with Crusaders returning from Palestine in the Middle Ages. The brown rat originally inhabited the tree-less steppes of Central Asia and probably started emigrating in large numbers before Roman times. Like the black rat, it eventually reached all parts of the world by living in the holds of ships, and has proved itself to be one of the most adaptable animals ever known.

Along with mice, another rodent which also lives wherever man does, rats have become popular pets. They are especially bred for this purpose and are not wild rats, although the basic colours and patterns of pet rats originate from wild specimens. White rats are actually albinos of brown rats. An albino of any animal is one which lacks normal pigmentation in its skin or hair. They are usually quite rare but man has specially bred albino rats for their "colour".

Pet rats need to be kept in cages, but they require quite a lot of room and cages with a ramp leading to a second level are recommended. Of course it is best to use metal cages as rats will gnaw their way through wooden ones if they get bored or want to escape. They will live on almost anything, but pet rats are best fed on rolled or crushed oats mixed with a little bird seed. They will live for as long as two or three years.

HORNED VIPER

An asp is simply a kind of snake. It belongs to a family of snakes called "vipers", which includes some of the deadliest poisonous snakes in the world. Some other snakes in this unpleasant group are: the rattlesnake,

WHAT IS AN ASP? the water moccasin, the copperhead, the South American bushmaster, the poisonous adder of Europe, the chain viper of India, and the horned viper of Africa.

The asp that is supposed to have killed Cleopatra was probably the horned viper of Africa. The poison, or venom, of such a snake destroys the capillaries in the body so a person dies of internal bleeding.

All vipers have thick bodies and flat, triangular heads. Their poison fangs, which are located in their upper jaws, are really very long teeth. There is a tube or channel in these teeth which connects to the poison glands, or sacs, located just behind the eyes.

When the snake wants to bite, it contracts the muscles of these sacs and the poison flows out through the fangs into the open wound which the snake has made by its bite. In a medium-sized snake, as much as half a teaspoon of this poison can be put into the victim at one time!

Removing the fangs of such a snake does not do much good. This is because new fangs are always developing behind the old fangs. So they simply take the place of the removed fangs!

The vipers are divided into two families: the true vipers, which are found only in Europe and parts of Africa, and the pit vipers, which are found in the Western Hemisphere and some parts of Asia.

The most deadly of all vipers is the chain viper of India, which is often 1.5 metres long. By the way, vipers will not strike unless they are molested or are seeking prey. But it is still wise to stay away from them!

It all depends on what we mean by "deadly". Should we consider it to be the snake that kills the most people? Or the snake that has the most poisonous venom?

WHAT IS THE DEADLIEST SNAKE?

Some experts have called the king cobra the world's deadliest snake. And they give several reasons for this. It is the longest venomous snake in the world. Its venom is very powerful. And it is a snake that does not hesitate to attack. There have been cases of people dying in less than an hour after being bitten by a king cobra.

Another candidate for "deadliest" is the tiger snake of Australia. Its venom is one of the most potent known. But this snake only has a limited amount of this venom.

There is also a snake in India called the krait which belongs to this group. There are records to show that about 77 per cent of all people bitten by this snake die. The spectacled cobra of India actually kills more people than any other kind, but less than 10 per cent of those bitten would die if they received treatment in time.

By the way, the largest snake in the world is not the deadliest. This is the anaconda of South America. It can be as long as 9 metres. But this snake is found in areas that are very hard to get to, so there may be even larger anacondas that have not yet been discovered.

In the United Kingdom there is only one poisonous snake, the adder, which is found in most parts of the British Isles, but not in Ireland.

To most of us, a snake is a snake. We know there are differences among them, but we do not realize how great these differences are.

The many different species of snakes reproduce in many different ways.

DO SNAKES LAY EGGS?
There are many species of snakes, including rattlesnakes, copperheads, water snakes, and garter snakes, that do not lay eggs, but give birth to living young. And many produce quite a few young at one time. Some snakes have been known to have more than 75 young at one time!

Then there is a big group of snakes that lay eggs. These eggs are usually deposited in hidden places such as under a rock or log, or in hollow stumps. The eggs are not the same shape as chicken eggs, but are a little longer and usually smaller. The eggs of the bull snake, however, and those of certain large snakes, are about the size of a chicken egg.

The shell of a snake's egg is tough and has a leathery quality. The number of eggs they lay depends on the species. The snake that lays the most eggs is probably the python. One Indian python was known to have laid 107 eggs at one time.

The eggs are hatched by the heat of the sun or by decaying vegetable matter which gives off a natural heat. In some cases, the snake guards the eggs by coiling about them.

Since some snakes can lay 100 eggs at a time, who takes care of the young when the eggs hatch? No one has to. All young snakes are able to care for themselves from the moment of hatching or birth!

If you have ever watched a snake move, there were probably two things about it that impressed you. The first, of course, was simply the mysterious ways in which a snake moves. You do not see any legs, the body does not

DO SNAKES HAVE BONES? seem to have anything to push or pull it, and yet there it is, moving! And the second thing is that the body seems to "flow" along the ground. It does not seem to have a bone in its body!

The fact is, however, that a snake is simply full of bones! A snake has a sectioned backbone, and to this backbone are attached pairs of ribs. Some snakes have as many as 145 pairs of ribs attached to that very flexible backbone.

Ball-and-socket joints attach the sections of the backbone to one another, and each rib to a section of the backbone. So great freedom of movement of that backbone and the ribs is possible.

The tips of each pair of ribs are attached with muscles to one of the scales that are on the "stomach", or abdomen, of the snake. Because of this, a snake can move each one of these scales independently. When the snake moves one of these scales, that scale acts like a foot.

Snakes also have bones in their heads and jaws. A snake can open his jaws very wide when it is swallowing its dinner. This is because all the bones around the mouth and throat are loosely attached so the mouth can be stretched very wide. In fact, most snakes swallow their catch without trying to kill it first. Later on they digest it.

So, you see, snakes do have bones in their body, even though their slithery bodies look as if there's nothing solid in them!

Just because snakes do not have legs now, does not mean they did not have them at sometime in their development. But how and why they came to lose their legs is not known to science.

WHY DON'T SNAKES HAVE LEGS? Some experts believe that the ancestors of snakes were certain kinds of burrowing lizards. There are many kinds of such lizards today, and all of them have very small legs or no legs at all. In time, the legs disappeared altogether. And despite this, snakes are able to move and get along very well indeed. One of the most helpful things for them in moving are the belly scales that cover the entire undersurface of most snakes.

There are four ways in which snakes move. One of them is called "lateral undulatory movement". In this method, the snake forms its body into a number of wavy, S-shaped curves. By pressing backward and outward against rough places on the ground, the snake slips forward on those scales.

A second way snakes move is called "rectilinear movement". In this case, small groups of the belly scales are pulled forward on part of the body, while other scales project backward to keep the snake from slipping back. Then the scales that have been holding the body are pulled forward. The scales that moved first hold the body.

A third way is a "concertina" method, which is used for climbing. The snake wraps its tail and rear part of the body around a tree, stretches out the forepart of its body and hooks it on the tree higher up. Then it releases the rear part and pulls the rest of its body upwards.

"Sidewinding" is another method by which snakes move. A loop of the forebody is thrown to one side. Then the rear part is shifted to the new position, and another neck loop is thrown out.

COACHWHIP SNAKE

SIDEWINDER

SCALES ON UNDERSIDE OF SNAKE

Snakes are reptiles, and all reptiles have skin that is dry and scaly. The snakes are thus related to the lizards, alligators and crocodiles, and turtles and tortoises.

WHY DO SNAKES HAVE SCALES? Since there are over 2,000 different species, or kinds, of snakes, there are some that live on land, some in the earth, others in water, and still others in trees. They inhabit practically all parts of the world except the polar regions and some of the ocean islands.

Since snakes have no legs (though the boas and pythons have the remains of hind legs), the scales help them move about. This is how this works. On the underside of the snake there are very broad scales. The snake can move them forward in such a way that the rear edge of each scale pushes against some irregularity in the ground. When they are pushed back against these irregularities, the whole snake moves forward.

All snakes, young and old, shed their skins. Even the film that covers the eyes is cast off. The skin is turned inside out during the process. The snake removes it by rubbing against rough surfaces. The shedding occurs several times a year.

All of us have seen pictures of "snake charmers" blowing on some musical instrument, while a snake rises up and seems to "dance" to the music. What is really happening?

CAN A SNAKE REALLY BE CHARMED? The truth is that the "snake charmer" is not charming the snake at all! He is just putting on a show to make people believe that his music is making the snake perform. To begin with, snakes are deaf, so they cannot even hear the music he is playing! But snakes can pick up vibrations with great sensitivity. Even when they lie in a basket, if there are any vibrations in the ground near them, they notice them and respond.

What the snake charmer does, therefore, is to tap the basket or stamp on the ground, pretending he is merely keeping time to the music. The snake reacts to this vibration. The snake charmer also moves his body constantly, and the snake "dances" because of these movements the man makes. In fact, what the snake is doing is keeping its eyes fixed on the man, and as he moves, it moves so as to keep him right before its eyes!

SWALLOWS

The British Isles have a wide range of physical regions which encourages a tremendous diversity of birdlife. More than 200 species of birds breed or winter here.

WHY DO BIRDS MIGRATE?

The most important reason why birds undertake migratory flights is simple. Winter cold reduces their food supply so much that they are in real danger of starvation. They need to seek warmer countries if they are to survive.

Birds become migratory only to ensure that more individuals of a species will survive, despite the risk of being blown off course during their travels, than if they stay to eke out a precarious living. If the risks of migration outweigh those of wintering, the species will be sedentary, but for some species, such as the lapwing and the song thrush, risks and disadvantages are so finely balanced that neither pattern dominates.

Time of departure of migratory birds is determined by the weather, wind direction and strength being more important to the birds than changes in temperature.

Many birds regularly return to the same small area of territory and ringed birds returning have been recorded passing the same locality on the same date in consecutive years.

Birds are able to navigate by means of the sun and stars, but how they do this has not yet been fully established.

Any way you look at it, the ostrich is a strange and remarkable bird. It is the largest of living birds—but it cannot fly. Its small wings are used for balance when it is running at high speeds.

DOES THE OSTRICH HAVE A VOICE? The head and neck of the ostrich are nearly bare of feathers. Its legs are long, with only two toes each. The plumage of the male (cock) is dark brown or black, with white tail and wing plumes. The female (hen) is much duller-coloured and smaller.

As you might imagine, a bird like this does not have a "singing" voice —but it does have a voice! Most of the year, ostriches make only a loud hissing noise. But during the mating season, the males make a loud, deep booming roar that can be heard from quite a distance away.

Three or four hens lay their eggs in one shallow hole scooped in the sand. The hens take turns sitting on the eggs to keep them warm. The male takes his turn at night. These are the largest eggs laid by any bird.

The ostrich is a greedy eater. Its food is mainly plants, berries, and seeds. But in order to help it digest its food, an ostrich will sometimes swallow large stones, bits of iron, and other objects!

Ostriches are raised commercially for their beautiful plumes. The cropping of the plumes does not harm the birds. The first cropping may be done before the bird is a year old. Each time it is done, the plumes will grow again.

There are about 50 different kinds of birds of paradise, but they are all found in the tropical islands of the Western Pacific and in Northern Australia.

WHAT ARE BIRDS OF PARADISE? Birds of paradise range in size from that of a crow to that of a sparrow, and each kind has its own special pattern of brilliant colours. It is this display of brilliant colours in their plumage that makes these birds so unusual. But these beautiful birds are actually related to the common crow.

The first Europeans to see these birds were the early Dutch explorers in the fifteenth century. They looked so beautiful that these men believed the birds were fed from the dews of heaven and the nectar of flowers, which explains their name.

Only the males have the brilliant plumage. The reason for this is not yet understood. It may be to attract the females, or it may be to draw natural enemies away from the nests of the mother and the young and so protect them.

Most birds of paradise build flimsy, platform-like nests in the tree-tops. In these they lay their streaked and spotted eggs. The birds eat almost anything they can find, from fruit to snails and insects.

During the mating season, the male birds gather and show off their fine feathers before the females. While these birds are usually wary, at this time they concentrate so much on showing off that hunters can shoot them at close range. The natives used to shoot them with blunt arrows so as not to injure the plumes.

Usually, the larger the bird the larger the egg it lays. But the size of a bird's egg is not always dependent on the size of the parent bird.

WHAT BIRD LAYS THE LARGEST EGG? It really depends on the amount of food necessary to nourish the growing germ up to the point of hatching. Birds that are able to take care of themselves a short time after hatching come from large eggs. In these eggs there was enough food yolk to bring them to a high state of development before they were hatched.

Birds that are born blind and helpless come from relatively small eggs, in which there was not enough food to develop them to the point of self-support at birth. Not all eggs are shaped like hen's eggs. Some birds lay cylindrical, spherical, and even pear-shaped eggs. The eggs of some birds nesting in high, exposed places are shaped in such a way that there is little danger of their rolling and breaking.

When it comes to size of egg, the ostrich is the champion. Ostrich eggs measure 15 to 17 centimetres long and 13 to 15 centimetres across. It has been found that an ostrich egg shell will hold from 12 to 18 hens' eggs!

While the ostrich lays the largest eggs of any birds living today, there have been birds that would have considered an ostrich egg tiny! The extinct elephant bird, or roc, of Madagascar, laid the largest eggs ever known. Complete shells of these eggs have been found and measured. Some of them are 33 centimetres long and 23 to 26 centimetres in diameter. The shell of these eggs will hold about eight litres, and that's six times as much as an ostrich egg will hold, and nearly 150 times as much as a hen's egg will hold!

The smallest eggs are produced by hummingbirds. Some species of hummingbirds lay eggs that are only six millimetres in length.

MYNA BIRD

AFRICAN PARROT

There are a great many birds which can be taught to say a few words. But the real "talking birds" can be taught to say long sentences! The best talking birds are parrots, mynas, crows, ravens, jackdaws, and certain jays.

WHAT BIRDS CAN TALK BEST? According to the experts the best bird talkers in the world are the African parrot and the myna bird of India.

Many people believe that the ability of a bird to "talk" depends on the structure of its tongue. A parrot, for instance, has a large, thick tongue. But many other talking birds have small tongues!

Do birds understand what they are saying? Most biologists believe birds do not understand the words they say, but they can sometimes form an association between certain expressions and actions.

214

P-BEAT

DOWN-BEAT

When man decided he wanted to fly, he had to create a flying machine. When you examine a bird, you can see that Nature has done everything possible to make the bird a perfect flying machine.

HOW CAN BIRDS FLY?

First of all, the bird has wings. The main flight feathers of the wings are attached to the bone of the outer arm by a tough cord of tissue called a "sinew". The supporting flight feathers are attached to the upper arm bone in the same way.

Each feather has its own set of muscles, so the bird can control each feather in flight. On the up-beat of the wing, the main and some of the supporting flight feathers are turned so the edges are turned up. The air can pass easily between the feathers. On the down-beat, all the flight feathers have flat sides down and air cannot pass through the wings. In this way the bird pushes himself into the air—and takes off in flight!

But a flying body must have the greatest possible lightness, compactness, and strength. So the large bones of a bird are hollow. Many of them have air sacs. The ribs of a bird are fused to make a firm support for the down-beat of the wings.

The head, tail, wings, and legs of a bird are extremely light. The bones of the skulls are very thin. A bird does not have teeth and jaws with heavy bones and muscles—it has instead a hollow beak.

The strong muscles that move the wings are attached to the breast-bone, bringing them closer to the centre of gravity. Even the fact that birds are warm-blooded is a help, because cold-blooded creatures become sluggish in winter. So you see, everything about the bird is "designed" to help it to fly!

The ability of certain birds to fly great distances and arrive "home", or at their destination, is one of the most remarkable things in nature. Do you know that carrier, or homing, pigeons were used to carry messages as

HOW DO PIGEONS FIND THEIR WAY HOME?

long as 2,000 years ago by the ancient Romans? And even now, when modern armies have all kinds of wonderful equipment for transmitting messages, they still train homing pigeons for use in those situations when other methods of communication fail!

Many scientists have studied this amazing ability of birds, but no one yet has the full answer. One theory, which is better known than the others, is that pigeons use the sun to help them find direction. As you know, there is a different angle towards the sun as the day progresses—it is low in the morning, high at noon, and then low again. But some scientists believe a pigeon can see which path the sun will follow through the sky, and can figure out direction from this. It seems almost impossible to believe—but so far no one has offered a better explanation.

Not all birds, or even all pigeons, can do this. In fact, there are 289 different kinds of pigeons and doves, and they vary quite a bit. Some kinds of pigeons like to live and travel alone; others are always found in flocks. Some feed and live mainly on the ground. But most kinds live in forested areas and build their nests among the tree branches.

Not everybody accepts the theory of evolution; but according to those who do, animal life (which includes fish, birds, and insects) began more than 500,000,000 years ago, after the earth's surface had cooled and the oceans were formed. Most scientists believe that there was life in the sea before there was any living thing on land. The land had no life for the next 160,000,000 years.

WHAT WAS THE FIRST LAND ANIMAL?

Then strange, fishlike creatures began to come out of the oceans on to the land. At first their movements were very awkward because they had no legs. They had to use their fins like feet for a long time. After many generations, their fins became legs and feet.

While these changes were taking place, the animals still laid their eggs and hatched their young in the water. These walking creatures, whose ancestors were fish-like, developed into "amphibians" (cold-blooded animals that live part of their lives on land after hatching from eggs laid in the water).

In time, some of the early amphibians no longer laid their eggs in the water. When this happened, the amphibians became "reptiles" (cold-blooded animals that reproduce by laying their eggs on land).

Reptiles ruled the earth for more than 100,000,000 years. Some of the reptiles developed feathers on their bodies, and their forelimbs became wings. In time they learned to fly, and birds came into being. Birds' feathers are the result of changes that took place in the reptile scales.

Other reptiles ceased to lay eggs and became mammal-like animals that gave birth to their young. They also became warm-blooded and developed into true mammals.

The name "amphibian" comes from a Greek word which means "living a double life". Most amphibians spend the early part of their lives in the water and the later part on land.

WHAT ARE AMPHIBIANS?

There are three groups, or orders, of amphibians. They are the frogs and toads, the salamanders, and the caecilians. Newts, efts, and mud puppies are salamanders. Caecilians are burrowing animals that have no legs or tail and are blind.

There are more than 1,040 species of amphibians. All are less than one metre long, except the giant salamander of Japan, which may grow to 1.5 metres in length.

Most of the amphibians are neither strong nor quick, though frogs can move fairly fast. The large majority are protected mainly by their retiring habits and their colouring. In addition, practically all amphibians are able to secrete poison in their skin glands, which is their best defence against enemies.

In adult life, most amphibians usually have lungs, but they also breathe through their skin. Amphibians are usually found only in hot and temperate climates. They generally cannot live in salt water.

Although typical adult amphibians live on land, they return to the water for the mating season. There the eggs are laid and fertilized, and there the young pass the first part of their lives as fishlike larvae, feeding mostly on vegetable material.

A few amphibians have developed strange methods of taking care of their eggs. The female of a certain Brazilian tree frog builds a nest of mud for her eggs while the male sits by and croaks. The Surinam toad hatches her eggs on her back. Amphibians that leave their eggs unprotected in the water usually lay hundreds at a time, joined in bands or masses by a gluey substance. Those that take care of their eggs lay fewer of them.

TOAD

FROG

SALAMANDER

In the way we usually think of a voice, the answer is no as far as most turtles are concerned, but there are giant tortoises who grunt, roar or even bellow! Turtle is the collective name for a family of reptiles which

DOES THE TURTLE HAVE A VOICE?

we call tortoises when they live on land, turtles when sea-going and terrapins when they live in fresh water! Did you know that as a family they are more ancient than dinosaurs?

Perhaps the reason is that a turtle does not really need a voice to protect itself. After all, it has that wonderful shell. These shells are made up of a "bony box" covered with horny plates.

The shell is divided into two parts, with one part covering the back, the other covering the underpart of the turtle's body. Through the openings between the two parts, the turtle can stick out its head, neck, tail, and legs.

Turtles can grow to tremendous size. The largest kind in the world today is the leatherback. It usually weighs about 450 kilograms.

But this is nothing compared to certain species of turtles which have become extinct. One such species is called "Colossochelys". It was a giant tortoise that became extinct about 5 million years ago and there is a complete skeleton of one in the Natural History Museum in London. The shell is about the size of a Mini and you could fit an engine and four wheels and drive it away into the London traffic!

Turtles are also supposed to live to a ripe old age. The giant tortoise lives longer than any other vertebrate animal (an animal with a backbone). There are many cases on record of such turtles having lived 100 years and longer, and there may be some that lived as long as 200 years!

If you've ever been fishing you probably feel that fish eat everything but what you use for bait! Little boys in towns often catch fish with a piece of bread on a bent pin. Country boys use worms. Trout fishermen use flies.

WHAT DO FISH EAT? And some fish are tempted to "bite" by other fish on the hook.

Since there are thousands of different kinds of fish, it is impossible to describe all the things they eat. But the struggle for life beneath the water is so great, that fish have learned not to be too particular about their diet.

Some fish are vegetarians and will not eat any other living creature, but most of them are "predacious", which means that they will eat other fish or aquatic animals, and insects. A curious thing is that many fish relish eating the small crustaceans, or shelled creatures.

While there is a great variety of fish, there are certain general things that can be said about them. As a general rule, for example, fish are long and tapering in shape because it is the most satisfactory shape for cutting through the water quickly.

Most fish use their tails as a power engine and guide themselves with both tail and fins. They breathe by means of gills through which water is constantly passing from the mouth.

Have you ever been fishing and tiptoed to the edge of the brook in order not to scare the fish away? If a fish hears you, the chances are he might decide it is safer elsewhere—because fish do have ears and can hear. But

CAN FISH HEAR? the ears of a fish are located internally, not externally as are the ears of so many other familiar creatures.

Many people imagine that fish somehow get along without performing some of the functions we know are necessary to life. This may be because fish are cold-blooded. And it may also be because we like to catch fish and prefer to think they do not know what is happening to them. But fish have a nervous system like other animals. When we make them uncomfortable, they feel it, and when we hurt them, they suffer pain.

Fish have a very keen sense of touch, and they taste, as well as feel, with their skin. They also have two small organs of smell which are located in nostrils on the head.

And just because a fish is cold-blooded does not mean it can go without "fuel" to keep the body going. This "fuel", of course, is food. It is burned in all the living tissue of the fish and provides the power of life, growth, and motion.

The blood stream carries not only this food to every organ of the body, but also oxygen to keep the "fires" going. So the fish has a heart to pump this blood, just as we have.

Fish, of course, live in so many different kinds of environment that they differ from each other in many ways. For example, lungfish actually have both gills and "lungs" for breathing in air! Some fish that live in caves are blind, and so they have developed feelers on their heads. Some live in salt water and some in fresh. And some fish live only on the bottom of the ocean.

The electric eel is one of a group of electric fish. These fish capture their prey and defend themselves from enemies by discharging electric shocks. They closely resemble and are related to other fish, but they just happen to have this electric power. Scientists still cannot explain the origin and development of the electric power in these fish.

WHAT IS AN ELECTRIC EEL?

The most dangerous of all the electric fish is the electric eel of South America, sometimes called "the Brazilian electric eel". This thick, blackish creature is an inhabitant of the rivers emptying into the Amazon and Orinoco rivers. It often grows to a length of 2 metres or more and by a blow of its tail, in which its electric organs are located, it can stun an animal as large as a horse! Human beings are also said to feel the effects of the shock for several hours.

Another kind of electric fish is the electric catfish. This is sometimes four feet long and may be found in all the larger rivers of tropical Africa.

Third in the group of electric fish is the electric ray, or torpedo ray, found in all warm seas. It lives mostly in deep water near the shore. The member of this family inhabiting the Atlantic Ocean is said to grow to a length of 1.5 metres and weighs 90 kilograms.

The electric ray is dark above and light below. It is round and flat and has a powerful tail. Its electric organs are situated between the head and gills. Experiments made on this fish have shown that its electric power can be used up and that the power will not return until the creature has rested and eaten.

Jellyfish are among the strangest sea creatures because they are almost entirely made of jelly. They do not look like fish and they are not related to them at all. They protect themselves with a sting that is unpleasant and can sometimes be very dangerous.

ARE JELLYFISH DANGEROUS?

Jellyfish are shaped like an overturned bowl. The digestive system is under the bowl. The digestive tract ends in a tube which hangs down from the centre and has a mouth at the lower end. Tentacles, hanging from the edge of the bowl, gather food and are sometimes used for swimming. Between the tentacles are nerve centres and sense organs.

The bowl of the jellyfish is made up of two thin layers of tissue with jelly-like material between them. If a jellyfish is removed from the water it dries up very quickly because 98 per cent of its body is water.

Of course, if the jellyfish is quite small, being stung by one may not be too dangerous. But when it comes to the big ones, that's a different story. Experts report that jellyfish exist with a bowl of nearly 4 metres in diameter and with tentacles more than 30 metres long.

When a jellyfish like this "embraces" you, it may make it hard for you to breathe and even partially paralyse you. The Portuguese man-of-war, which is one of the largest jellyfish, can kill and eat a full-sized mackerel. It can cause serious injury to human beings. There is a kind of jellyfish found off the coast of Australia called "the sea wasp", which has been known to cause death in many cases.

What makes the jellyfish dangerous are the tentacles. Some of them are barbed and pierce the body of its prey. The barbed cells are connected to poison glands which kill or paralyse the prey.

WHALE SHARK

WHITE SHARK

There are more than 150 different kinds of sharks. All of these live in salt water, except for one species. In Central America there is a lake called Lake Nicaragua, and there is a fresh water shark that lives there.

WHERE DO SHARKS LIVE?

Actually, sharks do not live in any one "spot", because they wander hundreds of miles looking for prey. Most big sharks are generally found living near the surface in the open sea. But there are some that live deep down at the ocean bottom. Smaller sharks usually live near the shore, and they are found in most warm and temperate seas around the world.

Most people think of sharks as very dangerous creatures. The truth is that some sharks are quite dangerous to man, and others are harmless. For example, the sharks that often follow ships are harmless scavengers, hoping to pick up food from the ships. Even small fish are not afraid of these sharks.

This is also true of some very big sharks, that is, unless they are attacked. One of these is the whale shark. This shark is found near the Cape of Good Hope and in the Mediterranean, Pacific, and Caribbean right up to Florida. It may be over 11 metres long and weigh more than 13 tonnes.

The other "safe" big shark is the basking shark. It is the biggest fish of the North Atlantic, and is over 13 metres long. It likes to bask in the sun with its back partly out of the water.

But the most dreaded of all fish is the great white shark, which is sometimes 12 metres long. It definitely attacks human beings.

OCTOPUS
CATCHING CRAB

If you ever run into an octopus underwater, it might be a good idea to take off in another direction! Octopuses are not as dangerous as they look or are made out to be, but they can be very unpleasant.

WHAT DOES AN OCTOPUS EAT?

This is due to the bite of the octopus, which can be poisonous. An octopus has two very tough jaws that look like the beak of a parrot. Not only can the bite be painful, the octopus can inject venom or poison with its bite.

Of course, this venom is very useful to an octopus in getting its dinner. For instance, it can make a crab helpless, and thus easy for the octopus to eat. Crabs, fish, and other living sea animals are the normal diet of an octopus. The animals are captured by the sucking discs and then torn to bits by the jaws. But when an octopus is very hungry, it stops being particular. It will eat practically anything it can capture and tear apart!

What makes an octopus so strange looking are eight tentacles, or arms. The tentacles are long and flexible with rows of suckers on the underside. These suckers enable the octopus to grab and hold very tightly to anything it catches.

The octopus does not use these long tentacles for getting about. In the back of the body there is a funnel-siphon with which it can shoot a stream of water with great force. This enables him to move backwards very quickly.

Did you know that the octopus has been hunted for food since ancient Greek and Roman times? It was considered a great delicacy by the Romans. And even today, Greeks, Italians, and Chinese enjoy eating pickled or dry octopus.

When you look at an oyster that has been opened, it seems to be formless. But it is really a complex creature with a mouth, gills, stomach, liver, intestine, and heart.

HOW ARE OYSTERS BORN? There are more than a hundred species of oysters. They vary widely in size, shape, habits, and flavour. But generally, oysters produce many young. Some of them spawn five or six times during a season.

A female oyster may discharge almost half a billion eggs in a single season! Luckily, less than 1 per cent hatch and reach maturity, otherwise the oceans of the world would be choked with oysters.

A young oyster begins to swim a few hours after it hatches from the egg. It is quite different in appearance from a fully grown oyster. In shape it resembles a small purse, with a circle of fine, vibrating hairs, or cilia, at its mouth end. These hairs fall off and the oyster grows in a year to about one inch across.

But before this, when the young oyster is only a few weeks old, it attaches itself to a rock or other submerged object. At the end of a month or two it is about the size of a one pence piece.

One of the greatest problems an oyster faces is simply to survive against all its enemies. Young swimming oysters are eaten by adult oysters and by fish. Even the larger oyster that has attached itself to something can be attacked by creatures called "drills". They bore holes through the valves and extract the soft parts.

About 4,000 years ago, a Chinese fisherman who decided that oysters might satisfy his hunger opened a few and was probably the first man to discover pearls!

HOW DO OYSTERS MAKE PEARLS? Pearls are made of the same material as the mother-of-pearl lining in the shells of the oyster. The body of the oyster is very tender, so to protect itself it secretes this mother-of-pearl lining to provide a smooth surface against its body.

When an irritating object, such as a grain of sand, manages to get inside the oyster's shell, the oyster coats it with layer after layer of mother-of-pearl—and this becomes a pearl!

When this happens naturally, the pearl may be perfectly shaped. But man has found a way to help the oyster along in the making of pearls. A bit of sand or a tiny piece of mother-of-pearl is inserted between the shell and the outer skin of the oyster. After two or three years, when these shells are taken from the water and opened, a pearl is found inside. These are called "cultured" pearls, and are not usually perfectly shaped.

In Japan, they have now learned how to make perfect cultured pearls. The irritating material is put right into the body of the oyster. This is really a surgical operation requiring great care and delicacy, because the oyster must be kept alive.

The largest pearl found is said to have been 5 centimetres long and 10 centimetres round. Because pearls are expensive, most of us buy artificial pearls. The French make beautiful artificial pearls by taking hollow glass beads, lining them with a substance that comes from the shiny scales of certain fish, and then filling the beads with wax.

Perhaps you have sometimes watched a snail moving slowly across the ground and wondered how it was able to move, since no "legs" were showing. The fact is that the whole bottom part of a snail's body is

HOW DO SNAILS WALK? really a "foot"! This foot is flat and smooth and contains muscles which the snail uses to glide along the ground. To help it move more easily, this foot has tiny glands which give out a slimy fluid, so the snail really glides over the surface with a wavelike movement.

Here's an amazing fact about this foot of the snail. It is so tough that a snail can crawl along the edge of the sharpest razor without hurting itself in the slightest! In fact, the snail is a remarkable creature in many ways. For instance, a snail never gets lost. It has an instinct that guides it back to its hiding place no matter how far away it has wandered. And even though a snail may weigh less than 15 grams, it can pull a weight behind it that weighs more than 450 grams.

Snails are chiefly of two types, those with shells and those without. The snail that lives in a shell has a body that fits right into the coil of the shell, and it has strong muscles that enable it to pull its body entirely into the shell when there is danger. As an added protection when the body is in the shell, a horny disc at the end closes the opening tightly.

Snails live on land or in fresh water. Most snails eat plants of various kinds. The snail has a tongue that is like a file, with hundreds of tiny teeth. It uses this to cut and shred its food.

Cats and dogs, elephants and bats, whales and horses, and monkeys and men belong to a zoological classification called "mammals".

WHAT IS A MAMMAL? Mammals are distinguished from all other types of life by the fact that their young are fed with milk from the mammary glands of the females. In most mammals the young are born fully formed, instead of hatching out of eggs as young birds do.

Mammals are also distinguished by the hair or fur they have on all or some parts of their bodies. They are warm-blooded, and they have a four-chambered heart and a diaphragm.

While most mammals live on dry land, a few, such as the whale and dolphin, live in the water. Some burrow in the ground, such as the mole and many rodents. And still others live in trees, such as monkeys and squirrels. The only mammals that can fly are the bats.

Scientists have arranged the mammals into a number of smaller divisions, or orders. The lowest of these orders, "the monotremes", are mammals that lay eggs. The next order, "the edentates", are toothless mammals. Then come the sea mammals. Then we find "the ungulates", or hoofed mammals.

The "carnivorous" mammals eat flesh. The "rodents" are gnawing mammals. The "insectivores" are animals that eat insects. The highest order is "the primates", or mammals with nails, instead of hoofs or claws. Monkeys, apes, and men are primates.

Nearly all flatfish are valued highly as food. The European sole is commonly considered to be the most delicious of all fish. The largest member of the flatfish family is the halibut. After it was discovered that halibut

WHAT ARE FLATFISH? liver oil was the richest natural source of Vitamin A, as well as possessing a high Vitamin D content, halibut fishing became specialized, and special "halibut ships" were built. By far the most commercially important flatfish is the plaice. This fish, easily recognizable by its characteristic red spots, is very common round our coasts. The flounder, which comes up many tidal rivers, is also common here.

Among the more than 500 different kinds of flatfish are sole, flounder, fluke, halibut, and turbot. They have bodies that are flat like a pancake, and they lie and swim on one side with both of their eyes up on top.

But long, long ago, the flatfish did not travel and rest on their sides. They lived and moved in an upright position, and as a result they were being destroyed by their enemies. Then some of them, in order to survive, began to travel and rest entirely on their sides, and after thousands of years all flatfish began to do this.

But there was one problem. This meant that one eye would be buried in the mud and the mouth was at a bad angle for eating. So for thousands of years these fish began trying to twist the buried eye around to where it could see. And gradually this eye developed on the top of the head on the upper side!

The fantastic thing is that today, each flatfish after it is born goes through this process. It repeats the whole process of its evolution during its own lifetime—its eye actually travels across the top of its head and comes out on top!

A manatee looks like a small whale and it is a mammal, not a fish. The American manatee lives in the rivers of Florida, Mexico, Central America, and the West Indies. It measures 2.5 to 4 metres in length. The

WHAT IS A MANATEE? body is somewhat like a fish, but the tail is quite different. It is broad, shovel-like, horizontal, and has rounded edges. It has a thick skin which is hairless, except for "whiskers" on the upper lip.

Manatees live in bays, lagoons, and large rivers, but not in the open sea. As a rule, they prefer to stay in shallow water. When they are not feeding, they lie near the bottom. In deeper water, they often float about with the body arched, the rounded back close to the surface, and the head, limbs, and tail hanging down.

Manatees live on the plants they find in shallow waters. They use their flippers to push food to their mouths, and a manatee may eat 27 to 45 kilograms of food a day. But then a grown manatee may weigh as much as 680 kilograms. Because manatees browse like cows in the shallow waters and often are seen in small herds, they are sometimes called "sea cows".

Manatees usually give birth to one calf, but sometimes there are twins. To nurse the young, the mother rises to the water's surface and, with her head and shoulders out of the water, clasps the youngster to her breast with her flippers.

Manatees move very slowly and are perfectly harmless. But in some places today, manatees are still being hunted because of their flesh, their hide, and the oil which can be obtained from them.

Man can move across the surface of the earth much faster than any other mammal . . . but not on his own two legs! Even the fastest runner of all time would rank as a pretty slow-moving creature compared with certain animals.

WHAT IS THE WORLD'S FASTEST MAMMAL?

In a short dash, man has been known to travel at a speed of 22 to 25 miles an hour. For a short dash, even an elephant or a rhinoceros can do about 25 miles an hour. A race horse, which we consider to be pretty swift, can go at about 40 or 50 miles an hour. The fastest a greyhound can go is about 35 miles an hour.

If we want to measure real speed of motion by a mammal, we have to go to such creatures as the antelope and the gazelle. These animals can do between 60 and 65 miles for a dash of a mile or so. The speed champion of the entire kingdom, however, is the cheetah or hunting leopard. These animals have been timed at a speed of 70 miles an hour! Of course, they can keep this up for only about a mile, after which they drop down to a slower speed.

Since a whale lives in the water and has a fish-shaped body, why isn't it considered a fish?

The fact is that the whale is a water mammal, and is descended from

WHY ARE WHALES CONSIDERED MAMMALS?

ancestors that lived on land. During the thousands and thousands of years they have been living in the water, whales have grown to resemble fish in their shape and other outside features, but they are built and they live like land animals.

A whale's flippers, for instance, have the bones of a five-fingered hand. Some whales even have the bones of hind legs in their flesh! The most important difference between whales and fish, of course, is that the baby whale is fed on its mother's milk like other little mammals. It is not hatched from an egg but is born alive. And for some time after it is born it stays close to its mother, who takes very good care of it.

Since all mammals have warm blood, and the whale has no fur coat to keep itself warm in the icy water, it has blubber instead. This is a layer of tissue under the skin filled with oil which retains heat and is as good as a fur coat!

Whales breathe differently from fish. Instead of gills, they have lungs and they take in air through two nostrils or "blow holes" on the top of their heads. When they go underwater, these nostrils are closed by little valves, so no water can get in. Every five to ten minutes, a whale rises to the top of the water to breathe. First it blows out the used air from its lungs with a loud noise. This makes the "spout" which we often see in the pictures of whales. Then it takes in fresh air and dives down into the sea to swim about.

BLUE WHALE

The biggest whale also happens to be the largest animal in the world. It is the blue, or sulphur-bottom, whale, which may be more than 30 metres long and weigh 125 tonnes.

WHAT IS THE BIGGEST WHALE?

It may be found in all waters but is most common in the Pacific Ocean. It belongs to the group of whales known as "the whalebone whales" (the other is known as "the toothed whales"). So whalebone whales have no teeth.

It is rather strange to think that the largest animal in the world is able to get along without teeth! How do these whales manage? They have developed a structure in their mouths made up of hundreds of bony plates, known as a "baleen". It grows down from the palate (roof of the mouth) and forms a sort of sieve.

The whale feeds by swimming swiftly through a school of its prey—mostly small molluscs, crustaceans, and fish, with its mouth wide open. When it closes its mouth, the water is forced out between the plates, but the food is caught. The mouth of the whale is like a huge bucket. The head is about one-third the length of its body!

Of the toothed whales, the largest are the sperm whales. They may be 20 metres long and they have huge heads. The grampus, or killer whale (which is really a large dolphin), is the only one that eats other warm-blooded animals. It is about 9 metres long and easily catches seals. Packs of killer whales even attack large whales.

Because whales live in the water and have fish-shaped bodies, we tend to compare them with fish. But the skeleton, circulatory system, brain, and other organs are quite unlike those of fish.

At one time, whaling was quite an important industry. To most of us, the idea of hunting for whales must seem a little strange. What can we get from this huge creature that can be useful to us?

WHAT DO WE GET FROM WHALES?

Well, the number of valuable products that come from whales is amazing. The blubber of the whale (an oil-filled layer of tissue under the skin) provides excellent oil. The oil is used for lighting in certain parts of the world and is often used in making soap.

Many whales furnish good meat to eat. Fertilizer is made from their ground flesh and bones. From the sperm whale comes spermaceti, an oil found in the cavity of the head. It is used in making ointments, candles, and cosmetics.

Also from the sperm whale comes ambergris, a very valuable substance produced by the intestine, which is used in making perfume. The teeth of the sperm whale and the tusk of the narwhal whale are both of valuable ivory. And the skin of the white whale is made into a kind of leather.

Did you know that all whales are mammals that have learned to live in the water? They are descended from mammals that once lived on land. In fact, they still have the bones of a five-fingered hand covered by the skin and flesh of their flippers. Some whales even have the bones of hind legs down in their flesh. But during the many thousands of years they have been living in the water, they have adapted themselves very well to this life.

Dolphins are such interesting creatures that people find it hard to believe that a dolphin is simply a whale!

There is an order of acquatic mammals that scientists call "Cetacea".

WHAT IS A DOLPHIN? To this order belong whales, dolphins, and porpoises. Dolphins are small whales that belong to the toothed-whale group. Porpoises are a kind of dolphin without beaks but with a triangular back fin and spade-shaped teeth.

The toothed whale lives on cuttlefish, squids, crabs, and many kinds of fish, which they chase and capture. The grampus, or killer whale, which is really a large dolphin, is the only cetacean that eats other warm-blooded animals. It is about 9 metres long and easily catches seals. The other dolphins are not often more than 3 metres long and their heads are quite small.

Dolphins live in great herds and seem to enjoy following ships. The common dolphin, which may be found in all temperate and tropical seas, has a tail shaped like a half moon. The black of the back contrasts with the white belly.

Scientists are very interested in the way dolphins move through the water avoiding danger, and in the call notes they use in communicating with each other. It is believed that porpoises and dolphins are capable of making sounds that have more "meaning" than any other creature in the sea.

There are few animals that depend on flying for moving about as much as a bat does. While birds and insects fly, too, they can manage to walk about if they have to. But the limbs and feet of a bat are not suited to walking.

WHY DO BATS HANG UPSIDE DOWN?

Which means they also cannot stand easily. So when a bat is in its roost, the easiest thing for it to do is to hang on, head down!

The bat does a great many things that are quite remarkable. To begin with, the bat is a mammal—the only mammal that can fly. The young are born alive and feed on milk from the mother. When the young are very small, the mother may carry them with her when she goes hunting!

Bats are nocturnal, which means they are active during the night and sleep during the day. Since they have to hunt for their food, you would imagine that bats would need exceptionally good eyesight. But actually, bats do not depend on their eyes for getting about. When bats fly, they utter a series of very high-pitched sounds. These sounds are too high to be heard by the human ear.

The echoes from these sounds are thrown back to the bat when it is in flight. The bat can tell whether the echo came from an obstacle near by or far away, and can change its course in flight in time to avoid hitting the obstacle!

Most people think all bats behave more or less the same way, but since there are more than 2,000 kinds of bats, you can see why this is not so. There are bats with a 15-centimetre wingspread and bats with a wingspread of nearly 2 metres.

Nobody except the Aboriginal people knew kangaroos existed until about 200 years ago. The first Australian explorers and settlers saw them then for the first time.

The kangaroo, of course, has a pouch, and in Australia many mammals have pouches. Australia and its neighbouring islands are where most of the pouched animals have been found. Pouched animals form the order of mammals called "the marsupials". This name comes from the Latin word *marsupium,* which means "pouch".

WHY WERE KANGAROOS FOUND ONLY IN AUSTRALIA?

The first mammals appeared more than 100,000,000 years ago, during the Age of Dinosaurs. Some of these were marsupial, and some were "placental". A placental mammal supplies food to the unborn young within the mother's body. In marsupial mammals, the pouch serves this purpose. The young are born very tiny and develop in the mother's pouch.

When the earth's climate changed, the dinosaurs died out. The mammals multiplied and developed in many ways. They became the ruling animals of the earth. But the placental mammals were more successful than the marsupials. Their brains were superior, and it was also better for the young to develop inside the mother's body than in a pouch.

In most parts of the world the marsupials disappeared. They could not compete for living places with the other mammals. But this did not happen in Australia and South America.

Scientists believe that Australia was once linked to South-Eastern Asia. This may have been with a chain of islands or an isthmus. So marsupials spread into Australia at a time when there were no advanced placental mammals there. They did not have any competition, so they flourished and evolved in many forms.

One of the strangest animals you could see is an echidna, or spiny ant-eater. The echidna has long claws, a tubelike snout, and a covering of short, stiff spines like that of a hedgehog or porcupine. But what makes

WHAT IS AN ECHIDNA?

it strange is that although it is a mammal, it lays eggs! This animal and the platypus, or duckbill, are the only mammals that lay eggs like birds and most reptiles.

Also, even though it is a mammal, like birds and reptiles it has only a single body opening. This serves both for the elimination of all body wastes and for laying eggs. The platypus and the spiny anteater are therefore called "monotremes", which means "a single opening".

The spiny anteater is equipped for a life of digging and for gathering ants and insects as its principal food. The echidna lives in Australia and New Guinea. It has legs that are short and powerful with long, curved claws for digging. The snout is long and narrow and shaped like a tube. It has a sticky, wormlike tongue that it can thrust out to catch insects.

At breeding time, the female echidna develops a pouch on her under-side. This pouch opens to the rear. No one is certain how the eggs get into the pouch. But at egg-laying time the female probably curls her body so that one or two eggs are laid directly into the pouch.

She carries the eggs until they hatch. The young live in the pouch until they become too big for comfort. Then the mother leaves them in the burrow or in some other safe hiding place while she searches for food.

If threatened, a spiny anteater digs straight down into the ground and presents only its sharp spines to the enemy. It can bury itself completely in a few minutes! The New Guinea spiny anteater can grow to a length of about 76 centimetres. The Australian species is a little smaller.

There are more than 2,000 kinds of bats, and so naturally there are many differences among them. Most bats eat insects, but there are bats in the warm tropics that eat fruit or the pollen of flowers. And there are still

DO BATS HAVE TEETH?

other bats that eat fish, or smaller bats, or blood.

Britain's biggest bat is the noctule, or great bat, but its extended wing span is only 33 to 36 centimetres and its length 13 centimetres. This bat lives in wooded districts and feeds on large insects.

The fruit-eating bats of the tropics alight on branches bearing fruit. They have broad, flat grinding teeth to crush the juices from the fruit. Pollen-eating bats have long tongues which enable them to reach into the flowers.

The vampire bat feeds only on blood. It gets the blood from horses, cattle, dogs, chickens, and people. With its two sharp upper incisors (the front teeth) it makes a shallow hole in the skin of its victim. It then laps the blood that comes from the wound.

Bats may have from 20 to 38 teeth. A curious thing is that there is no bat known to have 22 teeth. Some of the insect-eating bats have as many as 38 teeth! So you see that teeth are quite important to a bat.

Did you know that bats have been on earth for so long that they are one of the oldest established orders of animals? Fossil remains of bats have been found that are about 60,000,000 years old! The earliest known picture of a bat is in a tomb in Egypt. It was made about 4,000 years ago.

Chapter 3

Our Body and What Happens To It

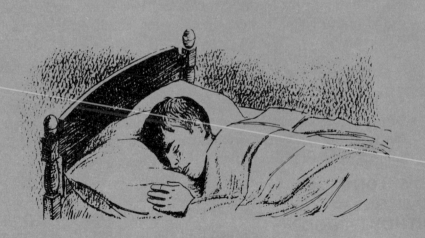

About 60 per cent of the human body is water! If you could squeeze out a human being like a lemon, you would obtain about 50 litres of water.

WHY DOES THE BODY NEED WATER?

This water, which is not like ordinary water because of the substances it contains, is necessary to the life of the body. About a gallon of it is in the blood vessels and is kept circulating by the heart. This blood water bathes all the cells of the body in a constant stream. The water also acts as a conductor of heat through the body.

Even if you drink no water during the day, you take in about a litre of water from the solid foods you eat. So when you eat fruit, vegetables, bread, and meat, you are getting water because they are from 30 to 90 per cent water. In addition, the average person takes in about two litres of water as fluids.

In the course of a day, about ten quarts of water pass back and forth inside the body between the various organs. For example, when you chew something and swallow it, you suck some saliva from the salivary glands and swallow it. In the next few moments, this water is replaced in the glands by water from the blood vessels. The swallowed water later goes from the stomach and intestine to the blood.

The amount of water in the blood always remains the same. Even though you may feel "dried out" after exercising on a hot day, the blood vessels contain the same amount of water. And no matter how much water you drink, it remains the same.

What happens to the extra water? It is stored away in various parts of the body. These include the intestine, the liver, the muscles, and the kidneys.

Most of us feel upset if we skip just one meal, and if we tried to go without food for 12 hours we would really be uncomfortable. But there are some people who seem able to "fast" for very long periods.

HOW LONG CAN MAN GO WITHOUT FOOD?

Various records are claimed for long fasts, but in most cases there is no medical proof and so the records are doubtful. One South African woman claimed that she lived for 102 days on nothing but water and soda water.

There are great differences among living things in the ability to survive without food. For example, a tick, which lives on animals, may

HUMMINGBIRD

TICK

SHREW

survive a whole year. Warm-blooded animals use up their stores of food in the body more quickly.

In fact, the smaller and more active the animal, the more quickly it uses up its reserves. A small bird starves to death in about five days, a dog in about twenty. In general, we can say that a warm-blooded creature will die when it has lost about half its normal weight.

This matter of weight is important. Man and other creatures live in a state of "metabolic equilibrium", which means maintaining the body weight once a certain point has been reached. This regulation of body weight is done by thirst, hunger, and appetite.

When your blood lacks nutritional materials, this registers in the hunger centre of the brain and you feel "hungry". The body is crying out for any kind of fuel (food). And it is our appetite that sees to it that we choose a mixed diet, which is the kind the body needs.

We might say that what the body does with food is "digest" it. But what exactly does this mean?

Our digestive system has two basic jobs to do with the food we take

WHAT DOES THE BODY DO WITH FOOD?

in. The first job is to break down large food molecules so that they can be carried through the body. It is impossible for large molecules to pass through the walls of the cells and tissues. Starch must be broken down to sugar, oil to soaps, and protein to amino acids before they can pass through the cell walls.

The second job of the digestive system is to transform the "foreign" molecules of food into human molecules. Don't forget that we take in food molecules of all kinds: milk, meat, coffee, potato, fish, and so on.

241

While we can swallow a piece of chicken, we cannot replace any part of the body with chicken protein. The human body is made up of molecules of human protein, and they are usually arranged in a special kind of way. So the body must break down the molecules of butter, flour, fish, fruits, and so on, into their elements. Then human proteins, fats, and starches must be built up from them.

The process of digestion is quite complicated. It begins in the mouth with the saliva, which helps break down starches. It then continues in the stomach, where most of the process of digestion takes place. Here, juices from the stomach wall are mixed with the food.

The food, now in liquid form, then goes into the small intestine. The breakdown of proteins is completed here; fats are split into their finer parts, and starch digestion is also completed here.

As the digested material passes over the surface of the small intestine, it is absorbed into the blood and lymph. In this way, nourishment reaches all the cells of the body.

In order for the body to carry on its functions, it needs energy. This energy is obtained through the process of combustion. The fuel for the combustion is the food we take in.

WHY IS THE BODY WARM? The result of this combustion in the body is not, of course, a fire or big heat. It is a mild, exactly regulated warmth. There are substances in the body whose job it is to combine oxygen with the fuel in an orderly, regulated way.

The body maintains an average temperature of 98·6 degrees Fahrenheit (37 degrees Centigrade) and this temperature is always maintained. This is done by a centre in the brain, known as the temperature centre, which really consists of three centres: a control centre which regulates the temperature of the blood; one that raises the temperature of the blood when it drops; a third that cools the blood when the temperature is too high.

What happens if the blood temperature drops? Part of the nervous system is stimulated into action. Certain glands send out enzymes to increase oxidation in the muscles and liver, and the internal temperature rises. Also, the blood vessels of the skin contract, so that less heat is lost by radiation. Even the tiny glands found on the surface of the skin help by sending out a fatty substance that prevents body heat from escaping.

Shivering is automatically activated by the temperature of the blood dropping too low. The heating centre of the brain makes you shiver in order to produce heat!

If the temperature of the blood rises, the cooling centre goes to work. It dilates (opens up) the blood vessels of the skin so that the excessive heat can be eliminated by radiation, and perspiration can evaporate more easily. Perspiration is a quick method of cooling off for the body. When a liquid evaporates it takes heat from wherever it is located.

Every living creature must breathe in some way. All animal life breathes by taking in oxygen. Man gets his oxygen by taking air into the lungs.

It seems a simple thing for us to breathe. We do not even think about it as we do it. But it involves quite a

HOW DO WE BREATHE?

complicated process. When a person breathes in, air passes into the body through a series of tubes called "the upper respiratory tract". This starts with the nose. Here, particles which could be harmful to the lungs are stopped or strained out. The nose also warms the air.

From the nose the air turns down through the "pharynx", or throat. From here, the air goes through two smaller tubes called "bronchi", one of which enters each lung. The lungs are large, soft organs. Around the entire lung is a thin covering called "the pleura".

The lung tissue is like a fine sponge in some ways. But in the lung there are spaces, or air sacs, and it is here that air is received from the bronchi, the proper gases are used, and unwanted gases are forced out. These air spaces are called "alveoli".

The air we take in contains oxygen, nitrogen, carbon dioxide, and water vapour. These same gases are present in the blood but in different amounts. When a fresh breath is drawn in, there is more oxygen in the alveoli than in the blood. So the oxygen passes through the very thin walls of the blood vessels (capillaries) and into the blood. Carbon dioxide goes from the blood into the air sacs of the lung and is exhaled.

While there is much more to the process of breathing, of course, this is the most vital part of it—the exchange of gases that enables all the cells to obtain oxygen and to get rid of carbon dioxide.

The colour of a human being's skin depends on three "pigments", or colour materials, found in the body. The first of these is called "melanin", which is a brown substance. The second is called "carotene", which is a

WHAT CAUSES DIFFERENT SKIN COLOURS?

yellow substance. And the third is called "haemoglobin", which is the red pigment of blood.

The differences in skin colour found in the races of the world depend almost entirely on the amount of melanin found in the skin. We know that sunlight causes the skin tissues to produce more melanin, so people who live in hot climates have darker skin.

If we go back to earliest times, we find that there were three chief groups of people developing at the same time. One was the Mongolian branch, which tended to have yellow to brown colouring. The second was the Negroid branch, which had dark to black colouring. And the third was the Caucasian branch, which had white to dark colouring.

In the course of centuries, these strains often became mixed together. This was less true of the Negroid branch, which was isolated until recently.

Despite this mixing up, it used to be believed that there were five clearly separated races of mankind: Caucasian (white), Mongolian (yellow), Malayan (brown), Negro (black), and American (red). Today, scientists do not believe the human race can be divided into five separate colours. There are too many ranges of colour, even in the same stock of people!

The white race, for instance, is a mixture of three principal stocks: Mediterranean, which has a dark complexion, Nordic, which has a blond complexion, and Alpine, which has a medium dark complexion!

An albino is a person without any colour, or pigmentation. All races have a certain amount of pigmentation, though some among the white race (especially the Scandinavian) have very little.

WHAT IS AN ALBINO? What causes colour, or pigmentation, in people? It is produced by certain substances in the body acting on each other. The substances are colour bases, or chromogens, and certain enzymes. When the enzymes act on the colour bases, pigmentation is produced.

If an individual happens to lack either of these substances in his body, there is no pigmentation and he is what we call an "albino". The word comes from the Latin *albus,* meaning "white".

A person who is an albino has pink eyes, and this is because of the red of the blood circulating in the retina of the eye. An albino's eyes are very sensitive to light. So such a person keeps the eyelids partly closed and is constantly blinking.

The hair of an albino is white over his entire body. Even tissues inside the body, such as the brain and the spinal cord, are white.

By the way, albinism is found not only in man, but in plants and all kinds of animals as well. It is even found among birds, and there is no race of man that may not have albinos.

It is believed that albinism may be inherited, so people who are albinos themselves may pass on the characteristics to their children.

Probably the albinos we are all most familiar with are white mice, rats, and rabbits. But there are people who have seen albino squirrels and even albino giraffes!

Human beings often expose their bodies to the sun to get a "tan". Very few people realize that sunlight has many important effects on the skin.

HOW DOES THE BODY TAN?

The most obvious is to produce redness or sunburn. This is caused by ultraviolet light. It transforms "histidin", a substance contained in the skin, into a substance that opens up (dilates) the blood vessels. And this is what causes the skin to become red.

There is another substance in the skin called "tyrosin". Ultraviolet light transforms this into the brown pigment called "melanin". This melanin is then deposited in the outer layers of the skin to protect it against further action of the light rays and we call this effect "tanning".

The sunlight also has a positive health effect. It destroys fungi and bacteria that may have settled on the skin. Sunlight also produces a substance in the skin which contracts the blood vessels. This results in raising the blood pressure.

Certain cells in the body which fight infection are stimulated to greater activity by the action of sunlight. Even the muscles of the body are "toned up" by the action of sunlight. And the nervous system seems to be stimulated. Also, the body obtains Vitamin D because ultraviolet light performs a chemical change that produces it in the skin.

If sunlight has all these good effects, shouldn't a person get as much of it as possible? The answer is that if sunlight acts like a medicine on the body, one should be careful about how much medicine to take. If you are out to get a tan, you should do it gradually; a few minutes the first day, five more minutes the next day, and so on. Too much exposure to the sun may actually injure the skin and the body.

Did you know that you have seen cells many times? When a section of an orange is broken open, the whole fibres that we see are cells. If the cell walls are broken, the juices will run out.

WHAT ARE CELLS?

According to scientists, the cell is the building block that makes up all living things. Everything that is alive is made up of one or more cells. Cells are also the units in which all life activities take place. Each cell in a plant or animal lives its own life and at the same time makes it possible for the living thing as a whole to carry on its life activities.

Living cells, both plant and animal, consists of a cell wall, a mass of jelly-like colourless material called "protoplasm", and a kernel-like part of the protoplasm called "the nucleus". It is the protoplasm which is the living matter.

In fact, this protoplasm is by far the most complicated chemical substance in existence. It carries on all the processes necessary for life. It takes in food and oxygen, changes some of the food into living matter, gives off waste, repairs its worn-out parts, and reproduces itself.

Each cell needs food and oxygen. To do work it must have energy. To carry the necessary supplies to every one of their cells, the higher forms of living things have developed a circulatory system. This circulates food and oxygen to the cells and removes waste products.

BLOOD CELLS

NERVE CELLS

MUSCLE CELLS

The cell is the building block that makes up living things. Everything that is alive is made of one or more cells. The simplest plants and animals consist of only one cell. Cells in more complicated living things work together. They are organized in groups, each of which has some special work to

WHAT DOES A CELL DO?

do for the plant or animal.

A tissue is a group of cells of a particular kind that does one particular type of work. For example, there is bone tissue, muscle tissue, or bark tissue. When tissues co-operate to perform a special task, such a group of tissues is called an "organ". An example of this is the human hand, which is composed of bone, muscle, nerve, and other tissues.

In the human body there are five important types of cells. Epithelial cells make up the skin and the glands, and line the blood vessels. Muscle cells make up the three kinds of muscles. Nerve cells make up the brain, spinal cord, and nerves. Blood cells are found in the blood and lymph. Connective tissue cells make up the framework tissue of the body.

The circulatory system, in higher forms of living, carries food and oxygen to every cell and removes waste products, like carbon dioxide. The individual cells combine the food and oxygen slowly, thus obtaining the heat and energy necessary for their life and work. It is because of this energy that muscles can contract, nerves can conduct messages, and the brain can think.

247

Every time we examine an organ of the human body, its structure and the way it works almost seems like a miracle to us. The liver is no exception. It is the largest gland of the body and, next to the brain, the heaviest

WHAT DOES THE LIVER DO?

organ. The average human liver weighs about one kilogram.

The liver has to be so large because of the work it does. It not only manufactures digestive juices, it is also a filter in which all the food received from the intestine (except fat) goes through a chemical process. It is like a blood-filled sponge which absorbs the food digested in the intestine.

What happens to food in the liver is that it is "reconstructed". The foreign protein is rebuilt to form human protein.

The liver also "detoxifies" food. When the body takes in nicotine and caffeine, the liver transforms these "poisons" into harmless compounds. Liver cells also destroy bacilli that may enter the body.

Because the liver is located between the intestine and the heart, it acts as a kind of dam for the liquids we take in. If you drink a large amount of liquid, the liver swells up soon after.

The liver cells manufacture the digestive fluid known as bile. (It is sometimes called "gall".) One of the things bile does is emulsify fat. It divides the large fats drops contained in digested foods into very fine droplets and thus makes it possible for the body to absorb fat.

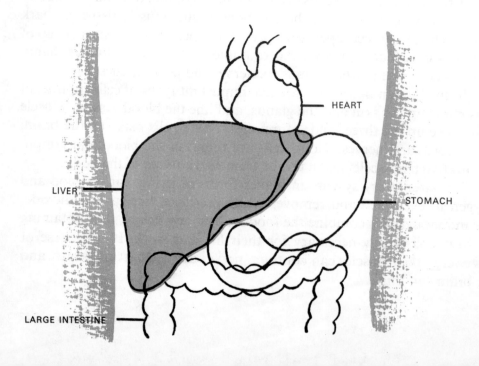

HEART

LIVER

STOMACH

LARGE INTESTINE

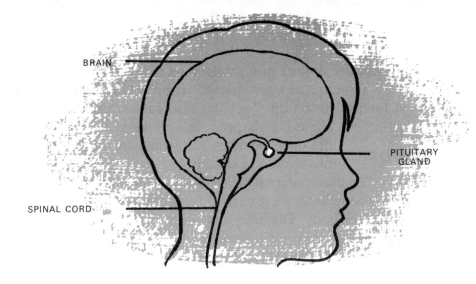

BRAIN

PITUITARY GLAND

SPINAL CORD

The pituitary gland is part of the endocrine system of the body, so let us start with that. The endocrine system consists of glands located in various parts of the body. These glands produce active chemical substances called "hormones".

WHAT IS THE PITUITARY GLAND?

These glands send their secretions directly into the blood stream to be distributed throughout the body. The endocrine system as a whole is involved with "regulating" many things that happen in the body. And the pituitary gland, which is part of this system, controls many of the functions of the body. In fact, it is the most important part of the body in regulating growth, the production of milk, and in controlling all other endocrine glands.

A truly amazing thing about this vital gland is that it is about the size of a pea and weighs about the same! It is joined to the undersurface of the brain and is protected by a bony structure.

Even though the pituitary is such a small gland, it is divided into two distinct parts called "lobes"—the anterior lobe and the posterior lobe. And into the posterior lobe, which is the smaller of the two, go more than 50,000 nerve fibres connecting it with various parts of the body!

The pituitary gland controls growth in children by acting on another gland, the thyroid. The pituitary also controls the sexual development of a person. And it regulates the metabolism of the body, which has to do with the transforming of food into various forms of energy. It is also involved with certain muscles, the kidneys, and other organs.

Tumours that may grow on this gland can make it overactive or underactive. And one result of this activity can be to make people grow to giants or develop so poorly that they will be dwarfs.

In the body there are organs that produce secretions. These organs are called "glands". Usually, the word "gland" is applied to endocrine glands, or glands of internal secretion. They are also called "ductless glands".

WHAT IS THE PINEAL GLAND?

These glands produce secretions which do not go into ducts or tubes, but which are absorbed directly into the blood stream.

The name for these internal secretions is "hormones". Hormones are chemical messengers that are carried by the blood stream and which affect all parts of the body. The body has many glands that produce these internal secretions, and the principal ones are the thyroid, the parathyroids, the thymus, the pineal, the pituitary, the adrenals, the sex glands, and parts of the pancreas.

So we see that the pineal gland is one of the endocrine glands and it is considered part of the endocrine system. Yet we do not know what hormone the pineal gland secretes. In fact, it is a rather mysterious little organ.

The pineal gland is about the size of a small pill and is located in the central part of the brain, towards the top of the head. Because of this location, physicians in ancient times thought the pineal gland was responsible for our thinking. Some writers believed that the pineal gland was the remnant of a "third eye" that man may have once had, similar to that found in reptiles.

Today we believe that this gland either produces some internal secretion or affects other endocrine glands in the work they do. For example, it is quite close to the pituitary gland and possibly has some effect on that gland.

The kidneys are two, flat, bean-shaped, solid organs that are among the most important in our body. They lie on each side of the spine near the waistline. They are about ten centimetres long.

HOW DO OUR KIDNEYS FUNCTION?

The kidneys help the body by removing unwanted substances. It is just as important for the body to be able to get rid of what it does not need and cannot use as it is for it to take in what it needs. But kidneys at the same time see that other materials are kept in the body. They also regulate the amount of water and other substances in the blood.

In the outer part of each kidney, capillaries form tiny loops that make up a ball-like shape covered by a delicate membrane. In each kidney there are about 1,500,000 of these tiny balls, called "glomeruli". More blood flows through the kidneys every minute than through any other organ. The glomeruli allow some of the fluid of the blood which carries the finest dissolved materials to pass through the membranes.

The fluid that passes through is called "urine". It is collected within a cuplike wall which covers each glomerulus. A very delicate tube, called a "tubule", drains the urine from the cups.

As the urine flows through the tiny tubules, the lining cells are busy exchanging materials between the blood and urine. Substances that the body needs are taken back into the blood. Much of the water in the tubules also returns to the blood. In this way the kidneys help to keep the body properly moist. The kidney tubules also help regulate the acid level in the blood.

All the small tubules collect in the inner part of each kidney and open into a delicate sac, the pelvis of the kidney. The urine then goes down two tubes, called "ureters", that connect the kidneys to the bladder.

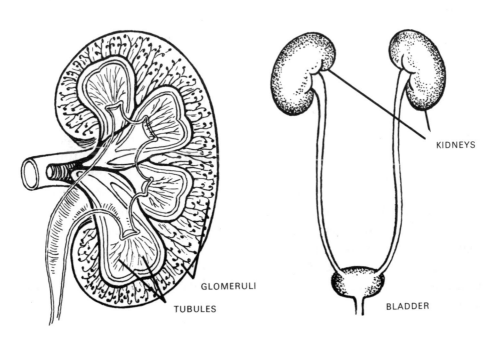

GLOMERULI

TUBULES

KIDNEYS

BLADDER

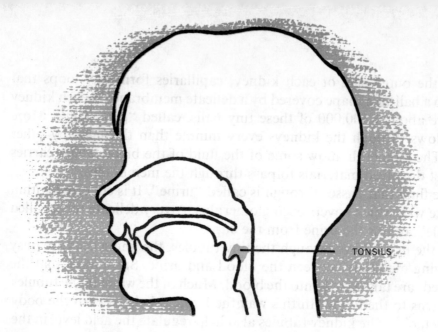

TONSILS

Most people think we just have two tonsils, located on either side of the throat just behind the tongue. But this isn't true.

There are several pairs of tonsils of different sizes. Tonsils are small bundles of a special kind of tissue called "lymphoid".

WHAT DO OUR TONSILS DO? Because of their location in the throat, they have a special job. They are the first line of defence against infections entering through the nose and mouth.

The largest pair near the palate are "the palatine" tonsils. High in the back of the throat are some smaller ones. These are called "the adenoids". Other small tonsils are found just below the surface in the back of the tongue, and there are still others in the back of the pharynx.

The tonsils are covered by the same smooth membrane that lines the mouth. In the tonsils, this membrane dips down to form deep, thin pockets called "crypts". The crypts trap germs and other harmful material from the mouth. The white blood cells surround the germs and help to destroy them. So fighting infection is the normal work of the tonsils.

Sometimes germs become active inside the tissue of the tonsils, and this may cause inflammation of the whole tonsil. This inflammation is called "tonsillitis". One or usually both palatine tonsils become enlarged, red, and sore. The crypts are swollen and sometimes discharge thick pus. This is acute tonsillitis. It is an infection that happens suddenly and usually goes away in four or five days.

Acute tonsillitis develops more often in childhood than in infancy or adulthood. It also happens more often during the winter months, when colds are common.

252

Man has two sets of teeth: a first (primary), or baby set, and a second, or permanent, set. In a full set of teeth there are four types, and each type has a special job.

HOW MANY SETS OF TEETH DO WE GROW?

The "incisors", in the centre of the mouth, cut food. The "cuspids", on either side of the incisors, tear food. The "bicuspids", just behind the cuspids, tear and crush food. The "molars", in the back of the mouth, grind food.

There are 20 teeth in the first set, 10 in each jaw. They begin to form about 30 weeks before birth. In most children the first teeth to appear are the lower incisors. They usually appear when a child is about six months old. Between the sixth and thirtieth month, the rest of the primary teeth appear. The primary teeth in each jaw are the four incisors, two cuspids, and four molars.

Of the 32 teeth in the permanent set, 28 usually erupt between the sixth and fourteenth years. The other four, the third molars, or wisdom teeth, erupt between the seventeenth and twenty-first years.

The permanent teeth are four incisors, two cuspids, four bicuspids, and six molars in each jaw. The twelve permanent molars do not replace the primary teeth. As the jaws become longer, they grow behind the primary teeth. The bicuspids in the permanent set replace the molars in the first set.

The first molars, which are often called the six-year molars, usually are the first to erupt. They are the largest and among the most important teeth. Their position in the jaw helps determine the shape of the lower part of the face and the position of the other permanent teeth. They come in right behind the primary molars and often are mistakenly thought of as primary teeth.

The human bone is so strong it's a wonder it ever does break! Bone can carry a load 30 times greater than brick can. The strongest bone in the body, the shin bone, can support a load of 1,600 kilograms.

HOW DOES A BROKEN BONE HEAL?

Yet, as we all know, bone sometimes breaks as a result of violence. Each type of break has a name, depending on how the bone has been broken. If a bone is just cracked with part of the shaft broken and the remainder bent, it is called an "infraction". If there is a complete break it is called a "simple fracture". If the bone is broken into more than two pieces, it is a "comminute fracture". And if the pieces pierce the muscle and the skin, it is a "compound fracture".

Mending a broken bone is somewhat like mending a broken saucer. The fragments have to be brought into as close alignment as possible. But the big difference is that the doctor does not have to apply any glue. This is produced by connective tissue cells of the bone itself.

Bone tissue has an amazing ability to rebuild itself. When bone is broken, bone and soft tissues around the break are torn and injured. Some of the injured tissue dies. The whole area containing the bone ends and the soft tissue is bound together by clotted blood and lymph.

Just a few hours after the break, young connective tissue cells begin to appear in this clot as the first step in repairing the fracture. These cells multiply quickly and become filled with calcium. Within 72 to 96 hours after the break, this mass of cells forms a tissue which unites the ends of the bones!

More calcium is deposited in this newly formed tissue. And this calcium eventually helps form hard bone that develops into normal bone over a period of months.

A plaster cast is usually applied to the broken limb in order to immobilize the bone and keep the broken edges in perfect alignment.

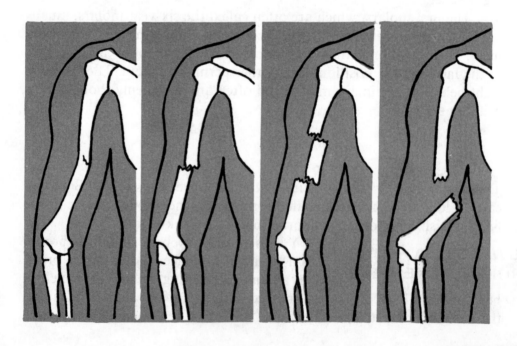

254

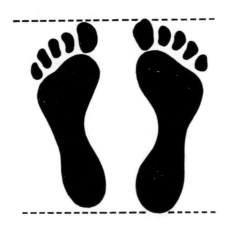

You probably noticed that when you buy shoes and the man measures your feet, one foot is larger than the other. Since one foot does not do any more work than the other, why should this be so?

WHY IS ONE OF OUR FEET BIGGER THAN THE OTHER?

It is related to the fact that our body is "asymmetrical", that is, it does not consist of two identical halves, right and left. You can see this for yourself in many ways. If you look at your face in the mirror, you will notice that the right half of your face is more developed than the left. The right cheek is more prominent, and the mouth, eye, and ear are moulded with greater precision.

The same applies to the rest of our body. The legs are not equal in strength and dexterity. The heart is on the left side and the liver on the right, so that internally the body is not exactly balanced. The result is that our skeleton develops in a slightly unbalanced way.

Now this slight difference can have a tremendous effect on how we do things. The uneven structure of the body causes us to walk unevenly. The result is that when we cannot see, as in a snowstorm, a fog, or when blindfold, we will walk in a circle. The same is true of animals, whose body structure is also uneven. And if anyone were to drive a car blindfold, he would end up driving in a circle, too!

When we come to the question of right-handed and left-handed people, we run into something curious. Ninety-six per cent of all people are right-handed. But this is not due to asymmetry of the body, it is due to asymmetry of the brain. The left half of the brain controls the right side of the body and vice versa. Since the left half of the brain predominates over the right half, this makes the right half of our body more skilled and makes most of us right-handed!

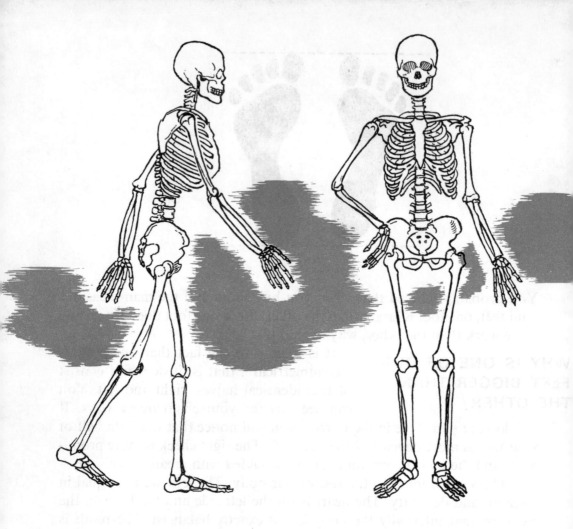

There are two main jobs that the skeleton does—it supports the body, and it protects delicate organs.

The skeleton is the frame that holds man erect. It is made mostly of bones. A baby is born with as many as 270 small, rather soft bones in his framework. A fully grown person usually has 206, because some bones become fused, or grow together.

WHY DO WE HAVE A SKELETON?

Bones fit together at joints and are held fast by ligaments, which are like tough cords or straps. Some joints can be moved freely. For example, when you run, you move your legs at the hip and knee joints. When you throw a ball, you move your arm at the shoulder and elbow joints.

Some joints cannot be moved at all. At the base of the spine the bones are fused, forming one bony plate that fits into another. Neither moves. The joints in your skull are solid, too, except for those in the jaw.

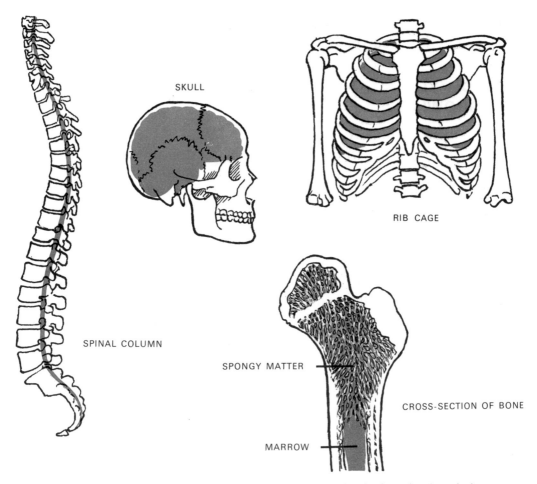

SKULL

RIB CAGE

SPINAL COLUMN

SPONGY MATTER

CROSS-SECTION OF BONE

MARROW

The protection that the skeleton provides includes the hard, bony cap of the skull. This protects the brain. The rib cage protects the heart and lungs. And the backbone, or hollow spinal column, protects the spinal cord, the body's trunk line of nerve cables. The backbone is actually a string of small bones.

It is hard for us to think of bone as living tissue, but it is. It grows when a person is young. For example, the thigh bone may triple in length between the time a person is born and the time he is fully grown.

Bones grow in length and thickness as calcium and other minerals are added to them. And since bone is living tissue, it must be fed. The outside of the bone is covered with a thin, tough skin. The skin holds many tiny blood vessels that carry food to the bone cells.

The middle of a bone is spongy and filled with marrow. Some of the marrow is a storehouse for fat, and other marrow makes red blood cells.

The average newborn infant is about fifty centimetres long. In 20 years, this little body more than triples in length. The average height of a man is 1.7 metres.

WHEN DO YOU STOP GROWING?

But man does not stop growing then. He actually continues to grow even after the age of twenty-five and reaches his maximum height at about the age of thirty-five or forty.

What happens after that? He does not just stop growing but begins to "shrink". The average person shrinks as much as ten millimetres every ten years after the age of forty. The reason for this shrinkage is the drying up of the cartilage in the joints and the spinal column.

Growth varies with the seasons. Children grow more rapidly during the summer than during the winter. Children of school age actually grow twice as fast during the summer months as during the winter! Better food, better modes of living, a whole group of circumstances are making the newer generations taller than the previous ones.

Our rate of growth is determined by four important sets of glands: the thyroid, the pituitary, the thymus, and the sex gland. When these glands operate normally and there is the proper balance between their functions, then growth is normal.

Did you know that every morning we are taller than we were the previous evening, but in the course of the day we begin to shrink?

Did you know that both hair and nails have the same origin? They both develop from the horny layer of our skin.

A hair develops when a part of this skin goes down into the lower layer and strikes roots there. Then it shoots upwards through the layers of the skin and comes out as a hair.

HOW DOES HAIR GROW?

In the roots of the hair there are four different layers of cells. They divide and multiply and push the shaft of the hair up through the skin. As they move farther away, the hair cells change into a horny material like that of our outer layer of skin.

On the outside surface of the hair, the cells become flattened out and lie on top of one another like shingles. Near the cells of the root there are big, round, fat cells from which come the materials to build the hair. By the way, the hair root is sort of "screwed" into the tissue. It cannot be torn out. So when you pull out a hair, you do not pull out the root.

Your hair grows at the rate of about 12 millimetres a month. And the surprising thing is, it does not grow at the same speed at all times. Hair grows very slowly at night, then speeds up in the morning, then slows up till late afternoon, then grows faster again!

The hair on a man's head lives about three to five years, and on a woman's it has a life of about seven years. Your eyelashes live only about six months! Altogether, an adult man has somewhere between 300,000 and 500,000 hairs in his skin.

WHY DO HUMANS HAVE HAIR?

Man is a mammal and all mammals have some hair. In the case of other creatures, we can see how having hair is useful. Its chief value is that it holds the heat of the body. Hair protects tropical animals from direct sunlight. A long mane can protect an animal's neck. The hair of a porcupine helps it fight its enemies. But why do human beings have hair?

To begin with, an infant at birth is covered with a fine down. When a child is in the process of becoming an adult, this hair coat is transformed into an adult hair coat. And the development of this adult hair coat is regulated by certain glands containing special hormones.

In the male, these hormones cause hair to grow on the body and face, and hold back the growth of hair on the head. In the female, the hormones act in just the opposite way. There is less hair on the body and face, more hair growing on the head.

These differences in the male and female hair growth are called "secondary sex characteristics". That is, they are another way of setting the two sexes apart. The man's beard not only indicates he is a man, but is supposed to give the male an appearance of power and dignity.

Charles Darwin, a famous nineteenth century naturalist, believed that as man developed, he needed the fine hairs of the body to help drain off perspiration and rain water. The hairs that appear in certain parts of the body, such as the eyebrows, lashes, and the hairs in the ears and nose, help guard these body cavities against dust and insects.

Medical science still does not really know what causes dandruff. Dandruff might be considered a disease of the scalp, which produces small flakes on the scalp and in the hair. The scientific name for this condition is *seborrheic dermatitis.*

WHAT CAUSES DANDRUFF?

There is a great deal of evidence that indicates an infection of some sort is the cause of this condition. But this has not yet been proved, and the agent that might be causing such an infection has not yet been found.

We know that where dandruff appears there is almost always an overactivity of certain glands which are connected to the roots of the hair. They are called "sebaceous glands", and they produce an oily material called "sebum". This oily substance makes the scales or flakes greasy. And this can make the scalp itchy.

Sometimes where there is a dandruff condition there are also more bacteria or fungi than are normally found on the scalp. But they do not seem to have much effect on the dandruff. They just complicate the condition. Of course, if the dandruff produces an intense itching and the person scratches, this may lead to an infection because of the germs that enter the broken area of the skin.

With mild cases of dandruff, washing the hair at least once or twice a week, and thorough massage, will help remove the excess oil and flakes. The preparations for dandruff "control" do help in many cases. But where there is a severe case, and where even washing the hair is irritating, the person should go to a doctor.

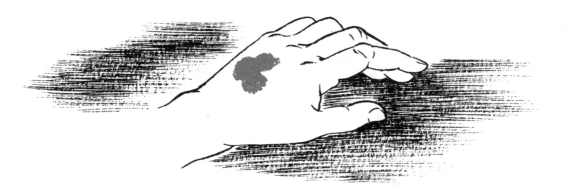

The technical name for a birthmark is "naevus" and it refers to a mole which is present at birth or develops shortly after birth.

WHAT ARE BIRTHMARKS?

Medical science still does not know what causes them and no way has been discovered to prevent their appearance. But one thing is known: they are definitely not caused by some frightening experience the mother had before the birth of the child.

Almost everyone has at least one mole somewhere on the body. They can appear on almost any part of the skin, including the scalp. They may vary greatly in appearance since this depends on the layer of skin in which they originate. Most moles develop before or right after birth, but in some cases they do not show up until the child is about fourteen or fifteen.

If left alone, birthmarks rarely cause any serious physical problems. The greatest danger associated with them is the possibility that, interfered with, they may be transformed into a cancerous growth. But this happens very rarely and most people who have moles do not worry about this.

There is a whole variety of other skin disorders that might be considered birthmarks. One of these is a reddish or purplish structure or stain that appears on the skin at birth or shortly after. Sometimes these are strawberry or raspberry in colour. They are actually an unusual formation of blood vessels, and usually disappear without treatment. But many doctors believe that strawberry or raspberry marks should be removed early in order to prevent leaving scars.

Medical authorities would even consider freckles to be "skin blemishes". They are caused by exposure to ultra-violet rays usually from the sun. People with blonde hair and fair skins are the ones who most often get freckles.

Nobody likes to have pimples and blackheads, and it would be nice if we could say this is what causes them and this is how to avoid having them. But the problem is not so simple.

WHY DO WE GET PIMPLES? Both pimples and blackheads start most often in the follicles of the hair. Certain glands, called "sebaceous glands", deposit an oily material there. When the hair follicle becomes plugged up and this deposit collects, it forms a blemish we call a blackhead.

Pimples are small, raised areas of the skin which often have collections of pus in them. But the cause of pimples is harder to explain than that of blackheads. This is because they may be due to many conditions, including an improper diet, a glandular imbalance, or tiny infections in the skin.

Pimples may also be a sign that a more serious skin disorder is developing, or they may even be a sign of some diseased condition in the body. This is why a person should consult a doctor when he has many pimples on the body. The doctor will try to determine what brought them on. If the pimples are caused by some internal condition, then medication applied to the pimples will not do much good and could even damage the skin permanently. Pimples should not be squeezed. This makes it possible for bacteria to get into the area.

Acne is a condition that occurs in many young people of adolescent age. Acne includes blackheads, pustules, cysts, and nodules, all of which appear together. While the cause of common acne varies from person to person, in some cases it is due to the eating of certain foods, and in others it may be due to the glands not working properly. A person with acne should consult a doctor for treatment.

Mumps is a contagious disease in which the salivary glands swell up. The parotid glands, which are located below and in front of the ears, are the chief ones affected.

WHAT CAUSES MUMPS? Mumps is caused when these glands are invaded by a virus. And it is spread almost entirely by direct contact with a person who is infected. The virus is present in the saliva and in the secretions of the nose.

Everybody knows what a person with the mumps looks like: there

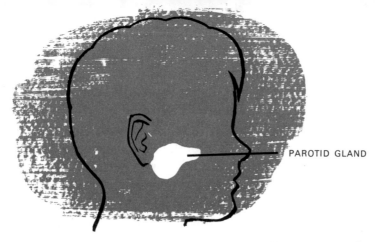

PAROTID GLAND

is a swelling about the ears and the jaws. The swelling appears first on one side and then the other. This is often the first recognizable symptom of the disease. There may also be a sudden rise in body temperature to about 40 degrees centigrade, and headache and vomiting.

Mumps is primarily a disease of children and young adults, though in rare cases it occurs in adults. Children usually get it between the ages of five and fifteen, and especially between the ages of seven and nine.

In almost all cases, after a person has had one attack of mumps he is immune to the disease.

Among children, mumps is considered to be a harmless disease if it is detected early and if there is proper treatment. And there is very little medical attention necessary except in severe or complicated cases. The patient is usually required to rest in bed as long as the glands are swollen and there is fever.

Because mumps spreads from one person to another, patients are usually quarantined to control the disease.

Meningitis is not a single specific disease. It is an inflammation (swelling and soreness) of the meninges. The meninges are the membranes (layers of tissue) that cover the brain and spinal cord.

WHAT IS MENINGITIS? Although many different germs can cause the infection, it is most often caused by the bacteria *meningococci*. Meningitis may follow head injuries and infections, or it may be a complication that comes with such diseases as tuberculosis, whooping cough, pneumonia, influenza, and scarlet fever.

In most cases, the bacteria enter the body through the throat. Some

263

people may carry the bacteria in their throats without becoming sick. These people, called "carriers", help to spread the infection.

Infants and children are more likely to be infected. Every five or ten years there may be an epidemic with many cases of illness.

The germs first grow in the blood, causing fever and chills and usually a red rash on the skin. Soon the germs settle in the meninges and cause the inflammation. When this happens there is pressure in the head which the patient feels as a severe headache. Next the neck becomes stiff. The patient holds his neck as still as possible; any attempt to bend it forward results in great pain.

The patient often becomes confused or even unconscious and vomits. He may have convulsions, twitchings, and jerkings of the body which he cannot control.

In fighting this condition, doctors usually use the "sulpha" drugs and antibiotics. They have cut the death rate of the disease to about 10 per cent. Without treatment, about three quarters of the patients would die.

Scarlet fever is a disease that attacks the mucous membranes of the nose and throat and usually produces a skin rash.

WHAT CAUSES SCARLET FEVER? The infection is caused by bacteria belonging to the *streptococcus* group. While the disease itself is no longer considered serious, it may be followed by other more serious illnesses. Two of the worst of these are rheumatic fever and nephritis (a kidney disease).

Scarlet fever occurs chiefly in the winter. Half the cases of scarlet fever occur among children between the ages of three and eight, and 90 per cent among persons under fifteen. One attack of scarlet fever usually makes a person immune to this disease.

Many people carry the germs of the disease in the nose or throat without being ill. They pass the bacteria to others by coughing or sneezing. Two to five days after a person has been exposed to it, the sickness begins with fever, chills, and vomiting. The throat becomes very sore. It is red, swollen, and covered with white patches. The tongue is also red and dotted with tiny swellings.

On the second day, small, bright red spots begin to spread over the body, arms, and thighs. This rash is caused by a toxic (poisonous) substance given off by the bacteria. This toxin acts on small blood vessels in the skin, and enlarges them.

After about seven or eight days, the rash fades, the fever lessens, and the throat clears. The skin on the soles of the feet and the palms of the hand forms thick scales which peel away. During the second week of the illness, much of the skin on the face and body also scales off.

About 10 to 12 per cent of all the people in Europe and America suffer from peptic ulcers at some time in their lives. What is an ulcer and what causes it?

WHAT CAUSES STOMACH ULCERS?

The gastric juice that is manufactured in the stomach contains hydrochloric acid, mucus, and an enzyme called "pepsin". Pepsin breaks down protein in the food into simpler substances.

Sometimes, however, the mixture of pepsin and acid acts on the wall of the digestic tract and the result is a peptic ulcer. These ulcers usually occur in the walls of the stomach.

People who develop such ulcers usually have a higher concentration of hydrochloric acid than is normal. There are other conditions that help in the formation of an ulcer, or hold back the healing process once one is formed. Tense, ambitious, hard-driving people are more likely to develop peptic ulcers than very calm people. Smoking may make an ulcer worse or delay healing of an ulcer. Coarse food also retards healing. But this disease may actually occur in any type of person at any age (though it is rare under the age of ten). Men get it four times as often as women.

How do you know if you have an ulcer? The pain tells you! The pain may occur from 30 to 60 minutes after eating. This pain rarely comes in the morning, but usually follows after lunch and dinner. And it may occur at night, after midnight.

The pain of a stomach ulcer is usually relieved by eating. When a patient has a peptic ulcer, his doctor puts him on a diet of soft foods with a lot of milk and cream, and orders him to rest and avoid fear and worry.

Rheumatic fever is a disease of the heart which usually affects only young people. Unfortunately, this disease may result in serious and permanent injury to the heart, so that a person who has had it may have to be careful.

WHAT IS RHEUMATIC FEVER?

But he should still be able to lead a fairly active life.

The cause of rheumatic fever seems to be an infection by certain bacteria. It is as if the person who gets this disease is allergic to these particular bacteria. And this may be a result of heredity.

The age of a person also seems to have a great deal to do with getting this disease. Those between the ages of six and nineteen get it most frequently. Those younger and older are not so likely to contract the disease.

Nearly all cases of rheumatic fever seem to come after an infection by the bacteria which are called *streptococcus*. So it is likely to happen after a "strep" throat, tonsillitis, nose infection, or scarlet fever. That is why it is important to treat such infections promptly under a doctor's care.

Often the symptoms of rheumatic fever are so slight that the person overlooks them completely. But a doctor may recognize the condition, and his treatment may help prevent it from becoming more serious. Sometimes when children suffer from what we call "growing pains", they may really be having a slight attack of rheumatic fever and should be examined by a doctor.

The pains associated with rheumatic fever usually occur in the joints, especially the knee and elbow. In acute cases, there may be very high fever. The joints swell up, become red, tender, and extremely painful. Sometimes, there are lumps beneath the skin, which is often a sign that it is a serious case. Treatment of this disease requires constant medical care.

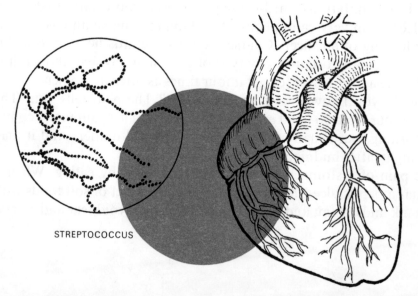

STREPTOCOCCUS

HEART

Rheumatism is actually a disease. It is an inflammation of the joints of the body. Unless the disease is checked, the condition becomes worse and eventually the person becomes disabled.

WHAT IS RHEUMATISM?

The disease begins by an inflammation of the membrane which lines a joint, such as a knee, elbow, or wrist. The cartilage is also attacked, and changes even take place in the bone itself. The bone loses certain minerals and becomes fibrous. There is a stiffening of the joint, and it may become unable to be used.

While there are many theories about what brings on rheumatism, none of them has yet been proved. One theory is that it comes from infection that attacks in three ways: by organisms (germs, bacteria) which reach the joint through the bloodstream; by toxins that come from some other infection; or because the joint is allergic to some organism.

Some doctors think that certain types of people are more likely to get rheumatism than others. These may be people between the ages of twenty and forty who are thin, not very vigorous, and who get overtired easily.

When the disease begins, a person usually has fever, pain, and swelling in one or more joints. The patient complains of being tired, loses weight, and has a feeling of numbness and tingling in the feet and arms.

One sign of this disease is warmth, pain, and swelling in the middle joints of the fingers. It may be painful just to move the fingers. In other cases, other parts of the body are attacked: the joints of the hands, toes, wrists, knees, elbows, shoulders, and hips. In fact, any joint in the body can be attacked by rheumatism.

Since we do not know the cause of this disease, and since it can be quite different in the way it develops in each person, there is no cure or single treatment that works. A doctor will treat each case differently.

There is always some alcohol in the body. The carbohydrates starch and sugar form alcohol when decomposed, so some alcohol enters the blood stream after every meal. There is always about a gram of alcohol in our body. But when we drink alcohol, this amount is increased.

WHAT IS INTOXICATION?

Alcohol is actually a narcotic, but a weak one. A narcotic is a substance that penetrates into the nerve cells and has a paralysing effect on them. But before the narcotic paralyses, it stimulates the nerve cells and excites them.

The first thing that happens when a person takes in alcohol is that it stimulates the mucous membranes of the mouth and the pharynx. This causes the salivary glands and the gastric glands to produce their secretion. This is why people drink some alcohol to stimulate the appetite before dinner.

Alcohol has an effect on the muscles of the body. It raises the percentage of the fuels that the muscles can transform into work-energy. So for a short period it seems to enable people to perform physical work better. But this is followed by a period of fatigue, so the total effect is not a good one.

Alcohol also seems to stimulate the brain. A person talks and acts with more vivacity. The skin gets redder, the blood pressure rises, and the heart beat and breathing are increased.

But actually, alcohol has a depressing effect on the brain. It affects the more important or higher functions such as thinking, observing, and paying attention. The controls a person has are relaxed and his judgment becomes poorer. How much alcohol a person has to take before this happens depends on many things. But this state, which we call intoxication, can be dangerous if the person still has to perform responsible actions such as driving or working.

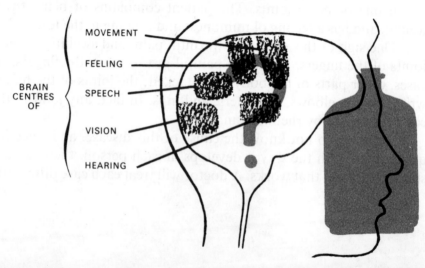

MOVEMENT

FEELING

BRAIN
CENTRES
OF

SPEECH

VISION

HEARING

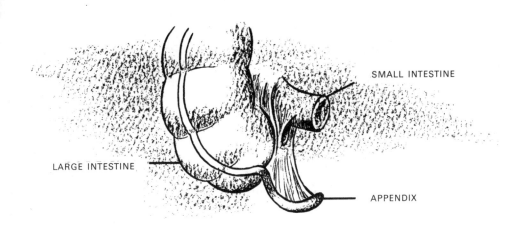

SMALL INTESTINE

LARGE INTESTINE

APPENDIX

The appendix seems to be a part of the body that we can manage without, and even if it is healthy it does not do anything important for us. The appendix is a hollow tube, about 8 to 15 centimetres long, closed at the

WHAT IS AN APPENDIX?

end. In other words, it is a "blind" tube that does not go anywhere. It is found at the beginning of the large intestine in the lower right part of the abdomen.

So it is a kind of off-shoot of the large intestine. The wall of the appendix has the same layers as the wall of the intestine. The inner layer gives off a sticky mucus. Beneath it is a layer of lymphoid tissue. It is in this tissue that trouble may sometimes occur.

This tissue may become swollen when there is infection in the body. The contents of the intestine enter the appendix but are not easily forced out. If the tissue is swollen the contents of the tube may remain and become hard. The veins of the appendix may be easily squeezed by the hardened material and swollen tissue. This cuts off the blood flow and may cause infection.

Since appendicitis, or inflammation of the appendix, occurs fairly commonly, many people are constantly on the watch for symptoms. The typical symptoms are pain, tenderness, and spasm in the right side of the abdomen. Sometimes the pain is first felt in the pit of the stomach and then is concentrated on the right side.

In children, the first symptoms of appendicitis may be crying, vomiting, and refusing to eat. Sometimes parents give their children a laxative when this happens, and this is a very dangerous thing to do. A doctor should always be consulted at once when such symptoms appear.

There is only one treatment when a person has acute appendicitis: immediate operation to remove the appendix. It is a simple procedure and can be done quite safely.

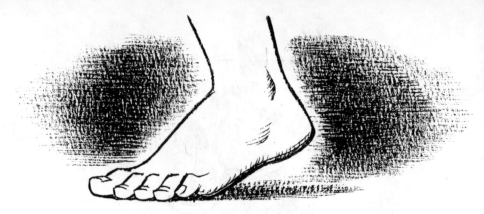

You do not have to be an athlete to have athlete's foot. This is basically a fungus infection of the foot, and most persons are liable to catch it to some degree, though some people are especially sensitive to the fungus. The name of this disease comes from the fact that it is often spread among athletes who share a common shower bath.

WHAT IS ATHLETE'S FOOT?

There are two chief types of athlete's foot. In the more common form, a crack appears in the skin, usually at the base of the fifth toe or between the fourth and fifth toes. There is also some loose dead skin clinging between the toes. When this loose skin is removed, the skin is red and shiny.

The second type of athlete's foot begins with a reddening of the skin between the toes, and it later becomes thick and begins to scale. Both these types may spread to cover part or all of the sole of the foot. And they may appear on both feet, though usually one foot is attacked more than the other.

There are several other diseases that can produce effects similar to athlete's foot. So a person who decides to treat himself with some medicine should be sure he really has athlete's foot. This is why it is safer to have a doctor examine your feet before you start your own treatment.

There are three types of fungi that cause athlete's foot. They are present on the skin at practically all times, so it is possible to get an infection at any time. But when the skin becomes warm and remains moist for long periods, the fungi get into the dead outer layer of the skin and begin to grow. The fungi produce certain chemicals in the skin while they grow, and if a person is not allergic or sensitive to these chemicals he may not be bothered by the fungi at all.

Some mild cases of athlete's foot require no treatment and disappear as soon as the weather becomes cooler. But in more serious cases, the feet should be kept dry, socks should be changed frequently, and certain lotions may be helpful.

Diphtheria is a serious disease. It is caused by bacteria, and illness starts a few days after the bacteria enter the body. The bacteria usually enter the body through the mouth and nose, and infect the throat first.

HOW IS DIPHTHERIA CONTROLLED?

Usually there is a sore throat, fever, and a feeling of being unwell. A grey or pale membrane appears over the tonsils and back of the throat. The infection may spread into the larynx (voice box) and block air passages there.

Diphtheria has serious effects on other parts of the body, too. They are caused by toxins, or poisons, given off by the organism. The heart and nerves may be seriously injured. Children, especially between the ages of two and five, are most likely to have diphtheria.

The cause of diphtheria is a tiny, rod-shaped bacillus (a form of bacteria). The bacillus was discovered in 1883. After it was discovered that this organism produced the toxin causing the disease, the next step was to prepare an antitoxin which could make the toxin harmless. This was done by a man called Emil von Behring in 1890. The antitoxin can prevent the serious poisonous effects of the disease although the bacteria and throat infection are still present.

Diphtheria is far less common now that it can be partly prevented. The toxin can be treated in a way that makes it harmless. When this harmless toxin (called "toxoid") is injected into a person, it causes antibodies to be formed which protect the body from the bacteria.

The amount of immunity to diphtheria that a child has is found by a test invented by Béla Schick in 1913. A small quantity of diphtheria toxin is put into the skin. If the child does not have enough antitoxin, a red spot appears there from four to seven days later. In this way, children who might otherwise get the disease can be treated to protect them from the bacteria.

DR BELA SCHICK

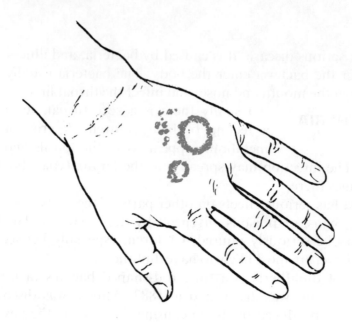

Ringworm is a very common disease of the skin. The medical name for it is "tinea", and it is caused by a fungus infection.

You usually see ringworm on the arms and legs. The most common

WHAT IS RINGWORM? form of it is one, or several, raised round sores on the skin. They seem to heal in the centre while the edges continue to grow outward. Sometimes the healed centre part becomes reinfected, and then a second "ring" develops and grows inside the original ring. In some cases of ringworm, the centre does not heal at all.

A ringworm sore starts as a small, slightly raised area with a reddish colour. Then it gets redder and there may be some blisters and a slight itching or burning sensation.

Another common type of ringworm is ringworm of the scalp. This is a very contagious form and children seem to catch it very easily.

It is very difficult to destroy the fungi that cause ringworm, so treatment of the patient usually consists of trying to prevent the infection from spreading, until it eventually ends.

Ringworm is a highly contagious disease, and it can be spread by animals as well as human beings. Objects that are handled by people with ringworm can infect other individuals.

The best way to treat it is to catch this disease in its first stages. Go to a doctor for treatment. He will see to it that it does not spread to other parts of the body and help you to get rid of it as quickly as possible.

Blood is necessary for the life of every part of the body. The first step in understanding this is to realize that the blood contains many different materials and cells. There is a fluid, or liquid, part of the blood which is

WHAT DOES BLOOD DO FOR THE BODY?

called "plasma". It contains many substances dissolved in it. Let's see what some of these are and what they do.

Carbohydrates such as sugars are in the blood to give the body energy. Fats are in the fluid for burning or storage. Many salts are also in the blood to meet the body's needs.

The blood plasma carries food from the stomach and intestine to the cells, which would starve without it. It also carries waste from the cells to the kidneys and intestine. The secretions of many glands are in the blood and are carried to various parts of the body.

The red cells in the blood, which give the blood its colour, contain a substance called "haemoglobin". The body has a great need for haemoglobin because it combines easily with gases such as oxygen and carbon dioxide. The red cells carry the oxygen in the arteries and capillaries to all cells of the body.

The white cells in the blood called "leucocytes" are very important to the body. They destroy bacteria. Other white cells, called "lymphocytes", are part of the body's process for fighting infections. Still other white blood cells, called "monocytes", take care of dead material and dirt that may get into the body.

In addition, the blood contains pieces of cells called "platelets" that help to form clots, so that when a blood vessel is cut you do not lose too much blood.

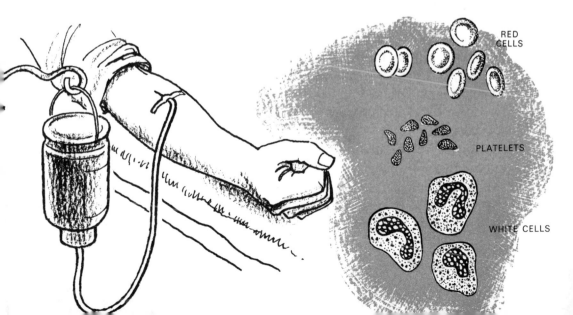

RED CELLS

PLATELETS

WHITE CELLS

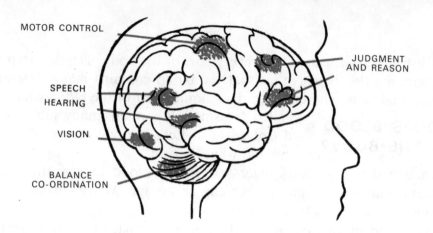

MOTOR CONTROL

SPEECH HEARING

VISION

BALANCE CO-ORDINATION

JUDGMENT AND REASON

A stroke is a form of injury to the brain. Another name for it is "apoplexy".

When a stroke occurs, the flow of blood to a part of the brain is suddenly cut off. As a result, all the structures connected with that part are injured.

WHAT IS A STROKE?

There are several things that can cause this failure of the blood to reach parts of the brain. A blood vessel may be ruptured and cause a haemorrhage. A clot may form within a blood vessel. This is called "thrombosis". There may be spasm of an artery. Or a blood vessel may become closed off because of a small particle, often a blood clot, floating in the blood stream. This is called an "embolus". An embolus is usually linked up with heart disease, but it may occur in other diseases too.

In terms of damage, it does not matter what causes the stroke. That part of the brain through which pass the nerves that control our voluntary motions, our sensations of pain, our temperature, touch, and vision may be damaged.

The most frequent cause of stroke is thrombosis. Strangely enough, a person can have this kind of a stroke after a period of inactivity. For example, a person might wake up in the morning to discover that an arm, or a leg, or even a whole side of the body is useless. Or he may find that he can hardly speak or speak not at all. People with this kind of stroke have a pretty good chance of recovery, but there is usually some permanent disability.

In treating a stroke, the doctor has to find out what caused it, so he needs a complete history of the illness of the person. People who become crippled in some way by a stroke can often be rehabilitated; that is, trained to regain the use of the function that was crippled. This includes use of muscles and the ability to speak again.

274

The human body has 639 muscles, each with its own name! If all the muscles are put together, they make up the flesh of the body.

Most muscles are fastened firmly to the bones of the skeleton. The

WHY DO MUSCLES ACHE AFTER EXERCISE?

skeleton forms the framework, and the muscles move the parts of the body. Without them a person could not live. Not only would it be impossible to eat, breathe, and talk, but the heart would stop because its beating is a muscular action.

All muscle is made up of long, thin cells called "muscle fibres". But muscles differ in what they do and how they do it. They also differ in shape, appearance, size, and in other ways.

When a muscle contracts, it produces an acid known as lactic acid. This acid is like a "poison". The effect of this lactic acid is to make you tired, by making muscles feel tired. If the lactic acid is removed from a tired muscle, it stops feeling tired and can go right to work again!

But, of course, lactic acid is not removed normally when you exercise or work. In addition, various toxins are produced when muscles are active. They are carried by the blood through the body and they cause tiredness—not only in the muscle, but in the entire body, especially the brain.

So feeling tired after muscular exercise is really the result of a kind of internal "poisoning" that goes on in the body. But the body needs the feeling of tiredness so that it will want to rest. Because, during rest, waste products are removed, the cells recuperate, nerve cells of the brain recharge their batteries, the joints of the body replace the supplies of lubricant they have used up, and so on. So while exercise is good for the body and the muscles, rest is just as important!

In an adult human body there are about 5.5 litres of blood. These litres form the most amazing transportation system imaginable.

HOW MUCH BLOOD IS IN OUR BODY?

The blood circulates through the body so that it reaches every one of the billions of cells that make up the body tissues. It brings food and oxygen to each cell, carries away waste products, carries hormones and other chemical substances, helps the body fight infection, and helps regulate body heat.

The blood is made up largely of a colourless liquid called "plasma", and it is the red corpuscles floating in this liquid that give blood its red colour.

It is when we consider how many of these blood cells there are in the ten pints of blood that our imagination is staggered. There are about 25 billion of them! In a single drop of blood there are some 300,000,000 red corpuscles. If the cells were joined together in a chain, keeping their actual size, the chain would go four times around the earth.

Even though the cells are tiny, they have a tremendous surface area. For instance, if you could weave them into a carpet, the total surface area of this carpet would be 4,090 square metres. Since at any one given moment one-quarter of the blood is to be found in the lungs, about 1,000 square metres of blood-cell surface are constantly being exposed to the air. Every second, 2 billion blood cells pass by the air chambers of the lungs!

Because the air in lowland regions is under greater pressure, it contains more oxygen than at high altitudes. So the higher up a person lives, the higher is the number of blood cells he has. A person living in the mountain regions of Switzerland may have 50 per cent more blood cells than one living in London.

High blood pressure involves a great many older people. It is believed that 15 to 20 per cent of all deaths in the United States in people over fifty years of age is due to high blood pressure!

WHAT IS HIGH BLOOD PRESSURE?

First of all, what is blood pressure? It is the amount of pressure exerted on the blood by the heart and the arteries. When the left ventricle of the heart contracts, it forces blood out into the arteries. The major arteries then have to expand to receive the blood. But the muscular lining of the arteries resists this pressure, so the blood is squeezed out into the smaller blood vessels of the body. So blood pressure is the amount of pressure the blood is under as a result of the pumping of the heart and the resistance of the walls of the arteries.

There is a way of measuring this, and a certain amount is considered normal for a person's age. But in some people this pressure becomes greater than normal, and it is then called "hypertension", or high blood pressure.

It can be caused by many things, such as nervous tension and disturbances of glands or the kidneys. Usually, it is difficult to know all the reasons. And in most cases a person can have it without any unpleasant symptoms. In some cases, the condition quickly becomes worse.

What is happening is that the smaller blood vessels of the circulatory system are resisting the flow of blood. Then certain symptoms may appear. There could be heart palpitations, headaches, dizziness, and a feeling of being tired.

Medicine has many ways of treating this condition, depending on the specific case. This ranges from rest, change of job, diet to lose weight, low salt diet, surgery, and so on.

Anaemia is a word used to describe many different conditions having to do with disorders of the blood. These conditions exist when the blood does not contain the normal number of red cells, or when the cells do not have the normal amount of haemoglobin.

WHAT IS ANAEMIA?

Anaemia can be caused by poor blood formation, the destruction of cells, or by too much loss of blood. And these conditions, in turn, may be caused by many different body disorders. So when a doctor treats "anaemia", he has to know exactly which type he's dealing with.

One kind of anaemia, for example, can be caused by an injury that results in great loss of blood. Other body fluids seep into the blood to make up the volume, the blood is diluted, and the result may be anaemia.

Another type of anaemia is caused by an increased destruction of red blood cells, which can be the result of several conditions in the body. In some cases it may be inherited, or it may come from a transfusion of blood of the improper type, severe burns, allergies, or leukaemia.

One kind of anaemia many of us know about is nutritional anaemia. The most common and least severe anaemia of this kind develops when there is not enough iron for the formation of red cells. Iron is necessary for the body to manufacture haemoglobin.

Many of the common foods we eat contain only small amounts of iron. Also, many people cannot afford foods that have a high iron content, such as meat, eggs, and leafy vegetables. So iron deficiency is not a rare condition.

The symptoms of this anaemia are generally a paleness, weakness, a tendency to tire easily, faintness, and difficulty in breathing. If the patient is able to get enough rest and a good diet, he is usually able to recover quite rapidly.

Our blood, as you know, is necessary to life. And there are many different substances and cells in the blood, each with a job to do. But sometimes something goes wrong with the balance of things in the blood.

WHAT IS LEUKAEMIA?

One such disorder of the blood is called "leukaemia". When a person has leukaemia, the white cells may increase as much as 50 or 60 times. This condition is very serious, because it is the result of a disorder in the blood-producing parts of the body.

Years ago, a person with leukaemia was considered to be hopeless. And while we still do not have a cure for it, a great deal of progress is being made, especially in helping such a person live longer and more comfortably.

There are several different kinds of leukaemia. Each form has a different symptom and has a different effect on the life expectancy of the person. That is why the treatment of a person with leukaemia varies in each case.

In general, leukaemia can be divided into two forms: acute or chronic. Acute leukaemia seems to come on suddenly and may progress very quickly. This type is seldom discovered until it has become well advanced. Acute leukaemia occurs in persons over 35 years of age.

Leukaemia also varies according to the particular type of white cell that is involved. Even though there are many kinds of leukaemia, the early symptoms may be quite alike. This is why it is important to have a diagnosis as quickly as possible. The diagnosis of leukaemia is made by examining the bone marrow and blood under the microscope.

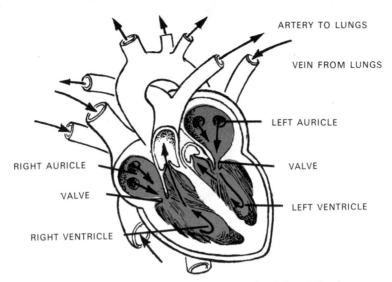

ARTERY TO LUNGS

VEIN FROM LUNGS

LEFT AURICLE

VALVE

RIGHT AURICLE

VALVE

LEFT VENTRICLE

RIGHT VENTRICLE

The adult human heart is about the size of a clenched fist. Yet it generates enough energy in 24 hours to lift 68,000 kilograms, or the weight of a locomotive, 30 centimetres off the ground. It pumps about 16,360 litres of blood in 24 hours.

HOW DOES THE HEART WORK?

This amazing organ, which only weighs 225 to 340 grams, is built like a double-storey house. Each part has a room upstairs, the right and left "auricles", and a room downstairs, the right and left "ventricles".

There are trap doors called "valves" between the auricle and ventricle on each side, but none between the two houses. There are also exits from the ventricles into arteries and entrances from veins into the auricles. All the doors in a healthy heart fit very snugly, because once blood is squeezed out of the heart, it must not flow back through the same door. The valves open and shut with each heartbeat.

Actually, the heart is two pumps, one on each side. The left side receives the oxygenated blood from the lungs and sends it through the body. The right side receives it back again with less oxygen and more carbon dioxide and sends it to the lungs.

The two upper rooms, the auricles, have thinner walls because they send the blood only a short distance to the lower rooms. The right ventricle has somewhat thicker walls, for it sends the blood to the lungs. The most important room in the heart is the left ventricle, with the thickest walls, for it sends the blood farthest.

The heart squeezes up and relaxes about 100,000 times each day. In a child it does this from 90 to 100 times a minute; in an adult, from 70 to 80 times a minute. When you make some special effort, such as running a race, the heart works about three and a half times as hard.

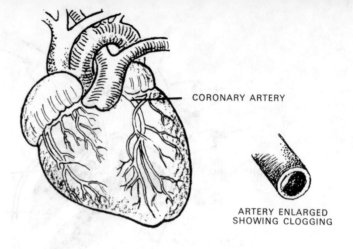

CORONARY ARTERY

ARTERY ENLARGED
SHOWING CLOGGING

What people call "heart attack" is one of the chief causes of death in the Western World. In three out of four cases, the victim is a man, and the age is usually between fifty and seventy years.

WHAT IS A HEART ATTACK?

A typical heart attack is often caused by "coronary thrombosis". In fact, many people simply call it a "coronary". This is because it starts with the coronary arteries, the two blood vessels that supply the heart with blood.

When one of these arteries become clogged, the blood supply of part of the heart is shut off. The tissue in this part of the heart begins at once to degenerate and die, just the same as if it had been wounded.

When one coronary artery becomes clogged, the smaller branches of the other artery take up the work over a period of time. After a while, most of the areas of the heart that have been cut off receive the blood they need.

If the second artery can carry on the work for both, the person lives. Fortunately, in most cases the second artery can do the job, providing the heart is spared from all strain during this period.

In many patients, a heart attack occurs after some unusual physical exertion, emotional upset, exposure to extreme cold, eating a heavy meal —or any situation where the heart is called upon to do a bigger job than usual. These things do not actually cause the heart attack, but there is some relationship. In many cases, however, an attack can occur while a person is at rest.

The symptoms of a heart attack usually include pain beneath the breastbone. But the pain may also first be felt in the arms, neck, or left shoulder. There is sweating and shortness of breath. The victim may become pale and be in a state of shock, and the pulse may become weak. A person should immediately call a doctor if such symptoms appear.

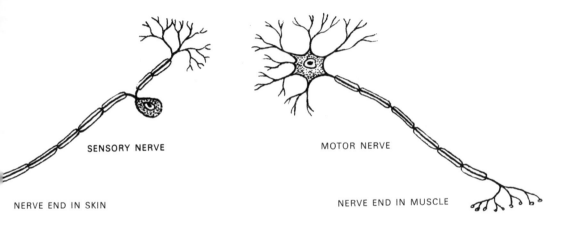

SENSORY NERVE

MOTOR NERVE

NERVE END IN SKIN

NERVE END IN MUSCLE

The cells whose job it is to keep our body informed of conditions in the outer world are the nerve cells.

In lower forms of life, nerve cells are located in the skin and they directly transmit messages to the deeper parts of the body. But in human beings and other complex organisms, most of the nerve cells are actually in the body, though they may pick up their "messages" in the skin by means of delicate "antennae".

WHAT ARE NERVES?

The purpose of the nerve cells is to transmit messages throughout the body, each message to the proper place. The nerve fibres along which these messages go are constructed like a cable, and are amazingly efficient.

Actually there are four chief types of nerve cells, or "nerves", or nerve units. These are the completely independent units of nerve cells in the body, each organized to do its special job. One type receives messages such as heat, cold, light, and pain from the outer world, and conducts them to the interior of the body. These might be called "the sensory units".

Another type might be called "the motor unit". It receives impulses from the sensory units and responds to them by sending a nerve current to various structures in the body, such as the muscles and the glands. The reaction that results is called a "reflex". A "heat message", for example, would make certain muscles react and pull a hand away from a hot surface.

A third type of nerve unit does a connecting job. It transmits messages over longer distances in the body. It connects motor cells in one part of the body with sensory cells in another part.

A fourth type of nerve unit has the job of carrying messages from the outer world, such as cold, heat, and pain, to the brain where we "translate" the message into feeling.

When you read, you look at certain symbols and are able to get some meaning from them. For example, a kind of "reading" is going on when you read symbols on a road sign, or when an engineer reads the markings on a blueprint, or when an Indian sees smoke signals!

HOW DO WE READ?

When we say "reading", we usually mean reading print or writing. But here, too, we must understand the symbols. The first thing we have to do in learning to read is to recognize the symbols or letters as being different from others. Then we must get the idea for which a word (or group of symbols) stands. But before we can understand fully, we must be able to relate the symbols or word to our own experience.

Over the years, children have been taught to read by various methods. The "spelling" method begins by teaching the child the names of the letters of the alphabet in order. Next he puts two letters together, then three letters, and then spells and pronounces syllables, and then these are joined into words, phrases, and sentences.

In the "phonetic" method, children learn the sounds of the letters then put the sounds together to make words. At first only short words are made, then longer ones. In still another method, the child memorizes the way a word looks. Other methods use both sounding out and remembering the way a word, phrase, or sentence looks.

But we can only learn to read when we are ready to begin learning. And for this we must be able to see words or symbols that are alike and different; remember the form of a word; remember ideas in the order in which they are given; bring to mind pictures of objects that the words describe; move eyes from left to right on a page—and many more things!

There are very few cases of people walking in their sleep. But while sleepwalking is a peculiar form of behaviour, there is nothing mysterious about it.

WHY DO PEOPLE WALK IN THEIR SLEEP?

To understand it, let us start with sleep itself. We need to sleep so that our tired organs and tissues of the body will rest and be restored. We still do not have an exact scientific explanation of how and why we sleep, but it is believed that there is a "sleep centre" in the brain which regulates the sleeping and waking of the body.

What regulates this sleep centre? The blood. The activity of our body all day releases certain substances into the blood. One of these is calcium. It passes into the blood and stimulates the sleep centre. And the sleep centre has been "sensitized" before by special substances so that it will react to the calcium.

When the sleep centre goes to work, it does two things. The first is it blocks off part of the brain so that we no longer have the will to do anything, and we no longer have consciousness. We might call this "brain sleep".

The second thing it does is block off certain nerves in the brain stem so that internal organs and our limbs fall asleep. Let us call this "body sleep". And normally these two reactions or kinds of sleep, are connected. But under certain conditions they may be separated! The brain may sleep while the body is awake. This might happen to a person whose nervous system does not react normally. So such people might get out of bed while their brain is asleep and walk about! The brain and body sleep have become disassociated, and they are sleep walkers.

Did you know that you really cry all day long? Every time you blink your eye you are "crying"! You see, there is a tear gland that is situated over the outer corner of each eye. Every time your eyelid closes, it creates a

WHY DO ONIONS MAKE YOU CRY?

suction which takes out some fluid from the tear gland. This fluid we call "tears".

Normally, this fluid has only one purpose. This is to irrigate the cornea of the eye and so prevent it from drying out. But suppose some irritating substance reaches the eye? The eye automatically blinks and tears appear to wash the eye and protect it against the irritant.

We are all familiar with the experience of having smoke get in our eyes. It makes us cry. Well, the onion sends out an irritating substance, too. The onion has an oil containing sulphur which not only gives it its sharp odour, but which irritates the eye. The eye reacts by blinking and by producing tears to wash away the irritant! It is as simple as that.

The onion is an interesting vegetable. It is a member of the lily family, and it is a native of Asia. The onion has been used as food for thousands of years, going back to the early history of man.

Onions belong to the genus Allium, and are, therefore, related to the milder leek and the very pungent garlic, both of which are cultivated extensively in Europe. Shallots have a rather milder flavour than garlic. Chives are smaller members of the same branch of this family.

The mildest and biggest onion popular in this country is the Spanish onion, which often weighs 450 grams or more.

TEAR GLAND

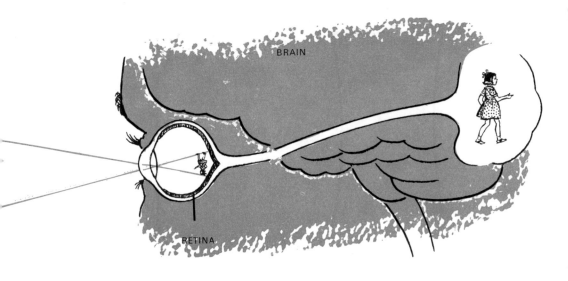

BRAIN

RETINA

Seeing, of course, is done by the eye. But our brain plays a very important part in the process we call seeing.

Mechanically, this is what happens. Light waves pass through the

HOW DOES THE BRAIN HELP US TO SEE?

pupil of the eye and form an image on the retina. The retina is a carpet-like screen of cells at the back of the eyeball.

Each of the retina's 130,000,000 cells is sensitive to light. When light strikes a cell a chemical change takes place. This starts an impulse in a nerve fibre, which travels through the optic nerve to the seeing portion of the brain.

But this is not all that happens. What the brain sees is very different from the pictures formed on the retina. For example, your eyes are seldom at rest. If you stand outdoors looking at the scene around you, your eyes stop for only a second at the grass, treetop, cloud, bird, or squirrel.

The brain does not see a series of quick snapshots. The seeing part of the brain records each picture and remembers it. It adds them together and gives them meaning, so that the whole picture is seen, not the parts. In a second, it draws upon the store of memories in the brain. A tree, a cloud, a squirrel—these have been seen before. It takes only a glance to recognize them.

So seeing includes the use of many parts of the eye, the optic nerve, and the parts of the brain that see and interpret the eye's messages. That's why a baby must learn to use his vision. Before long his visual mechanics work well. But his vision is still poor. Why? Because he understands little of what he sees. The brain is not yet playing its full part in seeing.

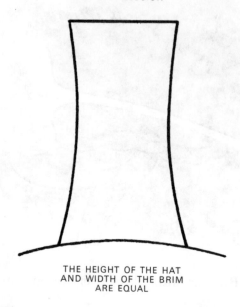

THE HEIGHT OF THE HAT
AND WIDTH OF THE BRIM
ARE EQUAL

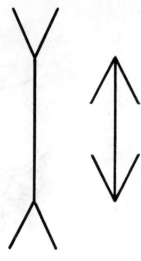

THESE TWO VERTICAL LINES
ARE OF EQUAL LENGTH

The simplest way to describe an optical illusion is that it is a "trick" that our eyes play on us. We seem to see something that isn't really so. Or we may be able to see the same object in two completely different ways.

WHAT IS AN OPTICAL ILLUSION? If our eyes are functioning properly, and they are instruments for seeing exactly what is before us, how can they play "tricks" on us? Here is what makes it possible. Vision is not a physical process. It is not like photography, for instance, which works mechanically. Vision is really a psychological experience, because it is not the eyes that see, but the brain!

The eyes are mechanical instruments for receiving impressions. But when those images reach the brain, a judgment takes place. The cells of the brain have to decide what they think this image is.

What helps the brain make that decision? One of the important things is the work that the eye muscles have to do in order to see a thing. In judging distances, angles, and the relationship of things in space, our eyes have to move back and forth. Our brain says that our eyes have travelled a certain distance because the brain has an idea of the amount of energy and the time it took for our eyes to move back and forth.

So now we have the possibility of one kind of optical illusion. Suppose there are two lines of equal length, but one is vertical and one is horizontal. The horizontal line will seem shorter to us because it is easier for the eyeballs to move from side to side than up and down. So the brain decides the horizontal line must be shorter!

286

When we look out across a field, how do we know one distant object is bigger than another, or that one is behind another? Why don't we see everything "flat", instead of in three dimensions, in proper relation to each other?

HOW DO WE SEE IN THREE DIMENSIONS?

The fact is that we "see" things not only with our eyes but with our minds as well. We see things in the light of experience, And unless our mind can use the cues it has learned to interpret what we see, we can become very confused.

For instance, experience has given us an idea about the size of things. A man in a boat some distance from shore looks much smaller than a man on shore. But you do not say one is a very large man and the other a very small man.

What are some of the other "cues" your mind uses? One of them is perspective. You know that when you look down the railway tracks they seem to come together. So you consider the width of the tracks and get an idea about distance. Experience tells you that near objects look sharply defined and distant objects seem hazy.

From experience you have also learned how to "read" shadows. They give you cues to the shape and relationship of objects. Near objects often cover up parts of things that are farther away.

Moving the head will help you decide whether a tree or pole is farther away. Close one eye and move your head. The object farther away will seem to move with you, while nearer objects go the other way.

The combined action of both eyes working together also gives you important cues. As objects move nearer to you and you try to keep them in focus, your eyes converge and there is a strain on the eye muscles. This strain becomes a cue to distance.

All sounds are caused by a vibrating object, that is, an object that is moving back and forth rapidly. These vibrations cause molecules in the air to move, and they make the molecules next to them move, and soon

HOW DO WE HEAR DIFFERENT SOUNDS?

there is a movement back and forth of the molecules in the air that produces what we call "sound waves".

But the vibrations differ from each other and they produce different kinds of sounds. There are three basic differences between one sound and another. The differences are in loudness, pitch, and tonal quality.

Loudness of a sound depends both on the distance of the vibrating object from your ear and on the distance the vibrating body moves in its to-and-fro motion. The greater this movement is, the louder the sound will be.

The highness or lowness of a sound is its pitch. This depends upon the speed of vibration (the frequency) of the sounding object. The tonal quality depends upon the number and strength of the "overtones" which are present in the sound. This happens when there are higher sounds at the same time as lower ones, and they blend.

We cannot hear until a sound wave passes into our ear canal to the eardrum. The eardrum acts like a drum membrane and causes three tiny bones in the middle ear to move in the rhythm of the sound. This causes a fluid in the inner ear to start moving. The sound waves move the fluid, and this makes tiny hair cells in the fluid move.

These hair cells change the movement into nerve impulses. They are carried to the brain, and the brain interprets them as sound. But it is the different kinds of sound waves that produce different motions in our ear, and different nerve impulses to the brain—and so we hear different sounds!

There is no musical instrument made that can compare with the human voice as regards the fineness of its strings or its ability to change range and achieve richness of tonal quality!

HOW DO WE SING?

The human vocal apparatus is quite a complicated mechanism. First, let us start with the larynx. This contains the vocal apparatus and consists of a framework of cartilages, which you can feel in the front of your neck. Inside the larynx are two "arytenoid cartilages', to which are attached our "vocal cords". Sixteen different muscles move these vocal cords, making them tense or slack, just as a violinists controls the tension of his strings. The vocal cords can assume about 170 positions!

When a certain amount of air is blown upwards by the diaphragm and other muscles, the vocal cords begin to vibrate, and this makes the column of air in the respiratory passages vibrate, too. We hear the vibration of the column of air as a sound. If the vocal cords are not too tense, so they vibrate about 80 times per second, the sound waves are heard as deep tones. If the cords are tensed so that they vibrate about 1,000 times per second, we hear the sound waves as high tones.

The pitch of the human voice depends on the length of the vocal cords. The range and quality of a voice depend on the form and size of the resonating spaces. These include part of the vocal cord, and the windpipe, the lungs, the thorax and pharynx, the oral and nasal cavities, and the nasal sinuses. People with beautiful voices have their resonating spaces shaped in such a way that they vibrate "musically".

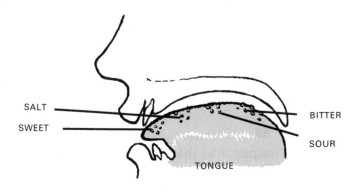

The tongue is one of the most amazing muscles and organs of the body. It is the only muscle we have that is attached at only one end. So it can move like no other muscle, and this is important for some of the work it has to do.

WHAT DOES THE TONGUE DO? When we speak and produce a whole variety of different sounds, the tongue assumes a variety of forms and positions to enable us to make the sounds. Just say the alphabet slowly and notice the different positions of the tongue for the different letters.

The mucous membrane that covers the tongue plays a part in the taking, holding, and grinding of food. In fact, the surface of the tongue is like a combination of graters, rolling pins, kneading boards, brushes, rakes, and points that act on food particles we take in.

289

The tongue is also one of the most delicate organs we have connected with the sense of touch. It is constantly telling us things, reporting on changes that take place in the mouth, and sending messages to the central nervous system about what we are eating and drinking.

Finally, of course, our taste buds are located on the tongue. The surface of the tongue is covered with little bumps that look like tiny warts. These are called "papillae", and the taste buds are located in the walls of these papillae.

Man has about 3,000 taste buds. A cow has about 35,000, and a whale has few or none. The number depends on the taste needs of the animal. Man's taste buds are able to register three different sensations: sweet, salt, and bitter. They may also register sour, but this is possibly a combination of the other three.

Different parts of the tongue are sensitive to different tastes. The back is more sensitive to bitter, the sides more sensitive to sour and salt, and the tip of the tongue picks up sweet tastes.

It seems like such a simple thing to us to sniff something and smell it. But the process of smelling, and the whole subject of odour, is quite a complicated thing.

WHAT IS SMELL? Man's sense of smell is poorly developed compared to that of other creatures. Man's organ of smell is located in the nose; at least, this is the place where the "messages" of smelling are received. This organ is quite small. Each side of the nose is only as large as a fingernail!

This organ is really a mucous membrane, containing nerve cells which are surrounded by nerve fibres, kept moist by mucous glands. Through the cells, delicate hairs stick out into the nasal cavity.

But the tips of these hairs are covered by a fatty layer of cells. If they become uncovered and dry, our ability to smell disappears. In ordinary breathing, the stream of air does not come in contact with the smelling area, so if we want to smell, we have to sniff. This sends the air to the right place.

The substance that we smell must actually be dissolved in the fatty layer that covers the hairs before we can smell it! This is why it takes us a bit of time to "get" a smell. It is also why substances that have an odour have to be both volatile, or able to move, and part of an oily substance

290

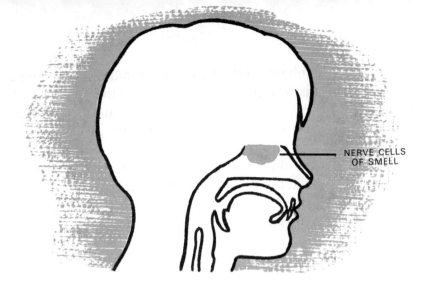

NERVE CELLS
OF SMELL

that can dissolve in that layer which covers the "smelling" hairs.

The way a thing smells depends on certain groups of atoms that carry odours. So that odour depends on a chemical formula, and each type of odour has a different chemical formula. And it takes only a very tiny amount of an odorous substance to excite our sense of smell.

There is a small smell centre in the brain which receives the "messages" from the nerves in the nose and tells us what we are smelling.

When it comes to the human body, you can be pretty sure that everything found in it has a purpose. This is also true of the mucus in the nose.

The nose is the passageway through which the air enters our body.

WHY DOES THE NOSE HAVE MUCUS?

A great deal has to be done to that air, however, before it enters our lungs. It has to be warmed, and it has to be cleaned. Many dust particles that enter with the air are removed by way of the nose.

The first cleansing of this air is carried out by the bristle hairs which are at the entrance to the nose. This is where the coarse dust particles are removed. Starting with the nose and extending to the air chambers of the lungs, the passageway is lined with cells which have delicate little hairs growing out of them. These hairs are called "cilia".

The mucus in our nose is clear as glass. The reason it becomes greyish green in colour is that tiny dust granules have been brought up from the windpipe by the cilia and carried into the nose, where they become mixed with the mucus.

A human being inhales millions of dust granules every minute of the day and night. This is true no matter where you live! The only air that is dust-free is the air over the ocean, once you get at least 600 miles from shore. Even a breath of pure country air contains about half a million dust particles!

Together with the dust, all types of bacteria enter our nose when we breathe. These bacteria stick to the mucous layer in our nose. And since the mucus is antiseptic, it kills many of the bacteria. So you see, the mucus in our nose really has the job of helping guard our health!

Does "thought" take place at the fastest speed possible? In times past, this was held to be true, which explains the expression "quick as thought".

WHAT IS THE SPEED OF THOUGHT? Today we know that thought is an impulse which must travel along a nerve fibre in our body, and this speed can be measured accurately. The surprising thing is that thought turns out to be a very slow process.

A nerve impulse moves at a speed of only about 155 miles an hour! This means that a message can be sent more quickly outside our body than from one part of our body to another! Television, radio, and the telephone all convey messages more swiftly than our nerves do. A thought travelling by nerve from New York to Chicago would arrive hours later than the same thought sent by telegraph, radio, telephone, or TV.

When something happens to our toe, for instance, it actually takes a while for that impulse to be received by our brain. Suppose you were a giant with your head in Alaska and your feet at the tip of South Africa. If a shark bit your toe on Monday morning, your brain would not know it until Wednesday night. And if you decided to pull your toe out of the water, it would take the rest of the week to send that thought back down to your foot!

Different kinds of "signals" make us react at different speeds. We react more quickly to sound than to light, to bright light than to dull light, to red than to white, and to something unpleasant than to something pleasant.

Everybody's nervous system sends thoughts at a slightly different speed. That is why certain people can react more quickly to signals than others.

292

How do we know what is going on in the world around us? We use our senses. Through them we can see, hear, feel, and taste.

But there are some scientists who believe that man can gain information without the use of senses. They believe the human mind has certain powers that have not yet been understood, and so it is possible to take in information that has not passed through the senses.

WHAT IS THE THEORY BEHIND ESP?

This process is called "extrasensory perception", or ESP. "Extrasensory" means "outside the senses". Many of the scientists who have studied this subject are psychologists. Their field of work is called "parapsychology". It is concerned with things that happen for which no physical cause can be found.

There are supposed to be three kinds of ESP. An example of one would be when someone seems able to read the thoughts in the mind of another person. A second kind of ESP is illustrated by this case: a woman living in one town dreams that her daughter, who lives in another town, had been hurt in an accident. The next day she learns that her daughter was hit by a motor car the night before.

A third kind of ESP would be the case of people who seem able to look into the future and know what will happen.

We know that some such cases really seem to happen, but many times it is difficult to accurately check the reports to see if they are true. Also, many people want to believe it and do not record very accurately what actually happened.

A great many experiments have been done to prove ESP exists, but the existence of ESP is still an open question for most scientists.

Fatigue can actually be considered a kind of poisoning! When a muscle in our body works, it produces lactic acid. If we remove the lactic acid from a tired muscle, it is able to start working again at once!

WHY DO WE GET TIRED?

There are other substances the body produces in the course of muscular activity. These are known as "fatigue toxins". The blood carries these through the body, so that the muscle itself, the entire body, and especially the brain feel tired.

Scientists have conducted interesting experiments on fatigue. If a dog is made to work until it is exhausted and falls asleep, and its blood is then transfused into another dog, the second dog will instantly become "tired" and fall asleep! If the blood of a wide-awake dog is transfused into a tired, sleeping dog, the latter will wake up at once, no longer tired!

But fatigue is not just a chemical process, it is also a biological process. We cannot just "remove" fatigue, we must allow the cells of the body to rest. Damages must be repaired, nerve cells of the brain must be "recharged", and the joints of the body must replace used up lubricants. Sleep will always be necessary as a way of restoring our body's energy after fatigue.

Very often, the best way to make a tired body part feel fresh again is to make other parts of the body active! We can actually rest by means of activity. Activity increases the respiration. The blood circulates faster, the glands are more active, and the waste products are eliminated from the tired part of the body. But, if you are totally exhausted, the best thing to do is sleep!

There is no living creature that does not need sleep or complete rest every day.

WHY DO WE SLEEP? If you want to know why, just try going without sleep for a long period of time! You will discover that your mind and body would become too tired to work properly. You would become irritable and find it hard to think clearly or concentrate on your work. So sleep is quite simply the time when the cells of your body recover from the work of the day and build up supplies of energy for the next period of activity.

One of the things we all know about sleep is that we are unconscious in sleep. We do not know what is going on around us. But that does not mean the body stops all activity. The vital organs continue to work during sleep, but most of the body functions are slowed down.

For example, our breathing becomes slower and deeper. The heart beats more slowly, and the blood pressure is lower. Our arms and legs become limp, and muscles that control our posture are at rest. It would be impossible for our body to relax to such an extent if we were awake. So sleep does for us what even the most quiet rest cannot do.

Your body temperature becomes lower when you are asleep, which is the reason people go to sleep under some kind of covers. And even though you are unconscious, many of your reflexes still work. For instance, if someone tickles your foot, you will pull it away in your sleep, or even brush a fly from your forehead. You do these things without knowing it.

Sleep, as we know, is important to us because it helps restore tired organs and tissues in our body. But how much sleep do we actually need?

HOW MUCH SLEEP DO WE NEED? For most of us, eight hours seems to be about the right amount. Yet we know that there are a great many people who get along perfectly with less sleep, and some who may even need more. A great deal depends on the way we live. But a good general rule to follow is to sleep as long as we have to in order to feel happy and be able to work at our best when we awaken.

There are actually different levels of sleep. There is a deep sleep and a shallow sleep. In a shallow sleep, our body does not get the same kind of rest it gets in a deep sleep, so that after eight hours of a shallow sleep we may still feel tired. But a short, deep sleep can be very restful.

Alexander the Great was able to get a deep sleep whenever he needed it. Once, during the night before an important battle, he remained awake longer than anyone else. Then he wrapped himself in a cloak and lay down on the earth. He slept so deeply that his generals had to wake him three times to give the command to attack!

Normally when we go to sleep, our "sleep centre" blocks off nerves so that both our brain and our body go to sleep. One prevents us from wanting to do anything, and the other makes our internal organs and limbs go to sleep. But sometimes only one goes to sleep and the other does not. A very tired soldier can sometimes fall asleep (brain sleep) and keep on marching, because his body is not asleep!

Dreams have interested, puzzled, and frightened people for thousands of years. And all kinds of strange explanations were developed about dreams.

IS WHAT WE DREAM OUR OWN IDEA?

At one time, people thought that the figures appearing in dreams were messengers from the gods. It was generally believed that dreams came from something outside the person dreaming and could be understood only by persons with special skills.

Today it is believed that dreams are created by the dreamer himself. And because dreams are something a person creates, they may have special meaning for the person who dreams them.

Just why you have a particular dream when you do may depend on many things. Your health may have an effect on your dreams. A person who is ill or uncomfortable will have different kinds of dreams than a person who is well and happy.

If a person is hungry, or cold, or very tired, his dreams may include this feeling. So that many dreams seem to be made up of disguised feelings. Also, the events of the day before may have a lot to do with what you dream.

Often the persons or situations in a dream are those that you met during the day. Or your emotions may make you have the kind of dream you have. Needing or wanting something may be expressed in a dream, and being frightened may become part of a dream.

The feelings of happiness or disappointment which come out in dreams were probably in the dreamer before. All the dream does is give them an outlet.

No person really knows how much he or she remembers! Just close your eyes and try to recall everything you have ever seen. All the people, all the houses, all the streets, all the objects you have ever looked at, and all the words and numbers you have ever learned. There seems to be no end to it.

HOW DO WE LOSE OUR MEMORY?

In our brain there is a visual memory centre where these millions of impressions are stored away, as neatly as in a good photographic library. We cannot yet explain how this miracle of filing away takes place. But we do know that it takes place in an orderly manner, according to subjects.

Because of this orderly arrangement, it is possible for one section to be injured or destroyed without harming other sections. For example, a person may have a brain injury or a haemorrhage and have his storehouse of certain memories wiped out. He may have "forgotten" how to use words, but he may still be able to use numbers!

Sometimes people have a "memory blindness" because of old age or an injury that prevents them from recognizing objects they see. They may look at a ball and not know what it is. But if they touch it, they are able to recognize it, because they are not depending on their visual storehouse of memory.

Our brain also has an auditory memory centre. Here are stored all the sounds we remember, just as if it were a vast library of gramophone records.

A person may also suffer from amnesia. This is usually caused by a state of great anxiety, and it makes a person forget certain associations which, unconsciously, he does not want to remember. When people with amnesia are treated, these associations can be restored and their memory may come back to normal.

Just being able to stand up or to walk, is one of the most amazing tricks it is possible to learn! It is a trick, and it must be learned.

If a four-legged visitor from another planet came to see us, he would marvel at the ability we have to do this. If he tried to do it, it would take him a considerable time to learn the trick, just as it took time for you to learn it when you were a baby.

WHY CAN WE BALANCE OURSELVES ON TWO LEGS?

When you stand still, you are performing a constant act of balancing. You change from one leg to the other, you use pressure on your joints, and your muscles tell your body to go this way and that way.

Just to keep our balance as we stand still takes the work of about 300 muscles in our body! That is why we get tired when we stand. Our muscles are constantly at work. In fact, standing is work!

In walking, we not only use our balancing trick, but we also make use of two natural forces to help us. The first is air pressure. Our thigh bone fits into the socket of the hip joint so snugly that it forms a kind of vacuum. The air pressure on our legs helps keep it there securely. This air pressure also makes the leg hang from the body as if it had very little weight.

The second natural force we use in walking is the pull of the earth's gravity. After our muscles have raised our leg, the earth pulls it downward again, and keeps it swinging like a pendulum.

When you see an acrobat walking across a tightrope and balancing himself, remember he is only doing a more difficult trick of balancing than you do every day. And like you, he had to learn and practice it for a long, long time!

If you press your thumb on an ink-pad and then on a sheet of white paper, you will have a print which no one else in the whole world can make!

The same would be true of each of your fingers. Your ten fingerprints are absolutely unique, and they remain practically unchanged from birth to death!

CAN TWO PEOPLE HAVE IDENTICAL FINGERPRINTS?

Nature has simply created a different pattern for the ridges of the skin on every single human finger. This fact was probably first discovered by the Chinese more than 2,000 years ago. At that time, Chinese emperors were signing important documents with their thumb prints.

In 1892, an English scientist named Sir Francis Galton was the first to prove that no two fingerprints were alike. And in 1901, Scotland Yard adopted a system for identifying criminals by their fingerprints that was developed by Sir Edward Henry. This system, with a few changes, is used by police departments all over the world today.

Here is how Sir Henry worked out his system. All fingerprints were divided into "types" of patterns: loops, central pocket loops, double loops, arches, tended arches, whorls, and accidentals. By counting the ridges between two points in the pattern, each of the ten fingers could be classified into a certain group. Then you take all the groups together as a unit, and you have a complete system of classifying fingerprints.

It works so well that fingerprints can be filed away by these groups, instead of by the name or description of the criminal. And even though millions of prints may be on file in an office, the right one can be picked out in just a few minutes!

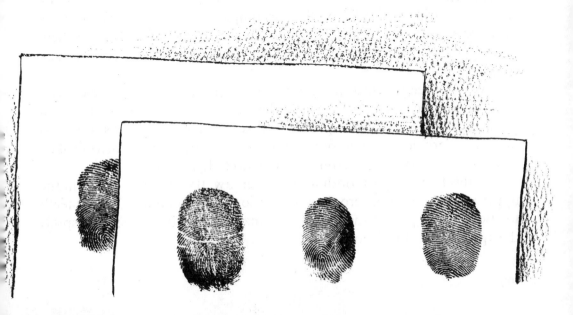

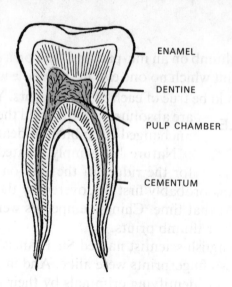

ENAMEL

DENTINE

PULP CHAMBER

CEMENTUM

Every tooth has the same two parts: a root, or roots, to anchor it in the jawbone, and a crown, the part that can be seen in the mouth.

There are four different materials in a tooth. The "enamel" is hard

HOW DO OUR TEETH GROW? and shiny and covers the crown. The "cementum" is a bonelike material that covers the root. The "dentine" is an ivory-like material that forms the body of the tooth. The "dental pulp" is in a hollow space called "the pulp chamber" inside the tooth. The dental pulp is made up of tissue that contains nerves, arteries, and veins. These enter the tooth through an opening at or near the root end.

Lack of calcium or Vitamin D in the diet will result in poor enamel, which will encourage early decay. The process of dental decay is also aggravated by the collection of sugary or starchy foods around the teeth, especially during the night. As they decompose in the mouth, these foods produce acids that will act on the calcium of the teeth and make them soluble, causing the teeth to soften, and thus allow bacteria to attack them.

Why do teeth sometimes grow "crooked"? The reason varies with each person, but scientists say that the way the jaws have developed in modern man can cause this problem. It seems that man's jaws today do not always provide enough room for his teeth. So they appear in a crooked position or become shifted during the period of growth.

If this happens to a tooth in the lower jaw, the opposing tooth in the upper jaw also becomes crooked in position. This sometimes causes teeth to stick out, or pushes the lips out, or makes the chin recede, and spoils the appearance of the mouth.

Chapter 4

How Things Began

Children in many parts of the world grow up chanting hundreds of jingles, verses, and rhymes which their great-great-grandparents chanted before them. For though the expression "nursery rhyme" was first used in 1824, such rhymes have existed for hundreds of years.

HOW DID NURSERY RHYMES ORIGINATE?

Nursery rhymes have a great variety of origins. Many of them have grown out of festivals, ceremonies, and rites used hundreds of years ago in Europe. Some have been made to explain the wonders of the world. Some repeat old chants for controlling rains, storms, droughts, and floods.

"London Bridge Is Falling Down" is said to date back to ancient days. Prayer rhymes, such as "Matthew, Mark, Luke, and John, bless the bed that I lie on," repeat ancient rites.

Rhymes may come from games centuries old. "Knick Knack Paddy Whack, give a dog a bone" comes from a game of knuckle-bones which started in Japan. It travelled to Rome and was carried to England and Europe by conquering Roman soldiers.

Rhymes sometimes come from street cries of peddlers who called out their service in rhymes. "Hot pease, hot, hot, hot" was such a street cry. Rhymed stories and songs were printed on long sheets of paper and sold for a penny. "Three Blind Mice" was printed in 1609 and sold in this way.

Some rhymes were learned from travelling actors who gave plays in the streets. Schoolboy actors used the verse "Thirty days hath September" as far back as 1602! About half of the 800 rhymes commonly used today are 200 or more years old.

"Zoo" is short for "zoological garden". And a zoological garden is a place where living animals are kept and exhibited.

Why do we keep wild animals in zoos? The most important reason is that everyone is interested in animals. Another reason is that scientists are able to learn many important things by studying living animals.

WHO STARTED THE FIRST ZOO?

The first zoo we know anything about was started as long ago as 1150 B.C. by a Chinese emperor, and it had many kinds of deer, birds, and fish in it. Even though it was somewhat like our modern zoos, there was one big catch to it. It probably was not open to the public but was kept for the amusement of the emperor and his court.

Since it costs a great deal of money to put together a zoo and maintain it, zoos in ancient times were assembled and owned by kings and rich lords. Many of them had collections of rare birds, fish, and animals of all kinds.

The first public zoological garden in the world was opened in Paris in 1793. This was the famous Jardin des Plantes. In it were animals, a museum, and a botanical garden.

The next big zoological garden to be opened was in 1829 in Regent's Park in London. Then came the Zoological Garden of Berlin, which was begun in 1844 and became one of the finest and best in the world.

In this country we have many zoos. At Whipsnade Zoo, in Bedfordshire, animals from all parts of the world thrive, free to roam, in the surrounding countryside, fenced in only for safety's sake. Other popular zoos are found at Bristol and Edinburgh.

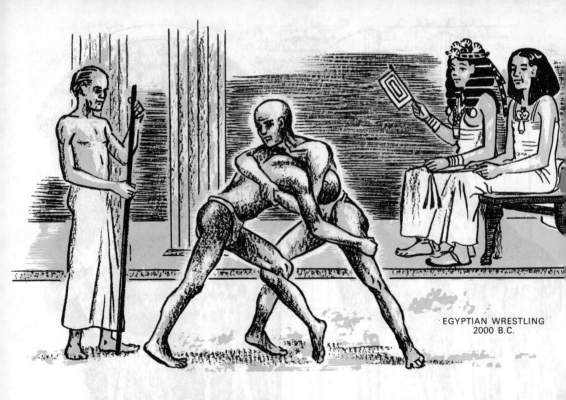

Wrestling is one of the earliest sports known to man. Many hundreds of scenes of wrestling matches are sculptured on the walls of ancient Egyptian tombs. And they show practically all the holds and falls known to us today. So wrestling was a highly developed sport at least 5,000 years ago!

HOW OLD IS OUR SPORT OF WRESTLING?

Wrestling as an organized and scientific sport was probably introduced into Greece from Egypt or Asia. But there is a Greek legend that it was invented by the hero Theseus.

Wrestling was an important branch of athletics in ancient Greece. The Greek wrestlers used to rub oil on themselves and then rub fine sand on the oil, to afford a better hold. The champion wrestler of the ancient world was Milo of Croton, who scored 32 victories in the national games, and had six Olympic victories.

In Japan, where wrestling is very popular, the first recorded wrestling match took place in 23 B.C. The Japanese have a style of wrestling called "Sumo", in which weight is very important. Some Sumo champions have weighed as much as 135 kilograms, and were tremendously strong, but still quite light on their feet.

In Britain, wrestling was cultivated even in earliest times. Did you know that King Henry VIII liked wrestling and was considered to be very good?

Today, "Hide and Seek" is played because it is fun. But the beginning of "Hide and Seek" really goes back a long, long time, when it had a different meaning to the people who played it.

HOW DID SOME CHILDREN'S GAMES BEGIN? In fact, it used to be played by grown-ups. In certain parts of Europe, it used to be the custom at springtime to go out into the woods and the country to find flowers and birds which appeared with the new season. Then these were brought back to the village so that everybody could see that spring was really there. Seeking for these signs of spring which were hidden in the woods was the real beginning of "Hide and Seek". And even though so much time has passed, in some countries today when this game is played, the person who is hiding still imitates the call of birds!

An interesting thing about practically all children's games is that each one started not as a game, but with something that happened in history, or a fable that people believed. Sometimes it started with a happy event, sometimes a tragic one.

"London Bridge Is Falling Down" is a game that started very seriously. It does not even have anything to do with London! It goes back to the days when people imagined that people must pass over a bridge after they died. Some people passed over the golden bridge into heaven, others had to pass over an old, tottering bridge to meet the devil. This game, played all over the world today, has a different name in each country!

Man has been skating in one way or another for more than 500 years! Ice skating is much older than roller skating, since roller skating goes back only to the eighteenth century.

WHO INVENTED SKATING? Wheeled skates were used on the roads of Holland about 200 years ago, and we cannot really know who was the first to make them or use them. A man in New York called J. L. Plimpton invented the four-wheeled skate in 1863. It worked on rubber pads and these were the skates that really made this sport popular.

The next development was roller skates with ball bearings. The wheels of roller skates were first made of turned boxwood, but the edges of the wooden wheels broke too easily. Soon wheels were made of hard composition or of steel. Roller skating races were very popular in America until about 1910, when motorcycle and sports car races took their place. But, of course, roller skating has remained a favourite sport with young people.

Ice skating goes back beyond the sixteenth century. At that time the Norsemen bound runners made of bone to their feet and skimmed over the icy surfaces.

Iron runners were next used in skating, followed by the steel runners of today. In early days, the skate-runner was attached to the foot by leather thongs, Later, the skate was clamped and strapped to the shoe. In the modern skate the blade is permanently attached to the skating boot.

You may think that skiing is a modern sport, but it is actually one of the oldest forms of travel known to man! The word itself comes from the Icelandic word *scidh*, which means "snowshoe" or "piece of wood".

HOW DID SKIING BEGIN? Some historians claim that skiing goes back to the Stone Age, and they have found ancient carvings that show people on skis. Long before Christianity appeared, the ancient Lapps were known in Scandinavia as *Skrid-Finnen*, or "sliders". They even had a goddess of ski, and their winter god was shown on a pair of skis with curved toes!

The first skis of which there is any record were long, curved frames, often made of the bones of animals, and held to the foot by thongs. And there is a picture carved on stone that is 900 years old that shows a ski runner.

Skiing as a sport began in Norway, in the province of Telemark. In fact, the town of Morgedal in this Norwegian province is known as "the cradle of skiing". Because this region would be snowbound for long periods at a time, it was necessary to use skis to get about. In winter, when the natives went hunting or trapping in the mountains, or to neighbouring villages to market or to visit, they had to depend on skis!

And if you think skiing meets are a modern development, it may surprise you to know that in Norway they were having skiing competitions for prizes as long ago as 1767!

Ice hockey is considered to be the fastest game in the world. It is played by two teams of six men in action at one time. Extra players, or substitutes, sit on the sidelines. Each team tries to do two things: put a small rubber disc, called a "puck", into the opponents' net, and prevent the opponent from scoring.

WHERE DID THE GAME OF ICE HOCKEY ORIGINATE?

Today, ice hockey is one of many games played with a stick and a ball. Such games are believed to have originated in Persia, where the game of polo began. We know that the ancient Greeks played a kind of hockey and even included it in their Olympic Games. There is a wall in Athens, Greece, which is about 2,400 years old that has carved pictures of young men playing a game that is much like the field hockey of today.

Ice hockey originated in Canada more than 100 years go. One claim is that English soldiers played an early form of ice hockey on the frozen surfaces of Lake Ontario at Kingston, Ontario, as early as 1867.

The first organized ice hockey leagues are claimed by both Kingston and Montreal. It is known that there definitely was an ice hockey league in Kingston in 1885. In 1890, the Ontario Hockey Association was organized with ten teams. In 1914, the Canadian Amateur Hockey Association was formed with a few thousand players.

So the birthplace of amateur ice hockey was Canada, but the United States organized ice hockey on a professional basis for the first time. In the winter of 1904–1905, a professional ice hockey league was formed at Houghton, Michigan. The world's only major professional league, the National Ice Hockey League, was started in 1910.

A duel, as we think of it today, is a pre-arranged encounter in accordance with certain rules, between two persons with deadly weapons, for the purpose of deciding a point of honour. According to this definition, cer-

HOW DID DUELLING ORIGINATE?

tain famous battles between two men were not really duels. For example, Hector and Achilles were supposed to have fought each other, but this was not a duel.

The reason for this is that in ancient times there was something called a "judicial duel". This was a legalized form of combat and it decided questions of justice rather than of personal honour. For instance, sometimes when a war was impending, a captive from the hostile tribe was armed and he fought with the national champion. The outcome of the duel was supposed to be an omen, since it was believed that the one who won deserved to win. At other times, such "duels" were a substitute for a trial in court.

In time, this form of duelling was abolished, and the duel of honour came into being. These began about the sixteenth century.

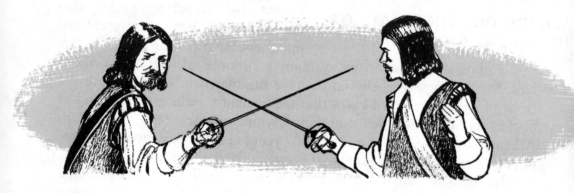

The custom of duelling became so popular that between 1601 and 1609, more than 2,000 Frenchmen of noble birth were killed in duels! The church and other officials protested against this custom, and in 1602 the French king issued an edict condemning to death whoever should give or accept a challenge to a duel or act as a second. This proved to be too strict, and in 1609 it was changed so that permission to engage in a duel could be obtained from the king.

Duels also became popular in England, and there, too, protests finally made them illegal. In Germany, however, student duels were a part of German student life until fairly recent times. It was considered an honour for a student to have participated in them.

Card games go back so far in history, that nobody really knows when or where playing cards originated. Most experts believe that playing cards came to us from Asia.

WHERE WERE CARD GAMES FIRST PLAYED? There is a tradition that both the ancient Hindus and Moslems used round playing cards for their amusement, but there are no records of this. In fact, the first records we have are from the fourteenth century. The Chinese claim that there were card games in China as early as the year 1120, and that during the reign of an emperor called Seun-ho they were invented to amuse people at his palace.

We do know that towards the close of the fourteenth century, cards were already quite popular in France. They were so popular that finally it was forbidden for working people to play card games on working days!

The first cards were generally rectangular or square, though sometimes people played with round cards. The early packs of cards usually consisted of 86 cards. One of the cards had no number and was called *fou*, which means "fool". This is the card we now call "the Joker".

During the fifteenth century, the art of wood engraving was introduced in Europe. Before that, cards were painted by hand and were very expensive, so that only wealthy people could afford to own cards. But with wood engraving it was possible to make cards more cheaply, and for the first time the poor classes were also able to enjoy card games.

In the sixteenth century in France, the four suits we use today—hearts, clubs, spades, and diamonds—were first used.

Golf, as we know it today, probably originated in Scotland. But in tracing the beginnings of golf we have to go back hundreds of years before that.

WHERE DID GOLF ORIGINATE? In the early days of the Roman Empire, there was a game known as "paganica". It was played with a leather ball stuffed with feathers, and a bent stick for a club. In England, there is evidence that a game like golf was played as far back as the middle of the fourteenth century. And in the British Museum there is a picture in a book from the sixteenth century which shows three players, each with a ball and club, putting at a hole in the ground.

During the fifteenth century, golf was becoming so popular in Scotland that laws were passed forbidding people to play because it was

SIXTEENTH-CENTURY GOLFERS

taking up too much of their time! Among other things, the interest in golf was causing people to neglect archery, and it was also interfering with attendance at church on Sundays.

Golf has been known since old times as the "royal and ancient" game. This is because royalty seemed to be very fond of it. James IV, James V, and Mary Stuart all enjoyed the game.

Golf clubs began to be founded in the eighteenth century. The first one was probably founded in 1744, The Honourable Company of Edinburgh Golfers. The Royal and Ancient Golf Club of St. Andrews, founded in 1754, frames and revises the rules of golf. Its decisions are accepted by clubs everywhere, except in the United States. In 1951, the Royal and Ancient and the U.S. Golf Association agreed upon a uniform code.

In the United States, golf was played as long ago as 1799. But another hundred years passed before golf began to be played in a regular and continuous way in the United States. The first golf club in the United States was founded in 1888 in Yonkers, New York.

There are many legends among many peoples of how music began. The Bible tells of Jubal, the father of musicians. An old Spanish book describes how Jubal listened to Tubalcain's forge and noticed that the sounds

WHAT WAS THE FIRST MUSIC?
made by pounding the anvil differed in pitch. He tried imitating these sounds with his voice and soon found himself singing high tones and then low tones.

The Greek myths tell of Pan, the inventor of the shepherd's pipe. Pan sighed through the reeds on a river bank and heard his breath produce a mournful wail as it passed through them. He broke them off in unequal lengths, bound them together, and he had a musical instrument!

Such tales are, of course, pure fancy. All primitive people do seem to have made music of some sort. But this music was not for pleasure alone. It had a meaning as part of their lives. Folk music, which is an ancient type of music, started when untrained singers made up songs.

The Greeks related music to poetry and the drama. They used instruments such as harps, lyres, and flutes.

The art of music owes a great deal of its growth to the early Christian church. In time, from church music there developed other forms and types, new instruments were invented, and music became an established art.

All primitive people seem to have made music of some sort. But the sounds they made were very different from those of modern music. This music often consisted of long and loud exclamations, sighs, moans, and

WHO FIRST WROTE MUSIC?
shouts. Dancing, clapping, and drumming went along with the singing.

Folk music has existed for centuries, passed from generation to generation by being heard, not by being written down.

Composed music is many centuries old. Ancient civilizations such as the Chinese, Hindu, Egyptian, Assyrian, and Hebrew all had music. Most of it was unlike ours. The Greeks made complicated music by putting tones together similar to present-day scales. For notation they used the letters of the alphabet written above the syllables of the words.

After the Greeks and Romans (who copied Greek music), the early Christian Church was important in the growth of the art of music. Saint Ambrose and Saint Gregory began a style of music known as "plain song".

This was a type of chant sung in unison. Tones followed one another in a way similar to the method developed by the Greeks. Churchmen also learned to write music down. The modern method of writing music developed from their system.

In 1600, the first opera, *Eurydice*, was produced by Jacopo Peri. Later on, men like Monteverdi wrote not only operas but music for instruments, such as the violin. Music began to be written for court dances, pageants, and miracle plays. And in time much of the great music we enjoy today was composed by such men as Bach, Handel, Haydn, Mozart, and Beethoven.

The accordion is an instrument made on the principle of the bellows. The sound is made by forcing air through metallic reeds. The development of this instrument can be traced over a period of many years.

WHO INVENTED THE ACCORDION? The metal reeds, that are part of the instrument, were first used by the ancient Chinese in a musical instrument known as a "cheng". In the sixteenth century, the idea of putting wooden frames on bellows was originated.

It is the opening and closing of bellows that causes a stream of air to vibrate the reeds. The keys of the reeds are depressed. The vibrating of the reeds produces the tone in an accordion.

Keyboards, such as are used on both pianos and accordions, are an invention that goes back to the twelfth century.

The first instrument that was the ancestor of the modern accordion was produced and patented by an Austrian man called Damian in 1829.

The piano accordion, as it was called, was well known in European countries only, until 1910. Then it was introduced on the American vaudeville stage. It has been developed in many ways since that time and in 1937 it was used for the first time in a symphony orchestra.

The piano accordion has 120 bass keys on one side, and 41 treble keys on the piano-type keyboard.

Unlike other musical instruments which came into being as the result of the work of one individual or several individuals, the drum has been in existence since the time of earliest man.

WHO INVENTED THE DRUM?

Many different kinds of drums have been used all over the world by the most primitive men, many of them races that long ago disappeared from the earth.

It is likely that the drum was first used as a means of calling together the scattered members of a tribe. It was a kind of war signal. In time, the drum became part of the music that primitive peoples used in their battles with "evil spirits". It had a religious significance to these primitive people. And since so many of their ceremonies involved dances, the drum furnished a perfect accompaniment.

Primitive people used drums made of various materials. Some were hollow tree trunks with animal skins stretched over them. Bamboo drums were made of long sections of the hollow reed, slit and beaten with sticks. Some people used to beat their own bodies on the ground to produce a drumlike sound!

Drums were commonly used by the ancient Egyptians. The typical Egyptian drum was small and was carried about in the hand. The ancient Hebrews also had drums, which were a sort of tambourine, sometimes beaten with the hand and sometimes with a stick. The Chinese and Japanese, too, have had drums from the earliest times.

The American Red Indians not only used the drum to send messages and to mark time for their dances, but they used drums to predict the weather! When rainy weather approached, the skins that covered their drums would become taut.

AMERICAN INDIAN DRUM

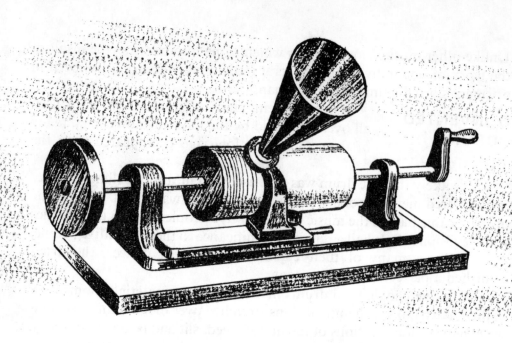

The first recording was made by Thomas Edison in 1877. His first machine had a cylinder turned by a hand crank. There was also a horn and a blunted needle, or "stylus". At the small end of the horn there was a flexible cover.

HOW WAS THE FIRST RECORDING MADE?

Sound waves that entered the large end of the horn moved this cover one way or another. To this the stylus was attached. It moved up and down with the sound waves, too.

The cylinder was covered by a layer of tin foil. The stylus pressed against this foil and gears moved the horn with its attached stylus slowly along the cylinder, as the crank was turned. In this way, as the stylus went around the cylinder many times, it made a crease in the tin foil.

When someone sang or spoke into the horn, it made the stylus move up and down. The stylus made a deeper groove in the tin foil when it was down, a lighter crease when it was in an upward position. The changing depth of the groove was the pattern of the sound waves made by a person singing or talking. It was the record of the sound.

To play the record, the stylus and horn were moved back to the beginning of the groove. As the stylus followed the groove, it caused the flexible cover in the horn to vibrate in the same pattern. This made the air in the horn move to-and-fro, and this made a sound like the original sound recorded!

Man's desire to be able to take photographs goes back hundreds of years. From the eleventh to the sixteenth century, there was a device called "the camera obscura", which was a forerunner of the photographic camera.

WHO MADE THE FIRST PHOTOGRAPH?

Its purpose was to show on paper an image which could be traced by hand to give accurate drawings of natural scenes.

In 1802, two men, Wedgwood and Humphry, took an important step forward. They recorded by contact printing, on paper coated with silver nitrate or silver chloride, silhouettes and images of paintings made upon glass. But they could not make these prints permanent.

In 1816, Joseph Niepce made a photographic camera, with which he could get a negative image. And in 1835, William Talbot was able to obtain permanent images. Talbot was the first to make positives from negatives, the first to make enlargements by photography, and the first to publish (in 1844) a book illustrated with photographs.

From then on, a whole series of improvements and developments came one after the other. The popular Kodak box camera was placed on the market in 1888, and photography as we know it was on its way.

Most photographic processes depend on the fact that the chemical silver nitrate reacts to light by turning black. And this was discovered way back in the seventeenth century by alchemists who were trying to find a way to turn common metals to gold.

WILLIAM TALBOT

It took man many thousands of years to reach the stage where he could produce anything that even remotely resembles a book as we know it.

So when we consider the first "book", we have to think of something

WHEN WAS THE FIRST BOOK WRITTEN?

quite different. In fact, the earliest books we know about were not really books in the modern sense of the word. Several thousand years ago, the Babylonians and Assyrians made tablets of clay. On these tablets they had inscribed records and writings which they wished to preserve.

With a sharp-pointed tool, they cut wedge-shaped, or "cuneiform", characters while the clay was still wet. To make the records more permanent, the clay tablets were placed in an oven and baked. Sometimes the record was a long one and occupied many clay tablets. Such a series of tablets, or "pages", might roughly be called a book.

The ancient Egyptians came a step closer to the modern idea of a book. They made a kind of crude paper from a reed called "papyrus". Flat sheets were made by hand, and these pale yellow sheets were pasted together into long strips, which were wound around cylindrical rollers of bone or wood.

Using sooty water as ink, the Egyptians wrote down poetry, stories, and records of all kinds in hieroglyphics, or picture writing. Since the rolls were not convenient to handle, the writing was sometimes done on separate sheets. These sheets were then laced together with cords to make a crude book.

Other ancient peoples, including the Greeks and Romans, made books which were wound around rollers.

The first printing of any kind was done by the Chinese and Japanese in the fifth century. At that time and for hundreds of years afterwards, books were so scarce and so hard to make, that few people could read or had

WHO MADE THE FIRST PRINTING PRESS?

books from which to learn.

The first printers used blocks of wood as the printing formes. Pictures were carved into their faces. The blocks were then inked and printed on the crude presses of the day. Later, words were added to the pictures, but these, too, had to be carefully carved into the wood.

A method was needed to shorten the long labour of hand carving each page. It took nearly a thousand years before any real change was made in the method used to reproduce the written word.

Many men were at work on the problem. Johann Gutenberg, a German printer living in Mainz, is generally believed to be the man who first solved the problem. Gutenberg hit upon the idea of using movable metal type. He printed his first book, the famous Gutenberg Bible, by this method between 1453 and 1456.

Gutenberg's type was cast in a mould, each letter separately. When taken out of the mould, the type could be easily assembled, or "set", in words, lines, and pages. Once set and printed, the pages were broken up, and the letters reset and used again to print other pages.

This system is still in use today, though later inventors have greatly speeded up the way in which the type is cast and set.

Many artists today paint pictures in which they make no effort to show the world around them. But when man began to paint pictures, that is exactly what he wanted to do. In caves, where early man lived thousands of years ago, paintings have been found that show animals as lifelike as can be.

WHO MADE THE FIRST PAINTINGS?

These were made by the people of the Old Stone Age of Europe. Many thousands of years later, when the Egyptians had created one of man's first civilizations, paintings were also lifelike. The Egyptians believed there was a life after death, so they painted on the walls of their tombs everything that went on in their lives. There were figures of men, women, and children with animals, boats, and other objects.

ANCIENT EGYPTIAN
TOMB PAINTING

The most artistic people of any age, except perhaps the Chinese, were the Greeks, who were at the height of their glory about 500 B.C. Their aim in sculpture was the imitation of life, but life in its perfect or ideal form.

Christianity, which originated in the Near East, brought an important change in art. The naturalism of ancient art was replaced by Oriental styles with flat designs and symbolism. During the Medieval period, which lasted from about 500 to 1500, the arts of fresco and of illuminating manuscripts were perfected.

Fresco is done by painting with a brush directly into fresh plaster, so that when it is dry the picture is a permanent part of the wall. The illustration of manuscripts or books, which is called "illumination", was practised by the monks. They made exquisite letters and pictures and full-page illustrations.

The first man-made writing material was papyrus, made from the papyrus plant. Papyrus was invented about 2000 B.C. by the Egyptians. For about 2,500 years or more, it was the only writing material used by man.

WHAT WAS PAPYRUS? Papyrus is a reedlike plant belonging to the family of sedges. It grows to a height of from 1 to 3 metres. The stems are soft, and sometimes as large as a man's wrist. At the tops of these stems are drooping, slender branches, like shaggy, coarse hair. The leaves are small and the roots are strong.

The Roman historian Pliny has left a description of how the ancient papyrus was made. The stems of the papyrus plant were peeled apart and flattened. The centre one was the broadest and most valuable.

These strips were laid side by side. Across them, at right angles, other strips were placed. The layers were glued together by the muddy water of the Nile or with a wheat-flour paste. The sheets thus formed were then hammered or rolled flat and dried in the sun.

At one time, papyrus writing material was one of Egypt's chief articles of commerce. All diplomatic papers for centuries were written on papyrus, until parchment took its place. Each piece was marked with a stamp to prove its value.

Baskets were also woven from the slender stalks of the papyrus plant. From its thicker stalks, mats and sails were made. Its pith, when boiled, furnished food for the poor, and when dried was used for fuel. So you can see how useful this plant was in ancient times.

A coin is a piece of metal of a given weight and alloy with the mark or stamp of those who issued it.

WHEN WERE THE FIRST COINS MADE? The first coins were made in the seventh century B.C. by the Lydians. They were a wealthy and powerful people living in Asia Minor. These primitive coins were made of "electrum", which is a natural composition of 75 per cent gold and 25 per cent silver. They were about the size and shape of a bean and were known as "staters" or "standards".

The Greeks saw these coins and appreciated the usefulness of a standard metal money, so they began to make coins, too. About 100 years later, many cities on the mainland of Greece and Asia Minor, on the

ROMAN COINS

islands of the Aegean Sea and Sicily, and in southern Italy had coinages of their own. Gold coins were the most valuable. Next came silver and finally copper.

Greek coinage lasted for about 500 years. The Romans adopted the idea and carried it on for about another 500 years. Then the art of coinage declined. From the year 500 to about 1400, coins were thin and unattractive. But in the fifteenth century, the art of coinage was revived. Metal became more plentiful. Skilled artists were employed to engrave the dies.

The first British coins were struck before the arrival of the Romans. By the Norman Conquest, there were 70 mints operating in this country, but, by 1850, the Royal Mint was a monopoly and an established part of the Civil Service.

Man got along quite a long time without money. He used what we call "the barter system". If a man wanted something he did not make or raise himself, he found another person who had what he wanted and offered

WHEN WAS MONEY FIRST USED?
him something in exchange.

The first kind of "money" used by primitive man usually consisted of things to wear or eat. The American Indians used carved shells called "wampum". Other types of "money" have been tobacco, grains, skins, salt, and beads.

Eventually, pieces of metal replaced the other kinds of money. The first people to use coined money were the Lydians, a people of Asia

Minor. In the eighth century B.C., they began to make pieces of metal money which were uniform in weight and design and which could be easily recognized.

Gold and silver had been used as money long before that, but not in the form of coins. They had circulated as bars from which pieces were cut and weighed, but there was no guarantee of purity or weight. It was the Lydians who first thought of stamping pieces of metal with some symbol as a guarantee. Other peoples imitated them and gradually the use of coins became widespread.

After the Middle Ages, it was found that a "promise" to pay money, if there was confidence in the person who made the promise, would serve as well as real money. So goldsmiths, merchants, and money lenders began to issue notes, which were written promises to pay cash on demand.

This "credit currency", since it was in the form of paper, was safer and more convenient to handle than gold. Soon banks, and then governments, began to issue such paper promises, and "paper money" came into existence.

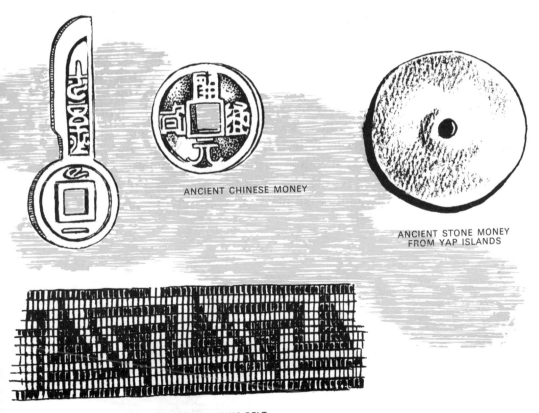

ANCIENT CHINESE MONEY

ANCIENT STONE MONEY
FROM YAP ISLANDS

INDIAN WAMPUM BELT

Mythology tells of humans who tried to fly; for example, Daedalus and Icarus, who flew on wings of wax and feathers. Their example has caused the death of many would-be fliers who, for hundreds of years, hurled

WHEN DID THE
FIRST AEROPLANE FLY?

themselves from high places with frail, home-made wings strapped to their backs. Gradually it was realised that man would never fly by copying the birds. Something new was needed. As far as we know, Roger Bacon (1214–92) was the first to suggest, "It's possible to make Engines for flying, a man sitting in the midst thereof . . ."

In the seventeenth century, man turned his attention to lighter-than-air flights and so began the first hot-air and hydrogen balloon flights. A big disadvantage of the balloon, however, was that the occupants were completely at the mercy of the weather and were constantly being blown off-course. Man was still a long way from real flying.

The first heavier-than-air machine to fly was a model glider built in 1804. It was a 994 sq. cm. kite, mounted on a rod, with a tail at the rear. John Stringfellow's 1848 steam-powered monoplane was launched down a 9-metres-long inclined wire. It gradually climbed, after release, until stopped by a canvas screen.

The Russians claim that Alexander Mozhaisky flew in a huge steam-driven aircraft in 1882. In 1896, Dr. Samuel Pierpont Langley flew successfully, covering 925 metres, a 5 metre-span tandem-wing model.

On the 17th December, 1903, Orville Wright started the home-made engine of his powered aircraft and took to the air. Not much of a flight by modern standards—only thirty six metres. But it was enough to establish Orville and his brother, Wilbur, as the first to build and fly an aeroplane that achieved controlled and sustained flight by power.

Preston Watson is reputed to have flown successfully in 1902 in a biplane fitted with a Santos-Dumont engine, but this claim has never been officially upheld.

The first people to cultivate tobacco—and smoke it—were the Indians of North and South America.

WHEN DID SMOKING BEGIN? When Christopher Columbus and other early explorers came to America, they found the natives using tobacco in many ways. For example, they smoked a pipe to symbolize peace among them. The Indians also believed that tobacco had medicinal properties so they smoked to help protect themselves against disease.

Tobacco was first introduced into Europe in the sixteenth century because of the idea that it was medicinal. The tobacco pipe was introduced into Europe by Ralph Lane, the first governor of Virginia. In 1586, he brought an Indian pipe to Sir Walter Raleigh and taught him how to use it. By 1619, so many pipes were being made in London that the pipe makers of that city formed a guild.

Today, of course, most tobacco is smoked in the form of cigarettes. Cigarette smoking is also quite old. The early Spanish explorers found the natives in the West Indies and Mexico smoking cigarettes. In the West Indies they used a thin palm bark to wrap the tobacco, and in Mexico they used corn husks.

The first people to use paper for cigarettes were the Spanish. Cigarette smoking spread throughout countries near the Mediterranean and Black seas, especially in those areas under Turkish influence. The English army, fighting in Crimea during 1854–1856, discovered Turkish cigarettes and brought them back to London. A few years later, the first cigarette factory was opened in London.

It is difficult to decide exactly who built the first petrol-driven car. Gottlieb Daimler, a German, built his first petrol-driven motor-car in 1887; in the same year, two Frenchmen patented a clutch and gearbox

WHO BUILT THE FIRST CAR?

which were basically the same as those fitted to the majority of English cars today. Nowadays, of course, some English cars have automatic transmission, though this modern feature is more popular in American cars.

The first great English pioneer in the development of the car was F. W. Lanchester, who produced his first car in 1895. Two "modern" innovations incorporated in his car were pneumatic tyres and wire wheels. Development from this date on was rapid.

At first it was difficult to raise the interest of possible investors in the manufacture of cars. One young American inventor, Henry Ford, designed a car to be sold at a popular price. Motoring in its early days was the privilege of the wealthy, and Ford's experiment proved successful. This led to the foundation of the world's largest car factory, the Ford plant, which proceeded to make comparatively cheap, reliable cars available to people all over the world. Henry Ford taught the motor industry its two principles of standardization and mass production.

If you had never seen a goldfish before and had to think up a name for it, what do you think it would be? Perhaps you would look at its bright colour in the sun and say it looks golden, so let's call it "goldfish"? Well,

HOW DID SOME FISH GET THEIR NAMES?

many fish got their names because of their appearance or some special quality about them.

For example, "shark" comes from the Greek *Karckarios* and the Latin *carcharus*, which mean "sharp teeth"! Does the porpoise resemble a hog a little bit? It gets its name from the Latin words *porcus pisces*, which means "hog-fish". The swordfish is an easy one. The upper jaw of this fish really looks like a sword.

The whale is simply the modern spelling of an Anglo-Saxon word *hwal*. The sunfish is so named because it has a round shape like the sun. That catfish got its name because of its large, glaring eyes. Is there any question as to how the flying fish got its name?

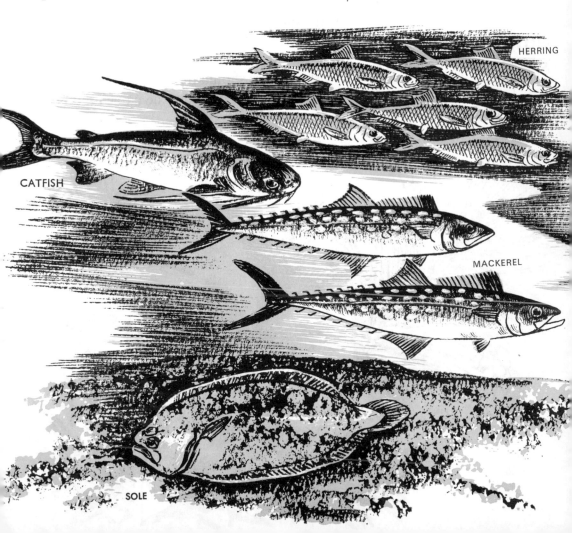

HERRING

CATFISH

MACKEREL

SOLE

The "sole" comes from the Latin word *solea*, which means "the bottom". Herring comes from an Anglo-Saxon word *haring*, which means "a multitude", or "many", and of course the herring is always found in multitudes.

Have you ever examined a mackerel? Then you probably noticed the spots on it. The word "mackerel" comes from the Danish word *mackreel* which means "spots"! A "smelt" got its name because it has a peculiar smell.

What's interesting about the salmon? The way it jumps over obstacles on its way upstream. So the word "salmon" comes from the Latin *salmo* which means a "leaping fish"! The trout loves to go after bait. And "trout" comes from the Latin *trocta*, which means "the greedy fish".

The names of many trees, plants, and herbs have interesting origins. Others, of course, have simply come down to us from other languages.

Let's look into some of the more interesting names of plants, trees

HOW DID TREES GET THEIR NAMES?

and herbs. The pine tree gets its name from the Latin word *pinus*, which means a "point". The spruce tree should really be called "Prussia Tree". It was long thought to be a native of Prussia. The name gradually became "spruce".

MAGNOLIA

SPRUCE

PINE

DANDELION

The magnolia is named after Pierre Magnol of France, who was a professor of botany. The cypress was first brought from the island of Cyprus in the Mediterranean. Willow comes from the old Anglo-Saxon word *wileg*. In Madagascar, there is a tree called "the Traveller's Tree'. It has large, fan-shaped leaves that catch the rain and passing travellers can quench their thirst at this tree!

Among plants with interesting names there is the Barber Plant which grows in the Orient. The natives rub its leaves on their faces to keep the beard from growing.

Mint owes its name to Menthe, a woman in an ancient fable who was transformed into a plant by her rival Prosperina. Thyme comes from the Latin *thymus*, which means "to sacrifice". This plant was burnt by the Romans on their altars. Dandelion comes from the French *dent de lion*, because the leaves of this plant were supposed to resemble the teeth of a lion. Arrowroot was said to be used by North American Indians for extracting the poison from arrow wounds.

The chief purpose of a name, of course, is identification. From the beginning of history, children have been given names at birth or soon afterwards to identify them.

WHAT DO OUR NAMES MEAN?

But when parents gave a child a name in ancient times, they also wanted the name to express something—to have a meaning. For example, it might describe his appearance or be a term of endearment.

Christian names are usually drawn from some older language. For example, Benjamin comes from the Hebrew; Andrew from the Greek; Amy from the Latin; Alfred from the Anglo-Saxon.

Originally, these names had a meaning. A girl born during a famine was sometimes called Una (Celtic for "famine"). A golden-haired girl might be called Flavia (Latin for "yellow") or Blanche (French for "white"). Other examples of names that have definite meanings are: David (beloved), Susan (lily), Deborah (bee), and Margaret (pearl).

In England and the United States any name desired by the parent can be given to a child. But in France and Germany, a name must be chosen from an official list.

When a name is translated from one language to another, it often undergoes interesting changes. For example, Henry is a Teutonic name meaning "head of the house". It becomes Harry, Hal, Henri (French), Heinrich (German), Enrico (Italian), and Hendrick (Danish).

Last names, or surnames, became common only about 900 years ago. They were added because it became too hard to identify people by just one name. Surnames developed in various ways: by including the father's name, or the town lived in, the occupation or business, and so on.

EDWARD JENNER

One day in the year 1768, a young milkmaid attended a Gloucestershire doctor's surgery for advice. Smallpox, the dreaded scourge of the country at that time, was mentioned in the waiting-room conversation, and the

WHO STARTED VACCINATION? milkmaid remarked that she could not catch it, as she had already had cowpox, a disease with symptoms similar to those of smallpox, though in very much milder form.

The importance of her remark did not escape the attention of Edward Jenner, a young medical student who was present. The idea occupied his mind constantly during the completion of his medical studies in London. After qualifying, he returned in 1773 to practise medicine in his native village in Gloucestershire, and devoted his spare time in the ensuing twenty years to investigation and research. He found that the milkmaid had been right: those people who had had cowpox very rarely caught smallpox.

In 1796, he made his first experiments, with the purpose of giving people a light dose of cowpox in order to ensure their subsequent protection from the horrible plague of smallpox. In 1798, he made his first really crucial test. Four children who had been inoculated with cowpox were now inoculated with smallpox. To his great joy, not one of them caught the dreaded disease. He had made the great discovery of vaccination, which today has almost completely wiped out this then frequently fatal disease.

Vaccination at first had many opponents, but eventually its value became so firmly established that vaccination for foreigners entering nearly all civilized countries is now compulsory. Vaccination is available to everyone in this country, and it is usually first performed when a child is about fifteen months old.

The dressing and decoration of hair by human beings is as old as civilization itself. It is a curious thing to notice how important the style of hair worn by men and women has been down through the ages. Savage tribes

WHO STARTED SHORT HAIRCUTS FOR MEN?

in all parts of the world have developed peculiar hair styles which have great significance for them.

The Chinese originally wore their hair in a knot at the top of the head. But when the Manchu conquered their country, they were forced to wear the pigtail as a sign of slavery. Eventually this style became popular among the Chinese and they kept it.

As civilization advanced, hair styles became more and more varied. In time, no two people wore their hair the same way. In certain countries

329

the hair hung down loosely, in other places it was the custom to brush it up high on the head.

It is only in fairly recent times that the custom developed for women to wear their hair long and men to wear it short. Up until the Middle Ages, men wore their hair quite long and treated it with the same care as women did. They curled it and wore ribbons in it. During the Renaissance they bleached their hair and even wore wigs to make their hair look longer.

Henry VIII finally decided to do something about this extreme style and ordered all men to wear short hair. But he allowed them to wear long beards and to curl their moustaches. When James I came to the throne, however, men returned to the custom of wearing their hair long.

In France, during the reign of Louis XIV, all the gentlemen of France competed with each other for the longest, curliest wigs!

The style kept changing back and forth until the nineteenth century, when the custom of short hair for men was established once and for all. Yet even today in the law courts, the judges and barristers wear wigs—a relic of the old days of long hair!

Honey is one of the most amazing products found in nature. It has been used since very ancient times, since it was practically the only way early man could get sugar.

WHEN WAS HONEY FIRST USED?

It was used by the ancients as a medicine, to make a beverage called "mead", and in a mixture with wine and other alcoholic drinks. In Egypt, it was used as an embalming material for the mummies. In ancient India, it was used to preserve fruit and in the making of cakes and other foods. Honey is mentioned in the Bible, in the Koran, and in the writings of many ancient Greeks. So you see, its use goes far back in history.

There are hundreds of ways in which honey is used today. It gives flavour to foods, fruits, sweets, and baked goods. It is used in ice cream. It is used in medicines and in feeding babies. It is given to athletes as a source of energy. Honey has antiseptic properties and has been used in healing wounds and cuts. It has been used in hand lotions, in cigarettes, in antifreeze, and even as the centre for golf balls!

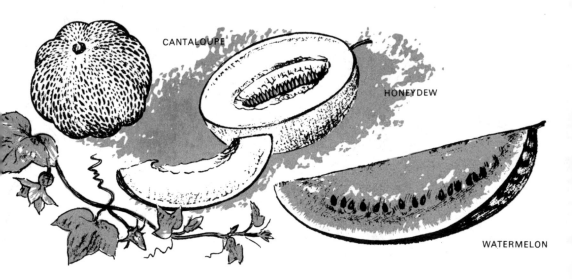

CANTALOUPE

HONEYDEW

WATERMELON

Almost everybody loves some sort of melon, whether it be muskmelon, honeydew melon, or watermelon. And when something is so popular today, it is hard to believe that it has actually been known and enjoyed for thousands and thousands of years!

WHERE DID MELONS ORIGINATE? The melon is a native of Asia, which means that it grows there without being planted by man. It is quite probable that many thousands of years ago the melon was introduced into other countries. The ancient Egyptians had the melon as one of their delicacies. The ancient Romans and probably the Greeks too enjoyed melons as much as we do! The first people to cultivate the melon in modern times were the French, and that was more than 300 years ago.

All melons belong to the gourd family, which also includes cucumbers and pumpkins. It is a trailing or trellis-climbing vine that grows best in rich, warm loam, well supplied with humus. In cooler climates, melons are grown in hotbeds or hothouses.

All melons come from two main varieties. Originally, muskmelons grew in Southern Asia and watermelons in tropical Africa. But during centuries of cultivation, they have spread to many countries, and many varieties have been developed from these two types.

Muskmelons get their names from the faint, musky perfume that they have. Muskmelons are also called "cantaloupes". Casaba melons are large, with smooth, yellowish-green rinds. They ripen late in the season and pack and keep better than other melons.

Honeydew melons have a very smooth rind and their flesh is a deep green. Watermelons are much larger than muskmelons, and much juicier.

CROSS-SECTION OF PINEAPPLE

When you look at a pineapple you may think you are looking at one fruit. Actually, the pineapple is a group of tightly packed small fruits! Each of these small fruits resembles a small apple. The central core is the stem

HOW DID THE PINEAPPLE GET ITS NAME? on which each individual small fruit is borne. And because the whole fruit somewhat resembles a pine cone, it has been given the name pineapple.

The Spaniards found the pineapple growing in South America during their first explorations and brought it back to Europe. For many years after that, rich Europeans carefully grew the pineapple in private greenhouses, and it was considered a great luxury. As transportation developed, it became possible for pineapples to be grown in the tropics and shipped to northern markets, so greenhouse-grown plants are now rare.

Today, pineapple fields exist in many parts of the world, including the West Indies, Florida, Northern Africa, Hawaii, the Azores, and Australia.

The pineapple plant grows about 1 metre high and bears its fruits at any time of the year. After the plant is mature, new shoots develop below it for the next crop. A single plant may live and bear fruit for many years. The leaves of the pineapple plant contain a fibre that can be made into cloth.

Pineapples are rarely raised from seed: they are grown from cuttings. These must be planted in thoroughly drained soil. Sandy soil only a few centimetres deep is suitable. Sometimes sheds are built over the plants to protect them from possible frost or too much heat.

332

The cabbage is a very ancient plant, and the food plants that have descended from it include many that you would never imagine have anything to do with the cabbage!

WHERE DID THE CABBAGE COME FROM?

Thousands of years ago, the cabbage was a useless plant which grew along the sea coast in different parts of Europe. It had showy yellow flowers and frilled leaves. From this wild parent plant, more than 150 varieties of cultivated plants have been developed. The best known kinds are the common cabbage, kale, Brussels sprouts, cauliflower, broccoli, and kohlrabi.

In the common cabbage there is one central bud and the leaves grow close together about it, fold over it, and form a large, solid head. Red and white cabbages have smooth leaves. Fresh white cabbage is eaten raw in salads or cooked as a vegetable.

Kale resembles the wild cabbage, since all the leaves grow to full size and remain separate from one another. Brussels sprouts combine features of both cabbage and kale. Tiny cabbage-like heads form on the stalk at the bases of the larger leaves, which are full and open.

In the cauliflower, it is the delicately flavoured flower buds and not the leaves which are eaten. These buds have developed into a solid mass with a few loose leaves around it. Because cauliflower was difficult to grow, the Italians developed a hardier variety called broccoli. Kohlrabi has a ball-shaped enlargement of the stem just above the ground, and these enlargements are eaten when young and tender.

CABBAGE   CAULIFLOWER   BRUSSEL SPROUTS

What is a flag? It is a symbol or sign made of cloth. It can be carried, flown, or waved. And it is used to say that the people who carry it or display it belong to a certain country or organization.

WHEN WERE FLAGS FIRST USED?

The idea of a flag probably originated thousands of years ago among early hunters and warriors. They wanted to be sure that both friends and enemies would be able to identify them and know whether to be ready to fight or to be friendly. Those first flags were probably made of animal skins or the feathers of a bird.

In ancient Egypt, the soldiers carried a pole with the metal image of a bird, animal, or some other object at the end of it. The first flags made of cloth were used by the ancient Chinese and East Indians. It is believed that the Chinese had cloth flags as long ago as 1100 B.C. In early Roman times, the soldiers also carried figures of different animals on poles. Then they began to use cloth flags, too.

During the Middle Ages, flags of all kinds were common in Europe. The Crusaders carried flags in their religious wars. Flags were used by noble or royal families, with special symbols that identified the family.

Probably the oldest national flag is that of Denmark. It has a white cross on a red ground and the legend is that it originated in 1219.

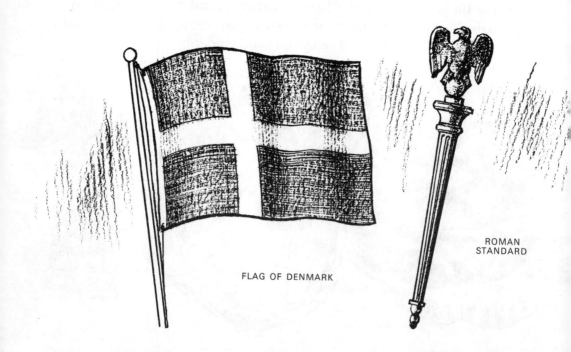

FLAG OF DENMARK

ROMAN STANDARD

The Chinese, as early as the fifth century B.C., had begun work on the Grand Canal of China, between Hangchow and Peking, a total length of 1,000 miles, and it is said to be the oldest existing canal. The principal part was built in the thirteenth century A.D.

WHO BUILT THE FIRST CANALS?

About 2000 B.C., the Egyptians built a canal joining the Nile and the Red Sea, thus anticipating the Suez Canal as we know it today. Later, Nebuchadnezzar built the royal canal of Babylon, which linked the Tigris and Euphrates. The Romans, too, constructed canals in many parts of their empire. Charlemagne, about the eighth century, began a system of canals to connect the Rhine, the Maas and the Danube. Later ages saw an extensive development of canal systems in Italy, France, Belgium and elsewhere in Europe.

The second half of the eighteenth century saw a time of great activity in canal-building in Great Britain for the transport of coal and other goods. This enthusiasm continued unabated until the advent of railways in the 1820's. The Manchester Ship Canal is a good example of how a waterway may be constructed to join an inland city with the coast. Between 1759 and 1830, no fewer than 4,790 miles of canals were cut in England. Many people invested money in them and some of the canal companies paid high dividends.

In earliest times, boats were pushed or pulled by men through canals; then horses and mules were used on a towpath along the bank. Today, boats move either under their own power or are hauled by horses.

Until the invention of the canal lock, canals could only be built where the country was level.

The idea of interplanetary travel is very old, but it is only during the past fifty years or so that astronautics have become a really practicable possibility.

WHO WAS THE FIRST ASTRONAUT? The Russian pioneer K. E. Tsiolkovsky suggested using rockets for space research as early as 1903, since rockets function by reaction motors and do not depend on a surrounding atmospheric medium. He also suggested liquid propellants because solid propellants were too weak and hard to control. In 1926, the first modern type liquid-propellant rocket was sent up by R. H. Goddard in America. In Germany, intensive research was undertaken, culminating in the liquid-propellant V2 rocket, which bombarded England during the Second World War.

After the war, serious work on the future development of rocket travel continued in the U.S.S.R. and the United States.

Before the Americans were ready to send up their first orbital satellite, *Sputnik 1* was sent up from the Soviet Union

In 1961, Russia took the world again by surprise by launching the first man into space—Yuri Gargarin, who completed a circuit of the Earth in free fall.

Piracy, which is robbery on the high seas, has been going on for thousands of years.

WHO WERE THE FIRST PIRATES? Even ancient Greek and Roman ships were often attacked by pirates in the Aegean and Mediterranean seas. In fact, the pirates became so powerful that they set up their own kingdom in part of what is now Turkey. The Romans had to send an expedition to destroy them in the year 67 B.C.

A great period of piracy lasted from the 1300's to 1830. Pirates established themselves in ports of northern Africa in what were called the Barbary States: Morocco, Algiers, Tunis, and Tripoli. They would capture and loot European ships that sailed the Mediterranean and sell their passengers and crews into slavery or hold them for ransom. This piracy did not stop until the French conquered Algiers in 1830.

One of the names we have for pirates is "buccaneers". These were the pirates who operated during the late 1500's and 1600's in the Spanish Main. Originally the term "Spanish Main" meant the Caribbean coast of Central and South America. In buccaneering days it usually meant the Caribbean Sea itself.

The buccaneers were mostly sailors and runaway servants from different countries who had gathered on the islands and in the harbours of the West Indies. They hunted wild cattle and dried the meat over grills called "boucans", and that's how the buccaneers got their name.

Pirates often buried their gold, silver, and jewels in the ground. They wanted to keep their hiding places secret. There are many people who believe that a great deal of buried pirate treasure is still to be found along the Gulf Coast from Florida to Texas.

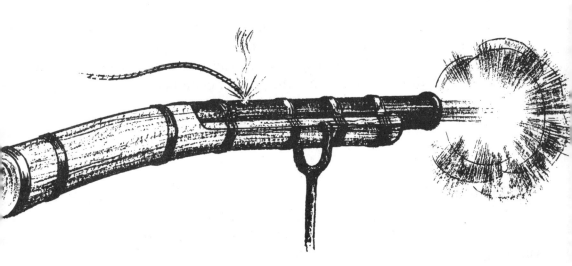

The first small firearms appeared late in the fourteenth century and were known as hand cannon. They had copper and iron tubes (barrels) closed at the rear. Near this end (the butt) was drilled a small "touch-hole" for setting fire to the powder inside. The butt ended in a hollow socket. Into this fitted a straight, wooden stick, or stock.

WHAT WAS THE FIRST GUN LIKE?

The mechanism that fires a gun is called "the lock". A forked piece of metal that pivoted to one side of the stock was added about 1425. It held a bit of smouldering wick or match. This piece could be worked back and forth to let the burning match down into the touch-hole and so fire the charge. Firearms shot this way were known as "matchlocks".

The next step (between 1475 and 1500) was to bend the stock downward. Then the user could hold it against his shoulder to take up the recoil, or kick. At the same time, he could aim along the tube or barrel at his target. This gun was called a "hackbut".

About 1515, the wheel lock was invented. A rough-edged steel wheel was spun against a flintlike piece of pyrites. This produced sparks in a small pan which sat on top of the wheel. The pan was filled with powder and a small hole connected it with the inside of the barrel.

Several forms of flintlock were developed in Europe; the earliest was known as "the snaphance". By the end of the seventeenth century, the flintlock had been improved as much as possible. It struck sparks with flint and steel like earlier guns. It was used with little change until about 1840.

In 1807, the "percussion" system was invented. There was now a small, hollow, metal tube, one end of which screwed into the barrel, while the other was a seat for an explosive capsule, or cap. When struck by the hammer, this flashed fire into the powder chamber.

One of the oldest customs of mankind is the celebration of the New Year. How did it begin? Some people say the Chinese were the first to start it, others believe it was the ancient Germans, and still others claim it was the Romans.

WHY DO WE CELEBRATE THE NEW YEAR?

We know that the Chinese have always had a great festival at the time of their New Year, which comes later than ours. The Chinese New Year festivals last several days.

The ancient Germans established a New Year festival because of the changing seasons. The German winter began about the middle of November. This was the time when they gathered the harvest. Because everybody came together at this time for the happy occasion, and because it meant they would have a period of rest from work afterwards, they would make merry and have a great holiday. Even though it was only November, they considered it the beginning of a new year!

When the Romans conquered Europe, they changed this time of celebration to the first of January. For them, the coming of the New Year was a symbol of starting up a new life with new hope for the future. This custom and this meaning has lasted to this day. We greet the New Year happily, hoping it will bring us a good, new life!

BURNSIDE

VANDYKE

IMPERIAL

There are many types of beards, of course, and each one has a different name for a special reason. A short, pointed beard is called a "Vandyke". This is because the Flemish painter Anthony Van Dyck's portraits showed men with this kind of beard. The English way of spelling his name was "Van Dyke", and this name soon came to be applied to the kind of beard he had painted!

HOW WERE BEARDS NAMED?

A "goatee" is just a little bit of a beard on the chin, and the name comes from the fact that it resembles the beard of a he-goat. A tuft of beard under the lower lip is called an "imperial", because Emperor Napoleon III of France used to wear one.

When a man has hair along the cheeks past both ears, he is said to have "burnsides". This is named after a general of the Civil War, General Ambrose Burnside. Sometimes this type of beard has the name twisted around and is called sideburns!

When we think of the millions of things that are held together by pins, we might wonder how man ever got along without them. It is quite likely that he never did; that pins made out of one material or another were in use from the very earliest times.

HOW DID PINS ORIGINATE?

The earliest form of a pin was probably a thorn. In fact, the word "pin" resembles the Latin word for "thorn" which is *spina*. Later on, man learned how to make pins out of the bones of fish or animals. In prehistoric times, Neolithic man was already making pins out of bronze.

Surprisingly enough, a safety pin, or a pin very much like it, seems to have been in use in Europe at the close of the Bronze Age, about 1000 B.C. It was made of bronze, very slender, and bent in such a way that the point was caught against the head.

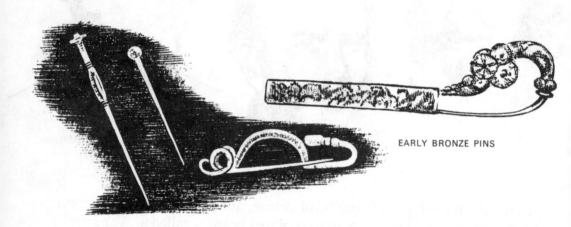

EARLY BRONZE PINS

Pins were used in Europe in very early times as a form of decoration, rather than for fastening clothes. It wasn't until the end of the fifteenth century that pins as we know them began to be manufactured. They were then considered so precious and valuable that a collection of pins was thought to be a wonderful New Year's gift. Sometimes, instead of giving the actual pins, an equivalent amount of money was given. And this is where we get our phrase "pin money"!

The first people to make modern-type pins were the French, who exported them to England. Soon we began making fine pins, too. In 1775, the Continental Congress in the American colonies offered a prize for the first 300 domestic pins equal in quality to those imported from England!

If you had to name the most long-lasting material made by man, would you say it was brick? Well, it happens to be so, and brick will outlast granite, limestone, or even iron!

WHEN WAS BRICK FIRST USED? Brick, of course, is a modern building material. It is being used today everywhere in the world. But actually, brick is as old as the history of civilization! The Babylonians and Egyptians made and used bricks at least 3,000 years before the birth of Christ. Some excavations suggest that it was used even earlier.

The making of brick in early times was very crude. Brick is made of clay or shale and baked or burned at a high temperature. In early times, raw clay was used to make brick, but no machinery to make it had been invented. The clay was crushed and mixed with water by workmen who trampled it with their bare feet. Straw was mixed with the wet clay to hold the bricks together. The mixture was then formed by hand into different sizes and shapes and placed in the sun to dry.

This crude method was followed for many years until it was discovered that burning the clay with fire made the bricks much harder and better able to withstand dampness. Straw was then no longer needed.

These sun-baked bricks would have been useless in England, but in the hot, Middle-Eastern countries they proved to be so durable that some of the bricks used in ancient Babylonia can still be seen today.

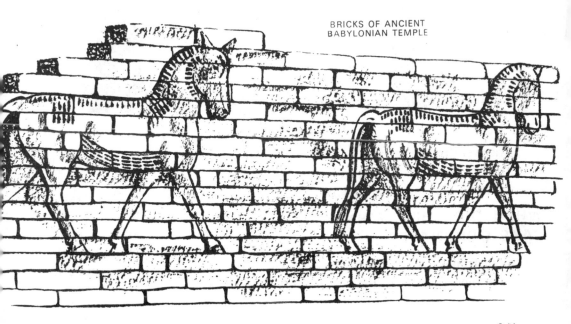
BRICKS OF ANCIENT BABYLONIAN TEMPLE

The origin of many customs is hard to trace, but this one has a definite beginning . . . and it reads like a fairy tale!

Many years ago, a beautiful girl in Holland wanted to marry a

WHO GAVE THE FIRST WEDDING PRESENTS? miller. He did not have much money, but he was loved by everyone because he used to give his flour and bread to the poor.

The father of the girl objected to the marriage and said that he would not give his daughter her dowry if she married the miller. The people whom the miller had befriended heard about this and decided to do something. None of them had much money, but they thought that if each one contributed some gift, the beautiful girl and the poor miller could marry after all.

So they got together and went to the girl's house with their gifts. Some brought utensils for the kitchen, and others brought useful articles for the house such as linen and lamps. They showered her with gifts, and she was able to marry the man she loved after all!

These were the first wedding presents and the custom has remained ever since.

The wedding cake goes back to Roman times. In those days, among the highest members of the rich families, a special kind of cake was used in wedding ceremonies. The bride and groom not only ate this cake to-

WHEN DID THE WEDDING CAKE ORIGINATE? gether, but treated the guests. It is even said that the cake was broken over the bride's head as a symbol of plentifulness! Each of the guests took a piece of cake so they, too, could have plentifulness in their lives.

Many peoples all over the world have used bridal cakes in their marriage ceremonies. Several of the American Indian tribes had special kinds of cakes made, which the bride would present to the groom.

In Europe, it became the custom for guests to bring to the wedding spiced buns which were piled up in a big heap on a table. The bride and groom were supposed to try to kiss each other over this mound of cake for good luck. The story is told that a French cook, travelling through England, thought it would be a good idea to make one mass out of this mound of little cakes . . . and that is how our present kind of wedding cake was born!

There are many different stories concerning how this custom began. All of them go back to very ancient times.

WHY DO BRIDES WEAR A VEIL?

We know that among many ancient peoples it was the custom to keep the bride hidden from her future husband until the wedding day. This was true in Egypt, where the groom never saw the face of his bride until the wedding day! Part of the wedding ceremony was the uncovering of her face. This custom was also in existence among the Arabs, the Hindus, and other peoples of Asia and Europe.

The early Romans and Hebrews also made the veil a part of the wedding ceremony. Some of these veils were so big that they enveloped the bride like a shroud. In fact, after the wedding, the veil was put away and taken out only when the woman was ready to be buried in it.

Today, of course, the reason a bride wears a veil is simply to make the wedding more romantic and attractive. It is a symbol of her loveliness and modesty!

The word "husband" originated from several sources. In Anglo-Saxon the word *hus* means "house". In Old Norse the word *bondi* means a "freeholder" or "yeoman". And the word *bua* means "to dwell". Put

WHY IS A MARRIED MAN CALLED A HUSBAND?

them all together and you have a word meaning a house-owner who is head of the household or family.

The word came to be used for a man who joined a woman in marriage and was, therefore, the head of his household. The word "husband", however, is still used to mean the managing of a household. For instance, a ship's husband is an official who is responsible for seeing that all the necessary equipment is safely on board before sailing, and that all the regulations relating to the trip are taken care of.

And when we say "husband one's resources", we mean to manage our affairs well!

A home is simply a place to stay, and human beings, like other creatures, at first found shelter and safety where they could. They stayed in a good sheltered place and considered it a "home".

WHEN DID PEOPLE BEGIN TO MAKE HOMES?

Later on, men began to improve their dwelling places in various ways. We cannot know which kind of home came first, but two of the earliest ones were the tree house and the cave house.

In a warm region, primitive man could live in a tree. He could bend the branches into a kind of framework which was tied or woven together.

It was then thatched, that is, covered with overlapping rows of bundles of grass. By living in this kind of home, early man was protected from sun, rain, flood, and any wild animals that could not climb.

But in a cold climate, a tree house would not do. So man used a cave, with a fire built outside the entrance. The cave man probably learned his first lesson in building a stone wall when he piled up loose rocks to make a doorway in front of his cave.

The next step was for man to make a cave by digging a hole in the side of a hill. Another development was to find a natural hollow on dry land, enlarge it, and build it up at the edge with stonework.

In different parts of the world, homes began to be built that suited the climate and activity of the people. In Europe, the first four-cornered house (instead of a round dwelling) was made with posts at the corners. Branches or young saplings were woven in and out between the stakes.

Man can obtain gas from places where nature has stored it away, or he can manufacture it.

WHEN WAS GAS FIRST USED?

Here is an illustration of how man can make gas. If a clay pipe is filled with powdered coal, covered with clay, and then heated in a hot fire, smoke will come from the end of the pipe stem. Soon the smoke stops. If a flame is held to the stem, the gas coming out will burn brightly and steadily. Magnified thousands of times, this little experiment shows the process of making coal gas.

In 1792, a Scottish engineer called William Murdock was the first to use manufactured gas. He purified the gas that escaped from burning coal and piped it off to use for lighting his home. Several years later, he used it to light a factory in Birmingham.

In the United States, manufactured gas was used for lighting before natural gas. In 1812, David Melville of Newport, Rhode Island, lit his home and the street in front with gas that he made from burning coal. In 1816, Baltimore, Maryland, lighted its streets with manufactured gas. Natural gas was first used at Fredonia, New York, in 1821.

Today, more natural gas is used than manufactured gas. This is because of the discovery of new gas fields, the development of new uses for gas, and the new kinds of pipelines that make it possible to link distant gas fields to large cities.

Furniture is anything on which people sit, sleep, or eat. So when the early cave man slept on a wolf skin on the floor, that was his furniture. When he made a crude box in which to keep his bone tools, he made the first chest.

WHEN WAS FURNITURE FIRST USED?

The first records we have of furniture as we think of it today come from the Egyptians. At least 4,000 years ago, they were using chairs, tables, stools, and chests. Some of the chairs had high backs and arms, decorated with carved animals' heads. Others were simple square stools with crossed legs which folded together like camp chairs. Egyptian beds were only a framework, often very low. The Egyptians did not use pillows. They used head-rests of wood and ivory.

The Babylonians and Assyrians also had elaborate furniture. Kings and queens rested on high couches with footstools, or sat in high-backed chairs while they ate from high stands and tables.

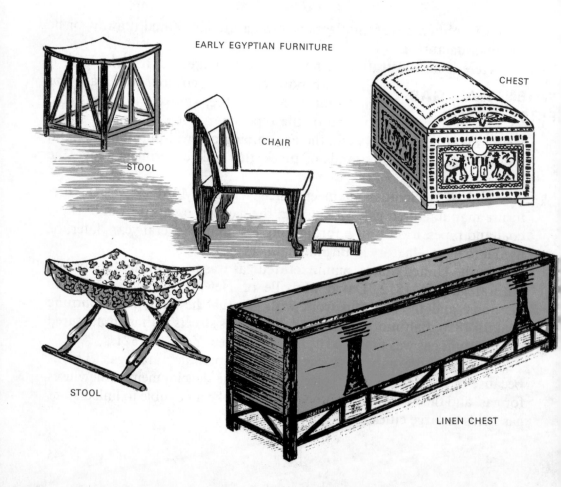

EARLY EGYPTIAN FURNITURE

STOOL

CHAIR

CHEST

STOOL

LINEN CHEST

Greek home life was very simple. The Greeks used only beds, chairs, and light tables for serving food. During meals the men rested on low beds and the women sat in chairs. The beds were like the Egyptian beds.

The Romans copied Greek styles. But they liked to fill their houses with objects for decorations, so they needed more kinds of furniture. They developed the cupboard, which they used for storing extra objects. They also used carved and painted wooden chests. The Romans made tables with metal, ivory, and stone decorations.

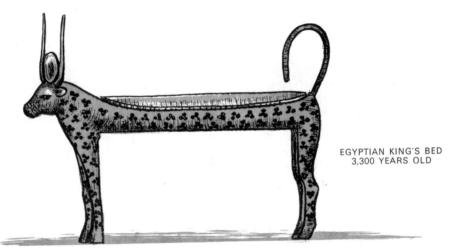

EGYPTIAN KING'S BED
3,300 YEARS OLD

Nobody knows who made the first bed. By bed we mean a special article of household furniture designed for sleeping. The ancient Assyrians, Medes, and Persians already had beds that were quite elaborate. They were made of stone, wood, or metal, and were often quite beautifully decorated.

HOW LONG HAS MAN BEEN MAKING BEDS?

The ancient Egyptians had wooden beds. The beds had frames similar to ones made today. The Greek beds had a wooden frame with a board at the head, and there were bands of hide laced across it, upon which skins were placed. Later on, these beds became quite "fancy". The bed frame was layered with expensive woods, or it was made of solid ivory with silver feet, or it would be made of bronze.

The Romans had bed frames that were high and could be reached only with the help of steps. They also probably had the first "double beds", arranged for two persons. They had rich hangings and were elaborately decorated. One Roman emperor had a bed of solid silver!

In the Middle Ages, many people slept on beds made by placing carpets on the floor or on a bench against the wall. Mattresses stuffed with feathers, wool, or hair were put on the carpets, and they would cover themselves with skins.

Then in the thirteenth century, beds became more luxurious. Bed frames were made of wood, which was painted and ornamented.

Later on, a kind of bed appeared that was hung from the ceiling or fastened to the walls. And soon all kinds of large and elaborate beds were designed for the wealthier people, and the bed became an important part of the furnishing in a house.

CRYSTAL PALACE

What we call a "world's fair" is really an exposition. The fair is one of the oldest and most popular means of selling and trading goods.

Expositions, on the other hand, are for a different purpose. These

WHEN WAS THE FIRST WORLD'S FAIR?

large displays are set up mainly to show the industrial and artistic development of a particular country or a particular period.

The first exposition, or "world's fair', was The Great Exhibition of the Works of Industry of all Nations. It was held in Hyde Park, London, in 1851. The exhibition was housed in one building, the Crystal Palace. This permanent building was made entirely of iron and glass, like a huge greenhouse. It was destroyed by fire in 1936.

The first United States international exposition was in New York City in 1853. Although nearly 5,000 exhibitors took part, about half of them from 23 foreign nations, it was not a success.

The United States' first great exposition was the Centennial in Philadelphia, Pennsylvania, in 1876. It commemorated the 100th anniversary of the signing of the Declaration of Independence. There, for the first time, thousands of people saw the products and manufactures of the entire nation brought together. Alexander Graham Bell exhibited his telephone publicly for the first time at the Centennial.

Other famous exhibitions include the "Festival of Britain", held in 1951 to celebrate the anniversary of the Great Exhibition of 1851, and the marvellously successful Expo'67 held in Canada.

A needle is a very slender tool that is sharp at one end and often has a little hole, or eye, at the other end to pass a thread through.

Man first thought of the needle so long ago that we cannot know when it was "invented".

WHO MADE THE FIRST NEEDLE?

We know that the earliest needles were made of bone, ivory, wood, bronze, or thorn. Some were really awls, such as a shoemaker uses, for they had no eyes. They were used to punch holes in the material. Well-finished needles of fish or bird bone have been found in remains of the Stone Age.

For thousands of years, bone needles pierced with eyes have been used among more civilized races. Even stone needles have been dug up in the ruins of ancient Egypt. Bronze and iron needles were known to the Romans. Many well-made needles have been found in the ruins of Pompeii.

Steel needles like those we use now are believed to have been first made by the Chinese. They were brought into Europe by the Moors in the Middle Ages. The first steel needles made in Europe were manufactured at Nuremberg, Germany, in the fourteenth century.

During the reign of Queen Elizabeth I, Elias Grouse, a German, taught the art of needle-making to the English. It is now an important industry here. The world's principal producers of needles are England and France.

Even though many machines are used in making needles, they are still not easy to make. A needle passes through the hands of more than 20 people before it is finished!

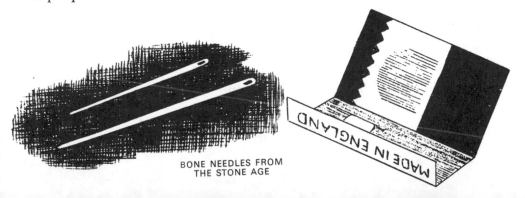

BONE NEEDLES FROM
THE STONE AGE

MADE IN ENGLAND

WILLIAM H. SEWARD

When white men first went to Alaska, they found Eskimos, Aleuts, and Indians living there. In fact, Alaska was one of the last large areas of the world to be discovered and explored by white men.

WHO DISCOVERED ALASKA?

In the early eighteenth century, the Russians were moving through Siberia to the Pacific Ocean. In 1728, Vitus Bering, a Dane in the service of the Russian navy, sailed east from Kanchatka. He drifted along St. Lawrence Island, but failed to reach the Alaska mainland. In 1741, Bering led a second expedition in two small ships.

One ship, the *St. Peter*, was under his command, and the *St. Paul* was commanded by Alexei Chrikov. The two ships were separated during a storm, but both reached Alaska.

For the next two hundred years, Russian fur traders hunted fur-bearing animals throughout Alaskan waters. They established many settlements, and in some of these places the quaint churches built by Aleuts and Indians under the guidance of Russian missionary priests can still be seen.

Later on, sea captains from Spain, France, and Great Britain explored the Alaska coast. But it was the Russians who used Alaska as a source of fur, and millions of these furs were sent by the Russians to European capitals. Then some of the fur-bearing animals began to be wiped out, and by the 1820's the Russians began to leave the Alaskan coast.

The Russian tsar, Alexander II, was not very interested in Alaska. William H. Seward, secretary of state under Abraham Lincoln, urged the United States to buy Alaska from the Russians. In 1867, the Alaskan territory was sold to the United States for $7,200,000. It was bought at less than two cents an acre! Today, Alaska is not only the 49th state in the United States, but its value to this country could hardly be measured in dollars!

You have probably heard people say that the only true "Americans" were the Indians. Everyone else has ancestors who went there from some other country. The Negroes, too, originally went there from other countries. But what most people do not know is that the first Negroes to come to America came as explorers!

WHEN DID THE FIRST NEGRO GO TO AMERICA?

They came with the Spanish, the French, and the Portuguese, who went there on voyages of discovery. There were Negroes with Balboa when he discovered the Pacific Ocean, and with Cortez when he explored Mexico. Negroes explored with the Spanish, French, and Portuguese into the interior of North America, going into New Mexico, Arizona, and the Mississippi Valley. It was a Negro who introduced the raising of wheat to the New World.

Later on, of course, Negroes went to the New World in quite a different way—they were brought there as slaves. In 1619, a Dutch vessel brought 20 Negroes to Jamestown, Virginia, who were sold by their captain for provisions he needed.

At the time, many white people went to America to work as "indentured" servants. This meant they sold their service for a set length of time. But when white indentured servants stopped coming from Europe, many Negro slaves were brought into the colonies. This started in 1688, and by 1715 there were over 58,000 Negro slaves there. By 1775, this number had grown to over 500,000.

In 1807, at the request of President Thomas Jefferson, Congress voted that no more slaves should be brought into the country. But many were brought in against the law. By 1860, just before the Civil War, the Negro population in the United States was about 4,400,000.

If there is one sight in London that every visitor wants to see it is the Tower. The history and grandeur of England seems to be present where-ever you turn.

WHEN WAS THE TOWER OF LONDON BUILT?

On the spot where the Tower now stands there was probably first a British fort, then a Roman one, and perhaps a Saxon one. William the Conqueror may have started building the White Tower, which is the oldest part of the present fortress. Most of the other buildings were put up during the reign of Henry III (1216–72).

William the Conquerer built the Tower in order to make the citizens of London afraid of him, but it has been used more as a prison than a fortress.

The Tower of London is still maintained as an arsenal. During the two World Wars, it was again used as a prison. It occupies a site on the old city of London and covers an area of about 5 hectares. The outer wall is surrounded by a deep moat, which was drained in 1843.

While there is a garrison of soldiers assigned to the Tower, the most interesting people tourists see there are the "Beefeaters". They are the "Yeomen Warders", a body of about 40 men specially chosen for this job of defending the Tower. They wear a special uniform which is said to date back to the time of Henry VIII or Edward VI. The reason they are known as "Beefeaters" is that in ancient times they were served beef every day as rations.

Hawaii is the most recent state to become part of the United States. It is made up of a group of islands in the Pacific Ocean, some 2,400 miles southwest of California. The state includes eight large and many small islands, and has a total area of about 6,420 square miles.

HOW WAS HAWAII FORMED?

According to Hawaiian legends, there was a volcano goddess called Pele who formed the islands. From time to time Pele returns to the island's craters and kindles her fires into eruptions.

The strange fact is that the Hawaiian Islands are actually the tops of great volcanoes which have been thrust up from the bottom of the ocean. For example, the island of Hawaii ("the Big Island"), which is twice as large as all the other islands together, was piled up by five volcanoes whose eruptions overlapped one another. Two of these are still active and they are still continuing the process of island building.

One of these volcanoes, Mauna Loa, erupts every few years. In 1950, it erupted for 23 days and lava flowed down into the sea. It turned the water into steam, killing many fish.

Another volcano, Mauna Kea, is dormant. It is the highest mountain in the Pacific. It rises over 4,200 metres above sea level, but its base goes down to about 5,480 metres under the ocean. If measured from under-water base, it is the world's tallest mountain.

On the island of Maui there is a volcano called Haleakala which rises to a height of about 3,055 metres. It is the world's largest inactive volcano. Its crater is about 20 miles around and some 830 metres deep.

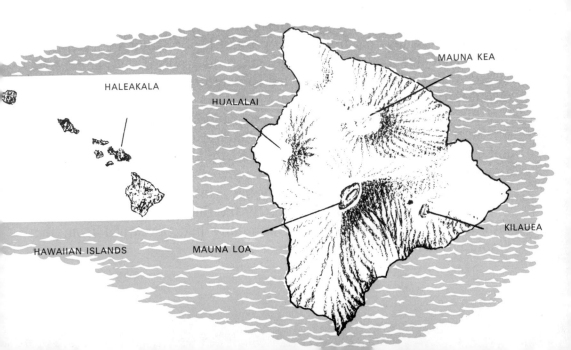

HALEAKALA

HAWAIIAN ISLANDS

MAUNA KEA

HUALALAI

KILAUEA

MAUNA LOA

NEOLITHIC LAKE DWELLERS

We think of cities as being part of civilization. Both the words "city" and "civilization" come from the same Latin word *civis*, meaning a person who shares in both the duties and privileges of the community in

HOW DID CITIES BEGIN?

which he lives. When many different kinds of people learned to work and play together, great cities grew.

The main differences between a city, a town, and a village, is size. In most cases the city is the largest. Nearly all cities were first villages.

No one knows just when or where the first city was started. It could have started when a wandering tribe of hunters found a spot they liked well enough to stay in. This happened as long ago as 6000 B.C., and probably even earlier. By 3000 B.C., men were already building and living in quite large cities.

At a very early time in history, men discovered that food was easier to get if they could capture and tame animals. Then they did not need to hunt them through the forests every time they got hungry. Men also learned that they could have more fruits and grains if the plants were cared for. In this way men started agriculture—farming and animal raising.

But people cannot farm and move around all the time. They must stay in the same place long enough to harvest crops. It is also difficult and slow to move a herd of animals across the country. As tribes settled down and stayed at one spot, a village or town began.

There is nothing left of the very first villages, since the buildings were made of skins, wood, or mud. By the time men learned to build with long-lasting materials, the community had developed from the simple agricultural village to a town or city.

Plastic means "capable of being moulded or modelled". When heated, plastics are like modelling clay. They can be moulded into shapes which last when the material is cooled.

WHO INVENTED PLASTIC? In making plastics, chemists start with the molecule. The chemist causes molecules from a certain material to form a long chain, the links being the molecules. The new "long-chain" molecule acts differently from the single molecule. The molecules are said to "polymerize" when they link into chains. By polymerization new materials are made.

The hard pieces of polymer are ground into fine powder or made into pellets. Colours are added, and chemicals are worked in to make it flexible.

Chemists knew and had worked with plastics about 125 years ago. Vinyl chloride was polymerized in 1838, styrene in 1839, acrylics in 1843, and polyester in 1847. But at that time there was no great need for these synthetic materials. Natural products such as wood, metals, rubber, hide, and ivory were plentiful.

The supply of ivory was first to be used up. So a prize was offered to anyone who developed a substitute for ivory. While working on this project, John Hyatt and his brother Isaiah Hyatt discovered celluloid, which they patented in 1870.

Celluloid had many defects, but their discovery led other chemists to think about developing synthetic materials. In 1907, Leo Baekeland discovered the phenolic plastic, which was the first entirely synthetic material to be produced in large quantities. Since that time many new plastics have been discovered.

The word "college" originally meant any society or union of persons engaged in some common activity. For example, there is a college of cardinals which elects the pope at Rome, and the United States has an

WHEN WAS THE FIRST UNIVERSITY STARTED? electoral college to choose the president and vice president.

In medieval times, any corporation or society organized for a common interest was called a "university". So the earliest educational universities were merely societies of scholars or teachers formed for mutual protection. There were no permanent buildings. Instructors and students simply rented a hall or a large room.

In time, these institutions grew, buildings were built, certain legal rights and privileges were obtained, and the universities became permanent. The first such university was in Salerno, Italy. As far back as the ninth century it was well known as a school of medicine. It was formally made a university in 1231.

Toward the end of the twelfth century at Bologna, Italy, a many-sided university was established. The school at Bologna taught law, medicine, arts, and theology.

The most famous of the medieval schools of higher learning was the University of Paris, officially organized in the last half of the twelfth century. It became a model for all the later universities of Europe.

Our two oldest English universities were modelled upon the University of Paris. Oxford and Cambridge were both legally recognized by the thirteenth century. A university, remember, usually includes a number of colleges. This means that degrees are given in many different fields at a university.

Many institutions start as colleges and later become universities. In the United States, the first college was Harvard, founded at Cambridge, Massachusetts, in 1636. Today it is a great university.

Arithmetic may be called the science of numbers. The word itself comes from the Greek "arithmos" which means numbers. At first, men may have counted their sheep and oxen on the fingers of their hands. The

HOW DID ARITHMETIC START?

word "digit", which means any single figure from 0 to 9 inclusive, reminds us of this, for "finger" in Latin is "digitus".

Then man got around to making notches on sticks and the next step was to invent a suitable notation—a system by which each number might be recorded using signs and symbols. The ancient Greeks used the letters of their alphabet for the purpose. The Romans carried this system a little further, dropping most of the alphabet and making seven letters do all the work. These letter systems were employed in writing sums, but, generally, calculations were made with the aid of an abacus.

The Arabs introduced the notation which we use today based on the Hindu system. This had the innovation of a nought to indicate

"place value" (as in distinguishing, say, 13 from 1030). This simplified calculations enormously. The Arabs called the figure 0 "sifr", a word meaning empty.

The first arithmetic to be written advising the use of the Arab notation was by an Italian in 1202. The first arithmetic to be printed was written in Latin, and came out in Italy in 1478. Other early arithmetics were printed in 1484 and 1496. They included adding, subtracting and multiplying.

In some Latin schools, arithmetic was studied only in the fifth and sixth years, and only then one hour a week was given to it.

It should be remembered that the early books of arithmetic contained most of the modern methods and we owe a great debt of gratitude to their authors and the Hindus who inspired them.

It cannot be too strongly stressed that a complete mastery of the fundamental facts (or tables) in addition, multiplication, subtraction and division is necessary to a basic understanding in simple arithmetic.

Men have lived together in groups since the very earliest times. Each group tried to keep together and to find ways that would keep the group going after its individual members were gone.

WHY DID PEOPLE START TO HAVE SCHOOLS?

In order for the group and its values to survive, it was necessary for the older members to teach children all that they had learned so that they could solve the problems they would face. Young people had to be trained to carry on the customs, knowledge, and skills of the group. So the idea of "education" existed long before there were actual schools.

But when letters were invented, schools became a necessity. Special learning was required to master the symbols. And the existence of these symbols made it possible to accumulate and transmit knowledge on a scale that had never been possible before.

Ordinary life in the group did not provide this type of education. So a special organization was needed to take over the job of providing it. And this was the school.

Nobody knows when the first schools appeared. We do know that they were in existence in Egypt and perhaps in China and in some other countries 5,000 to 6,000 years ago.

Actually, it was not until the eighteenth century that the idea of education for all as a way of improving man and his society began to spread. And it was only about 100 years ago that people began to consider an education as the right of every child.

The principal religions in the world today are the Hindu, Buddhist, Confucianist, Taoist, Shinto, Zoroastrian, Mohammedan, Jewish, and Christian faiths.

HOW DID THE MAJOR RELIGIONS START?

The Hindu religion of India was formed about 3,000 years ago. Founders of this faith considered that Brahma was the first great god. Brahma created all forms of life and multiples of other gods.

Buddha was a great religious teacher who lived about 3,000 years ago. In its original form Buddhism does not depend upon a god or gods

BIRTH OF BRAHMA

BUDDHA   ZOROASTER

but teaches that man can purify himself of all desires and thus do away with evil and suffering. There are various sects and modifications of Buddhism.

Confucianism, based on the teachings of Confucius, a sixth century B.C. philosopher, is concerned almost wholly with man's right conduct toward his fellow man.

Taoism sprang from a little book called *Tao Te king*, which was written by Lâo-tse in the sixth century B.C. It calls upon its followers to find and follow the natural way of life.

Shinto is the primitive religion of Japan. It has been modified by many later contacts and teachers, mostly Chinese.

The Zoroastrian religion stems from the teachings of Zarathustra, or Zoroaster, prophet of Iran, born probably in the seventh century B.C. This religion elevates Ahura Mazda (Wise Lord) as the great One God. The Mohammedan religion is based on the teachings of Mohammed, prophet of Arabia in the sixth century A.D.

Judaism is the oldest one-god (monotheistic) religion. Originating in Palestine, which was the early home of the Jews, it went with the Jewish people wherever they travelled. The Christian religion is based on the teachings of Jesus Christ. He was born in Palestine between 8 and 4 B.C.

"Monasticism" means a way of life devoted to religion. A "monastery" is a house where men who have taken religious vows live. These men are usually monks, but priests and brothers also may live in monasteries.

WHO WERE THE FIRST NUNS?
A "convent" is a house where women who have taken religious vows live. These women are called "nuns".

Monasticism was practised long before Christian times. A group of Jews, the Essenes, lived a community life and shared their property. Christian monasticism began in Egypt during the third century A.D. Groups of men left society to live alone and pray.

Religious orders of women have also existed since very early times. In fact, some people believe there were organized convents for women before there were any for men! In the year 270, St. Anthony, considered to be the founder of monasticism, is said to have placed his sister in a nunnery. So there must have been nuns as early as that time.

In Christian history, when an order of monks or friars began, a branch for women was usually formed.

Most religious orders of women today follow the rule of St. Augustine or St. Francis. They take vows just as men's orders do. They live in convents, each of which has its own habit (style of clothing).

Until the seventeenth century, nuns usually stayed in the convent and spent their lives in prayer. But since that time, many orders of nuns have gone out to work with people in schools, hospitals, orphanages, and homes for the aged.

On a hot day in June, 1859, at the close of the battle of Solferino, fifteen thousand dead and wounded lay on the battle field. There were few surgeons, and many of the wounded died before they could receive medical attention. A young Swiss, Henri Dunant, travelling through the battle area, was appalled by the carnage and the cries of the wounded. He gathered a volunteer band of women from a nearby Italian village, and under his guidance and example, they nursed the wounded.

WHEN DID THE RED CROSS START?

Henri Dunant wrote a pamphlet about the terrible scenes he had witnessed. He claimed that much death and suffering could be avoided if an organization were founded to protect the wounded in battle, "without distinction of nationality".

Thanks to Dunant's humanitarian concern, the Red Cross Treaty was adopted by fourteen nations at an international conference at Geneva in 1864, and was revised in 1906. It provides for the protection, in time of war, of relief societies to be organized in various nations. The Swiss flag, with its colours reversed, was adopted as the Red Cross emblem. Now, under the Red Cross banner, the hearts of many nations unite in the service of humanity in times of war or national disaster. In every war, this banner of mercy is respected by friend and foe alike.

The British Red Cross Society was founded in 1870, and incorporated in 1908. Although the British Forces have medical services of their own, in time of war the Red Cross provides necessary further assistance.

HENRY DUNANT

Today there are millions of people who believe that if a black cat crosses their path, bad luck will quickly follow. The superstition actually goes back thousands and thousands of years!

WHY IS A BLACK CAT CONSIDERED BAD LUCK?
The ancient Egyptians worshipped the cat and considered it sacred. They had a goddess called Pasht, who had the head of a cat. The Egyptians believed their goddess Pasht had nine lives, and this explains why many people still think a cat has nine lives. When a black cat died in ancient Egypt, the mummy of the cat was preserved. A cemetery has been found in which there were thousands of mummies of black cats!

When people believed in witches, they associated the black cat with witches. They believed black cats were witches in disguise, and that killing the cats did not mean killing the witches, because a witch could take on the body of a cat nine times!

In the Middle Ages, it was believed that witches and witch doctors always used the brain of a black cat in cooking up their mysterious potions. Through all these associations, the black cat came to be a sign of bad luck!

To us, the right to a trial by jury is one of man's most sacred and natural rights. But it took man a long time to reach the point where this right was recognized.

HOW DID TRIAL BY JURY BEGIN?
When the Normans conquered England in 1066, they started a kind of jury. But the men on a jury were not there to listen as witnesses. They were supposed to decide a case on the basis of their own knowledge of the facts.

It was not until the reign of Henry II in the twelfth century that a big change was made. It was decided that the jury must decide a case solely on the evidence heard in court.

And this, of course, is the whole basis of the trial by jury system we have today. Twelve members of the trial jury listen to the evidence given by witnesses, to the arguments of the lawyers, and to the instructions of the judge. They then retire to a room to decide on their verdict. There seems to be no special reason why the number of jurors is 12, simply that Henry II in 1166 so decided and it has been that way since.

Before jury trials, trials were conducted in different ways. One method was "trial by compurgation". This meant that an accused person brought into court a number of neighbours who were willing to swear that he was innocent.

A second method was "trial by ordeal". The accused was subjected to all kinds of ordeals, like plunging his hands into burning oil, or carrying a piece of red-hot iron. If he survived the ordeal, he was declared innocent.

A third method was "trial by combat". Here a man had to do battle and defeat his enemy. If he won, he was innocent!

Thousands and thousands of years ago, primitive man started the custom of using a headpiece of stone to mark the grave of the dead. If we observe what many primitive people do today, and believe it is done for the

WHY DO WE HAVE GRAVESTONES?

same reasons, then the custom seemed to have this purpose: to keep the evil spirits that are supposed to live in dead bodies from rising up!

The gravestone was also a way of warning people away from the spot where those evil spirits lived. Over the centuries, of course, the purpose of a gravestone changed. The Greeks ornamented their gravestones with sculpture. The Hebrews marked their graves with stone pillars. The Egyptians built great tombs and pyramids to mark the places where their dead were buried.

When Christianity appeared, the marking of graves became a common practice. Christianity took over the sign of the cross and ring, which to primitive people was a symbol of the sun. Later on, this was changed to a simple cross, and it is still used today.

Man is afraid of many things. When he cannot understand why things happen, especially if he feels frightened or is injured by them, he tries to explain it in some mysterious way. The belief in witchcraft was one

WHY DID PEOPLE BELIEVE IN WITCHES?

way of explaining such things as drought, thunder and lightning, and mental and physical illness.

A witch was supposed to be a person of great power and authority, who used that power to do harm. Some people believed that the Devil helped witches do their evil work. Usually the witch was a woman, and she would ride about at night on a broomstick. If the witch was a man, he was called a wizard or warlock.

Witchcraft had a firm hold on the imaginations of the common people hundreds of years ago. They lived in ignorance, superstition, and fear. But the surprising thing was that many educated people believed in them, too. This was because it was a very easy way of explaining unforeseen disasters.

In early Christian times, witches were believed to have sold their souls to the Devil, a pagan god, or other evil masters in return for supernatural powers.

In 1484, Pope Innocent VIII issued a papal bull formally condemning witchcraft, partly because the terrible plagues that swept Europe were blamed on witchcraft.

During the seventeenth century, both Roman Catholics and Protestants began a witch hunt that brought death to thousands. In England, there were professional witch-finders who went about the countryside looking for marks of witches and identifying persons as witches. Between 1647 and 1663, hundreds of people in Massachusetts and Connecticut were accused of witchcraft.

Today, doctors believe that many of the dreams and visions that were blamed on witchcraft were really the products of hysteria or mental illness.

HEAD-HUNTER
OF THE
PHILIPPINES

Head-hunting goes back to the Stone Ages and perhaps even before that. It has been practised in one form or another practically all over the world. And it actually survived until the early twentieth century in the Balkan peninsula in Europe! While the reasons for doing it may have differed from place to place and from time to time, it had one general basis.

WHY ARE SOME PEOPLE HEAD-HUNTERS?

This was the belief that the soul was made up of matter and that all life depended on it. It was believed that in human beings this soul matter was located especially in the head.

When a community or a tribe was able to get hold of some heads, they believed that the souls within the heads were captured. They thus felt they were adding to the stock of soul matter belonging to the community, and this would make the people, the cattle, and the crops more fertile.

Many of us think of head-hunting as being carried on chiefly in Africa, but this is not true. Head-hunting did occur there, especially in Nigeria. But in the British Museum there is a bas-relief which shows a battle taking place in the seventh century B.C. and the Assyrians are cutting off and taking away the heads of their enemies. In many parts of India, head-hunting was widely practised.

In North America, the Indians did not take the head, they just took the scalp, probably because they believed the soul was located in the hair. In South America, there was not only head-hunting, but they developed the practice of shrinking the head and preserving it as a trophy.

Another name for oil is "petroleum", and this gives us a clue as to how it was formed. The word "petroleum" means "rock oil". Scientists think that petroleum was formed from plants and animals that lived ages ago in and around warm seas that covered much of the earth.

HOW WAS OIL FORMED?

As the plants and animals died, they piled up on the sea bottom. In time, millions of tons of sand and mud covered them. Under pressure, the mud and sand changed to rock.

The plants and animals turned into a dark liquid trapped in the pores of the rocks. When parts of the earth's crust moved upward, sections of the old sea floor became dry land. Some of the liquid oozed to the surface of the earth and so men came to notice it.

Petroleum, or crude oil, has been used for thousands of years. The ancient Egyptians and Chinese used it as a medicine. In India, it was burned long before the Christian Era.

But until the middle of the nineteenth century, the only way man got this oil was by collecting it when it seeped naturally from the earth. Sometimes it was skimmed from the surface of streams or soaked up in rags.

Crude petroleum, as it comes from the well, is of little use. It must be refined. A distillation process separates the different things nature put into crude oil. In this process we obtain petrol, kerosene, lubricating oils, fuel oil, and asphalt.

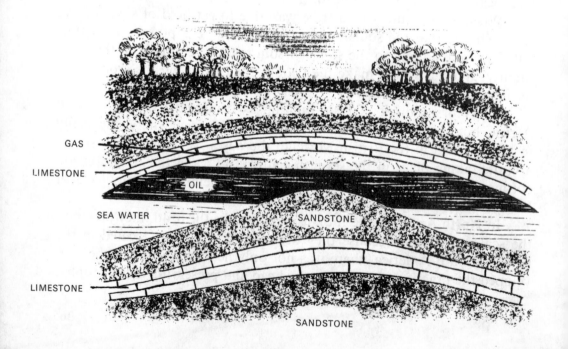

It is almost certain that gold was the first metal known to man. One reason for this is that gold is found in the free state, uncombined with other metals or rocks. The bright yellow colour and shining appearance

WHEN WAS GOLD DISCOVERED?

of gold probably attracted the attention of primitive man. Exactly when this happened cannot be known, because it was long before recorded history.

Some of the earliest records of gold have to do with the treasure of European kings. These records are more than 5,500 years old. The next records are of the ancient Assyrians who, in the year 2470 B.C., conquered their neighbours and carried away stolen gold.

The Greek and Roman kings also loved gold. They obtained as much gold as possible by stealing from conquered countries and by using slaves to dig in the mines.

GOLD BRACELETS FROM PREHISTORIC IRELAND

GOLD NECKLACE FROM ANCIENT ASSYRIA

During the Middle Ages, men were so anxious to have gold that they tried to find a way to change other metals to gold. They mixed and melted many different things, but they never found a way to do it.

Still later, Spain sent many explorers to all parts of the world to search for gold.

The discovery of gold anywhere in the world has always caused a rush of people to that place. Gold was discovered in California in 1848 and the Gold Rush of '49 followed. The same thing happened when gold was discovered in Australia in 1851, in British Columbia in 1856, in South Africa in 1886, and in Alaska in 1896.

SIBERIA

ALASKA

The Eskimos are just one more kind of North American Indian. They look Mongolian, but no more so than some other native peoples of North and South America.

WHERE DID ESKIMOS COME FROM?

Like the rest of the Indians, the Eskimos came from Asia. It is believed that the first Eskimos came to North America by way of the Bering Strait and Alaska 2,000 to 3,000 years ago.

Some then moved along the western coast of Alaska and then along the southern coast as far as the place where the city of Anchorage now is. Others moved out upon the Aleutian Islands. But most of them moved east along the northern coasts of Alaska and Canada.

The first known meeting of Eskimos and Europeans was around the year A.D. 1000, when the Norse discoverers of America saw Eskimos, probably in Labrador or Newfoundland. The Eskimos later met the Norsemen in Greenland.

During the twelfth and thirteenth centuries, there was a great deal of intermarriage between the Europeans and the Eskimos in Greenland. Many of the Eskimos there today are now practically European in appearance.

As a matter of fact, it is important to realize that Eskimos differ among themselves almost as much as Europeans do. Some of them look like blond Scandinavians or Germans. Others look like dark southern Italians.

The reason Eskimos live in the north is probably that they are a hunting people and their country is one of the best for hunting in all of North America.

Posters are so named because they contain messages that are "posted" for people to see. Most posters call attention to a product, an event, or a service. They are placed at a point where many people pass. And, in

WHEN WERE THE FIRST POSTERS USED?

a way, they are the first examples of advertising.

Posters have been found in certain ruins of ancient Egypt. Of course, they were in the form of wall paintings, but their purpose was the same. They are the first posters we know about. And in ancient Rome, when certain events were going to take place in the Colosseum, posters were displayed all over Rome to advertise these events.

When printing was developed in the fifteenth century, it became much easier to make many copies of the notice or advertisement. Some were passed out by hand ("handbills"), and some were pasted up (posted) on walls or fences.

The modern poster as we know it was born with the invention of lithography in 1796. This made it possible to add coloured pictures to the type.

Do you know what kind of poster you see most today? It is the outdoor advertising billboard, and you usually see it along the highroad. Since people go by these posters rather quickly and do not have time to stop and read them, this means that a poster has to follow certain basic rules. Its message must be presented so it can be read in a glance. It should have few colours, few words, and a simple design.

The Canadian people are made up of different national stocks and races. The first known inhabitants of the country were the Indians.

It is believed the Indians crossed into this continent across the

WHEN DID PEOPLE SETTLE IN CANADA? Bering Strait and Sea from eastern Asia at least 10,000 years ago. When Europeans first explored the country, Indian bands were living in most of the forested areas. There were only a few Indians in the provinces near the Atlantic Ocean.

The second group of people to enter Canada were the Eskimos. They crossed the Bering Strait from Asia less than 3,000 years ago. There are few records of their early movements.

The first white settlers in Canada were the French. They came in greatest numbers to Quebec, but also to Nova Scotia, where they cleared farms on the southern side of the Bay of Fundy.

The French built their citadel at Quebec City, where the St. Lawrence River narrows, and carved farms out of the forests in the territory. By the time of the British conquest in 1763, there were about 60,000 French in Canada, living chiefly between Quebec and Montreal.

There were not many British in Canada until the American Revolutionary War drove large numbers northward.

Throughout the nineteenth century, thousands of British immigrants came to Canada. The descendants of these peoples from England, Scotland, and Ireland now make up about half the population.

Around the turn of the century, immigrants came in increasing numbers from Europe, and the largest numbers came from Central and Eastern Europe—Germans, Czechs, Poles, Rumanians, and Ukrainians.

The sailor who rolls up his sleeves and shows an arm tattooed with anchors, hearts, and mottoes, is actually wearing a form of body adornment that has been used by the most primitive peoples.

WHEN DID TATTOOING BEGIN? Tattooing goes back to very ancient times. The Egyptians, Southern Chinese, East Indians, and others all knew of tattooing.

In those olden days, the art of tattooing was made to seem important and dignified because it was accompanied by elaborate ceremonies. The

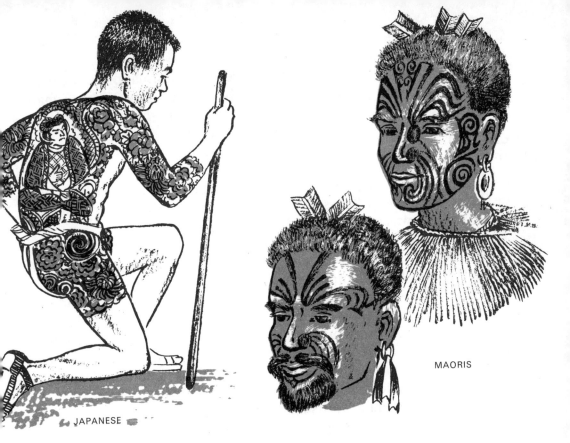

JAPANESE

MAORIS

Maoris of New Zealand used to cover their faces with very complicated tattooed patterns, and sometimes they still do it today.

In Japan, the practice of tattooing chrysanthemums, dragons' faces, and whole landscapes has gone on for centuries. Tattoo designs used to take the place of clothing for some of the Japanese. The American Indians used tattooing as a way of identifying themselves with certain tribes.

Tattooing has also had, in many parts of the world, a religious and social importance. Among some peoples, young girls are not considered ready for marriage until they have been decorated with fancy tattooing. Tattooing has been used to designate mourning among some people. And warriors have had themselves tattooed in order to show their courage or to look more frightful to their enemies.

Today, tattooing is usually done by pricking the skin in dots and lines with a sharp instrument, such as a needle of steel, shell, or bone. Then colouring matter is put in to form a design. A less usual method is that of "sewing" in the pattern by drawing through the skin a thread which has been dipped in colouring matter.

If we think of advertising as a way of spreading information in order to do business—we might say advertising began ages ago. When a man brings some of his crops to market and stands there shouting his wares, isn't he really delivering a "commercial"?

WHEN DID ADVERTISING BEGIN?

Long before printing was invented, traders would make signs on walls to call attention to their products. And merchants hung out signs with pictures of boots, or gloves, or whatever they sold, as a way of "advertising" their business. The town crier was also used to advertise in olden times.

Advertising as we know it, however, really began with the invention of printing. A small poster advertising a certain religious book was actually printed by William Caxton in 1480.

With the coming of printing, and especially the newspaper, advertising developed from just being an announcement about something to being an argument and suggestion to make people buy the product. Weekly papers printed in England as early as the 1650's had advertising for coffee, chocolate, and tea. In June, 1666, the London Gazette actually issued a supplement, an addition to the regular newspaper, that contained nothing but advertising!

Today, advertising is considered a "science" as well as an art. Research is done, studies are made of consumer tastes and habits, and ads are tested and checked, so that there will be the greatest return for the money spent.

WILLIAM CAXTON

SILKWORM MOTH

COCOON

RVAE ON
ERRY LEAVES

Silk is the thread or cloth made from the fine web of the silkworm, a certain kind of caterpillar. The web is actually a cocoon that the worm spins during a stage of its development into a moth.

WHEN WERE SILKWORMS FIRST USED? The secret of making silk thread and cloth was known to the Chinese about 4,000 years ago. There is a legend that a young Chinese empress called Si-Ling-Shi accidentally dropped a caterpillar cocoon into her hand basin and discovered that shining threads could be unwound from the cocoon.

She is said to have experimented with the raising of silkworms and the use of silk threads for weaving. For hundreds of years, the Chinese guarded the secret of raising the silkworms and making silk.

Traders from other countries would come to the border of China to obtain the precious silks and other goods. Sometimes, in regions such as ancient Persia and the Greek islands, the silk cloths would be taken apart and rewoven in new designs.

The secret of silk raising was brought to Japan about the third century A.D. About the year 550, Justinian, Emperor of Byzantium, is said to have sent two Persian monks to China to bring back eggs of silkworms in a bamboo tube. This small beginning started a silk industry in the region around Constantinople.

From there the raising of silk spread slowly throughout South-Eastern Europe. Italy became famous for lovely brocades, damasks, and velvets made of Italian-grown silk.

To us it seems so natural to put up an umbrella to keep the water off when it rains. But actually the umbrella was not invented as protection against rain. Its first use was as a shade against the sun!

WHEN WAS THE UMBRELLA INVENTED?

Nobody knows who first invented it, but the umbrella was used in very ancient times. Probably the first to use it were the Chinese, way back in the eleventh century B.C.!

We know that the umbrella was used in ancient Egypt and Babylon as a sunshade. And there was a strange thing connected with its use: it became a symbol of honour and authority. In the Far East in ancient times, the umbrella was allowed to be used only by royalty or by those in high office.

KING DARIUS OF
ANCIENT PERSIA
500 B.C.

In Europe, the Greeks were the first to use the umbrella as a sunshade. And the umbrella was in common use in ancient Greece. But it is believed that the first persons in Europe to use umbrellas as protection against the rain were the ancient Romans.

During the Middle Ages, the use of the umbrella practically disappeared. Then it appeared again in Italy in the late sixteenth century. And again it was considered a symbol of power and authority. By 1680, the umbrella appeared in France, and later on in England.

By the eighteenth century, the umbrella was used against rain throughout most of Europe. Umbrellas have not changed much in style during all this time, though they have become much lighter in weight. It wasn't until the twentieth century that women's umbrellas began to be made, in a whole variety of colours.

Some form of handkerchief has been used by man since the very earliest times. Probably the first form of handkerchief was the tail of a jackal which was mounted on a stick. Primitive people used this as both a handkerchief and a fan.

HOW LONG HAVE HANDKERCHIEFS BEEN USED?

We know that many savage races made little mats of straw which they wore on their heads and used to wipe away perspiration. This was probably the chief early use of the handkerchief.

In Greek and Roman times, there were not only handkerchiefs but napkins, too. Napkins were used for drying the hands at the table. Handkerchiefs were made out of small linen squares which were put inside the clothes and taken along on journeys.

In the seventeenth century in France, handkerchiefs became very elegant. They were made of lace and often decorated with gems. When snuff became popular in the eighteenth century, women began to use handkerchiefs of coloured cloth.

Marie Antoinette persuaded Louis XVI of France to issue a law that handkerchiefs had to be square in shape, instead of round, or oval, or oblong!

The wearing of gloves is a very old custom. They were invented for protection by ancient peoples who lives in cold regions.

HOW DID THE WEARING OF GLOVES BEGIN?

We know that the ancient Persians and Romans wore gloves. In the *Odyssey*, there is reference to Laertes' wearing gloves while walking in his garden.

In early times, gloves were of leather only and were worn chiefly in war and in the chase to protect the hands. But by the eighth and ninth centuries, practically everybody in Germany and the Scandinavian countries wore gloves during winter months for protection against cold.

It wasn't until the thirteenth century that women began to wear gloves for ornament. They were usually made of linen and reached to the elbow. Queen Elizabeth, years later, created the fashion for wearing jewelled and embroidered gloves. Kid gloves first appeared in France during the reign of Louis XIV, and the women of the time wore gloves of netted silk.

Stockings were originally made of leather to cover the legs for protection. But even the idea of protecting the legs in this way was not a common practice until after the beginning of the Christian Era.

WHO INVENTED STOCKINGS? The first people who tried to make a stocking anything like the ones we wear today were the French, and in the seventh century, French men wore leather stockings for protection and warmth.

Soon people began to want to make the stockings more attractive. So fabric stockings appeared, made of pieces of cloth, silk, or velvet sewn together. They were often decorated with gold embroidery, and were worn by fashionable people.

The first knitted worsted stockings appeared in London about the year 1565. Queen Elizabeth received a gift of silk knitted hose, which pleased her so greatly that from that time on she wore silk stockings. These silk stockings were made in Italy, and only the very rich could afford them.

It wasn't until the beginning of the twentieth century that silk stockings really became available for the average person to wear.

FULTON'S CLERMONT

An engine is a machine that produces motion. It changes energy, usually heat energy, into motion or movement so that work may be done.

WHO MADE THE FIRST ENGINE? Men had tools for a long time before they had engines to power them. First they had to depend on manpower or animal power to help them work their tools. Then they learned to harness the wind with sails and with windmills. When a windmill pumped water and ground grain, it was a kind of engine. The energy of falling water did work by turning water wheels.

But when men learned how to harness heat in an engine, our whole civilization began to change. Actually, the first known use of the heat from fire to power an engine took place about 2,000 years ago. A Greek philosopher named Hero made the first steam engine. However, it was too small to do any work.

In 1705, Thomas Newcomen, an Englishman, invented a practical steam engine. It was used for pumping water out of coal mines. However, it used too much fuel.

In the eighteenth century, James Watt made an improved engine. He made valves that worked automatically, so that no one had to stand by and operate the valves which made the piston move up and down.

In 1803, Robert Fulton used Watt's steam engine to drive a boat. In the 1820's, George Stephenson built a steam engine in England.

The steam engine was heavy, however, because the burning took place in a furnace outside the boiler.

The petrol engine, which was developed by Nicholas Otto of Germany in 1878, was the first step toward solving the problem of weight. This engine did not need a separate furnace, and was much lighter than a steam engine of the same horsepower.

ROBERT BOYLE

Chemistry is the science used to find out what things are made of and how they can be changed.

It was actually the desire to make certain changes that was the beginning of chemistry. Modern chemistry grew out of a study called "alchemy". In the Middle Ages, alchemists searched for a "philosopher's stone" which could change other metals into gold. They carried on many kinds of experiments in their work.

WHEN DID CHEMISTRY BEGIN?

One of the first men to collect and organize all that was known about chemistry and science was Robert Boyle, who lived in the seventeenth century. He knew that compounds can be broken up into parts.

Other chemists followed Boyle and made new discoveries. Joseph Black studied gases and air. Henry Cavendish discovered hydrogen, one of the elements that make up water. Joseph Priestly discovered oxygen, which is the element commonest in nature. Antoine Lavoisier was the first to clearly explain fire. He also proved that nothing can be destroyed, only changed from one form to another.

John Dalton had an idea that all substances are made of tiny bits of matter. Scientists came to believe that chemical changes came about through the combination of these tiny bits. They are now called "atoms". The idea of atoms made most of the mysteries of chemistry seem simple and reasonable.

The science of chemistry thus continued to develop and today the chemist has become a creator of new materials. He has learned how to take molecules apart and put them together in different ways.

ALESSANDRO VOLTA

Today, of course, it is almost impossible for us to imagine living without electricity. But man has been able to use electricity only since 1800.

In 1800, Alessandro Volta invented the first battery, and so gave

WHEN DID MAN FIRST USE ELECTRICITY?

the world its first continuous, reliable source of electric current. Soon it was discovered that an electric current can be used to produce heat, light, chemical action, and magnetic effects.

Volta's discovery that there is a continuous "flow" of electricity was a great step forward. Various types of machines had been developed, but they would only provide a surge of electricity. Volta's discovery led to many developments in the use of electricity.

Sir Humphry Davy found that electric currents would decompose various substances in solution. From these experiments have come processes that led to the production of low-cost aluminium, pure copper, chlorine, various acids and fertilizers, and special steels.

Then it was discovered that magnetism could be produced by an electric current. A coil of wire through which an electric current is passing acts like a bar magnet. This discovery led to all kinds of electrical devices in which some kind of mechanical motion is produced..

Later on, Michael Faraday found a way to do the opposite—produce electric fields by magnets in motion. This eventually led to the development of electric dynamos and transformers.

So you see that man began to use electricity for practical purposes only recently in his history—and new discoveries and developments are still taking place.

What comes to your mind when you think of a scientist? You think of someone who studies something in the world or about man, who makes observations and conducts experiments, and then who comes up with certain principles or rules.

HOW DID SCIENCE BEGIN? But before the seventeenth century, if men wanted to solve a problem or understand something, they simply read what had been written about it, or asked some authority for his opinion.

Soon after the year 1600, Galileo started a new method. He started trying things out to see what happened. In other words, he "experimented". Little by little, more people began trying things out and writing down what they had observed. As more facts became known, it was found that some of the facts were related to one another. These relationships were then summarized into scientific principles and used as guides for other experiments.

In this way the body of knowledge called science began to grow rapidly. As it grew, the natural relationships between facts broke up the large field of science into smaller divisions. Today, there are many different divisions of knowledge in science.

The "natural sciences" deal with our natural surroundings. The "social sciences" are subjects that give information about the way human beings act and live together. All of these sciences are basic, or pure, sciences. They are concerned with facts and principles. In the "applied" sciences, these facts and principles are applied to doing and making things. Pharmacy, medicine, forestry, electronics, and civil engineering are examples of applied sciences.

Wherever man lives, "doing the laundry" is a problem that must be coped with.

The word "laundry" has a curious origin. In the old days, when

HOW DID LAUNDRIES START? clothes were washed, lavender used to be put on fresh-washed linen to make it fragrant. The French word for lavender is *lavande,* and in time a woman who washed clothes came to be known as a *lavandière.* It was from this we got the English words "laundress' and "laundry"!

Early civilization used different methods of washing garments. In an ancient Egyptian tomb is a picture of two slaves laundering. The slaves are working wet clothes between a block and an inclined table. The water runs into a trough below.

The clothes of the Romans were made mainly of wool, and they needed skilful handling to keep their size and shape. They were sent to public laundries, where laundrymen were known as "fullers". The fuller did two kinds of jobs. He wove new cloth and he cleaned garments that had been worn.

Fullers were still working at their trade many centuries later when a fuller's guild was organized in England. In laundering clothes at that time, they removed the dirt by beating it out of the cloth with clubs. In earlier times, it had been done by trampling the cloth with the feet!

For centuries, washing methods used in most British laundries were much like those used in early Greece and Rome. They worked without soap, because soap was expensive. But the beating of the cloth gradually came to be done more and more by machines.

Just before the days of telegraphs and railways, the United States Government established a mail system that came to be known as the Pony Express. It started in 1860, and ran from St. Joseph, Missouri, to the Pacific coast.

WHAT WAS THE PONY EXPRESS?
To carry the mail, a fleet of horses was used. Each horse would be ridden for 10 to 15 miles, and then the rider would jump on a fresh horse for the next stage. A rider would travel three stages, or 30 miles, before passing on the mail bag to the next rider.

These riders were tough men with a great deal of courage. They braved all kinds of weather and the danger of attack by Indians to get the mail through. But they actually rode horses, not ponies, so the name "Pony Express" is not accurate!

When the Queen was crowned in Westminster Abbey, there was a stone under the throne called the Coronation Stone, and it has a long and glorious history.

WHAT IS THE CORONATION STONE?

Until 1286, this stone had been kept in the abbey of Scone where the Scottish kings were crowned. It had great significance in the Coronation Service for the king stood on the "Stone of Destiny", as it was called, while the Bishop, in God's name, placed the crown upon his head.

Why is the year 1286 important? Well, in that year, King Alexander III was killed by a fall from his horse. His whole family had died before him, and his only living descendant was his grand-daughter Margaret, who was born in Norway. This left two distant connections of the king fighting it out between them—an Englishman, John Balliol, and Robert Bruce. Edward I was king of England at the time, and he decided to intervene in the struggle for power by offering to act as guardian during Margaret's childhood, and proposed that she should marry his son and unite the two kingdoms. Everyone agreed to this statesmanlike plan, but, unfortunately, the little girl died two months later on her way to Scotland. Edward claimed to be overlord in Scotland and allowed John Balliol to be king. Within three years, Balliol was in armed revolt against his master and Edward invaded. He easily defeated the Scottish army and annexed the country, denying it even the status of vassal kingdom—this was symbolized by the removal of the "Stone of Destiny" to London, where it was put under the English Throne in Westminster Abbey, and it has stayed there ever since.

As you know, Robert Bruce eventually became king of Scotland and spent his whole life in revolt against the English, but that's another story.

If you own a chair, motor car, or farm tool, it can be stolen, lost, or destroyed. If you went to court to recover such property, you could only be compensated for it if it were lost or destroyed. But if you owned land, and for some reason the land was taken

WHAT IS REAL ESTATE?

from you, the courts could restore the land itself to you. The thing itself, in Latin, is *res*, from which comes our word "real". In other words, land was "real" property, or a "real" estate, as compared to personal property.

It was based on this difference that the English law in ancient times established two kinds of property, real property (or real estate, as we now call it), and personal property. In early times, land (real property) was considered to be of the greatest value. Today, there may be other kinds of property that are considered of greater value by some people. For example, owning shares of stock in a company, or the right to use patents in manufacturing goods and machinery may sometimes be of more value.

In feudal days when the laws were being established, real property was not only land, but everything fixed to it, such as trees, buildings, and everything fixed to the buildings. And this distinction still holds today. For example, a lamp on a table is not fixed to the house, and is personal property, removable should the house be sold. If you screw it to the wall, and intend it to remain there, it then becomes a fixture and goes with the house.

In transferring real estate from one person to another, a deed must be officially recorded with the Land Commission for assessment. The law recognizes transactions concerning real estate in the order in which they are recorded. For this reason, before a person buys land he has the public records examined to make sure that the title is "clear"—that is, that there are no claims against the land or rights held on it by other persons.

We assume it is perfectly natural for the government to undertake the job of delivering our letters and packages. But this idea of government service was very slow in developing.

HOW DID THE POSTAL SYSTEM START?

In ancient times in Persia and Rome, the government did arrange for the sending of messages, but these were only concerned with government business. During most of the Middle Ages, merchant guilds and associations and certain universities maintained a limited messenger service for the use of their members.

It was in the sixteenth century that governments began to have regular postal services. They had three chief reasons for doing this. One was to enable them to inspect suspicious correspondence. The second was to produce revenue. And the third was to provide a service for the public. This last reason is practically the only purpose of the postal service today.

Henry VIII had a government postal service in England, and this was enlarged by later rulers. In 1609, no one was allowed to carry letters except messengers authorized by the government. But in 1680, a London merchant started his own penny post for the city and suburbs, and it became quite successful. So the government took it over and continued the service till 1801.

The whole system was finally changed in 1840. Stamps were introduced, and rates made uniform for all distances within the country, varying only according to the weight of the piece of mail. All other countries modelled their postal systems on that of Great Britain.

ENGLISH
POSTMAN
1840's

EARLY GREEK

Today it seems perfectly natural for us to shake hands when we greet someone or say goodbye. But like so many things that we do without thinking, such actions at one time probably symbolized something.

HOW DID THE HANDSHAKE ORIGINATE?

For example, in primitive life the hand was probably a symbol of power and strength. The hand was used to fight enemies, kill animals, and make spears and implements. So when the hand was extended to someone, it could have represented good will, since it showed that the person was not armed or ready to fight.

We know that the hand was an important symbol in early religions, probably as a mark of power. The Greeks prayed to their gods with raised hands. Presenting the hands palm to palm was at one time the way an inferior person paid respect to a superior one.

Among the Arabs, it was customary at one time to kiss the hand of a superior. Later on, polite Arabs began to resist the efforts of people to kiss their hands, and sometimes they would end up clasping hands as each tried to prevent the other from showing this mark of "inferiority".

The early Greeks held out the right hand when they wished to indicate friendship to a stranger. So we can see that the hand, and what was done with it, was full of meaning to people down through the ages. And while we shake hands without thinking, we are really carrying on a custom that has been handed down to us from ancient times.

Income includes just about everything a person earns: wages and salaries, interest on bonds and savings bank accounts, dividends on stock, and rents. It also includes the payments that are received by doctors, lawyers, authors, inventors, and other professional persons.

HOW DID INCOME TAX START?

Income tax in this country was first levied by William Pitt the Younger, in 1799, to pay for the French Wars. Today, income tax is a personal tax on all annual income from investments or employment. The amount due is assessed on an annual return of income, with the rate of tax graded in accordance with the size of income and with a differential between earned and unearned income. A proportion of income is left free of tax, according to a scale of allowances for personal or family expenses.

In Britain, rates of tax are fixed by an Annual Finance Act and the people who manage the income-tax system are called Commissioners of Inland Revenue. Inspectors of Taxes control local tax districts. General or Special Commissioners hear appeals against tax assessments or refusals of allowances.

Income tax, when first introduced, was intended to be only a temporary measure!

BROOM MADE
OF TWIGS

BROOM CORN

A broom and a brush are somewhat alike. A broom, of course, is used for cleaning only, but many brushes serve this purpose, too. However, the brush was invented many thousands of years before the broom.

WHO INVENTED THE BROOM?
The cave man used brushes made of a bunch of animal hairs attached to the end of a stick. The kitchen broom was originally a tuft of twigs, rushes, or fibres tied to a long handle. In colonial times in America, this was the kind of broom that was used. And in many parts of Europe today, you can still see streets and floors of homes being swept with such brooms.

The kitchen broom as we now know it is made from stalks of corn, and this kind of broom is an American invention. There is a story about the origin of it that may or may not be true. According to this story, a friend in India sent Benjamin Franklin one of the clothes brushes made and used in that country. It looked very much like a whisk broom.

A few seeds still clung to its straws, and Franklin planted them. They sprouted—and within a few years broom corn was being cultivated. One day an old bachelor of Hadley, Massachusetts, needed a new broom. He cut a dozen stalks of broom corn, tied them together, and swept out his house. After that he never again used a birch broom.

In fact, he began to make corn brooms and sell them to his neighbours. When he died in 1843, broom making was an important industry, and the town of Hadley was growing nearly a thousand acres of broom corn a year! Today, much of the work of broom making is still done by hand.

387

When you think about the Government, you usually have in mind the politicians, who sit in the House of Commons and some of whom are heads of Departments of State. But behind these prominent statesmen is

HOW DID THE CIVIL SERVICE ORIGINATE? an army of men and women without whose support the whole administrative structure of the country would grind to a halt!

In Whitehall, and in offices all over the country, Civil Servants of many grades act their part in the machinery of government. In ancient times, soldiers were almost the only people who served the state or government. Often the "government" was merely the monarch, who delegated certain powers to a privileged few. But as the number of people in government increased, certain jobs had to be done by specially trained people. Government employees not in military service came to be called "civil servant employees".

Entry into the Civil Service is almost entirely by competitive examination, and vacancies are regularly advertised in national and local newspapers.

It may surprise you to know that the postman, the attendants at the National Gallery, officers in Customs and Excise, prison warders, receivers in bankruptcy, keepers of Records, examiners of patents, public inspectors of factories and mines and quarries, and the Prime Minister's private secretaries are all servants of the vast body called Civil Service! And it is obvious that as the Civil Service grows, so does its power.

An interesting thing about man is that he has always liked to be entertained. From the very beginning of civilization there have been acrobats, jugglers, animal trainers, and clowns to provide this entertainment. So

WHEN DID ACROBATS FIRST APPEAR? we cannot really know when the first acrobats appeared.

But when we think of acrobats today, we think of the circus. And by going back to the first circus, we can get an idea of how today's kind of acrobats originated.

The first and largest circus of ancient times was the Circus Maximus in Rome. It was first begun in the third century B.C., and was chiefly built for chariot races. But the atmosphere of that circus was very much like some of ours today. It was a great big entertainment for the masses.

At the same time, in other theatres, all kinds of entertainment were available such as we associate with the circus today. There were jugglers, acrobats, ropewalkers, and animal trainers.

For about a thousand years after Roman times, the "organized" kind of circus disappeared. There were wandering groups of performers —and they included acrobats, jugglers, and ropewalkers.

The first time acrobats appeared in a regular kind of circus again was in England in 1768. They appeared together with clowns and ropewalkers, and people who did trick riding on horses.

So you see that acrobats have been entertaining people for thousands of years—and are still among the favourite performers in a circus.

The dream of a flying machine that would rise straight up is an old one. Leonardo da Vinci made drawings for a gigantic screwlike helicopter about A.D. 1500. He never tried to build one because he had no motor to drive it. No one knows where it came from,

WHO INVENTED THE HELICOPTER?

but a toy helicopter known as "the Chinese top" was shown in France in 1783. In 1796, Sir George Cayley made experimental forms of Chinese tops and also designed a steam-driven helicopter.

For the next 100 years, a number of people made designs for helicopters. Some were fantastic, others almost practical, and a few of them actually flew. But there were no powerful, lightweight engines. It was not until such engines were made during World War I that anyone made a helicopter that got off the ground with a man aboard.

Igor Sikorsky built two helicopters, in 1909 and 1910. One of them actually lifted its own weight. Towards the end of 1917, two Austro-Hungarian officers built a helicopter to take the place of observation balloons. It made a number of flights to high altitudes but was never allowed to fly freely.

Work on helicopters continued in many countries, but none of the machines were what the inventors had hoped for. In 1936, an announcement came from Germany that the Focke-Wulf Company had built a successful helicopter. In 1937 it flew cross-country at speeds close to 70 miles an hour and went up more than 335 metres.

In 1940, Sikorsky showed his first practical helicopter and it was delivered to the United States Army in 1942.

INDEX

Numerals in *italics* refer to pictures

A

Accordion, 312
Achilles, 154, 308
Acne, 262
Acrylics, 355
Acrobats, 388–89
Adenoids, 252
Advertising, 369, 372
Aerolites, 84
Aeroplane, first flight of, 322
Africa:
  drums, *313*
  head-hunters, 365
  meteorites, 84
Air, 44
  carbon dioxide, 13–14, 52
  currents and clouds, 99, 100
  dust, 50–51
  gases, 44, 53
  moisture, 106–7
  molecules in cubic inch, 43
  pollution, 51
  pressure, 44, 102, 105
  vacuum and, 40–41
  See also Atmosphere; Weather
Alabaster, 49
Alamo, 118–19
Alaska:
  Eskimos, 368
  glaciers, 76–77
  gold, 367
Albinos, 245
Alcohol, 27, 59
  intoxication, 268
Algae, 13
  Antarctica, 63
  lichen and, 29
Allosaurus, 160
Alloys, 45, 46
Alpha rays, 54

Altitude:
  air pressure, 44
  temperature, 109
Aluminium, 60
Amazon River, 80, 137
Amazons, 137
Ambergris, 233
America, 111
  Negroes, 351
  pins, 340
  See also United States
American Indians, 148, 371
  Aztecs, 147
  cannibalism, 126
  cliff dwellers, 144–45
  Custer's Last Stand, 143
  drums, 313
  Eskimos, 368
  scalping, 365
  smoking, 323
  tattooing, 371
  wampum, 320
Amnesia, 297
Amphibians, 217–18
Anaemia, 277–78
Anglo-Saxons, 125
Angora, 176
Animals:
  albino, 245
  Antarctica, 63
  counting by, 164–65
  desert, 161
  evolution, 12, 166, 217
  eyes, 168, 174
  fallout and, 48
  first land, 217
  food, need and use, 241
  fossils, 64, 160
  Ice Age, 68
  instincts, 167, 173
  learning and training, 164–65, 167, 178
  manlike, 166
  man learns to use, 67
  minerals needed by, 46

moulting, 169
  mythical, 162, 163
  rabies, 174–75
  reasoning, 167
  salt, need for, 164
  seed distribution, 18
  sounds, 175, 181, 187, 219
  speeds, 230
  talking, 165–66, 234
  totems, 120
  vision, 168, 174
  water, need for, 240
  See also names, types
Antarctica, 62–63, 68
Anthropoid apes, 166–67
Antifreeze, 59
Antitoxins, 271
Ants, 193
  aphids and, 198
Apes and monkeys, 166–67
  colour vision, 174
  reasoning, 167
Aphids, 198
Appendix, 269
Arachnid, 191–92
Archaeology, 65
Archimedes' Principle, 34–35
Arctic, 71
Aristarchus, 84
Arithmetic, 356
Arteries, 32
Artesian well, 74
Arthur, King, 150–51
Arts, 128
Asia:
  apples, 23
  bridal veil, 343
  typhoons, 103
  See also specific country
Asp, 205
Asparagus, 19
Ass, 177

Assyrians:
  furniture, 346, 347
  gold, 367
Astronaut, first, 336
Astronomy, 83–84, 153
Athlete's foot, 270
Atlantis, 121
Atmosphere:
  clouds, 99, 100
  moon, 97
  ozone, 96
  sunspots, effect on, 96
  See also Air; Weather
Atomic energy, 53–54
  sun, 92, 94
Atomic number, 45
Atomic weight, 43
Atoms, 42, 378
  carbon, 52
  in molecules, 42, 43
  number, 45
  radioactive fallout, 48
  uranium, 54
  weight, 43
Aubrey, John, 139
Aurora borealis, 96
Australia:
  gold, 367
  kangaroos, 236
Aztecs, 147

B

Babylonians:
  brick, 341
  furniture, 346
  umbrella, 374
Bachelor's degree, 128–29
Backbones, 32–33
  See also Skeleton
Bacon, Roger, 322
Baekeland, Leo, 355
Balance:
  centrifugal force and, 34

walking, 298
Banyan tree, 23–24
Barbarism, 127
Bark, 15–16
products, 16, 27, 29
Basalt, 73
Bats, 235, 238
Battery, 378
Bauxite, 60
Beards, 259
styles, 330, 339
Beavers, 185
Beds, 346, 347–48
Beefeaters, 352
Bees, 202
Behring, Emil von, 271
Bell, Alexander Graham, 349
Beta rays, 54
Birds:
albino, 245
Antarctica, 63
eggs, 212, 213–14
evolution, 217
flying, 215
migration, 211
moulting, 169
talking, 214
training, 165
wings, 33, 212, 215
See also names
Birds of Paradise, 213
Birthmarks, 261
Black moulds, 31
Blood, 273
amount in body, 276
cells, 247, 273, 276
circulatory system, 32, 247
clots, 273, 274
disorders, 277–78
pressure, 276
Body, asymmetry of, 255
See also specific subject
Bones, fractures, 253–54
See also Skeleton
Books, 316–17
Botany, 12
Boycott, 112
Boyle, Robert, 377
Brahma, 358
Brain:
Neanderthal man, 68
thought, speed of, 292
vertebrates, 32
vision, 285–87

Bread moulds, 31
Breathing, 243
nose, 291–92
Brick, 341
Britain:
See England
Broccoli, 333
Brontosaurus, 159, 160
Brooms, 387
Brownies, 142
Brussels sprouts, 333
Buccaneers, 337
Buckingham Palace, 130
Buddhism, 358–59
Bumblebees, 202
Burial:
embalming, 330
graves, 363
Burro, 177
Butterfat, 51
Butterflies, 198–99
migration, 196

C

Cabbage, 333
Cabinet, government, 119
Cacti, 161
Caecilians, 217
Camel, 16, 181–82
Canada:
Eskimos, 368, 370
gold, 367
ice hockey, 307
settlers, 370
Canals, 134, 335
Cannibalism, 126
Carbon, 52
diamonds, 52, 56
Carbon dioxide, 44
plant use, 13–14, 52
Carbon monoxide, 52
Card games, 309
Carnivores, 164, 227
See also names
Carrier pigeons, 216
Cashmere, 176
Cat family, 175
black cats, 362
colour vision, 174
sounds, 175
speeds, 230
Caterpillars, 196, 198
Caucasians, 244
Cauliflower, 333

Cave men, 66
Cavendish, Henry, 377
Cavy, 183
Caxton, William, 372
Cayley, Sir George, 390
Cells, 246–47
cambium, 15
leaves, 14
osmosis, 20
wood, 14, 15
Celluloid, 355
Census, 115–16
Centaurs, 162
Centrifugal force, 34
Cetacea, 234
Chemistry, 377–78
plastics, 355
Chewing gum, 29
Chimera, 158
Chimpanzee, 166, 170–71
China:
accordion, 312
cards, 309
drums, 313
fingerprints, 299
flag, 334
hair style, 329
New Year, 338
painting, 318
printing, 316
religions, 359
schools, 358
silkworms, 373
tattooing, 370
umbrella, 374
zoos, 302
Chinese top, 390
Chlorophyll, 12
Chrikov, Alexei, 350
Christianity, 358, 359
graves, 363
monasticism, 360
music, 311, 312
orders, 360
witchcraft, 364
Cicada, 187
Cigarettes, 324
Circulatory system, 32, 247
Circus, 388–89
Cities, 354
Civil service, 388
Civilization, 67, 126–27
cities, 354
Cliff dwellers, 144–45
See also Indians

Clothing:
washing, 380
See also names
Clouds, 99, 100, 106, 10[
Coal, 52, 62
Coconut, 25
Coinage, 319–20
See also Money
Colleges, 355–56
degrees, 128–29, 357
Colorado River, 71, 75
Colour:
blindness, 174
insects attracted by, 3[
rainbow, 37–38
snow, 108
stars, 88, 91
vision, 174
Comets, 85
tails of, 85
meteors, 84
Compounds, 42, 377
metals, 45–46
Condensation, 106–7
Confucianism, 358, 359
Conservation, 70
Continent, lost, 121
Copernicus, 84, 153
theories of, 153
Cork, 16
Corona, sun's, 92
Coronation Stone, 382
Counties, system of, 145
Country, smallest, 131–3[
Credit currency, 321
Cro-Magnon man, 66, 67
Crude oil, 366
See also Petroleum
Crying, 284
Cryolite, 60
Crystal Palace, 348
Cullinan diamond, 55
Currency, credit, 321
See also Coinage;
Money
Current, electric, 378
Custer's Last Stand, 143
Cyclones, 102, 105

D

Dalton, John, 378
Dandruff, 260
Darwin, Charles, 12, 259
Davy, Sir Humphry, 378

Days, length, 80–81
Dead Sea, 122–23
Degrees, academic,
    128–29
Deserts, 71, 161
Diamonds, 52, 56
    cutting, 56
    famous, 55
    industrial, 55
    value, 55
Digestive system, 241–42
    liver, 248
    vertebrates, 33
Dimensions, sight and,
    286–87
Dinosaurs, 159
Dionysus, 162
Diphtheria, 271
Diseases:
    antitoxins, 175
    insect-borne, 189
    plant, 12, 18
    rats and, 204
    virus, 32
    worm-caused, 203
    See also names
Doctorate degree, 128–29
Dogs, 172
    bones, burying, 173
    instinct, 173
    learning, 167
    rabies, 174–75
    speeds, 230
    vision, 168, 174
Dolphin, 234
Donkey, 177
Dragons, 158
Dreams, 296–97
Drugs:
    See Medicines and
        drugs
Druids, 139
Drums, 313
Duelling, 308
Dunant, Henri, 351
Dust, 50–51
Dust storms, 51, 103
Dwarfs, 143
Dynamos, 379

E

Earth:
    as centre of universe,
        83–84
    atmosphere: see Air,
        Atmosphere
    eclipses, solar, 94–95
    gravity and weight, 97
    solar system, 82–83
    See also Earth's crust
Earth's crust, 73
    aluminium, 60
    basalt, 73
    faults and earthquakes,
        76
    granite, 57, 73
    temperature, 73
Earthquakes, 76
Earthworms, 203
Easter Island, 138–39
Echidna, 237
Eclipse, solar, 94–95
Ecology, 12
Edentates, 227
Education, schools, 357–
    58
    See also Colleges and
        Universities
Eggs:
    birds, 212, 213–14
    mammals, 237
    snakes, 207
    See also Reproduction
Egypt:
    brick, 341
    burials, 363
    camels, 182
    cats, 362
    donkeys, 177
    drums, 313
    embalming, 330
    flags, 334
    furniture, 346, 347
    granite, 57
    laundering, 380
    melons, 331
    needles, 349
    Nile, 71, 131
    painting, 318
    papyrus, 319
    posters, 369
    religion, 362
    schools, 358
    soapstone charms, 61
    tattooing, 370
    umbrella, 374
    wrestling, 304
    writing, 316
Electric fish, 221
Electricity, 378–79
lightning, 106
tidal power, 72–73
Electrons, 42
    sunspots, 96
Elements, 45, 377–78
    atoms and, 42, 45
    chemical families, 45
    periodic table, 45
    sun, 88
    See also names
Elephants, 178–79, 230
Elves, 142
Embalming, 330
Endocrine system, 249,
    250
Energy:
    forms, 38
    perpetual motion, 40
    matter, 42
    sun, 92, 93, 94, 96
    tidal, 72–73
Engines, 376–77
England:
    Anglo-Saxons, 125
    Arthur and Round
        Table, 150–51
    cabinet, 119
    circus, 389
    clothing, 375
    Coronation Stone,
        382–83
    crown, 55
    golf, 309
    Great Exhibition, 348
    gipsies, 134
    hair styles, 330
    juries, 362–63
    laundries, 380
    needles, 349
    pins, 240
    pixies, 142
    postal systems, 384
    property laws, 383
    Robin Hood, 156
    steam engines, 377
    Stonehenge, 124
    Tower of London, 352
    universities, 356
    Whigs, 117
    wrestling, 304
Epithelial cells, 247
Era of Reptiles, 159–60
Ermine, 184
Erosion, 75, 80
Eskimos, 368, 370
Ethyl alcohol, 59
Eucalyptus, 16–17
Europe:
    apples, 23
    clothing, 375
    gold, 367
    head-hunters, 365
    Ice Age, 68
    tobacco, 323–24
    umbrella, 374
    See also Middle
        Ages; country
Evaporation, 106–7
Evolution:
    animals, 12, 166, 217
    flatfish, 228
    man, 166
    plants, 12–13
Expositions, 348–49
Extrasensory perception,
    293
Eyes:
    animals', 168, 174
    compound, 201
    tears, 284

F

Fairies, 142–43
Fairs, 348
Fallout, radioactive, 48
Faraday, Michael, 379
Fat:
    digestion, 248
Fatigue, 294
Feet, 255
    athlete's foot, 270
Feldspar, 57
Ferns, 13, 64
Figs, 27
Fine arts, 128
Fingerprints, 299
Fire, 378
Firearms, 337–38
Fish, 220–21
    dangerous, 221, 222,
        223, 224
    Dead Sea, 123
    electric, 221
    fins, 33
    hearing, 220–21
    names, 325–26
Flags, 334
Flatfish, 228
Flatworms, 203
Flavourings, 16

Flies, 199–201
Floating, 34–35
Flowers:
  plants without, 29
  pollination, 27, 36
Flying, 215
Folk music, 311
Foods:
  digestion, 241–42, 248
  moulds, 31
  need for, 240
  nitrogen, 53
  See also names, types
Force and motion, 34
Fossils, 12, 64, 75
  dinosaurs, 160
  Neanderthal man, 68
France:
  cards, 309
  cave paintings, 66
  clothing, 375, 376
  duelling, 308
  hair styles, 330
  handkerchiefs, 375
  pearls, artificial, 226
  pins, 340
Franklin, Benjamin, 387
Freckles, 261
Freezing, 35
Fresco, 318
Frogs, 217
Frost, 107
Fruit trees, 13, 14
  apples, 23
  figs, 27
Fullers, 380
Fulton, Robert, 377
Fungi, 13
  Antarctica, 63
  lichens and, 29
  moulds and mildews, 31
Furniture, 346–47
  beds, 347–48

G

Galaxies, 81, 83
Galileo, 86, 87, 96, 379
Galton, Sir Francis, 299
Games:
  card, 309
  children's, 305
  See also names of
    sports

Gamma rays, 54
Gargarin, Yuri, 336
Garnets, 60
Gas, 345
Gases:
  air, 44
  breathing and, 243
  comets, 85
  condensation and
    evaporation, 106–7
  molecules, 43
  rare, 44
  stars, 88
  weight of, 44
Gems, 60
  diamonds, 52, 55, 56
Genetics, 12, 37
Germany:
  duels, 308
  fairies, 143
  petrol engine, 377
  gloves, 375
  Rhine maidens, 136–37
  New Year, 338
Gibbon, 166–67
Gipsies, 134–35
Giraffe, 180–82
Glacial Period, 68
Glaciers, 76–77
Gladiators, 140
Glands, 249–50, 258,
  260, 262
Gloves, 375
Gnomes, 143
Goats, 176
Gobi Desert, 71
Goblins, 143
Gold, 367, 377
Golf, 309–10
Government:
  cabinet, 119
  civil service, 388
  taxation by, 386
Grain alcohol, 59
Grand Canyon, 75, 80
Granite, 57, 73
Graphite, 52
Grasses, pollination, 36
Grasshoppers, 190
Gravestones, 363
  See also Burials
Gravity:
  moon, 97–98
  weight and, 97–98
Great Britain:
  See England

Greece:
  asparagus, 19
  astronomy, 83–84, 91
  coins, 319–20
  day, 81
  furniture, 347
  gravestones, 363
  handkerchiefs, 375
  hands, use of, 385
  hockey, 307
  Homer, 141, 375
  melons, 331
  music, 311–12
  myths and legends,
    121, 134, 136–37,
    149, 154, 162
  napkins, 375
  painting, 318
  pirates, 336
  religion, 150
  Socrates, 155
  steam engine, 377
  taxes, 386
  umbrella, 374
  universe, 83–84
  wrestling, 304
Green moulds, 31
Greenland, 68, 368
Griffins, 163
Grinding wheels, 55
Growth:
  body, 249, 257, 258
  trees, 14, 15, 16, 24
  See also specific subject
Guinea pigs, 183
Gum tree, 16–17
Guns, 337–38
Gutenberg, Johann, 317
Gypsum, 48–49

H

Hail, 108
Hair, 258–60
  dandruff, 260
  styles, 329–30
Hall, Charles Martin, 60
Handkerchiefs, 375
Hands:
  right- and left-
    handedness, 255
  thumb, opposable, 166
Handshake, 385
Hardest substances, 52,
  55, 56

Hearing, 288
  See also Sounds
Heart, 279
  attack, 280
Hawaii, 353
Head-hunters, 365
Heat:
  of condensation, 107
  in vacuum, 41
  See also Temperature
Height, body, 258
Helicopter, 390
Helium, 43
  in sun, 92, 94
Henry, Sir Edward, 299
Herbivores, 164
Hercules, 149
Herodotus, 65
Hinduism, 358
Hockey, 307
Homer, 141, 375
Homes, 344–45
Honey, 330
  insects, 36, 202
Hope diamond, 55
Hormones, 249, 250
Hornblende, 57
House flies, 199
Hurricane, 103
Husband, 344
Huygens, Christian, 38,
  86
Hyatt, John and Isaiah,
  355
Hydra, 149, 158
Hydrogen, 377
  compared with
    helium, 44
  in sun, 92, 94
Hypertension, 277

I

Ice:
  floating, 34–35
  freezing, 35
  glaciers, 76–77
Ice Age, 66, 67, 68
Ice hockey, 307
Ice skating, 305, 306
Icebergs, 35, 77
Igloos, 108
Igneous rock, 57
Iliad, 141
Incas, 146

Income tax, 386
India:
  conquests of, 55
  diamonds, 55
  head-hunters, 365
  religions, 358–59
Indians:
  See American Indians
Inertia, 34
Inorganic matter, 42
Insectivores, 227
Insects, 197
  antennae, 198, 201
  deadly, 192
  fossils, 64, 75
  honey-making, 36, 202
  life span, 187
  plants that eat, 188
  pests, 189, 194, 195,
    198, 199–201, 203
  pollination, 27, 36
  reproduction, 187,
    193, 200
  See also names
Instincts, 167, 173
Intoxication, 268
Invertebrates, 32
Ireland:
  boycotts, 112
  leprechauns, 142–43
Islands, volcanic, 353
Isotopes, 54
Italy:
  Pompeii, 123, 349
  universities, 356
  Venice, 134

J

Jackass, 177
Japan:
  pearls, 226
  printing, 316
  Shintoism, 358, 359
  silk, 373
  tattooing, 371
  wrestling, 304
Jardin des Plantes, 303
Jellyfish, 222
Jennet, 177
Jews:
  bridal veils, 343
  drum, 313
  graves, 363
  monasticism, 360

music, 311, 313
religion, 358, 359
taxes, 386
Jubal, 311
Judaism, 358, 359
  See also Jews
Judicial duel, 308
Juries, 362–63

K

Kale, 333
Kangaroos, 186, 236
Katydids, 190
Kidneys, 250–51
Koh-i-noor diamond, 55
Kohlrabi, 333

L

Lactose, 53
Lane, Ralph, 323–24
Languages:
  Anglo-Saxon, 125
  gipsies', 134, 135
  Latin, 112–13
  See also Speech
Lâo-tse, 359
Latin, 112–13
Latitude and longitude,
  61–62
Laundries, 380
Lava, 78
Lavoisier, Antoine, 378
Laws:
  juries, 362–63
  real estate, 383
  trials, 362–63
Lead:
  pencils, 52
  uranium, 54
Leather, tanning, 16
Leaves, 13–14
  plants without, 29
  shapes, multiple, 29
  transpiration, 20
  uses for man, 17, 27
Legumes, 53
Leprechauns, 142–43
Leukaemia, 278
Lichens, 29
  Antarctica, 63
Life:
  Antarctica, 63

carbon and, 52
Dead Sea, 122–23
desert, 161
metals and, 46
nitrogen and proteins
  and, 53
sun and, 93
viruses, 32
  See also Evolution
Light:
  analysis, 88
  corpuscular theory, 38
  energy, 38
  moonlight, 97
  speed, 38
  stars and planets,
    90–91
  sunlight, 93
  wave lengths and
    colours, 37–38
  year, 38
Lightning, 106
Limbs, vertebrates, 33
Lions:
  See Cat family
Liquids, osmosis, 20
  gases, 45
  See also Water
Liver, function of, 248
Livingstone, David, 117
Loam, 72
Locusts, 190
London, Tower of, 352
Longitude and latitude,
  61, 62
Loudness, 39
Lydians, 319, 320–21
Lymph, 247

M

Mace, 30
Magma:
  granite, 57
  lava, 77–78
Magnetism, 379
Mails:
  See Postal systems
Mammals, 217, 227
  marsupials, 236
  placental, 236
  reproduction, 227, 229,
    231, 236, 237
  speeds, 230
  See also names

Man:
  See subject
Manatee, 228–29
Manioc, 27–28
Marsupials, 186, 236–37
Master's degree, 128–29
Matter, 42–43
  vacuum and, 40–41
  See also subject
Medicines and drugs:
  alcohol, 59
  antitoxins, 175, 271
  penicillin, 31
  petroleum, 366
  quinine, 16
  trees and, 16, 17
Melons, 331
Melville, David, 345
Memory, 297
Mendel, Gregor, 37
Meningitis, 263–64
Meridians, 62
Mermaids, 136–37
Mesozoic Era, 159–60
Metallurgy, 46
Metals, 45–46
  alchemy, 377
  man-made, 54
  most abundant, 60
  necessary to life, 46
  radioactive, 53–54
  refining, 60, 378
  weights, 58
  See also names
Meteors and meteorites,
  84
Middle Ages:
  alchemy, 377
  beds, 348
  flags, 334
  gold, 367
  hair styles, 330
  painting, 318
  postal system, 384
  taxes, 386
  umbrella, 374
  universities, 355–56
  witchcraft, 362
Mildews, 31
Milk, 41
Milky Way, 81, 83
Minerals:
  Antarctica, 62
  Dead Sea, 122
  milk, 51
  softest, 61

Missing Link, 166
Missouri–Mississippi
  Rivers, 80
Mohammedanism, 358,
  359
Molasses, 59
Mould, 31
Molecules, 42–43
  plastics, 355
  See also specific
    substance
Moulting, 169
Monasticism, 360
Money, 319–20
Mongolian peoples, 244
Monkeys:
  See Apes and monkeys
Monotheism, 359
Monotremes, 227, 237
Monsoon, 104–5
Moon, 97–98
  solar eclipse and,
    94–95
Mosquitos, 189
Mosses, 13
  Antarctica, 63
Mother of pearl, 225–26
Moths, 199
Motion:
  centrifugal force and,
    34
  inertia, 34
  perpetual, 40
Mountains:
  granite, 57
  tallest, 353
Mucus, nose, 291–92
Mule-Killer, 190–91
Mumps, 263
Murdock, William, 345
Muscles:
  cells, 247
  exercise and, 275
  vertebrates, 33
Mushrooms, 26
Music, 311–12
  singing, 288–89
  sounds and overtones,
    39
  See also specific
    instruments

N

Names, 327–28

plants and trees, 326–
  27
Napkins, 375
Neanderthal man, 66, 67,
  68–69
Needles, 349
Negroes, in America, 351
Negroid peoples, 244
Nelson, Horatio, Lord,
  152–53
Neolithic Age, 67
Nerves, 281
  cells, 247, 281
  thought, speed of, and,
    292
  vertebrates, 32
New Year, 338–39
Newcomen, Thomas, 377
Newspapers, advertising,
  372
Newton, Sir Isaac, 34, 38
Nile River, 71, 131
Nitrogen:
  air, 44, 53
  legumes, 53
  proteins, 53
Noise, 39
  See also Sounds
Norse:
  See Vikings
North America:
  Ice Age, 68
  vikings, 152
Northern Hemisphere:
  seasons, 109
  tornadoes, 102
Northern Lights, 96
Nose, mucus, 291–92
  smell, sense of, 290–91
Nuclear explosions,
  fallout, 48
Nuns, 360
Nursery rhymes, 302
Nut trees:
  coconut, 25
  hazelnuts, 21
Nutmeg, 30

O

Oceans, 79
  monsoon winds, 104–5
  salt dust, 50–51
  tides, 72–73
Octopus, 224

Odyssey, 141, 375
Oil, whale, 233
  See also Petroleum
Old Stone Age, 67
Onions, 284
Opera, 312
Opossum, 186
Optical illusion, 286
Organic matter, 42
Osmosis, 20
Ostrich, 212, 214
Otto, Nicholas, 377
Oxygen, 378
  air, 44, 53
  carbon compounds, 52
Oysters, 225
  pearls, 225–26
Ozone, 96

P

Painting, 318
  cave, 66
Paleobotany, 12
Pan, 311
Papal States, 132
Paper money, 321
Parasites:
  viruses, 32
  weeds, 18
  worms, 203
Parathyroids, 250
Paris, University, 356
Pathology, plant, 12
Pearls, 225–26
Penicillin, 31
Periodic Table, 45
Perpetual motion, 40
Persians:
  beds, 347
  gloves, 375
  postal system, 384
Perspiration, 243
Pests:
  See names, types
Petroleum, 366
  engine, 377
Philately, 113–14
Philosopher's stone, 377
Photosynthesis, 14
Physiology, plant, 12
Piedmont Plateau, 57
Pigeons:
  homing, 216
  training, 165

Pimples, 262
Pin money, 340
Pineal gland, 250
Pineapple, 332
Pins, 340
Pirates, 336–37
Pit vipers, 205
Pitch, sound, 39, 150,
Pitcher plant, 188
Pituitary gland, 249, 2
Pixies, 142
Placental mammals, 2
  37
Planets, 82–83
  light from, 90
  Saturn, 86–87
  See also Stars; Sun
Plant lice, 198
Plants, 12–13
  age, 29
  algae, 13
  Antarctica, 63
  carbon dioxide use,
    13–14, 52
  chlorophyll, 12, 14
  desert, 161
  diseases, 12, 18
  distribution, 12, 18
  fallout and, 48
  food for, 12, 13–14
  food plants, 19
  fossils, 12, 64
  fungi, 13, 31
  green, 12–14
  heredity, 12, 37
  Ice Age, 68
  insect-eating, 188
  leaves, 13–14
  lichens, 29
  life span, 29
  moulds and mildews,
    31
  names, 327
  non-green, 13, 245
  nitrogen and, 53
  parasites, 18
  photosynthesis, 14
  poisonous, 18, 22
  pollination, 27, 36
  protective devices, 22
  reproduction, *see*
    Reproduction
  roots, 13, 14
  sap flow, 20
  sugars, 13–14
  symbiosis, 29

transpiration, 20
See also names
lasters, gypsum, 49
lastics, 355
latinum, 58
latypus, 237
limpton, J. J., 305
liny, 319
lutonium, 54
ollination, 36
  insects and, 27, 36
  wind and, 36
olyesters, 355
olymers, 355
ompeii, 123, 349
opulation census, 115–16
orpoises, 234
ostal systems, 384
  Pony Express, 381
osters, 36
otstone, 61
raying mantis, 190–91
Priestly, Joseph, 378
Primates, 170, 227
Printing:
  advertising, 369, 372
  posters, 369
  presses and movable
    type, 316–17
Property, 383
Proteins, 53
  digestion, 241–42, 248
  milk, 51
Protons, 43, 45
Protoplasm, 12, 247
Proxima Centauri, 90
Psychical research, 293
Ptolemy, 84, 153
Purring, 175
Pythagoras, 83–84, 150

Q

Quarrying, ice used in, 35
Quicksand, 47
  fossils in, 64
Quinine, 16

R

Rabies, 174–75
Races, mankind, 244
Radio, 96

Radioactivity:
  fallout, 48
  uranium, 54
Radium, 54
Rain:
  clouds, 99, 100
  condensation and
    evaporation, 106–7
  monsoon, 104–5
  rivers and, 79, 80
  sleet, 108
Rainbows, 37–38
Raleigh, Sir Walter, 324
Rats, 204
Reading, 282
Real estate, 383
Rearhorse, 190–91
Regent's Park, 303
Religions, 358–59
  cannibalism, 126
  head-hunters, 365
  monotheism, 359
  Pythagoreans, 150
  See also specific names
Reproduction:
  amphibians, 217, 218
  birds, 212, 213–14
  by bits, 29
  insects, 27, 187, 193, 200
  heredity, 37
  mammals, 227, 229, 236, 237
  nuts, 25
  pollination, 27, 36
  seeds, 13, 18
  snakes, 207
  spores, 13, 26, 31
  underground stems, 18
Reptiles, 210, 217
  See also Snakes
Resources, conservation
  of, 70
Respiration, 243
Rheumatic fever, 266
Rheumatism, 267
Right- and left-
  handedness, 255
Rings, tree, 14–15
Ringworm, 272
Rivers, 79
  desert, 71
  drainage basins, 80
  erosion by, 75, 80
  longest, 131
  See also names

Robin Hood, 156
Rocks:
  artesian wells, 74
  drilling, 55
  faults, 76
  granite, 57
  ice splits, 35
  igneous, 57
  lichens and, 29
  magma, 57, 77
  oil, 366
  sedimentary, 64
  shale and slate, 50
  soil and, 29, 57, 72
  volcano formation, 77–78
  water, 74
Rocky Mountains, 57
Rodents, 227
Roller skating, 305, 306
Romans:
  apples, 23
  asparagus, 19
  bridal veil, 343
  circus, 389
  coins, 320
  day, 81
  flags, 334
  furniture, 347
  gladiators, 140
  gloves, 375
  gold, 367
  handkerchiefs, 375
  language, 112–13
  laundries, 380
  melons, 331
  napkins, 375
  needles, 349
  New Year, 339
  pigeons, 216
  pirates, 336
  postal system, 384
  posters, 369
  sports, 140, 309
  umbrella, 374
Roots, 13, 14
  banyan tree, 24
  bark, 15

S

Sagas, 152
Sahara, dust from, 51
Salamanders, 217

Salt, coconuts grow in
  salt water, 25
  Dead Sea, 122–23
  dust in air, 50–51
  need for, 164
Sap flow, 20
Sapphires, 60
Saturn's rings, 86–87
Scarlet fever, 264
Schick, Béla, 271
Schools, 357–58
  See also Colleges
    and Universities
Science, 379
  See also names
Scorpion, 192–93
Scotland:
  brownies, 142
  golf, 309–10
  Whigs, 116
Sea cows, 228–29
Sea level, 44
Seasons, 100
  temperatures, 109
Sebaceous glands, 260–62
Sedimentary rocks, 64
Seeds, 13, 14
  distribution, 18
  fig, 27
  pollination and, 27, 36
  weed, 18
Segmented worms, 203
Selenite, 49
Shale and slate, 50
Sharks, 223
  name, 325
Shells, fossil, 64
Shintoism, 358, 359
Ship of the Desert, 181
Shooting stars, 84
Siberia, Ice Age, 68
Sidereal day, 81
Sierra Nevada, 57
Sight:
  See Vision
Sikorsky, Igor, 390
Silk:
  silkworms, 373
  spiders, 191
Singing, 288–89
Sirius, 90
Skating, 305–6
Skeleton, 256–57
  apes, 166, 171
  limbs, vertebrates, 33
Skiing, 306

Skin:
  birthmarks, 261
  cells, 247
  colour, 244, 245
  disorders, 262, 272
  freckles, 261
  hair, 258–59
  tanning, 246
Slate, 50
Slavery, 351
Sleep, 295–96
  dreams, 296–97
  walking in, 283
Sleet, 108
Smell, sense of, 290–91
Smoking, 323–24
Snails, 226–27
Snake charmers, 210
Snakes, 33, 205
  anatomy, 208–10
  deadliest, 205, 206
  largest, 206
  moulting, 169, 210
  movement, 208–9, 210
  poisonous, 205, 206
  reproduction, 207
Snow, 100, 107–8
Soap, from whales, 233
Soapstone, 61
Socrates, 155
Soil:
  classifying, 72
  erosion, 75, 80
  fallout and, 48
  formation, 29, 57, 72
  water in, 12, 13–14, 72
Solar system, 82–83
  Pythagoras' theory, 150
  See also Universe;
    subject
Sole, fillet of, 228
Sooth-Sayer, 190–91
Sound(s), 39, 288
  animal, 175, 181, 187,
    219, 234
  birds, 212
  hearing, 288
  human voice, 288–89
  noise, 39
  tongue and, 289
  waves, 288
South America:
  head-hunters, 365
  Incas, 146
Southern Hemisphere:
  seasons, 109

tornadoes, 102
Space:
  matter and, 42
  size and curvature,
    81–82
Spain:
  cave paintings, 66
  cigarettes, 324
Spanish Main, 337
Spectroscope, 88
Spectrum, 37
  stars, 88, 91
Speech:
  animals, 165–66, 171,
    234
  birds, 214
  children, 166
  human voice, 288–89
  See also Language
Spices, 16
Spiders, 191–92
Spiny anteater, 237
Spores, 13, 26, 31
Sports:
  See names
Springs, water, 74
Stamps, 113–14
Starches:
  alcohol, 59
  digestion, 241–42
Stars:
  brightness and
    magnitude, 91
  colours, 88, 91
  distances, 90
  light from, 90
  Milky Way, 81, 83
  names, 89
  number, 83, 88–89
  shooting, 84
  size, 90–91
  temperatures, 88, 91
  time measurement and,
    81
  See also Sun
Steam:
  condensation heat, 107
  engines, 377
Stephenson, George, 377
Stoat, 184
Stockings, 376
Stone Age, 67
  needles, 349
  painting, 318
Stonehenge, 124
Storms: eye, 102

wind direction, 102,
    105
  See also names
Street lights, 345
String-bark tree, 16–17
Stroke, 274
Styrene, 355
Sugars:
  alcohols, 59
  milk, 51
  plant, 13–14
Sun, 92
  eclipse, 94–95
  elements, 88
  energy, 92, 93, 94, 96
  life of, 94
  moon affected by, 97
  origin, 93
  rotation, 92
  seasons and, 109
  solar system, 83–84
  sunspots, 96
  tanning, 246
  temperature, 93
Sundew, 188
Sunlight, 92, 93
  rainbows, 37–38
Sunspots, 96
Superstitions:
  black cat, 362
Swallows, migration, 211
Symbiosis, 29
Synthetics, 355

T

Tails, vertebrates, 33
Talc, 61
Tanning:
  leather, 16
  skin, 246
Taoism, 358, 359
Tapioca, 27–28
Tastebuds, 290
Tattooing, 370–71
Taxes, 386
Tears, 284
Teeth, 253, 300
Telescopes, 87
Temperature:
  altitude and, 109
  body, 242–43
  coldest recorded, 62
  core of earth, 73
  desert, 71

moon, 97
  seasonal, 108, 109
  stars, 88, 91
  sun, 93
Termites, 194
Theseus, 304
Threadworms, 203
Thought, speed of, 2
Thumb, opposable, 1
Thunderstorms, 106
Tides, 72–73
Tiger:
  See Cat family
Time:
  See subject
Toads, 217
Toadstools, 26
Tobacco, 323–24
Tongue, 289–90
Tonsils, 252
Tools, primitive, 67, 6
Tornadoes, 102–3
Tortoises, 210, 219
Totems, 120
Totemic tribes, 120
Tower of London, 35.
Transformers, 379
Transpiration, 20
Trees:
  age, 14
  bark, 15–16
  circumference, 24
  flowers, 21, 25, 30
  giant, 23–24
  grafting, 23
  growth, 14, 15, 16, 2
  leaves, see Leaves
  names, 326–27
  products, 16, 17, 24,
    30
  reproduction, 25
  rings, annual, 14
  sap flow, 20
  See also names
Trials, 362–63
  duels, 308
Trojan War, 141, 154
Trolls, 143
Tropical storms, 103
Turtles, 210, 219
Tyrannosaurus, 159

U

Ulcers, stomach, 265

Umbrella, 374
Ungulates, 227
Unicorn, 163
United States:
  cabinet, 119
  colleges and univer-
    sities, 356
  dust, settling on, 51
  dust storms, 51
  expositions, 348–49
  golf, 310
  gypsum, 49
  hockey, 307
  hurricanes, 103
  Indians, see American
    Indians
  Pony Express, 381
  tornadoes, 103
Universe, 143
  distances, 90
  earth as centre, 83–84,
    153
  galaxies, 81–82, 83
  See also Planets;
    Solar system; Sun;
    Stars
Universities, 355–56
Uranium, 53–54
Urine, 251

V

Vaccination, 328–29
Vacuum, 40–41
Valley glaciers, 76–77
Vampire bat, 238
Vatican City, 131–32

Veils, bridal, 343
Veins, vertebrates, 32
  See also Circulatory
    system
Venice, 134
Venus flytrap, 188
Vertebrates, 32–33
  See also names,
    subjects
Vespucci, Amerigo, 111
Viking, 151–52
  Eskimos, 368
Vinyl chloride, 355
Vipers, 205
Virus, 32
Vision:
  animal, 168, 174
  brain and, 285
  colour blindness, 174
  dimension, 287
  optical illusion, 286
Vitamins, milk, 51
Vocal cords, 288, 289
Voice:
  See Sound(s); Speech
Volcanoes, 77–78
  Hawaii, 353
  eruptions, 123
  largest inactive, 353
Volta, Alessandro, 378

W

Walking, 298
Wampum, 320
Water:
  artesian well, 74

  body needs, 240–41
  condensation and
    evaporation, 106–7
  freezing, 35
  ice, 34–35
  molecules, 43
  osmosis, 20
  river sources, 79, 80
  saltiest body, 122
  soil and, 72
  springs, 74
  table, 74
  temperatures and, 109
  transpiration, 20
  See also Oceans
Watt, James, 377
Weasels, 184
Weather, 100
  fronts, 100, 105
  rings, tree, and, 14–15
  See also specific
    conditions
Webs, spider, 191–92
Wedding:
  cake, 342
  presents, 342
Weeds, 18
Weevils, 195
Weight:
  air pressure and
    altitude, 44
  density of matter and,
    42
  of elements, 45
  gravity and, 97–98
  molecules, 43
Whales, 230–31, 234
  Antarctica, 63

  largest, 232
  products, 233
Whigs, 116–17
White elephants, 179
Wigs, in court, 330
Wind, 101
  direction in storms,
    102, 105
  hurricane, 103
  monsoon, 104–5
  pollination by, 36
  prevailing, 101
  speeds, 103
  tornadoes, 102
Windmills, 376
Windstorms, 103
Wings, 33, 215
Witchcraft, 364
  black cats, 362
Wood, 14, 15
World's fairs, 348–49
Worms, 203
Wren, Sir Christopher,
  133
Wrestling, 304
Writing, 67, 127
  books, 316

Y

Year, New, 338–39

Z

Zoos, 302–3
Zoroastrianism, 358, 359